Minoan, Etruscan, and Related Languages: A Comparative Analysis

Sergej A. Jatsemirskij

Copyright © 2020 Ljudmila Jatsemirskaja

All rights reserved. No part of this book may be used or reproduced in any manner without written permission, except in the case of brief quotations.

Edited by
Peggy Duly, David V. Kaufman, and S. C. Compton

Cover design by Emma Lysy
Phaistos Disc cover photo by Aserakov

ISBN: 978-0-9995486-2-2

Library of Congress Control Number: 2020936806

Exploration Press
Chicago, IL
ExplorationPress.com

TABLE OF CONTENTS

Forward — i
Editor 1 Comments — iii
Editor 2 Comments — v

Chapter One
The Structure of Minoan and the Tyrrhenian Group of Languages

The Minoan Language — 2
The Eteocretan Language — 6
The Names "Tyrrhenians" and "Tyrrhenian Languages" — 6
The Earliest References to the Tyrrhenians — 7
The Tyrrhenian Languages of the First Millennium BCE — 8
    The Etruscan Language — 8
    The Rhaetic Language — 11
    The Aegean-Tyrrhenian Language — 13
    The Eteo-Cypriote Language — 16
    The Ibero-Tyrrhenian (South Lusitanian) Language — 18
    Possible Localization of Other Dialects — 19

Chapter Two
Sources

The Minoan Language — 23
The Eteocretan Language — 29
The Etruscan Language — 30
"Minor" Tyrrhenian Languages — 41
    The Rhaetic Language — 41
    The Aegean-Tyrrhenian Language — 42
    The Eteo-Cypriote Language — 44
    The Ibero-Tyrrhenian (South Lusitanian) Language — 45

Chapter Three
Writing

Cretan Hieroglyphs	48
Linear Writing Systems	49
The Tyrrhenian Alphabetic Script	59

Chapter Four
The Interpretation of the Vocabulary   68

Chapter Five
Phonetics

The Minoan Language	86
Vowels	86
Consonants	87
The Tyrrhenian Languages of the First Millennium BCE	89
Vowels	89
Consonants	96

Chapter Six
Morphology

Morpheme Structure	121
General Information About Morphology	123
Noun	127
Gender	127
Number	130
Case	133
Pronouns	143
Numerals	147
Verbs	157
General Information	157
System of Tenses	160
Hortative Forms	171
Conjectural Periphrastic Forms	173

Chapter Seven
Word Formation

General Characteristics	175

Prefixation	177
Main Name Formants and Their Combinations	178
Special Formants	187
Minoan Suffix –op-	187
Adjective Suffixes	188
Suffix of Belonging	190
Diminutive Suffixes	194
Forms with Enclitics	196

Appendices

1.	Phaistos Disk Inscription	201
2.	Eteocretan Inscriptions	203
3.	Tabula Cortonensis	205
4.	Bilingual from Pyrgi	207
5.	Lemnos Stele Inscription	211
6.	Main Eteo-Cypriote Inscriptions	213

Technical Resources

Index of Minoan and Tyrrhenian Words Preserved in Greek	215
Glossary	239
Abbreviations	253
Alphabetical Bibliography	255
Categorical Bibliography	267
Index	279

Figures

1.	Mediterranean Map	3
2.	Etruscan Script in Tarquinia Tomb	9
3.	Eteo-Cypriote Script	17
4.	Tartessos Script of Iberia	18
5.	Phaistos Disk	24
6.	Seal CHIC 314	25
7.	Tablet HT 6, Hagia Triada	26
8.	Inscribed Gold Ring from Mavro Spelio	27
9.	The Lemnos Stele Inscription	43
10.	Minoan Tablet HT 116	54
11.	Vase with Etruscan Alphabet	62

Tables

I.	Repertoire of Phaistos Signs	49
II.	Some Possible Acrophonic Parallels	51
III.	Linear A	56
IV.	The Varieties of the Etruscan Alphabet	60
V.	Etruscan Consonants	119
VI.	Nominal Declension	142
VII.	Pronominal Declension	142
VIII.	Etruscan Numerals	154
IX.	Examples of Comparison with Etruscan Numerals	156
X.	Known Paradigm of Tyrrhenian Verbs	172

FOREWORD

This work marks the completion of research that I have conducted for many years—namely, a study in the field of Tyrrhenian languages: Etruscan, several closely related idioms of the first millennium BCE (represented by a much smaller number of inscriptions), and the ancient language of Crete, known as Minoan to the specialists in Mediterranean linguistics, classical philology, and ancient history (Sir A. Evans's "Linear A"). To a certain degree, this publication continues my doctoral thesis, defended a few years ago in the Russian State University for the Humanities (Moscow).

The solution of both of the main problems as proposed in my doctorate (the comparative description of phonetics, vocabulary, and morphology of the Tyrrhenian languages of the first millennium BCE, and the demonstration of their genetic relationship)[1] has never been objected to by classical philologists or by specialists in comparative and general linguistics. Therefore, I decided not only to expand and edit the available material but also to conduct a further comparison on a new level—namely, to use for this comparison also the much older Minoan language (second millennium BCE) of Crete. This language has always seemed to me to be genetically related to the Tyrrhenian languages but to use it for my doctorate would have been logically premature: extensive research in this field has never been undertaken.

Naturally, the parts of my study that deal with the Minoan language are much shorter than those dedicated to the Tyrrhenian languages. However, by combining both types of data, I have tried to put the reader into an integrated linguo-historical context, showing that we are dealing not with a handful of isolates (or, for that matter, with two or three closely related dialects of a given isolate), but with a group of languages that can be studied both synchronically and diachronically and that have both a center and a periphery. Besides, such partitions allow us to solve several concrete tasks, such as reading and

---

1. It is important to keep in mind that preliminary comparisons of any two Tyrrhenian languages have been done before: as early as the beginning of the twentieth century several scholars had concluded that Etruscan is related to the language of Lemnos. In the 80s and 90s, Rix had genetically tied both the Etruscan and the Rhaetic languages to members of the Tyrrhenian language group. Seventy years ago, Schulten compared the South Lusitanian, Lemnian, and Etruscan languages, and Xarsekin had identified some clear Etruscan-Eteo-Cypriote cognates in the 70s. But a comparison of all five idioms on a sufficient basis has never been undertaken. As for Xarsekin's and Schulten's comparisons, they were simply forgotten. One of my aims was to rectify these oversights.

understanding a number of inscriptions, defining many borrowings in Greek, and explaining various problems in the history of writing.

The lack of a comprehensive comparative study and the problem of the relationship between the Tyrrhenians and the Cretans themselves made it necessary to present in the main text various results, concerning extralinguistic data: general information about both Tyrrhenians and Cretans and data about known written documents and the appropriate writing systems. I hope that this publication can be used as a short introduction to the state of contemporary Etruscan and Minoan research.

I would like to express my deep gratitude to my teachers, colleagues, and friends who have constantly helped me during all these years. They analyzed in detail many concrete problems, read voluminous parts of my MS, asked serious questions during conferences and in correspondence, indicated omissions of mine, and provided me with scholarly publications: Dr. V. A. Dybo, Dr. V. V. Shevoroshkin, Dr. V. P. Neroznak, Dr. A. V. Dybo, Dr. A. S. Kassian, and others.

My special thanks go to Ms. Peggy Duly (Benicia, California) who not only made this publication possible but was also generously providing me, over a number of years, with many scholarly editions (first of all, those concerning Crete). Without her help this study would not appear even in the form of a manuscript.

S. A. Jatsemirskij, October 2010

EDITOR 1 COMMENTS

I never had the privilege of meeting Sergej Jatsemirskij, but his brilliance was evident in his e-mails as well as his academic publications. He found every language fascinating and never stopped studying until his last days. His sense of humor and his care for others were as great as his insatiable linguistic curiosity! I still smile when I see his ironic (!) marks in the text. His passing at the age of thirty-seven from pancreatic cancer is a great loss to the world as well as to the field of linguistics.

Several years ago, I told Prof. Vitalij Shevoroshkin that I would like to know what Linear A was, and he immediately suggested that I contact Sergej. That was the beginning of a marvelous e-mail friendship and collaboration. I have no linguistic training myself, but I would proofread the translation to try to make it "flow" in English.

We were going through a final proofreading when he became ill, but he continued working until the end. There was a transcription problem with Tables V, VI and X, but I have tried to put them in a chart form that summarizes his findings. If there are any mistakes, they are my own! I would appreciate any suggestions and corrections. Because Sergej's research was completed over fifteen years ago, some of the concepts and references are not up to date, but the conclusions are still very relevant.

I wish to thank Prof. Shevoroshkin for introducing me to Sergej, since without him I would never have been involved with this fascinating project. My great appreciation also goes to John Bengtson who has mentored me through the publication process with great encouragement and patience! And thanks also to Dr. David Kaufman and S. C. Compton for re-editing and reformatting all this information into what you see here. Thanks, too, to Emma Lysy for the beautiful cover and to Dr. Pamela Gaber for her suggestions after reviewing the text.

Thanks also to Sergej's friend Dmitrij Gushchin for help in checking Sergej's original text after his passing, and to their friends Valerij Podchishchaev and Alexander Kozlov who were all of great support to Sergej since their university days.

And my great personal thanks to Sergej's mother Lyudmila Jatsemirskaja, whose encouragement kept him going throughout his life.

Peggy Duly, 2019

EDITOR 2 COMMENTS

The Etruscan and other indigenous pre-Indo-European cultures and civilizations of Europe have long been a mystery to us. We are only now beginning to learn much more about Etruscan culture and language. Sergej Jatsemirskij's linguistic insights indicate that the Etruscans probably had much more influence on Western culture and civilization, as well as on the Roman culture and the Latin language, than previously known. The insights found through the linguistic examinations in this book may well alter our perceptions of European, and especially pre-Indo-European, history.

I also never had the privilege of meeting Sergej in person or of communicating with him in any form. However, since I was invited to be coeditor of this book, I have been enormously impressed with the broad range of Sergej's linguistic and historical knowledge. It is unfortunate that Sergej passed on at such an early age (thirty-seven). Had he lived, I'm sure he would have given us many more stunning insights on these ancient languages and civilizations. Since having the honor of coediting this volume, I feel that I've developed a special bond with Sergej, and I am sure that, had I known him personally, we would have been good friends!

I would like to thank Peggy Duly for the opportunity to assist in editing this great work. I also want to thank my good friend and colleague S. C. Compton for taking on the monumental task of formatting and organizing what you hold in your hands. Sergej brought us together as a team to bring his book to fruition!

David V. Kaufman, PhD, 2019

SERGEJ A. JATSEMIRSKIJ
1980–2017

CHAPTER 1

THE STRUCTURE OF MINOAN AND THE TYRRHENIAN GROUP OF LANGUAGES

For a long time, Etruscan was the only extinct non-Indo-European epigraphic language of Mediterranean Europe known to scholars; particularly, all the non-Latin and non-Greek inscriptions had been declared as Etruscan. Thus, Osco-Umbrian, Faliscan, Rhaetic, and other inscriptions found themselves among the "Etruscan" texts; for example, the correct attribution of the famous Iguvine Tablets (discovered in 1444) to Umbrian was established only in the nineteenth century.

By the end of the nineteenth century, scholars had succeeded in delineating the actual Etruscan inscriptions and the first scientific assessments of the origin of the Etruscans had appeared. Already in the eighteenth century, N. Fréret put forward the so-called "Nordic" hypothesis of their appearance in Italy that was later supported by B. Niebuhr and W. Helbig (Nemirovskij 1983, 7–9). Although the hypothesis itself was rather far-fetched and did not at all prove its value in the future, it drew scholars' attention to the Rhaetic epigraphic material (in turn, rather miscellaneous). In 1885 on the Island of Lemnos, an inscription was found in a language, the proximity of which to Etruscan had already been noted by early scholars. After the Cypriote syllabary had been deciphered (1911) it turned out that some of the local inscriptions were also made in a non-Indo-European language, the affinity of which to Etruscan was noted by A. I.

Xarsekin (Xarsekin 1976 [2]). On the whole, by that time the horizons of studying the new language group had been expanded considerably.

To date, one can confidently state the relation of Etruscan to a number of extinct idioms that existed in ancient times in various Mediterranean regions (see Figure 1). It is evident that at some stage those languages were denser and much more widespread than at the time of the creation of the existing written texts, and subsequently, those languages were superseded by the languages of the Indo-Europeans. In this study, these languages will be denoted as "Minoan" and "Tyrrhenian" (see the explanation below).

As for the cradle of European civilization itself—the Aegean—pre-Indo-European written texts were found there at the turn of the nineteenth-twentieth centuries. During his famous excavations in Crete, Sir A. Evans discovered three scripts at once, among which only the latter one named "Linear B" used the Greek language; in 1909 the script of the Phaistos Disk, an inscription remaining unique up until now, joined them (published by L. Pernier). Furthermore, the most ancient script of Cyprus (being the intermedium between Linear A and the classic Cypriote Syllabary) became known; it was also used for the non-Indo-European language.

All these languages and scripts will be discussed below.

THE MINOAN LANGUAGE

According to long-established tradition, the Minoan language refers to the language of the most ancient and, beyond any doubt, pre-Indo-European population of Crete. It was they who created the culture that is also named "Minoan" after the semi-legendary "king" Minos (Μίνως)[2] who was known to the ancient writers as the ruler of Crete, the founder of an all-Cretan state and its naval supremacy (the so-called Minos' thalassocracy). It is evident that this language was present on Crete already in the mid-third millennium BCE; the dating here depends directly on the dating of the existing written texts made with the most ancient local writing systems: hieroglyphic (from the twenty-first or twentieth century BCE) and perhaps the inscription of the Phaistos Disk, which is likely to date from the seventeenth century BCE (for details see below in Chapter 2: Sources and Chapter 3: Writing.) We shall employ the name "the Minoan language" being aware of its conditional character; on the other hand, there is a name preserved in the inscriptions of Linear A but not used specifically anywhere (also see below).

The period of the development of the ancient Cretan culture of the twentieth to nineteenth centuries BCE, which includes the earliest inscriptions found so far, is denoted as Middle Minoan I, according to the accepted chronological scale. Neither the archaeological artifacts nor the testimony of ancient writers suggests that the bearers of the Ancient Cretan culture of Middle Minoan I differed significantly by ethnicity from the inhabitants of Early Minoan Crete. The absence of noticeable changes that could be occasioned by external factors enables us to state the total continuity in the development of these periods of Ancient Cretan culture.

---

2. This very form is likely to be a title rather than a proper name.

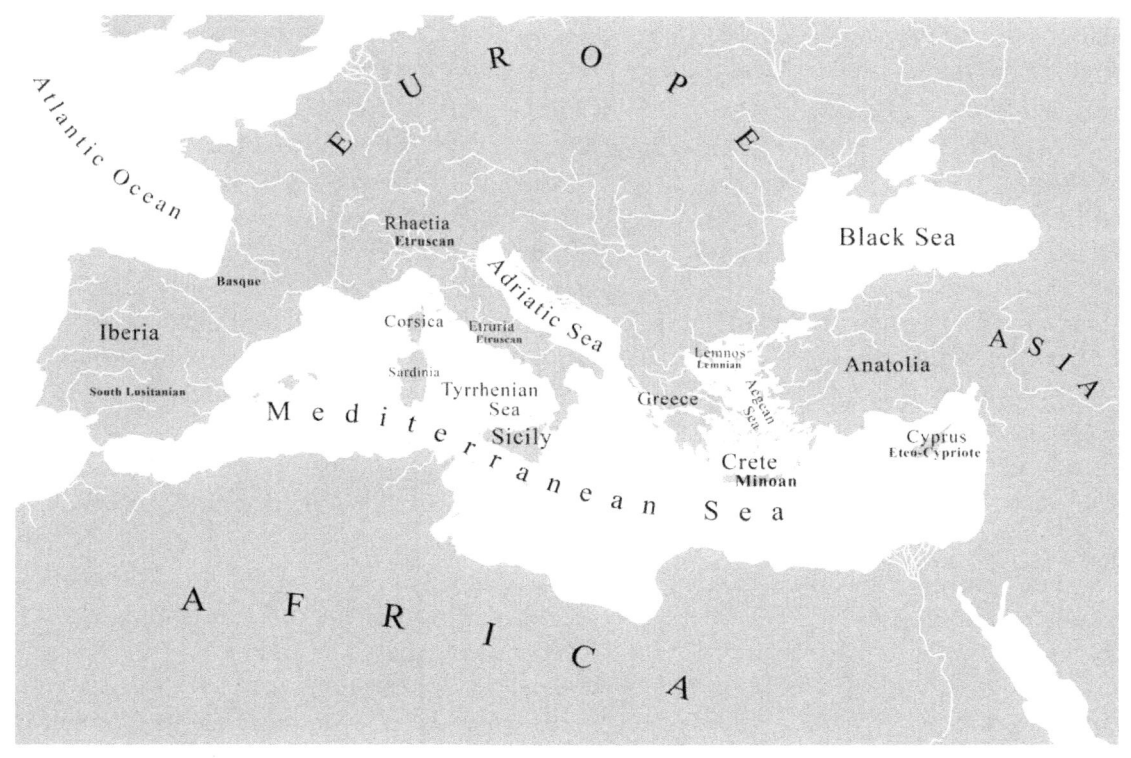

Figure 1. Map of Mediterranean languages and regions mentioned

Thus, we have serious reason to believe that the creators of the first written relics spoke the same language as the inhabitants of Crete of 2500-2000 BCE (the Early Minoan I Period), with natural diachronic changes. It is most likely that Minoan toponyms preserved in Greek sources (from the inscriptions of the Linear B script to late ancient writers) had been in use long before the classical writing appeared, thus being contemporary with the Minoan civilization. Subsequently, some of them were replaced by Greek ones. Anatolian forms are found there as well.

The chronology of the Minoan language of the written period is still not satisfactorily developed. This is primarily due to the fact that we do not have a convincing reading of Early Minoan (i.e., the hieroglyphic) inscriptions (and there is no certain reading of a single character for the text of the Phaistos disk). The records of the Linear A script, originating in the hieroglyphs, still need to be the basic subject of study as before.

The synchronous facts of Minoan (i.e., the material of the Linear A inscriptions) enable us to note certain occasional lexical parallels to Asia Minor (Anatolian), Middle Eastern (Semitic), and Egyptian areas. The type of interaction with Anatolian languages during the described period is still in question. Adaptations from Anatolian are seen in certain forms from Linear A inscriptions. It may well be that the bearers of the Hittite-Luwian languages penetrated to Crete during the Minoan period; on the other hand, it is quite possible that these lexemes had been adopted by the ancestors of the inhabitants of Crete earlier on the continent. Only the presence of Anatolian toponyms and anthroponyms in the Cretan inscriptions of Linear B is known for certain. The

Anatolians penetrated to other islands as well (cf., particularly the testimony of Herodotus [I, 171] concerning the fact that the Carians lived earlier on the islands and were named "the Leleges" (Λέλεγες < Hittite *lulah=h=i-* "barbarian").[3]

The parallels to the Semitic languages are no less mysterious. The Minoan derivational suffixes are clearly distinguished in the most significant of them, whereas, within the Semitic group, they do not have regular equivalents, and it enables us to consider them as early adoptions from the Minoan language. As for the period and place of contacts, however, it is hardly possible to discuss them. In addition to the suffixes, there are a few Egyptian-Cretan parallels which evidently appeared during the flourishing of Cretan maritime power. (The Cretans, *kftjw*, are also mentioned in Egyptian sources).[4]

The population of Crete became a fairly mixed picture over time. In particular, Homer (Od., XIX, 175-79) states that in the island, besides the Eteocretans, that is, the "True Cretans" (the Minoans, as well as their descendants), there also lived the Cydonians, the Pelasgians, the Achaeans, and the Dorics "divided in three tribes" (τριχάϊκες).[i]

The testimony given by Homer cannot be a cogent argument when describing the ethnic situation in Crete in the early period. We know that the Achaeans were not on the island until 1450 BCE, and the Dorics appeared even later, thus it is clear that the information about the dominion of Minos is evidently erroneous here. Homer actually describes the population of Crete in the period after 1200. Consequently, the mention of the Pelasgians does not necessarily attest to their earlier presence on the island. There is no reason, therefore, to state (in the current relative interpretation) the presence of the Pelasgo-Thracian people on the island in the period preceding the decline of Minoan Crete (i.e., until 1450 BCE). The Paleo-Balkan toponymy does not seem to be materially attested for in the earlier period.

Whatever the case, the Indo-European dialects of Paleo-Balkan origin are outside the subject area of our study. Here it is only important that the western tribe, the Cydonians (Κύδωνες) are mentioned as contemporaries of the Minoans by Homer and other sources. The stem of this toponym and ethnonym is attested clearly in the Linear A inscriptions (cf., *ku-do-ni* [HT 13, HT 85], *ka-u-do-ni* [HT 26] and apparently from the same stem *ka-u-de-ta* [HT 13]).

It is evident that the Cydonians and the Minoans were kindred tribes speaking related dialects. The Cydonians, along with the Minoans, were seen as the autochthonic population of Crete (note that there is no similar evidence of the Pelasgians). Their immediate relation is confirmed by a genealogical myth as well (an explanation that is a characteristic of the Hellenic tradition as a whole) which says that the eponymous ancestor of these people Κύδων (most likely a fictional character) was Minos's grandson. Judging by the testimony of Homer, the ethnic independence of the Cydonians continued at least to the Greek Dark Ages. It would be of particular interest to trace its

---

3. Hesychius gives similar information. The testimony of Stephen is quite mysterious: "Φύσκος δέ, ἀφ' οὗ οἱ Λέλεγες οἱ νῦν Λοκροί" (see Φύσκος).

4. Presumably, precisely because of the Cretans, a certain number of Egyptian words penetrated the Greek language. These forms were explored in detail by Ernstedt (1953).

material remains (i.e., dialect differences) among which there may be several phonetic fluctuations, above all, the differences in alternate vowels of some suffixes (see Chapter 7: Word Formation). Molchanov's supposition that "the All-Cretan Minoan language" took its shape by the sixteenth century BCE (Molchanov et al. 1988, 171) thus does not seem reliable.

In principle, such a state of affairs is also supported by the situation of the rivalries between Knossos and Cydonia as the major cities of Crete. Later on, Knossos holds a dominant position, while the palaces of Cydonia, Phaistos, and other cities would never reach the level of development of the Palace of Knossos. We can also assume that Knossos and Cydonia were originally the centers of two major tribes, and the original native name of the "Minoans" was paronymous with *ko-no-sa* (by analogy with Κύδωνες, Κυδωνία). The facts of the rivalries between Knossos and Cydonia continued to the last period (Strabo, X, 4, 11). In the Classical period, the third city, the position of which could appear decisive, had an Indo-European-derived but Tyrrhenian name, Γόρτυν, *ko-tu* in Linear B[5]; however, its native name is Ἐλλώτια (with a Minoan root that will be considered below).

Homer says that ninety cities existed in Crete. Although the quantity here certainly is a poetic overstatement, it should be admitted that we must recognize that the number of urban settlements in Crete was very impressive. The major cities of Crete bore mostly non-Indo-European Minoan names, a large number of which remained until the Classical period. In Linear B inscriptions, there are such cities mentioned as *a-mi-ni-so* (Ἄμνισος), *a-pa-ta-wa* (Ἄπταρα), *di-ka-ta-de* (Δίκτη), *ko-no-so* (Κνωσσός, Κνωσός), *ku-do-ni-ja* (Κυδονία), *pa-i-to* (Φαιστός), *tu-ri-so* (Τυλισσός), *u-ta-no* (Ἴτανος). These names have parallels in the texts with Linear A, but they are few so far.

The question of the boundary of the distribution of the Minoan language is extremely complicated. It is unknown whether we should consider the divergence of Minoan from the group of the related Aegean dialects on Crete itself, or a gradual expansion of the area of this language as the Cretan maritime power expanded (cf., in particular, the supposition that Linear A was introduced to Melos and Thera) (Pope 1976, 85). The pre-Greek inhabitants of Cyprus, being evidently part of the group under study, may also be an independent branch where the Cretan influence showed itself in the adoption of the writing system as well as the descendants of Cretan settlers (the second version is supported by Molchanov [cf., the chapter with a title that speaks for itself, The Minoans on the Island of Aphrodite] [Molchanov 1992]).

After the Thera eruption of the mid-fifteenth century BCE to which the majority of scholars link the decline of the Cretan state, the Minoan population steadily decreased being forced out at first by Achaean and from the twelfth century BCE by Doric settlers. The time of the disappearance of the last remains of Cretan speech is now defined according to Greek sources and the inscriptions of alphabetic writing (see below, in The

---

5. Compare the identical Etruscan *curtun* with contemporary Italian *Cortona*, Arcadian Γόρτυς, Macedonian (Emathia) Γορτυνία, Thessalian Γυρτών, Arcadian Κορτύνιοι (from Hesychius: "οἱ Ἀρκάδες· ἡ γὰρ Κόρτυς τῆς Ἀρκαδίας"), Boeotian Κυρτώνη (from Stephen) with Pamphylian Κορδυτός, Macedonian Γορδυνία, and the Thessalian coin legend ΓΟΡΔΙΑΣ.

Eteocretan Language section of Chapter 2). This language, recorded in inscriptions for almost two thousand years, is one of the most difficult riddles in linguistics. Being alien to the territory of Europe, it became the language of the oldest European civilization, but its origin, history, and internal structure are still to be revealed.

THE ETEOCRETAN LANGUAGE

When the "True Cretans" caught the eye of Greek historians, they had become small islands of the autochthonic population that had been gradually switching to the Greek language. The few records of them that exist are difficult to consider as linguistic information sources; it is only their peculiar origin that is pointed out.[6] It is known that the "True Cretans" inhabited the area of the cities of Dreros and Praisos not far away from the revered mountain of Dikti. It is the same place from which their fragmentary inscriptions come, made in the Greek alphabet.

By that time, the differences between the descendants of the inhabitants of Knossos and the Cydonians surely had already been lost. It is possible to speculate that the period of the last inscriptions—fourth century BCE—concurs approximately with the final extinction of the Cretan language.

THE NAMES "TYRRHENIANS" AND "TYRRHENIAN LANGUAGES"

The term "Tyrrhenian" (also Tyrsenian) was first used by Rix (1998). Its necessity became quite apparent after clear parallels between Etruscan and Lemnian, on the one hand, and Etruscan and Rhaetic, on the other, had been clarified. Besides its scientific, linguistic usage, this term has general cultural value as it makes it possible for the first time to present Etruscan as a member of a group of closely related languages, which is not large, but has demonstrated potential for a further comparison.

By referring to the languages under study as "Tyrrhenian," we follow the Greek name for these people: Τυρσηνοί, Doric Τυρσανοί, Attic Τυρρηνοί; in fact, Italic names also originate from this stem; Umbrian *Turskum*, Latin *Etrusci* (it is known that the prosthesis *e-* existed in the Etruscan language itself), *Tusci*, from which the later Greek Θοῦσκοι comes; the same stem is preserved today in the name of Tuscany (Latin *Tuscania*). It is evidently found in an abridged form on the Etruscan inscription on an amphora from Milan TLE 720: [1]*trskmetr* [2]*LXXVIs*.

The Greeks used the name "Tyrrhenians" for the Etruscans of Italy and their relatives in the Aegean (e.g., it is not always possible to trace whether the glosses that were kept by Greek sources have something to do with the Etruscan or the inhabitants of the Aegean). We do not have any other general name yet. It may well be that the

---

6. This very name became a common one. For example, Hesychius makes the following comment: "Ἐτεόκρητες· οἱ αὐτόχθονες."

original native name of the Etruscans, *rasna*, Ῥασέναι (Dion. Hal., I, 30), could claim a similar role. However, it has not been attested yet outside Italy. In our study, we shall use five designations of different languages: Etruscan, Rhaetic, Eteo-Cypriote, South Lusitanian and Aegean-Tyrrhenian. Their common stable features will be referred to as "Tyrrhenian."

THE EARLIEST REFERENCES TO THE TYRRHENIANS

The first evidence of the Tyrrhenians dates from a much earlier time than the inscriptions that have been deciphered/read. This evidence comes from Egypt. Under Merneptah, a pharaoh of the nineteenth dynasty (according to different datings, 1213-1203 [most likely] or 1224-1204 BCE), the invasion of the Libyans (rbw) took place led by King m-r'-ḥ'-ḥw-ḥ[7] in alliance with the Sea Peoples. They were defeated by the Egyptians. These events are described in four texts: the Great Karnak Inscription, The Cairo Column, the Athribis Stele, and the so-called Hymn of Victory. Among the Sea Peoples that are mentioned in the texts are groups from Asia Minor and the Aegean basin as well as three ethnic groups from the western Mediterranean.

Let us consider several extracts from the inscriptions listed (from J. Breasted's edition). From the Karnak Inscription: "[Beginning of the victory which his majesty achieved in the land of Libya] . . . Ekwesh ('-ḳ'-w'-š'), Teresh (tw-rw-š'), Luka (rw-kw), Sherden (š'-r'-d-n-n'), Shekelesh (š-k-rw-š'), Northerners coming from all the lands" [ARE, III, § 574].[8] The same peoples are also mentioned further (cf., § 579, § 588). In the list of the enemies killed and captured (§ 588) are the Libyans (6359) and '-ḳ'-w'-š' (6111), as well as 222 š-k-rw-š', 742 tw-rw-š'; the number of š'-r'-d-n-n' and rw-kw is unknown. Besides, there are 218 captives tw-rw-š' and š-k-rw-š' mentioned together. Undoubtedly, the number of the first two groups is overstated. The enumeration of ethnic "minorities" is more verisimilar.

In the Cairo Column inscription, š-k-rw-š' are referred to as the Libyans' allies (§ 595), but the remaining text is damaged. In the Athribis inscription there is the enumeration of captives as well (§ 601): 6200 Libyans, 2201 '-ḳ'-w'-š', 200 š-k-rw-š', 722 tw-rw-š', whereas The Hymn does not include the names of the Sea Peoples. Under Ramesses III (the twentieth dynasty, 1194-1162 or 1188-1156 BCE) the Sea Peoples again attacked Egypt; tw-rw-š' are mentioned in the inscription from Medinet Habu and in the inscription of the so-called "Rhetorical Stele."

Laying aside the question of '-ḳ'-w'-š' and rw-kw who are more likely to be Greeks (Achaeans) (Ἀχαιϝοί; here most likely "Ahhiyawa" of Hittite texts) and Lycians (Anatolian *Lukka*, Greek Λύκιοι), we shall consider the remaining names. The only convincing equivalents for š'-r'-d-n-n' and š-k-rw-š' are Σαρδόνιοι and Σικελοί (i.e., the inhabitants of Sardinia and Sicily). As for tw-rw-š', it is appropriate to see them only as Τυρσηνοί.

---

7. In the following, we will use the old transcription from Breasted's edition [ARE].

8. It is obvious that the author's restoration of the vowels is utterly relative. We shall not use it hereafter.

It is significant that "Tursha"—the Tyrsenians—are mentioned at such an early period along with peoples of the western Mediterranean (by š-k-rw-š' one should certainly understand not the later Sicels [Latin *Siculi*] whose language belonged to the Italic group, but the inhabitants of Sicily in general—this very meaning was also used for the Greek name "Sicels" or some Pre-Italic people [the Sicanians?]).[9] However, it is unclear whether we should limit them only to the western regions, because we know that during the later period the Tyrrhenians also inhabited the eastern Mediterranean (Cyprus in particular). Presumably the smaller numbers in the lists (cf., the number of the Sicilians) can point to "Tursha" as western (i.e., the most remote from Egypt) people, whereas the Libyans and "Achaeans," being nearest to Egypt, are quite numerous. Further conclusions about historical and geographic aspects are hardly possible now. In the future, we shall have to solve the problem of the settlement of the Tyrrhenians in the western and eastern Mediterranean.

We know that the Tyrrhenian languages attested in the records from the seventh to the first century BCE were certainly quite similar to each other. This gives us grounds to assume that the language of the much more ancient "Tursha" could hardly have been divided in the period described. If the records or at least the traces of this language are found some day, it certainly may be referred to as "Proto-Tyrrhenian." In this case, the key question will be its relationship with Minoan.

THE TYRRHENIAN LANGUAGES OF THE FIRST MILLENNIUM BCE

Among the languages related to Etruscan and attested by written relics, there is Aegean-Tyrrhenian (the language of the inscription of the famous Lemnos stele and the relic vocabulary of the Aegean), Rhaetic (represented by a few inscriptions from Alpine valleys), Eteo-Cypriote (i.e., the language of "true Cypriots," the pre-Greek population of the island), and South Lusitanian (the language of isolated inscriptions, not mixed with the core group of relic languages of the Iberian Peninsula). Besides, relic vocabulary, similar to the Etruscan one, not only covers most of the Aegean basin but also is evidenced in Cyprus. It makes sense to study also the substratum of Sardinia and Corsica to identify individual Tyrrhenian lexemes.

THE ETRUSCAN LANGUAGE

The Etruscan language (see Figure 2) is a language of the ancient pre-Roman population of Italy, originally widespread in Etruria (to the north of Latium, on the coast of the body of water referred to as the Tyrrhenian Sea; this area corresponds roughly to modern Tuscany). We have a quite detailed knowledge of the geographical description of Etruria and its tribes from ancient traditions (cf., for example, the information given by Pliny the Elder). It is easy to see that it is rich in properly Tyrrhenian names (including

---

9. Whose language does not belong to the group studied. Blažek with the reference to Diodorus Siculus (I, 22) gives the hypothesis of its link with Iberian (Urbanová and Blažek 2008, 211).

some not attested in the Etruscan inscriptions), as well as foreign names.[ii] Subsequently, the Etruscan language spread widely to the north and east.[iii] The influence of the Etruscans (and, accordingly, their language) reached also Latium and Campania. Traces of the Etruscans are found also in North Africa (near Carthage[10]) due to the development of trade and their maritime hegemony that existed for some time.

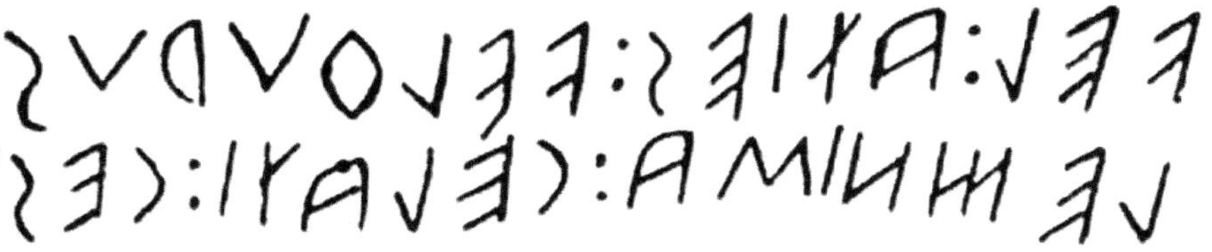

Figure 2. Script in Tarquinia Tomb.

The orientalizing Etruscan archaeological culture itself appears in Italy approximately in the eighth century BCE. It sharply differs from the local Villanovan archaeological culture (named after the site where an exemplary inscription was found—the Villanova di Castenaso cemetery near Bologna), which was first distributed in Emilia, eastern Romagna, Capua and Pontecagnano. The Villanova culture is usually associated with the Osco-Umbrian group of the Italic peoples.

The early Etruscan colonization was mainly in the south (up to Naples [Pfiffig 1969, 8 the map]); the most ancient inscriptions are found in Latium (including Rome, Praeneste, Satricum). In Campania they appear in the first third of the sixth century BCE, in Capua and Nola in 550-450 BCE (Nemirovskij 1983, 72).

Judging by the ancient authors, the Umbri were the most ancient people who inhabited the territory of Etruria. For example, Herodotus reports that the Tyrrhenian settlers arrived in the country of "Ombrikoi"[iv]; there is also more evidence of a wider dispersal of the people. The inhabitants of Clusium were formerly referred to as *Camertes Umbri* (*Camars, Camers* being the old Etruscan name of the city); one of Etruria's rivers kept the name *Ombro*. We can agree that all these facts "enable us to suggest the presence of the Umbrian substratum in Etruria" (Tronskij 1953, 68).

It is possible that the relatives of the "classical" Umbri are also the people Ἄμβρωνες who participated in the invasion of the Cimbri [Plut., Marius, 15, 5],[11] but the situation here is highly controversial. Besides the Italic version, there are two more to consider: Zhirmunskij, appealing to the names of *Amrum* (an island in the Frisian archipelago) and *Ymbrum* (Widsið 32), suggested that this name is also a German one (Žirmunskij 1964, 259). These parallels seem too few in number, and, apparently, there are no equivalents in ancient writings (only Tacitus mentions some *Gambrivios* [Germ., II, 4], but this also presents an obvious phonetic contrast).

---

10. The earliest being inscription TLE 724, containing the ethnicon *karθazie* (for details, see below).
11. In 114-101 BCE.

It is significant that all three of the tribal names (i.e., the Cimbri, Teutones, and Ambrones) are not peculiarly German (the link between the name of Cimbri and the ancient Cimmerians was already obvious to Plutarch in the passage given. At the same time, the Cimbri chief bore a Celtic name, *Boiorix*).

On the other hand, Festus (from Paul the Deacon) points directly to the Celtic origin of this people: "*Ambrones fuerunt gens quaedam Gallica, qui subita inundatione maris cum amisissent sedes suas, rapinis et praedationibus se suosque alere coeperunt.*" Here we are dealing with an ethnonym which is fairly widespread in western European languages (up to the name of the island Ἴμβρος near the coast of Chersonese in Thracia) as well as the result of Gallo-Umbrian contacts in northern Italy. Obviously, this issue requires special study.

Judging by the lexical borrowings in the early period, Italic words got into Etruscan from Umbrian; the latter, in turn, contains some Etruscan words. We do not have Etruscan written inscriptions that could be confidently dated to the eighth century BCE. Clearly dated inscriptions appear in the next century.[12] In general, the chronology of Etruscan texts has not been satisfactorily developed, which is attributed to a number of difficulties of historical, archaeological and paleographic character. On some principal indicators of dating, see below in Chapter 2: Sources and Chapter 3: Writing. Only a few texts have been accurately dated to within a century. A more precise determination of the age is possible only in isolated cases. In the existing publications (primarily Pallottino, see below), the age of inscriptions is usually marked with ant. "*Titulus antiquior*" or rec. ("*Aetatis recentioris*"). The publication of Pallottino contains 177 inscriptions of the seventh to the beginning of the fifth centuries. However, the number of inscriptions that can be attributed to the seventh century is insignificant. They are rare in subsequent publications of REE as well. It is also significant that the greater difficulty arises with the exact dating of later inscriptions. One has to note that we do not know the upper limit of the creation of Etruscan inscriptions.

It is known that the process of displacement of the Etruscan language by Latin lasted for centuries. The geographic distance to various cities from Rome defined the greater or lesser intensity of Romanization. The victory over Veii exaggerated by Roman historians (396 BCE)[13] indicated only the early stage of the Roman expansion. It resulted in the collapse of the Etruscan city closest to Rome but not that which was the most powerful. The fact that Veii got *civitas sine suffragio* ("citizenship without the right to vote") did not lead to the spread of the Latin language. Intensive Romanization took place much later.

Dionysius I, tyrant of Syracuse (406–376 BCE), destroyed the ports of the Tyrrhenian coast. In 384 BCE, the maritime power of the Etruscans came to its end with the Samnites displacing them from the Campania. The terrible damage inflicted on Etruria by the Gauls and the army of Hannibal contributed significantly to the rapid submission of Etruscan cities to Rome (in fact, Rome became the master of Etruria

---

12. Apparently, the Etruscan written inscriptions appear before the Latin (the inscription on the Praeneste fibula (CIL 1^2 3) is dated to the seventh century). This supports the view that we share concerning the Etruscan mediation in the formation of the Latin alphabet.

13. Cf. from Livy (V, 1–23).

early in the First Punic War [264 BCE]). It is obvious that Romanization was particularly noticeable afterward in Etruria, as there are many colonists sent by Sulla (reported by, *inter alia*, Sallust). Undoubtedly contributing to the Romanization was the Julian law (90 BCE) in which the residents of the united Italic cities, including the Etruscans, were granted Roman citizenship. Therefore, the exact dates for the latest written inscriptions are unknown. The first century BCE will be our reference point here.

Judging by the testimonies of the ancients, the Etruscan language had existed at least until the second century CE (for example, Aulus Gellius writes about it as a living language).[v] Etruscan rites, especially the practice of divination, existed under Constantine, Julian, Valentinian, and Gratian. Haruspicy was finally forbidden by Theodosius (d. 395 CE). We assume that, even at that time, the language had been preserved residually in some religious communities (although we cannot judge the extent of the haruspices' proficiency in it [cf., for example, the hymns of the Salii and the Arval Brethren, which became obscure to priests themselves in the very early days]).[14] The last time Etruscan haruspices appeared on the historical scene was in 408 CE. Rome had been besieged by the hordes of Alaric, and its people, who had despaired of the Christian god's help, again summoned haruspices who tried "praying to gods, according to ancestors' custom, to turn forthcoming barbarians back with frightening lightnings and sudden whirlwind."[vi]

Etruscan inscriptions had been created for a very long time (as compared with other Tyrrhenian languages). The Etruscan language survived the Tyrrhenian languages of the eastern Mediterranean for several centuries, as well as its closest idiom, which is Rhaetic.

The special position of the Etruscan language hardly needs explication. It is obvious that the materials of the "minor" Tyrrhenian languages are considered almost exclusively by being compared to it. The prospects for the study of the Tyrrhenian family largely depend on progress in the study of Etruscan, and fortunately, the prospects opening up now before the scholars of Etruscan itself are very high.

THE RHAETIC LANGUAGE

The Rhaetic language (or dialect) was spread in northern Italy, in Rhaetia (Latin *Raetia*), and incorporated into the Roman Empire only in 15 BCE by Drusus and Tiberius. Subsequently, with the Romanization of the Rhaetians, their language was superseded by Vulgar Latin, and therefore it can be considered as a substratum for the Rhaeto-Romance dialects. Perhaps the study of their peculiarities will contribute to some extent to the clarification of the facts of the Rhaetic language. In so doing, it should be borne in mind that Rhaeto-Romance belongs to the Gallo-Romance periphery and is placed in the Celtic substratum.

Ancient authors refer to many Rhaetian tribes. The most detailed description is again by Pliny, quoting the famous inscription from Tropea.[vii] It is easy to see that most of the names listed here either indicate the Celtic tribes, or they are unreliable. Tagliavini

---

14. Pfiffig assumed for the Etruscan language of this time the same cult status as that of Sumerian in Babylonia or Hattic for the Hittites (Pfiffig 1969, 9).

described the situation with the Rhaetian tribes quite accurately: "the Rhaetians possibly were a conglomeration of very different tribes, and it is quite probable that their name had rather a political meaning than ethnic or linguistic" (Tagliavini 1959, 93).

A comparison of maps of the distribution of contemporary Rhaeto-Romance dialects (Borodina 1969, 7)[15] and the dispersal of the ancient Rhaetian tribes (Krasnovskaja 1964, 100) shows that the dialect of the Suanets acts as a substratum of the Silvan subdialects (Sursilvan, Sutsilvan, and Surmiran), and the dialect of the "Rugians" as the Engadines (in the terminology of Krasnovskaya) (i.e., *Ruginates* according to the Roman designation).

Self-evident Tyrrhenian names (mostly with the suffixes *-na-te*) will be given later in Chapter 7: Word Formation. Here it should be noted that we should consider the dialect of a Tyrrhenian tribe (i.e., *RVCINATES* of Pliny) as a substratum of the modern southeastern Swiss Rhaeto-Romance dialect of Engadine.

It is obvious that the inscriptions originating from Rhaetia (primarily from *Val Camonica,* a valley inhabited by the *Camunni* people in ancient times) will be Indo-European in considerable (if not the major) part. The same applies to the sole "Rhaetic" gloss *ploum* "plow" (see below). Such a proportion of inscriptions, as well as Indo-European ethnonyms, support the viewpoint of the Indo-European character of Rhaetic (or more exactly, "all the tribal dialects of Rhaetia"). On the other hand, there are a number of authentic Tyrrhenian inscriptions and testimonies of the ancients that indicate the relationship of some of the Rhaetians' with the Etruscans.

The language of these Rhaetic tribes probably should be considered a northern Etruscan dialect. The previously disputed (cf., Whatmough 1933) kinship between the Rhaetians and Etruscans can be supposed proven now. The fundamental proposition of Rhaetic as a part of the pre-Indo-European layer must prevail after the works of Pisani (1953, 303–4).

Already the ancient authors had no doubt of the common origin of the Etruscans and the Rhaetians. For example, the evidence of Pliny the Elder: "*Raetos Tuscorum prolem arbitrantur a Gallis pulsos duce Raeto*" (NH III: 133). At the same time, the ancients also noted dialect differences. Titus Livy refers to the Rhaetians as an offshoot of the Etruscans, who, however, did not retain anything of the latter, "besides the sound of their tongue, but not in clear form" ("*praeter sonum linguae nec eum incorruptum*") (V: 33).

It is significant that Pliny's list does not have a name consonant with the common one, "Rhaetians." It is possible that it includes only Tyrrhenian tribes. Accordingly, the question also arises about the origin of the ethnonym itself. The opinion of the kinship **ras(n)-* : **rait-* (with which some scholars attempted to back up the "Nordic theory" as well) does not seem convincing (firstly, no equivalence of Etruscan **s* : Rhaetic **t*, has yet been elicited, and, secondly, in Etruscan *rasna*, Ῥασέναι there is not a diphthong registered anywhere).

The Rhaetian highland tribes, who stood at a low level of social development, did not leave any significant written record. Their contribution is less than not only Lemnian

---

15. Here we are not taking into account the earlier prevalence of Rhaeto-Romance, which was appreciably wider (Borodina 1969, 8).

but even Eteo-Cypriote inscriptions in their importance for the study of Tyrrhenian morphology. Apparently the Rhaetians underwent rapid Romanization. The dates of the existing inscriptions show that they may have stopped being drawn up after the Roman conquest.

Phonetically and morphologically, Rhaetic forms are considered only in comparison with Etruscan ones. Serious discrepancies with Etruscan have not been noted yet. As for the known ones, they are of a particular character.[16] Glaring distinctions in vocabulary may turn out to be inessential since we lack any Rhaetic texts of a length sufficient for conclusive comparisons.

THE AEGEAN-TYRRHENIAN LANGUAGE

The term "Aegean-Tyrrhenian language," designed to combine geographic and genetic characteristics, has been suggested by us to designate the Tyrrhenian language (or a group of related dialects), which are represented by toponyms, by the inscriptions of the Lemnos stele, and by the complex of the relic Aegean vocabulary that penetrated the literary Greek language, and was also preserved in glosses (primarily found in the dictionary of Hesychius). We do not have any reason for the separation of a special "Lemnian" language from this Aegean community. It is preferable to speak of closely related dialects. However, with regard to the language of the written records, it is permissible to use the traditional term "Lemnian language." The obsolete name "Etruscan Lemnos" goes back to the time when the inscriptions of the Lemnos stele were considered an inscription that had been left by Etruscan settlers.

Aegean-Tyrrhenian was a language of the Tyrrhenian people whose presence is evidenced by the ancient writers (Herodotus, Thucydides, etc.) and also by the relic vocabulary on the islands of Lemnos,[17] Imbros, Crete, Lesbos, Euboea, and others, as well as in Attica and Chalcidice. The early dating of the existing written records is now being rejected. They are dated to the sixth century BCE by the majority of scholars (cf., Xarsekin 1976[1]). According to Thucydides, the Tyrrhenians were evicted from the isle of Lemnos during the Greco-Persian wars. Diodorus reports that they took flight "for fear of Persians."[viii] Other chronological indications are virtually absent.

In general, there are certain difficulties in the interpretation of the Greek evidence concerning the Tyrrhenians of the Aegean primarily because of the fact that the Tyrrhenians are often associated with the "Pelasgians." This identification is found in Hellanicus of Lesbos[ix] and is supported by some other authors. It can be seen especially clearly in Thucydides (cf., for example, the following: "[the peninsula of Akte] is inhabited mostly by . . . Pelasgians who originated from the Tyrsenians, who once lived in Lemnos and Athens" [IV, 109]). Naturally, the records of the "Pelasgians" (though often mythologized) are longer than the references to the Tyrrhenians of the Aegean.

---

16. For example, in Rhaetic inscriptions the use of the "attributive" verbal form retains its importance from the tense-aspect type in [k:], which is a characteristic of archaic Etruscan (see Chapter 6: Morphology).

17. The name Λῆμνος itself is apparently Tyrrhenian. This root is present in Etruscan inscriptions (TLE 105 *lemniśa*, etc.).

However, we can postulate the following: the name "Pelasgians" can hide the Tyrrhenians as well, but the reverse mixing (i.e., the designation of the Pelasgians as "Tyrrhenians") apparently does not take place. In addition, the Etruscans of Italy are also referred to as "Tyrrhenians."

In many Greek works, from the poems of Homer to *Ethnica* of Stephen, another name has been preserved that conceals the Tyrrhenians of the Aegean: "Sinties." In most cases, these references are not original. Rather, they are quotations of Homer (in Strabo in particular [VII, I: 46]). Homer mentioned the Sinties once in the *Iliad* (I: 593-94) and once in the Odyssey (VIII: 294). The latter reference where they are described as people with "a rough speech" is very typical: "ἐς Λῆμνον μετὰ Σίντιας ἀγριοφώνους." Basically, such a perception of Tyrrhenian speech is quite natural to the Greek ear. Also, noteworthy references are found in Hellanicua and Philochorus, a historian of Attica (the third century BCE). Philochorus refers to the Sinties as Pelasgians[x] (which, strictly speaking, reflects the previously considered mixing of the latter with the Tyrrhenians), whereas Hellanicus uses this name for the inhabitants of Lemnos (there are only three references (cf., "Σίντιες ἐκαλοῦντο οἱ Λήμνιοι, ὡς Ἑλλάνικος ἱστορεῖ ἐν τῶι Περὶ Χίου Κτίσεως τὸν τρόπον τοιοῦτον" [Schol. Hom., Od. VIII 294]). In the late period, the Sinties of Lemnos are sometimes called the descendants of the Thracians (cf., for example, in Hesychius: "Σίντιες· Θρακῶν τι γένος. οἱ δὲ τοὺς τὴν Λῆμνον οἰκοῦντας"). It is obviously connected with the mixing of the original ethnonym with the name of the Thracian tribe Σιντοὶ (cf., [Strabo, VII, 1, 46]) at a time when the actual knowledge of the Tyrrhenians of the Aegean was already lost.

The references of Apollonius of Rhodes are extremely valuable. He refers to the Sinties as the eponyms of Lemnos (the island itself used to be called "Sinteis"), as well as definitively shows their Tyrrhenian origin: "οἳ πρὶν μέν ποτε δὴ Σιντηΐδα Λῆμνον ἔναιον Λήμνου τ' ἐξελαθέντες ὑπ' ἀνδράσι Τυρσηνοῖσιν" (Arg., IV, 1759). The same is indicated in the scholia on Apollonius [608]: "Σιντηΐδα: ἐπιθετικῶς Σιντηὶς ἡ Λῆμνος· Τυρσηνοὶ γὰρ αὐτὴν πρῶτοι ᾤκησαν βλαπτικώτατοι ὄντες."[18]

Some hold the opinion that Herodotus did not mention the Tyrrhenians of the Aegean at all (Nemirovskij 1983, 21). From this it is concluded that he subdivided the kindred peoples, referring to the Etruscans as "Tyrrhenians" and to the inhabitants of the Aegean as "Pelasgians." This hypothesis is unlikely to reflect the actual situation. There are few records of the Tyrrhenians in Herodotus' work. The name "Tyrsenia" (i.e., Etruria, is found three times [I: 94; I: 163; VI: 22]). As for the corresponding ethnonym, we find it only four times: in chapter I, 94 (where the traditional version of the origin of the Tyrrhenians from the Lydians and their resettlement to Italy is given); in chapters I, 166-67 and VI, 17 in connection with the mention of a piracy (doubtless the Etruscans are meant here); and in chapter I, 57. This last passage is most interesting, and we shall give it in full:

> I am unable to state with certainty what language the Pelasgians spoke, but we could consider the speech of the Pelasgians who still exist in settlements above Tyrrhenia in the city of Kreston,

---

18. With a folk etymology; in Hesychius σίντης, "βλαπτικός, κακοῦργος."

formerly neighbors to the Dorics who at that time lived in the land now called Thessaliotis; also the Pelasgians who once lived with the Athenians and then settled Plakia and Skylake in the Hellespont; and along with those who lived with all the other communities and were once Pelasgian but changed their names. If one can judge by this evidence, the Pelasgians spoke a barbarian language. And so, if the Pelasgian language was spoken in all these places, the people of Attica being originally Pelasgian, must have learned a new language when they became Hellenes. As a matter of fact, the people of Krestonia and Plakia no longer speak the same language, which shows that they continue to use the dialect they brought with them when they migrated to those lands.

In general, the passage is quite transparent, and we have no reason to doubt the presence of the Tyrrhenians in some northern areas (as they are called the neighbors of the Dorians), in Chalcidice (Kreston) and along the Hellespont in particular. However, in the corresponding passage in Dionysius of Halicarnassus, in place of Creston, Κρότων is named, a city on the east coast of Bruttium: "καὶ γὰρ δὴ οὔτε Κροτωνιῆται ὥς φησιν Ἡρόδοτος "οὐδαμοῖσι τῶν νῦν σφεας περιοικεόντων εἰσὶν ὁμόγλωσσοι οὔτε Πλακιηνοί σφίσι δ' ὁμόγλωσσοι. δηλοῦσι δὲ ὅτι, τὸν ἠνείκαντο γλώσσης χαρακτῆρα μεταβαίνοντες ἐς ταῦτα τὰ χωρία, τοῦτον ἔχουσιν ἐν φυλακῇ." καίτοι θαυμάσειεν ἄν τις, εἰ Πλακιανοῖς μὲν τοῖς περὶ τὴν Ἑλλήσποντον οἰκοῦσιν ὁμοίαν διάλεκτον εἶχον οἱ Κροτωνιᾶται, ἐπειδὴ Πελασγοὶ ἦσαν ἀμφότεροι ἀρχῆθεν, Τυρρηνοῖς δὲ τοῖς ἔγγιστα οἰκοῦσι μηδὲν ὁμοίαν,"[xi] and this reference is extremely strange for several reasons. First, this city is remote from Etruria, and the presence of the Tyrrhenians is not attested there,[19] and second, there is no reason to say that the language of the inhabitants of this Greek city is different from the neighbors' language (which is self-evident in respect of a Greek colony in Italy). And, most importantly, the record of the Italic city completely falls out of context in the narration (especially since it is ranked with Skylake and Plakia). We can assume that Dionysius meant the Tyrrhenian (i.e., Etruscan) city (Etruscan *curtun*, Latin and modern Italian *Cortona*).[20] However, his reference is not logical for the same reasons. It seems to us that Dionysius was a prisoner of his own views on the autochthony of the Etruscans. Considering them to be residents of Italy, he could not understand the reference to the Tyrrhenians in the Aegean and suggested the replacement of Kreston in the text of Herodotus by the city in Italy.

Thus, the mixing of the Tyrrhenians and Pelasgians, coupled with unconvincing stories about the resettlement of the latter to Italy, was peculiar to the Greek tradition in general and had continued for a long time (cf., also in Diodorus of Sicily;[xii] we cannot consider this matter in more detail at present).

The upper chronological limit of existence of this language is unclear, due to the lack of written records after the text of the Lemnos stele. There are no convincing hypotheses about the time of extinction of Aegean-Tyrrhenian at all.

---

19. Not including the statement of Pliny about the Pelasgians' presence in Bruttium: "*A Silero regio tertia et ager Lucanus Bruttiusque incipit, nec ibi rara incolarum mutatione. tenuerunt eum Pelasgi, Oenotri, Itali, Morgetes, Siculi, Graeciae maxime populi, novissime Lucani Samnitibus orti duce Lucio*" (NH, III: 71).

20. Actually, Kroton and Cortona as Pelasgian cities are mentioned by Dionysius in the same passage (I: 26).

Aegean-Tyrrhenian is very closely related to other members of the Tyrrhenian group (i.e., Etruscan, Rhaetic, Eteo-Cypriote, and South Lusitanian). On the other hand, there are certain differences between Aegean-Tyrrhenian and Etruscan in particular that make it possible to refute the viewpoint concerning the Etruscan settlers on the isle of Lemnos. Thus, within the Tyrrhenian family one should not exaggerate the relationship between Aegean-Tyrrhenian and Etruscan (Aegean-Tyrrhenian was clearly not as close to the latter as was Rhaetic. Moreover, it has specific similarities with Minoan).

These issues are not so important for the restoration of the Tyrrhenian morphological system (although, apparently, more important than it might be for Rhaetic). These forms are most valuable for the study of phonetics, vocabulary, and some issues of word formation.

THE ETEO-CYPRIOTE LANGUAGE

The Eteo-Cypriote (i.e., "true Cypriote") language is the language of the local population of the island, later displaced by Greek. The terms "Eteo-Cypriotes," "Eteo-Cypriote" have been introduced into scientific use on the analogy of "Eteocretans," "Eteocretan." So far as these terms are not found in the Greek sources, some of the evidence, where Κύπριοι appear (in particular, the group of Hesychius's glosses) may be attributed precisely to this ethnic group. Unfortunately, this language is rarely mentioned in Etruscological literature, although its relation to Etruscan was already noted by the Russian Etruscologist Xarsekin several decades ago (Xarsekin 1976[2]).

Figure 3. Eteo-Cypriote script, Amathus, Cyprus

Eteo-Cypriote (see Figure 3) is attested in the records of the sixth to fourth centuries BCE (see Chapter 2: Sources). We have no evidence for the time of its extinction. It is not quite clear what the relationship of this language was with an idiom attested to in the inscriptions of the so-called Cypro-Minoan syllabary. If there is a real kinship between them, it would add appreciably to our view of the whole group, since a language with the same ancient status as the Minoan would then appear in front of us. (In particular, a clay tablet from Enkomi, discovered in 1953, is apparently dated to the end of the sixteenth to the beginning of the fifteenth centuries BCE). However, this assumption is purely hypothetical so far, although it does not contradict the available data on the settlement of the Tyrrhenians (i.e., on the presence of "Tursha" in the eastern Mediterranean). In 1966, J. Friedrich, a prominent scholar of ancient written records in his "*Geschichte der Schrift,*" opines that the Cypriot-Minoan syllabary was created for the language that was later present in non-Greek inscriptions made with the classic Cypriote syllabary (Friedrich 1979, 92).[21]

Prospects for studying the morphology and vocabulary of the Eteo-Cypriote language are not clear. Classic lexical comparisons with Etruscan (such as *a-na ma-to-ri*, Etruscan *an, meθl*) are few. Interpretations of the vocabulary different from the known Tyrrhenian one (which is mainly Etruscan) may run into insuperable difficulties. The same applies to the morphological elements: about five to seven case, verbal, and derivational suffixes, about which one can speak more or less definitely, correspond to the Etruscan ones. Formants different from the latter have not been interpreted so far.

Figure 4. Tartessos script of Iberia

---

21. Russian translation.

However, it seems to us that progress in the study of Eteo-Cypriote may well be achieved, and the existing texts will reveal interesting grammatical forms. Apparently, the Eteo-Cypriote language (in case of a successful analysis of the inscriptions) will reveal an interesting picture of the coincidences and differences with respect to the other Tyrrhenian languages. Already one can say that some of the existing forms show certain peculiarities in word formation in comparison with the other languages of the group under study. If the relationship of the language attested in the Cypro-Minoan inscriptions to Minoan and Tyrrhenian is proven, it will be a most noticeable enrichment of the linguistic material, at least in quantitative terms.

THE IBERO-TYRRHENIAN (SOUTH LUSITANIAN) LANGUAGE (CONJECTURAL)

South Lusitanian is the westernmost, little-known Tyrrhenian idiom preserved in a few short inscriptions (see Figure 4). The dating of the latter is disputed, which has an influence on our understanding of the Tyrrhenians' settlement as a whole. Judging from the paleographic peculiarities, local Tyrrhenian inscriptions date from a very early time (for details, see Sources; Friedrich 1979, 92, see the upper limits of the existence of the language). However, the assertion that we have no reliable extralinguistic data indicating the Tyrrhenians' presence in Iberia would be premature. The evidence of Diodorus of Sicily (V, 20, 4) can be interpreted in such a way that the Tyrrhenians during their sea voyages went beyond the Pillars of Hercules (i.e., Gibraltar). Schulten put forward the view that they even reached Madeira (Schulten 1941, 17). On the other hand, this scholar, to whom we owe all the main results in the identification and study of the Tyrrhenian inscriptions of the Iberian Peninsula, clearly overstated the role of the Tyrrhenian people in Iberia, considering the city of Tartessos to be a Tyrrhenian colony, which has provoked a lot of debate (Schulten 1941, 28). The Tyrrhenians' presence on the Peninsula is proved also by some parallels in the toponymy and onomastics (perhaps these parallels form two layers with the earlier one related to the independent local language,[22] and the later one explained by contacts with the Etruscans). We can assume that the Tyrrhenian population of Iberia was not, however, numerous in comparison to the unrelated Iberian tribes surrounding them and eventually dissolved into the latter.

The Iberian material shows significant differences from the Etruscan in vocabulary, while the known morphological features (primarily in the morphology of the noun, since verb morphology is almost completely unknown) are close to the Etruscan ones (cf., in particular, the "redetermination" of genitive/adjective affixes).

There is a typical lexical coincidence to Aegean-Tyrrhenian: the stem of the verb *śar-on-* meaning "buried," which is totally unknown in Etruscan (despite the fact that, in the latter, the terminology associated with burial is well studied). It appears that Schulten,

---

22. Compare, for example, the name Ἀργανθώνιος (the king of Tartessos, according to Herodotus [I: 163, 165]; see also Hesychius among others) : Ἀργανθών (Stephan gives: "ὄρος Μυσίας ἐπὶ τῇ Κίῳ") : Etruscan *arcnti*(*-s*) (CIE 1900, 2555, Cl.).

who was first to connect the rare Iberian idiom to the Tyrrhenians, drew attention to precisely that stem that enabled him to make a preliminary conclusion about the relation to Etruscan and Lemnian (i.e., Aegean-Tyrrhenian). Further progress in the study of this language depends on the discovery of new inscriptions.

POSSIBLE LOCALIZATION OF THE OTHER DIALECTS

It may well be that with time other idioms included in the group under study will be found, but for the present there are no reliable "applicants" in view. It is now known that the pre-Indo-European languages of Mediterranean Europe form several independent groups, and ill-grounded comparisons between all the relics no longer appear in prestigious publications.

Since the Tyrrhenian peoples are originally related to Asia Minor, it is not surprising that, in different areas of the peninsula (Lydia, Mysia, Paphlagonia), we find toponyms which clearly belong to this layer, but, apparently, no written records of Tyrrhenian languages have been discovered in the area.

There are specific parallels to the known Tyrrhenian vocabulary in Sicily. They are few, but quite obvious. Similar examples will be presented below, in Chapter 6: Morphology and Chapter 7: Word Formation. In principle, they may be considered as loanwords, dating back to the period of Etruscan sea power.

It is possible that some traces of the Tyrrhenian language, which is different from Etruscan—or quite related to it—may be discovered in Sardinia or Corsica. However, the existing material is insufficient for making any conclusions (cf., also Urbanová and Blažek 2008, 212-16). The few suppositions on the Tyrrhenian character of Proto-Sardic rely mainly on extralinguistic data, among which one should primarily note the information from Tacitus,[xiii] who directly points to the common origin of the Sards and Tyrrhenians. However, it is not very reliable. Apparently, Tacitus substantiates the affinity between the Etruscans and Sards with the third element, the Lydians, and, in this case, it was the consonance with the name of the Lydian capital, Σάρδεις (also Σάρδιες, Σάρδις) that evidently served as the foundation for his supposition of that relationship. Using this information as a basis, Nemirovskij even made a guess about the Etruscans' migration from Sardinia (Nemirovskij 1983, 49-61), which was obviously premature.

More interesting is the information from Servius on the direct participation of the inhabitants of Corsica in the foundation of Populonia[23] and, apparently, Volterra.[xiv] However, these data are too few and scattered. In fact, the only real basis for comparison may be the substratum vocabulary in modern Sardinian and Corsican, but it is drawn more from the Iberian and Libyan-Berber language groups (i.e., associated with immigrants from the Pyrenean peninsula and North Africa; the ancient authors also point to these relations). In any case, it is necessary to determine the relation of the substratum of "Archaic Romance" (i.e., of Sardinia, Corsica, and some dialects of the

---

23. In this case, such an influence is quite possible. Among the major Etruscan cities, Populonia was the only maritime one.

extreme south of Italy) to Tyrrhenian. For the present, we have found only one reliable Etruscan parallel to the Sardinian vocabulary which is a common name *serθur* (Latin *Sertorius*).

CHAPTER ONE NOTES

[i] "ἄλλη δ' ἄλλων γλῶσσα μεμιγμένη· ἐν μὲν Ἀχαιοί, ἐν δ' Ἐτεόκρητες μεγαλήτορες, ἐν δὲ Κύδωνες Δωριέες τε τριχάϊκεί δῖοί τε Πελασγοί· – τῇσι δ' ἐνὶ Κνωσός, μεγάλη πόλις, ἔνθα τε Μίνως ἐννέωρος βασίλευε Διὸς μεγάλου ὀαριστής."

[ii] "*Adnectitur septima, in qua Etruria est ab amne Macra, ipsa mutatis saepe nominibus. Umbros inde exegere antiquitus Pelasgi, hos Lydi, a quorum rege Tyrrheni, mox a sacrifico ritu lingua Graecorum Tusci sunt cognominati. primum Etruriae oppidum Luna, portu nobile, colonia Luca a mari recedens propiorque Pisae inter amnes Auserem et Arnum, ortae a Pelopidis sive a Teutanis, Graeca gente. vada Volaterrana, fluvius Caecina, Populonium, Etruscorum quondam hoc tantum in litore.*

Hinc amnes Prile, mox Umbro, navigiorum capax, et ab eo tractus Umbriae portusque Telamo, Cosa Volcientium a populo Romano deducta, Graviscae, Castrum Novum, Pyrgi, Caeretanus amnis et ipsum Caere intus m. p. VII, Agylla a Pelasgis conditoribus dictum, Alsium, Fregenae, Tiberis amnis a Macra CCLXXXIIII p. intus coloniae Faliosca, Argis orta, ut auctor est Cato, quae cognominatur Etruscorum, Lucus Feroniae, Rusellana, Seniensis, Sutrina.

De cetero Arretini Veteres, Arretini Fidentiores, Arretini Iulienses, Amitinenses, Aquenses cognomine Taurini, Blerani, Cortonenses, Capenates, Clusini Novi, Clusini Veteres, Florentini praefluenti Arno adpositi, Faesulae, Ferentinum, Fescennia, Hortanum, Herbanum, Nepet, Novem Pagi, Praefectura Claudia Doroclodi, Pistorium, Perusia, Suanenses, Saturnini qui ante Aurini vocabantur, Subertani, Statonienses, Tarquinienses, Tuscanienses, Vetulonienses, Veientani, Vesentini, Volaterrani, Volcentani cognomine Etrusci, Volsinienses. in eadem parte oppidorum veterum nomina retinent agri Crustuminus, Caletranus.

Tiberis, ante Thyberis appellatus et prius Albula, e media fere longitudine Appennini finibus Arretinorum profluit, tenuis primo nec nisi piscinis corrivatus emissusque navigabilis, sicuti Tinia et Clanis influentes in eum, novenorum ita conceptu dierum, si non adiuvent imbres. sed Tiberis propter aspera et confragosa ne sic quidem, praeterquam trabibus verius quam ratibus, longe meabilis fertur, per CL p. non procul Tiferno Perusiaque et Ocriculo Etruriam ab Umbris ac Sabinis, mox citra XVI p. urbis Veientem agrum a Crustumino, dein Fidenatem Latinumque a Vaticano dirimens" (NH III: 50-53).

[iii] "*Iungetur his sexta regio Umbriam conplexa agrumque Gallicum citra Ariminum. ab Ancona Gallica ora incipit Togatae Galliae cognomine. Siculi et Liburni plurima eius tractus tenuere, in primis Palmensem, Praetutianum Hadrianumque agrum. Umbri eos expulere, hos Etruria, hanc Galli. Umbrorum gens antiquissima Italiae existimatur, ut quos Ombrios a Graecis putent dictos, quod in inundatione terrarum imbribus superfuissent.*

Trecenta eorum oppida Tusci debellasse reperiuntur. nunc in ora flumen Aesis, Senagallia, Metaurus fluvius, coloniae Fanum Fortunae, Pisaurum cum amne et intus Hispellum, Tuder. de cetero Amerini, Attidiates, Asisinates, Arnates, Aesinates, Camertes, Casuentillani, Carsulani, Dolates cognomine Sallentini, Fulginiates, Foroflaminienenses, Foroiulienses cognomine Concupienses, Forobrentani, Forosempronienses, Iguini, Interamnates cognomine Nartes, Mevanates, Mevaniolenses, Matilicates, Narnienses, quod oppidum Nequinum antea vocitatum est, Nucerini cognomine Favonienses et Camellani, Ocriculani, Ostrani, Pitinates cognomine Pisuertes et alii Mergentini, Plestini, Sentinates, Sarsinates, Spoletini, Sestinates, Suillates, Tadinates, Trebiates, Tuficani, Tifernates cognomine Tiberini et alii.

Metaurenses, Vesinicates, Urvinates cognomine Metaurenses et alii Hortenses, Vettonenses, Vindinates, Visuentani. in hoc situ interiere Feliginates et qui Clusiolum tenuere supra Interamnam et Sarranates cum oppidis Acerris quae Vafriae cognominabantur, Turocaelo quod Vettiolum, item

Solinates, Curiates, Falinates, Sapinates. interiere et Arinates cum Crinivolo et Usidicani et Plangenses, Paesinates, Caelestini. Ameriam supra scriptam Cato ante Persei bellum conditam annis DCCCCLXIII prodit.

Octava regio determinatur Arimino, Pado, Appennino. in ora fluvius Crustumium, Ariminum colonia cum annibus Arimino et Aprusa, fluvius Rubico, quondam finis Italiae. ab eo Sapis et Utis et Anemo, Ravenna Sabinorum oppidum cum amne Bedese, ab Ancona CV, nec procul a mari Umbrorum Butrium. intus coloniae Bononia, Felsina vocitata tum cum princeps Etruriae esset, Brixillum, Mutina, Parma, Placentia.

Oppida Caesena, Claterna, Fora Clodi, Livi, Popili, Druentinorum, Corneli, Licini, Faventini, Fidentini, Otesini, Padinates, Regienses a Lepido, Solonates Saltusque Galliani qui cognominantur Aquinates, Tannetani, Veleiates cognomine Vetti Regiates, Urbanates. in hoc tractu interierunt Boi, quorum tribus CXII fuisse auctor est Cato, item Senones, qui ceperunt Romam" (NH III: 112-16). On the northern border of the Etruscans' settlement: "*Mantua Tuscorum trans Padum sola reliqua*" (NH III: 130).

[iv] "ἀποπλέειν κατὰ βίου τε καὶ γῆς ζήτησιν, ἐς ὃ ἔθνεα πολλὰ παραμειψαμένους ἀπικέσθαι ἐς Ὀμβρικοὺς ἔνθα σφέας ἐνιδρύσασθαι πόλιας καὶ οἰκέειν τὸ μέχρι τοῦδε" (I: 94).

[v] "*Aspexerunt omnes, qui aderant, alius alium, primo tristiores turbato et requirente voltu, quidnam illud utriusque verbi foret; post deinde, quasi nescio quid Tusce aut Gallice dixisset, universi riserunt.*"

[vi] "τῇ πρὸς τὸ θεῖον εὐχῇ καὶ κατὰ τὰ πάτρια θεραπείᾳ βροντῶν ἐξαισίων καὶ πρηστήρων ἐπιγενομένων τοὺς ἐπικειμένους βαρβάρους ἀποδιῶξαι" (Zosimus, V: 41).

[vii] Cf., the following: "*Incolae Alpium multi populi, sed inlustres a Pola ad Tergestis regionem Fecusses, Subocrini, Catali, Menoncaleni iuxtaque Carnos quondam Taurisci appellati, nunc Norici. his contermini Raeti et Vindolici, omnes in multas civitates divisi. Raetos Tuscorum prolem arbitrantur a Gallis pulsos duce Raeto. verso deinde in Italiam pectore Alpium Latini iuris Euganeae gentes, quarum oppida XXXIIII enumerat Cato.*

Ex iis Trumplini, venalis cum agro suis populus, dein Camunni conpluresque similes finitimis adtributi muicipis. Lepontios et Salassos Tauriscae gentis idem Cato arbitratur; ceteri fere Lepontios relictos ex comitatu Herculis interpretatione Graeci nominis credunt, praeustis in transitu Alpium nive membris. eiusdem exercitus et Graios fuisse Graiarum Alpium incolas praestantesque genere Euganeos, inde tracto nomine. caput eorum Stoenos.

Raetorum Vennonienses Sarunetesque ortus Rheni amnis accolunt, Lepontiorum qui Uberi vocantur fontem Rhodani eodem Alpium tractu. sunt praeterea Latio donati incolae, ut Octodurenses et finitimi Ceutrones, Cottianae civitates et Turi Liguribus orti, Bagienni Ligures et qui Montani vocantur Capillatorumque plura genera ad confinium Ligustici maris.
Non alienum videtur hoc loco subicere inscriptionem e tropaeo Alpium, quae talis est: IMP : CAESARI DIVI FILIO AVG : PONT : MAX : IMP : XIIII : TR : POT : XVII : S : P : Q : R : QVOD EIVS DVCTV AVSPICIISQVE GENTES ALPINAE OMNES QVAE A MARI SVPERO AD INFERVM PERTINEBANT SVB IMPERIVM P : R : SVNT REDACTAE : GENTES ALPINAE DEVICTAE TRVMPILINI : CAMVVNI : VENOSTES : VENNONETES : ISARCI : BREVNI : GENAVNES : FOCVNATES : VINDELICORVM GENTES QVATTVOR : COSVANETES : RVCINATES : LICATES : CATENATES : AMBISONTES : RVGVSCI : SVANETES : CALVCONES : BRIXENETES : LEPONTI : VBERI : NANTVATES : SEDVNI : VARAGRI : SALASSI : ACITAVONES : MEDVLLI : VCEENI : CATVRIGES : BRIGIANI : SOGIONTI : BRODIONTI : NEMALONI : EDENATES : VESVBIANI : VEAMINI : GALLITAE : TRIVLLATI : ECDINI : VERGVNNI : EGVI : TVRI : NEMATVRI : ORATELLI : NERVSI : VELAVNI : SVETRI" (NH III, 133-7).

[viii] "Ὅτι οἱ Τυρρηνοὶ διὰ τὸν τῶν Περσῶν φόβον ἐκλιπόντες τὴν Λῆμνον" (Diodorus, X, 18).

[ix] Cf., the following: "Ἑλλάνικος δὲ ὁ Λέσβιος τοὺς Τυρρηνοὺς φησι Πελασγοὺς πρότερον καλουμένους" (FHG, Hell., fr. 1).

[x] "Σίντιες ἄνδρες Φιλόχορός φησι Πελασγοὺς αὐτοὺς ὄντας οὕτω προσαγορευθῆναι, ἐπεὶ πλεύσαντες εἰς Βραύρωνα κανηφόρους παρθένους ἥρπασαν" (Schol. Bt. Hom., A 594).

[xi] Cf., also I, 28: "τοῦ Πελασγοῦ τοῦ βασιλέος αὐτῶν καὶ Μενίππης τῆς Πηνειοῦ ἐγένετο Φράστωρ, τοῦ δὲ Ἀμύντωρ, τοῦ δὲ Τευταμίδης, τοῦ δὲ Νάνας. ἐπὶ τούτου βασιλεύοντος οἱ Πελασγοὶ ὑπ' Ἑλλήνων ἀνέστησαν, καὶ ἐπὶ Σπινῆτι ποταμῷ ἐν τῷ Ἰονίῳ κόλπῳ τάς νῆας καταλιπόντες Κρότωνα πόλιν ἐν μεσογείῳ εἶλον καὶ ἐντεῦθεν ὁρμώμενοι τὴν νῦν καλεομένην Τυρσηνίην ἔκτισαν."

[xii] "τούτους δ' ἔνιοί φασιν ἀπὸ τῶν ἐν Τυρρηνίᾳ δώδεκα πόλεων ἀποικαισθῆναι· τινὲς δέ φασι Πελασγοὺς πρὸ τῶν Τρωικῶν ἐκ Θετταλίας φυγόντας" (Diodorus, 14, 113).

[xiii] "*Sardiani decretum Etruriae recitavere ut consanguinei: nam Tyrrhenum Lydumque Atye rege genitos ob multitudinem divisisse gentem; Lydum patriis in terris resedisse, Tyrrheno datum novas ut conderet sedes; et ducum e nominibus indita vocabula illis per Asiam, his in Italia*" (Ann. IV, 55).

[xiv] "*Populonia est civitas Tusciae. matrem autem eorum qui venerant, patriam dixit, ut alibi "insignem quem mater Aricia misit." quidam Populoniam post XII. populos in Etruria constitutos populum ex insula Corsica in Italiam venisse et condidisse dicunt: alii Populoniam Volaterranorum coloniam tradunt. Alii Volaterranos Corsis eripuisse Populoniam dicunt*" (Aen., X, 172).

CHAPTER 2

SOURCES

THE MINOAN LANGUAGE

The sources for the study of the Minoan language are divided into two substantially different groups which are, firstly, written records themselves, made with Phaistos signs (see Appendix 1), Cretan hieroglyphics, Linear A and the Greek alphabet (see Appendix 2 for the texts of the latest Eteocretan period) and, secondly, the complex of the relic vocabulary, preserved in Greek. The sources of the first type, which are synchronous and come from the Cretans proper, contain information about the Minoan language, which is known to be more complete, but they still remain virtually unread for a number of reasons which will be discussed below.

The stratum of the relic vocabulary includes words that have penetrated into the Greek literary language, as well as rare (often recorded only once [ἅπαξ λεγόμενα]) glosses of Greek authors. Since it is almost impossible to distinguish them from the Aegean-Tyrrhenian relics, they will not be considered separately here. Their basic characteristics will be given in Chapter 4: Interpretation of the Vocabulary.

Minoan written records as such are quite numerous (among the languages of the group under study only Etruscan inscriptions exceed them quantitatively), and they are relatively diverse. They became known due to many years of archaeologists' work in Crete, which began in the late nineteenth century, became famous because of the excavations by Sir A. Evans, and continue to this day.

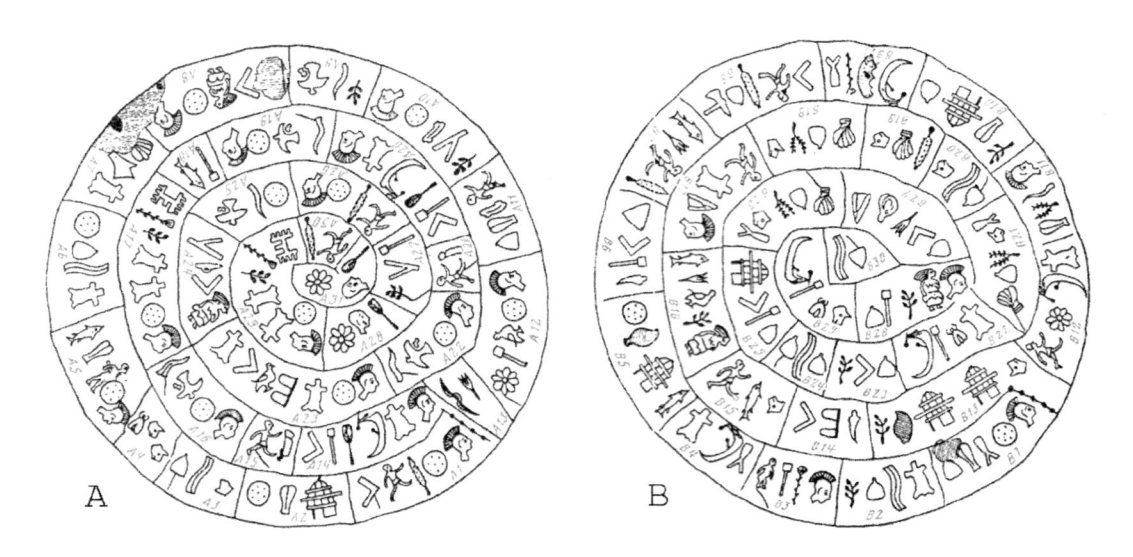

Figure 5. Phaistos Disk, front and back sides

It is quite probable that the world's most famous Cretan artifact, the Phaistos Disk (see Figure 5), conceals the Minoan language. The style of individual signs bears a particular resemblance to the later systems of local writing. Subsequently, the principle of drawing the inscriptions in a spiral is also found in Crete (see below the inscription on the ring of Mauro Spelio). On the other hand, there is no plausible similarity with any other well-known script, so the opinion that the disk could have been brought to Crete is purely speculative. "The relic is a disk of burned clay measuring a palm . . . It is found among the utensil remainders in the Phaistos palace ruins. The place where it was found and the objects around indicate the time about the seventeenth century BCE (i.e., the beginning of the 'Second Palace period' in Aegean culture")" (Ipsen 1976, 32).

The repertoire of the disk consists of forty-five signs, and both sides contain 242 characters. Word boundaries are nowhere in doubt, as all the supposed word forms are inserted into rectangular slots. The inscription of the Phaistos disk in the accepted numbering system is presented in Appendix 1. Unfortunately, over the century that has elapsed since the publication of the disk, no convincing reading of a single word has been offered.

The quantitative and geographical distribution of other existing inscriptions is rather uneven over different periods. The known hieroglyphic inscriptions come mainly from the east and northeast of the island with almost none found to the west of Knossos. A separate group is formed by the inscriptions from the area of Phaistos: Gortyna and Hagia Triada. Isolated finds come from Cythera and Samothrace.

For the present one cannot speak of "reading" hieroglyphic inscriptions as such. Any such attempts, in fact, would be based on an external comparison with the signs of Linear A and B, but it has not yet given clear results. Fortunately, in many inscriptions of larger dimensions word boundaries are regularly observed, which should be of great help to scholars.

Texts, written in Cretan hieroglyphics, are not infrequent (331 in CHIC edition), but most of them are very short inscriptions, or inscriptions containing only one to three characters. They are mainly seal stones (interestingly, many of them have not been found in excavations, but bought from the local population, since the Evans expeditions) and clay medallions with holes that were used as tags. As an example of a relatively "large" inscription of this type, we can offer a medallion from Knossos CHIC 039, which contains four groups of two characters each, a group of three characters and the number 120. Somewhat longer inscriptions were drawn on the tetrahedral clay "sticks" ("barres" by CHIC), which were used for economic record-keeping. The inscription of this type from Knossos contains nine groups of two or three characters and a series of numerals up to 6400 (!).

Isolated seals vastly exceed in length most of the inscriptions of this type. Of great importance is a four-sided seal from the National Archaeological Museum in Athens (CHIC 294), containing up to thirty-five characters, as well as some others. One should definitely note an octagonal seal of agate (CHIC 314) as well, which is now kept in the Ashmolean Museum (Great Britain). Its text contains twelve characters (see Figure 6). The inscription is, apparently, written in boustrophedon (this is partly taken into account also in the numbering adopted by the compilers of CHIC). Such a direction is indicated by upside-down images of heads, spears, axes, and vegetable characters emerging across the line. A detailed study of the octagonal seal was conducted by the Russian scholar Molchanov, who determined the direction of the script, the beginning and the end of the inscription, and suggested a number of interesting readings (Molchanov 1992, 33 et seq.).

Figure 6. Rendering of the boustrophedon inscription on octagonal seal CHIC 314 from the Ashmolean Museum

Of particular value is the inscription on a fragment of a stone vessel from Mallia (CHIC 328), containing sixteen characters. In fact, this is the main text on which one can pin the hope of finding the words, or at least concrete stems, related to the cult.

The fundamental edition of the hieroglyphic inscriptions of Crete was undertaken by Godart and Olivier (Godart and Olivier 1996) and was based on the preliminary material (Godart and Olivier 1978). It contains excellent photographs and detailed drawings, paleographic tables, detailed indices, etc. There is a unified numbering system used in the edition.

The main part of the Minoan texts is written in Linear A. Several hundred Linear A inscriptions have been found, which are very different in purpose, length, and degree of secure interpretation. We know best the clay tablets containing the palace household accounts (which, in principle, is similar to the situation with the records of Greek Linear B). Among the items containing noneconomic inscriptions, attention is drawn to ceramic and stone vessels, fragments of altars and slabs for libation, jewelry, and other artifacts. Besides these, there are numerous seals, clay labels, and owners' stamps, which are of much less significant interest for the study because of the extreme brevity of the inscription (although all groups include "texts" of a single syllable sign or a logogram). As relatively large inscriptions, we should mention the labels HT Wa 3017 and ZA Wa 2, containing seven characters each.

Vague mentions in Greek sources may indicate that, at the time when the Linear writing system was current as a medium for the records of noneconomic character, leather may have been used. Accordingly, such artifacts are unlikely to survive. On the other hand, peculiarities of the development of the Linear writing system, which will be discussed below, suggest that there were relic inscriptions composed in Crete, which may eventually be found.

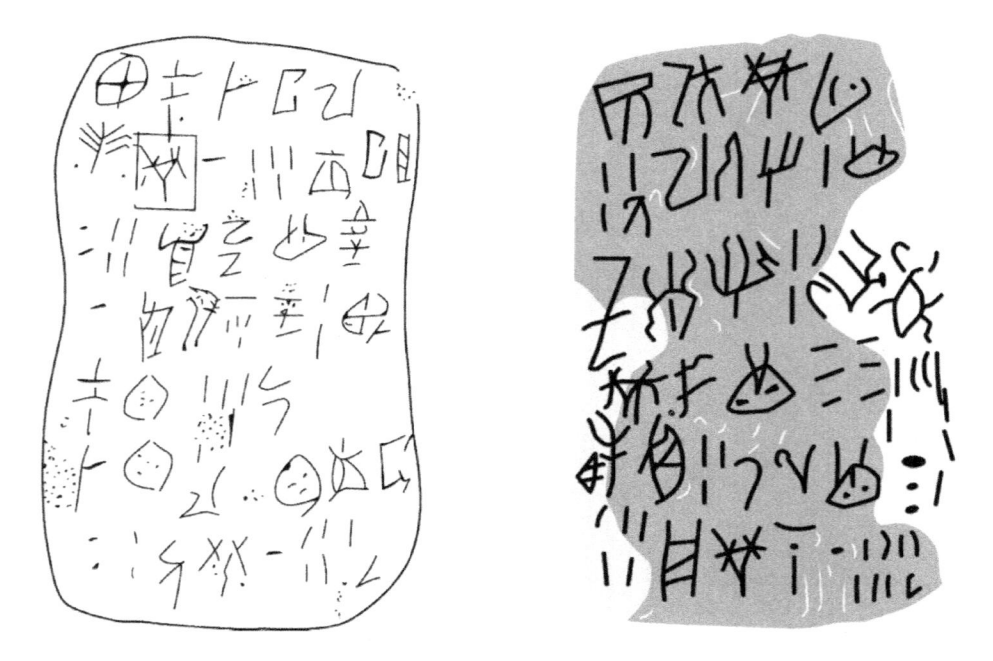

Figure 7. Tablet HT 6 from the ancient Minoan settlement at Hagia Triada.

Clay tablets come from different areas of Crete, with the greatest number coming from the famous archives discovered near the modern village of Hagia Triada. In the first volume of GO (for publications of inscriptions, see below) 154 tablets are listed from Hagia Triada, thirty-two from Knossos, thirty-one from Phaistos, nine from Mallia and one each from Kea, Palaikastro, Papoura, Pyrgos, Tylissos, and Zakros. The third volume includes 126 plates, mostly fragmented. The length of texts varies greatly; it can be minimal for the fragments. One of the largest one-sided plates, the plate from Palekastro, includes twelve groups of signs, presumably whole words, with a total of forty-two signs. For a detailed drawing of the intact tablet HT 6, see Figure 7.

In the economic records word boundaries are used irregularly, but this irregularity is largely compensated for by the wide distribution of logograms and numerical signs separating the categorematic words (which may even yield logograms and numerals. For example, in the inscription HT 116, eighteen logograms are made up of twenty-one syllabic signs, and each logogram is followed by a numeral, the designation of weight or quantity). It is clear that these inscriptions are very poor, both lexically and grammatically. Their content cannot exceed the limits of the ethnogeographical and socioeconomic realities of Crete in the late third to middle second millennium BCE. As a typical example of an economic tablet, one can cite the aforementioned inscription HT 13, which is read as follows: (1) *ka-u-de-ta* (2) *VIN te-re-za 5 1/2* (3) *te-tu 56 te-ki* (4) *27 1/2 ku-do-ni 17 1/2* (5) *da-?-? 19* (6) *no-du-ne-dwo(?) 5* (7) *ku-ro 130 1/2*, the word *ku-ro*, as was established long ago, means "a total, in all."

On the other hand, the regular abundance of ethnonyms and toponyms often enables us to correlate them with the forms occurring in Greek. Because of this, one can make very important observations about word-formation models.

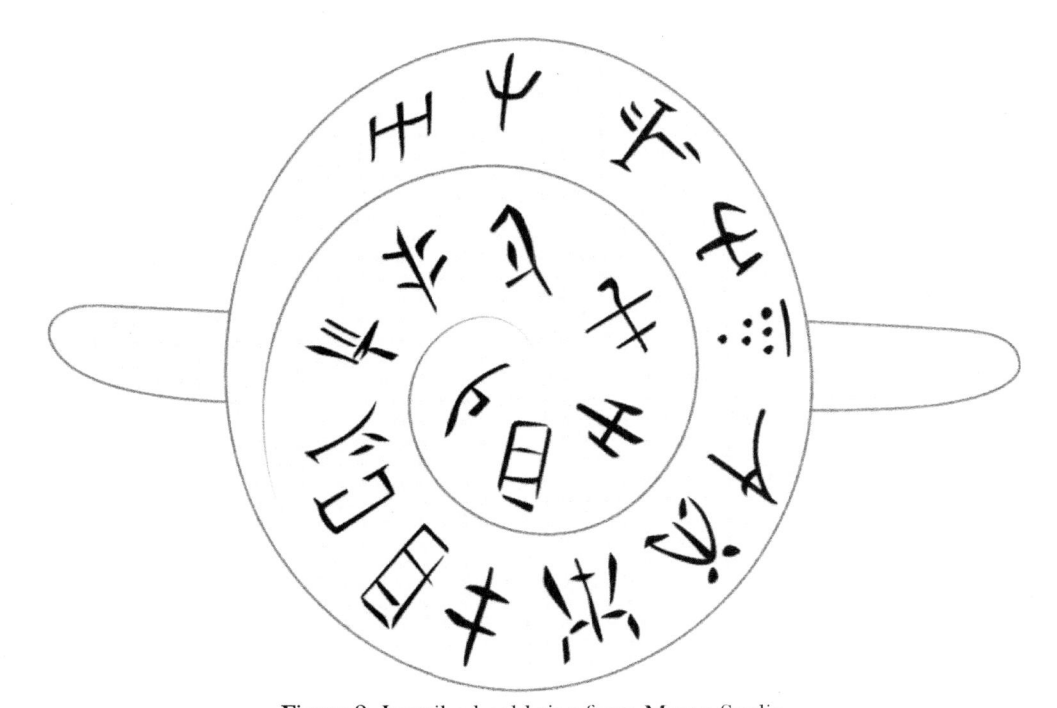

Figure 8. Inscribed gold ring from Mavro Spelio

The less numerous inscriptions on various objects (a total of seventy-six in the fourth volume of GO) are much more interesting. Provided that they are well preserved, they often contain more extensive texts. Thus, the inscriptions on the stone vessels TL Za 1 and PK Za 11 contain twenty-six and forty-two characters, respectively; the inscriptions on the silver hairpin KN Zf 13 contain nineteen characters, etc.

The inscription on the gold ring from Mavro Spelio (KN Zf 13, see Figure 8) requires very careful examination. Given that all noneconomic inscriptions should include more complex and interesting constructions, the inscription on such a valuable artifact stands out even more among them. Moreover, this inscription is the second, after the text of the Phaistos disk, which is made in a spiral (accordingly, it is also read from the outside to the center). It suggests that there was a tradition of inscribing the signs of Cretan writing on round objects that had a particular importance.

The text of the inscription (nineteen characters) will be discussed below. There are no difficulties in reading the particular syllables (except for the sign 301, which also will be discussed separately), but there are no word boundaries (it seems that even with their presence, the disclosure of the structure of the inscription would not be fundamentally different).

The type of the artifact enables us to make assumptions about which components are most likely to be found here: one or two proper names (of the master, owner, or the deity, to whom it was devoted, in any combination); a pronoun, a personal one (of the first person if the text is drawn up on behalf of the object, which is normal, for example, for Etruscan inscriptions) or a demonstrative one (if the text is drawn up on behalf of the master, owner, or the giver); and at least one verbal form, etc.

In general, we can say that the inscriptions available to scholars can expand the work in at least four ways: comparing the stems with the relic pre-Greek vocabulary, reading new signs using the combinatorial method, analyzing word-formation models, and accumulating initial material on morphology. It is obvious that the epigraphy in particular should be a major source for the study of this language in the future, because, as it most often occurs, it retains synchronous forms and constructions, free from distortion and modernization, which are inevitable in any tradition.

There are relatively few published editions of Linear A inscriptions. One of the first was the edition of the corpus produced by G. Pugliese Carrattelli (Carrattelli 1945). As can be seen, it was published before the decipherment of Linear B by Ventris (i.e., there was no possibility of even a conventional reading at that time). Afterward, this publication was extended and supplemented (Carrattelli 1963). There are other publications that are generally difficult to access.

The basis for the work of modern scholars on this topic is the fundamental five-volume corpus of Godart and Olivier (1976–1985), in this study, GO. The sophisticated classification of the inscriptions encouraged the editors to abandon the continuous numbering system by grouping the inscriptions according to type. Thus, the first volume includes economic inscriptions discovered up to 1970; the second includes the inscriptions on the seals, tags, and so on, also discovered up to 1970; the third the findings of 1975–76; the fourth, being most interesting for us, all other documents; the fifth, appendices and indices. The first is built on a geographical basis,[24] and the fourth lists the place of discovery and type of artifact.[25] In the fifth volume, there is a sort of "dictionary," where, in accordance with the accepted numeration of signs, under each sign is written all the forms starting with this sign, then all the forms where the sign appears in the noninitial position. There is no doubt that this exemplary edition will be of paramount importance for a very long time.

One should mention separately the corpus of inscriptions where the sequences of the numbers of the Linear A signs are given in accordance with the accepted classification, instead of photos or drawings (Raison and Pope 1994). It is a concise volume and is certainly useful to formalize the texts, for example, for machine processing, but one should use it with great care. The impossibility of checking the reading based on a graphic image puts the scholar into a total dependence on the authors' reading which is not always reliable.[26]

THE ETEOCRETAN LANGUAGE

After a long interval called the "Greek Dark Ages" (1200–800 BCE), beginning approximately from the end of the seventh century, inscriptions in a language that can be called Late Minoan reappear in Crete. They are made with the Greek alphabet. These inscriptions had been written before the end of the fourth century BCE by the Eteocretans, and they come from the same areas where the presence of the latter is recorded by Greek tradition, primarily from the cities of Praisos (Πραισός, Πραῖσος, Πρᾶσος) and Dreros (Δρῆρος).

The main Eteocretan inscriptions originate from Praisos. They were first published by M. Guarducci (*Inscriptiones Creticae*, etc. III. Roma 1942, 134–42). We will list and describe them here (for the reading, see Appendix 2):

1. Discovered in 1884; a stone measuring 27 × 34 cm. contains the left (for the viewer) side of the inscription; it does not seem possible to determine its initial size. The inscription is made with the archaic alphabet. It dates back to the end of the seventh to the beginning of the sixth centuries BCE, and its direction is boustrophedon.

2. The inscription of the end of the fifth to fourth centuries BCE. It is made with the standard Ionian alphabet but with the Cretan *lambda*.

3. The relatively large inscription of the fourth century BCE, discovered in 1904. It is a fragment of the right (for the viewer) side of the original monument, with the maximum dimensions of 41.5 × 20 cm. The text is made with the Ionian alphabet with a *digamma* added.

4. Besides the above enumerated, there are smaller fragments of the inscriptions from Praisos. They contain very few signs. Two Eteocretan texts from Dreros were found

---

24. In other words, HT, the inscriptions from Hagia Triada, KN from Knossos, etc.

25. For example, AP Za 1, an inscription on a stone vessel from Apodoulou, KN Zb 3, an inscription on a ceramic vessel from Knossos.

26. Thus, the sign 052 *no* here is read everywhere as 028 *i*, the sign 014 *do* was attributed to the unknown, because the name of a great Cretan city, *ku-do-ni*, was unread.

by the Temple of Apollo Delphinius together with six Greek texts. To our great regret, during the Italo-German occupation of Crete, the unique inscriptions were lost.

5. The Dreros bilingual. A piece of slate measuring 75 × 26 cm contained a boustrophedon inscription. It can be determined by special features of the paleography that it dates back to the seventh century BCE. The Greek part is damaged and cannot be fully translated.

6. "Short bilingual." The inscription on a long piece of slate (99 × 23 cm) of an irregular shape dates back to the seventh century as well. Word boundaries are absent. There are no associations with the known vocabulary.

7. The so-called inscription "Epioi" is unique. Its origin is unclear (moreover, it was in a private collection). There are three characters in it after the Greek part (1 ΕΠΙΟΙ 2 ΖΗΘΑΝΘΗ 3 ΕΝΕΤΗ ΠΑΡΣΙΦΑΙ). They resemble the linear ones,[27] but there are doubts about the authenticity of the inscription.

THE ETRUSCAN LANGUAGE

The published sources of information about Etruscan written inscriptions, including the literary ones, are very diverse, relatively numerous, and, on the other hand, only to an insignificant extent reflect the situation with the extant sources. It is known for certain that there were extensive written works in the Etruscan language. However, statements about the literature in the modern sense would be premature (we have, in fact, only the mysterious evidence of Varro: "*Volnius, qui tragoedias Etruscas scripsit*" [lL V, 55]).

It is obvious that a certain part of those texts was translated also into Latin. Some religious instructions may be considered a direct translation from Etruscan, and moreso because sometimes there are indications of the source. The apogee of this written work was, obviously, both original works and the work of the emperor Claudius in the history of Etruria in twenty books (compiled in the 40s of the first century CE)[xv] and "*Libri rerum Etruscarum*" by Verrius Flaccus (the first century BCE). Neither the mentioned Etruscan originals nor their Latin translations have reached us.

Judging by the testimony of ancient writers, the Etruscans had books of different types, an accurate grouping of which does not seem possible yet. Among the texts relating to the cult, they name "Books of Divination," "Books of Lightning," "Ritual Books," and "Books of the Augurs."[xvi] References to the Acherontic books are very diverse (it is believed that they also include such titles as "Acherontic Sacrifice" and "On the Deified Souls" [Nemirovskij 1983, 165]) (cf., in particular, the evidence of Servius [Serv. Aen. III, 168; VIII, 398]). It is not quite clear to which of the above enumerated categories the "libri Tagetici," the books of the prophet Tages, whose emergence and prophecy is also described by Cicero[xvii] could be assigned. One may find some parallels between Etruscan and archaic Latin writings. For the latter, see in particular Modestov (1868). In any case, the remnants of this vast complex of texts are insignificant.

---

27. Of course, knowledge of the linear writing could not have been preserved to that time. Nevertheless, the local population must have been acquainted with age-old artifacts and may have already used the obscure signs as *tamgas*.

The only nonepigraphic inscription of the Etruscan language is the Zagreb mummy text (also referred to as the text of the Zagreb ritual or the Agram mummy). In the literature, this artifact is often denoted by its class, *Liber Linteus* (i.e., "a linen book"). In the main publication, it appears as TLE 1, in the references to Pfiffig (1969) AM. The mummy of a young girl was bought in 1848 or 1849 in Egypt by a native of Slovenia, M. de Baric. The time and place of discovery, as well as the circumstances of the purchase, are not known. In 1862, it went to the National Museum in Zagreb. Only in 1891, the Austrian Egyptologist J. Krall determined that the language of the text is Etruscan (Krall 1892). It is the only linen book which has been preserved from the ancient world. It is made in the form of a scroll (*volumen*). The total length of the text cut in strips is about 3.5 m. It has 12 columns, each, except the last one, has twenty-five lines. The linen book leaves far behind any other Etruscan texts in terms of size: it contains about fifteen hundred words, among which about 1185 can be clearly read. At the same time, only about five hundred lexemes are known in the book. Many combinations (sacred formulas) are persistently repeated. The assumptions about the original size of the text are entirely speculative. It is characteristic that, in the existing calendar dates, June and September are mentioned (the interpretation of other menonyms is unreliable), but we do not know anything about what part of the text the duties distributed by months took.

There is no connection of the text with the ritual of mummification. The linen book was cut into strips and used to wrap the mummy for unclear (mundane?) reasons. The assumptions about the Egyptian nature of the inscriptions were rejected almost at once. This text is typical Italic and devoted to Neptune and some other gods (in particular, Tin). Though there are certain difficulties with the reading of Tin's name, we find here some of the epithets which in the Italic languages were given to Jupiter: *crap-śti*, which is comparable with the epithet of Jupiter, Mars, and Vofio *krap-*, occurring in the Iguvine Tables),[28] and *veive*: Latin *Ve-iovis*, *Ve-diovis* "Jupiter as a god of vengeance." The book was written on behalf of the institute *śacnicleri cilθl śpureri meθlumeric enaś*. By the peculiarities of its graphics, it is usually dated to the first century BCE, which, however, says nothing about the age of the text itself. It appears that this inscription is very heterogeneous and, at least in some of its parts, goes back to a quite early time. The different age of individual passages are indicated, in particular, by numerous spelling variations, especially in the confusion of the writing of simple voiceless (intense) consonants and aspirates, and the reduction of vowels (*aisuna-* : *aisna* : *eisna*), etc. By its paleographic features, the Zagreb text can be related to the area of Lake Trasimene (i.e., one can assume its origin in Clusium, Perusia, or Cortona). The reasons for the appearance of the book in Egypt can only be guessed at. Agreeing to the supposed dating, one cannot exclude the possibility that the flight of some Etruscan groups might have been connected with Sulla's repressions in the 80s; before that the Etruscan cities had been giving support to the populares, and thus they incurred the dictator's wrath upon themselves. The participation of Clusium (cf., the possible localization!) along with

---

28. Pfiffig compared Umbrian *iuve krapuvi* with *Juppiter Appenninus* (CIL XI 5803) with the Roman epithet *Juppiter Lapis* (Pfiffig 1969, 174, footnote 221); here among them also the theonym *Grabovius*, preserved by the Romans.

Volsinii and Arretium on the side of the Italics in the Social War in 90 BCE, followed by their defeat, adds evidence to such a possibility.

A common assertion in the literature that the text of the Zagreb mummy is the most valuable source for studying the Etruscan language does not seem quite correct. Actually, almost all the major (known) grammatical forms and lexical meanings have been established by other sources, in particular, "disparaged" brief epitaphs. The detailed analysis of the Zagreb text with the obviously more complex constructions and abstract meanings could be initiated only after the clarification of these basic categories. The statement would be true if we specify that the book is extremely important for better understanding of the language (although even here we must add that some of the inscriptions contain no less complex and peculiar constructions).

The interpretation of the Zagreb book is complicated by the abundance of specific religious vocabulary (for example, we can say that the terms *zeri, vacl, faśe, eśvi, zuśleva* designated various rites and ritual objects and kinds of sacrifices, and the forms *farθan, θezin, tut* were probably verbs denoting the religious actions and seldom anything more). However, the positional analysis of individual formulas, especially recurring ones, can lead to valuable observations.[29] Despite the fact that it is extremely difficult to study this vocabulary through other inscriptions, it is doubtless that this text is the most complicated and interesting that remains to us from the Etruscan language.

Frequent repetitions of certain formulas, as well as the use of deities' names (primarily Neptune's and some others), made it possible for the earliest scholars to establish that we are dealing with a text of religious content. Apparently, the ritual instructions that were contained in the *Liber Linteus* are in principle comparable with such an outstanding Italic text as the Iguvine Tables in the Umbrian language. However, attempts to use the latter as a quasi-bilingual have not led to noticeable results (the most significant in this regard were the works by K. Olzscha (cf., [Olzscha, 1939]; subsequently he proposed a complete translation into Latin of the seventh column of the book [Olzscha, 1962]).

In the structure of the texts, there are certain differences. For example, in the Iguvine Tables, there is no calendar division, which is characteristic of the Etruscan artifact. On the other hand, unconditional denial of the parallelism between the Zagreb book and the Iguvine Tables would be ungrounded. For example, we offer the opinion of Nemirovkij, "The Zagreb text was a liturgical book containing the list of sacrifices according to days and months of a year. Iguvine Tables are a description of the rites and hymns devoted to gods and concerned with cleansing of the city" (Nemirovskij 1983, 81). We cannot agree with such an approach for several reasons. First, we do not know the original size of the text and the part it had in the liturgy. Accordingly, the existing text may consist of heterogeneous fragments. Second, the Collegium itself, mentioned in the text, conducts ceremonies (possibly including purifying) "for the city and the state" (*spureri meθlumeri-c*, see below in Chapter 6: Morphology). Finally, there are some

---

29. Thus, it was established, for example, that *hamφe* meant "right-sided" (Gianecchini 1996, 281–310) in opposition to *laive* "left-sided" (from Latin *laevus*).

reasons to see the hymns or at least their excerpts in different passages of the Zagreb book.

It is known that Roman writers mention the poetic form of a certain part of the Etruscan ritual books. In particular, Lucretius mentions "Tyrrhenian chants" to refer to the Etruscan religious doctrine.[xviii] Even more interesting is the evidence of the later author John Lydus, directly pointing to the "Tages' poetry" "ἐκ τῶν Τάγητος στίχων" (Ost., 54). It is likely that John Lydus was referring to the verse translations into Latin, but it is quite consistent with the assumption of the poetic character of the original. Obviously, we should try to find verse fragments in the text. In this context, we present a characteristic passage from *Liber Linteus* (Col. VII):

(^{1} ce[ia hia]...) // (^{2} ceia hia etnam ciz vacltrin veltre) // ^{3} male ceia hia etnam ciz vacl aisvale // ^{4} male ceia ceia hia trinθ etnam ciz ale // ^{5} male ceia hia etnam ciz vacl vile vale // ^{6} staile itrile etc.

In this passage, it is easy to notice the rhythmic text, even rejecting the division into lines. Especially significant is that the lines in the original coincide with the rhythm and even rhyme in the modern (not peculiar to antiquity), sense of the word. We do not know the structure of Tages's books, but the very mythological claim of his "foundation" of the Etruscan doctrine indicates a fairly heterogeneous complex. This variety of liturgical texts, hymns, and other passages we also meet in the Zagreb book. We can well assume that *Liber Linteus*, at least in some parts, originated in *libris Tageticis*.

In the absence of other nonepigraphic inscriptions, some Latin passages can aspire to the role of their partial replacement, since, as we believe, they are made up according to the Etruscan principles or they may even be translations from Etruscan. Such fragments should be searched for in the inscriptions of the sacred style. The most striking of them is the so-called "Vegoia's prophecy" that was kept in the translation of the early Roman gromatics (Grom. vet., 350). This is the prophecy of the nymph Vegoia,[30] titled *Idem Vegoiae Arrunti Veltymno* ("The Same from Vegoia to Arruns Veltimnus"). The dating of the text is very controversial. The mythical version attributes the prophecy to very remote times, while the likely time of recording is the mid-third century BCE (Turcan 1976, 1107). The text of the prophecy was used by many scholars of the social history of Etruria (cf., Nemirovskij 1983, 137). For us, it is very interesting from a linguistic point of view. It seems that the Latin translation of the Etruscan text fully reflects the characteristics of the Etruscan use of reflexive and passive verb forms as well as syntax. In addition to that, the style and vocabulary of this prophecy, which establishes a set of rules and predicts the retributions for their violation, may contribute to the clarification of such an inscription as a tablet with curses from Monte Pitti (see below).

It is very likely that excerpts from the works of some authors—Etruscans by origin— are translations from the Etruscan original. These include, for example, a writer with the typical Etruscan name Tarquitius Priscus, a fragment of whose work is given in Pliny.[xix]

---

30. The variants: Begoe, Bigois; Etruscan *lasa vecu(via)*; at the same time, the word "nymph" for the translation of *lasa* is not quite correct.

Although Etruscan syntactic features in such passages are not apparent, they can be clarified with a successful study of Etruscan inscriptions.

All other Etruscan written records are inscriptions on solid objects. The known texts are extraordinarily diverse. By the beginning of the nineteenth century, less than three hundred inscriptions had been found; by the end of the century, more than five thousand (Nemirovskij 1983, 62). Currently, about eleven thousand diverse Etruscan texts have been found. We know of inscriptions of a sacred and (presumably) legal style, official texts of the rulers (the latter include a bilingual from Pyrgi, see below), epitaphs, signatures of owners and manufacturers of various items, votive inscriptions, coin legends and inscriptions on the landmark stones, ritual curses and other miscellaneous texts.

The size, proportion, content, and scientific value of these texts are extremely variable. Most inscriptions are brief epitaphs, containing primarily proper names and kinship terms, less frequently numerals (see the inscription TLE 93, which reads as follows: *θui clθi mutniaθi vel veluśa avil cis zaθrumisc seiθialiśa*)[31] and has little value for grammatical analysis. To this group of texts belong all the known Etruscan-Latin bilinguals. By Tronskij's estimate (Tronskij 1953, 83), short epitaphs made up approximately 80% of the inscriptions. (It should be noted that, by that time, about nine thousand inscriptions were known, but the fundamental proportion has not changed in subsequent years). The grammatical categories occurring in most of the epitaphs are very few. Primarily they are the means of expressing ownership (with the terms of kinship), and verbs with the meaning "died," "buried," "lies," etc. On the other hand, these texts are of paramount importance for the study of phonetics (including dialecticisms), distinctive features of graphics, comparisons of stems occurring in names, as well as for any other studies that rely on mass comparisons.

Another significant group of texts that are similar to each other in structure consists of the signatures of owners or manufacturers of various objects or their dedications. At the same time, the signatures of owners and masters are also simple in grammar (they include, first of all, the same formulas of ownership and, in many cases, the personal pronoun "I," "me," used on behalf of the object). A lot of dedications are more interesting, because here there are such structures as "I have been produced by such a person for such-and-such a deity," "I have been brought by such a person as a gift to the deity," and so on.

As a special group of inscriptions, one should name the very common signatures for images of mythological characters on the pottery, mirrors, gems, frescoes, etc. However, there is nothing of grammatical interest in them.

All other types of inscriptions are extremely rare. Especially disappointing is the lack of significant official texts, which must have existed in the Etruscan cities, and in addition, must have had in some cases Latin parallels (after the conquest of the Etruscan city-states by Rome). Pallottino explains that such a proportion of inscriptions is connected not so

---

31. "Here, in this grave (lies) Vel, (son of) Vel, aged 23, (from the kin of) Seithies."

much with a fundamental lack of complex, nonfunerary, and dedicatory texts as with the specific situation of the archaeological excavations that exists in modern Italy.[32]

Let us list the most important and largest epigraphic texts:

- The inscription on the tile from Capua (tabula Capuana, TLE 2): discovered in 1899 in present-day Santa-Maria-Capua-Vetere, now kept in the Berlin Museum. The text contains some three hundred words in sixty-two lines, of which twenty-five have been read. The inscription dates back to the fifth to fourth centuries BCE, and the direction of the writing is boustrophedon. The beginning of the text is well preserved. As for the lower part of the inscription, it is almost completely destroyed. Despite the fact that quite a lot of literature is devoted to the text from Capua, its content in general remains unclear. (Compare the selected works Cristofani 1995, Pallottino 1948, and Stoltenberg 1952–53).

- The stone pillar from Perusia (cippus Perusinus, TLE 570): found in 1822 and located in the Museum of Perugia, containing 130 words in forty-six lines. The inscription is made on different sides of a quadrangular column. It has reached us in perfect condition; all the words are readable, the divergences among the various scholars are minimal. Apparently, this is a text of a nonreligious (legal?) content. The inscription on the column is extremely rich in a variety of grammatical forms. It appears that, based on the structure of the text, one will achieve significant progress in its understanding.

- The inscription on a bronze tablet from Cortona (tabula Cortonensis, tavola di Cortona, further TC): This inscription was discovered in 1992 and was not included in the basic edition of the Etruscan texts (there are special publications [Agostiniani and Nicosia 2000; Rix 2000]). Therefore, we put it in Appendix 3 (according to the first edition). The text of the bronze plate, which is damaged on both sides, contains (in total) forty lines and about two hundred words. Note that, in the publications, they sometimes give numbers 1–32 to the lines of "side B," and 33–40 to the lines of "side A." The estimated dating is the third century BCE. The text is a precept to hold a ceremony and includes the enumeration of a number of individuals. It is characteristic that participation in the priestly collegium was hereditary, originally assigned to the gens Cusu. Apparently, as a quasi-bilingual to this inscription, one can use certain excerpts from the Iguvine Tables. The construction of the inscription is not very clear, and therefore a number of questions arise concerning word boundaries. A unique feature of the spelling is the use of the two options of [e], the simple (𐌄) and the "reverse" (𐌄),

---

32. In Italy, a commercial enterprise is responsible for archaeological sites, and it has the right to sell a part of its "products." Accordingly, excavations of cemeteries rich in various objects are preferred rather than searching in urban areas, which are poorer in finds but are the right sites in which to discover extensive texts, including formal and bilingual (in the era of domination by Rome).

the distribution of which is not yet possible to explain in terms of Etruscan phonetics. The text contains a number of very interesting and important grammatical forms and verbal phrases, which will be repeatedly cited below.

- The lead tablet from Magliano (ancient Heba, TLE 359): The inscription is scratched on both sides in a spiral, running in the direction from the outside toward the center. Word boundaries here are somewhat complicated. In the text there are clearly about eighty words. It is likely that the part on the front side (over fifty words) is earlier, the continuation on the back of the plate was added later. The general dating is in the fifth to fourth centuries BCE. It is an inscription of a religious character. The names of gods repeatedly occur in it, and there are the names of various rituals. The grammatical forms are very interesting. The calculation of years is not clear (the word itself *avil* "year" appears four times).

- The lead tablet from Volterra (TLE 401): The inscription consists of two columns: the first has eleven, the second fifteen lines, in all up to eighty words (including reductions of personal names). It seems that the text was inscribed by two or even three people. Some words, usually at the end of the line, are obviously added later. In the inscription there are a few people mentioned (in principle, it may be a contract). Grammatical constructions are not rich and, in general, are not clear. It is possible that they could be clarified only by comparison with similar inscriptions.

- The lead plate from Monte Pitti (TLE 380): The inscription contains about sixty words. It is fairly late. This is one of the most peculiar Etruscan inscriptions. This text is nothing more than a *tabella defixionis*, a type of inscription of spells, which were widely known in the ancient world. The inscription, composed on behalf of a freedwoman *titi setria*, in addition to listing a number of persons, contains peculiar grammar constructions, including repeated ones. It seems that a comparison of the Etruscan version with similar Latin spells, as well as with the prophecy of Vegoia, might lead to some success in interpreting the text.

- The epitaph of a high-ranking priest or haruspex Laris Pulena from Tarquinii (TLE 131). (Of more than sixty words): The inscription is of a unique design, carved on the scroll in the hands of the statue of Laris Pulena himself, who is carved reclining. The final part of the text is slightly damaged (there are no more than three to five words missing). The text contains some major combinations that will be discussed below. The final part of the inscription, which describes the rituals performed by the deceased, is almost entirely incomprehensible. See also the special report (Cataldi 1988).

- The lead plate from Santa Marinella (TLE 878): A very old (fifth century BCE) inscription, found in 1967, contains more than sixty words. The damage to the inscription is great. There are no unharmed combinations so that one can only operate here with separate forms. Therefore, one cannot speak definitely about the content of the text.

- The bronze model of a liver from Piacenza (ancient Placentia; TLE 719): with the names of gods and calendar dates, used, obviously, as a manual for soothsayers. The artifact, which has great importance for the study of Etruscan mythology, cosmology, and ritual, has almost no forms which are interesting from the grammatical point of view. (Compare selected works dedicated to the inscription: Nemirovskij 1986; Colonna 1994; Maggiani 1982.)

- The inscription from San Manno, near Perugia (TLE 619) (third to second centuries BCE): The text contains twenty-seven words, written in three lines. For a long time, this inscription was the lengthiest of the famous Etruscan texts and even was called the "queen of Etruscan inscriptions." The inscription is carved on the wall of an underground tomb. The formulas are substantially different from the usual burial ones. The grammatical forms are extremely interesting and unique in many aspects. In particular, distributive numerals appear only in this inscription. (See the special report, Buonamici 1928.)

Most of the other inscriptions are much shorter, which, however, does not indicate how meaningful they may be. Some epitaphs, belonging to relatives, form groups with partly overlapping forms and lend themselves to a more detailed analysis and fairly complete translation. Among such "series" the most interesting are epitaphs from the area of Tarquinii, belonging to the gens Alethna (TLE 169–75). These texts (especially the first three) are relatively detailed and very transparent from the grammatical point of view. Further, in Chapter 6: Morphology, the forms containing them will often be presented.

The bilinguals form a special, though small, group of inscriptions, the Etruscan-Phoenician (or rather, Punic) bilingual from Pyrgi and its "abstract" (TLE 874, 875, see Appendix 4). The gold plates with the text found in 1964 are perhaps the most important epigraphic finds of the twentieth century for Etruscologists. The Etruscan inscription contains thirty-seven words in sixteen lines. The text dates from the fifth century BCE. One observes a proximity of the Punic alphabet to the forms attested in the inscriptions of Tabnit and Eshmunazar, kings of Sidon, which belong to the end of the sixth to the beginning of the fifth century BCE (Xarsekin and Geltzer 1965, 114). A notable epigraphic peculiarity of the Etruscan epigraphic version is the use of two signs for the sigma, ⟩ and ⟨, with the absence of M (ś).

The inscriptions were made on behalf of the ruler of the city of Caere (ancient Pyrgi was the port of Caere), Tiberius Veliana, in honor of the dedication of a sanctuary and land to the goddess Uni (Juno, in the Punic section, Astarte). While the Punic version does not cause any difficulties for translation, the analysis of the Etruscan text is very difficult. It is noted that the contents of the two parts are somewhat different (in particular, the word order is significantly different, some lexemes [primarily Etruscan] have no equivalents). In this connection, some scholars even propose to consider the inscription TLE 874 as a quasi-bilingual (Pfiffig 1972, 12). Compare selected works dedicated to the bilingual from Pyrgi (Xarsekin and Geltzer 1965; Colonna 1989-90; Olzscha 1966).

Another text from Pyrgi on a gold plate, TLE 875, joins with the inscription we've been considering, TLE 874. It is appropriate to call the inscription TLE 875 a "summary" of the bilingual, even though it contains only fifteen words. Apparently, it mentions a rite of driving the "one-year nail" (if this is exactly how we should interpret the combination *cleva etanal*; it seems that the Etruscan *cleva* shows a link with the Latin *clavus*, the rite of driving a nail [as the calculation of years][33] in the temple of Nortia in Volsinii, as described by Livy).[xx] The inscription TLE 875 is also fully preserved.[34]

The other bilinguals (only Etruscan-Latin) are few in number and very short. Besides proper names, they contain (but not always) the terms of kinship and rarely some other noteworthy lexemes. Compare, for example, some typical bilinguals:[1] *C. LICINI. C. F . NIGRI*[2] *v . lecne . v . hapirnal* (TLE 455);[1] *leucle φisis lavtni*[2] *L . PHISIUS . L*[35] *. LAUCL* (TLE 470);[1] *vl . alfni . nuvi*[2] *cainal*[3] *C. ALFIUS . A . F*[4] *CAINNIA . NATUS* (TLE 554), etc.

The most interesting is the bilingual from Pisaurum TLE 697. Its text seems to read as follows: [*L . CA*]*FATIUS . L . F . STE . HARUSPE*[*X*] *. FULGURIATOR cafates . lr . lr . netśvis . trutnvt . frontac*. Apparently, it helps to clarify the title of the diviner.[36] In turn, a comparison of *netśvis* with the combination *ziχ neθsra-c* in the epitaph of Laris Pulena made it possible to translate the latter as "a book of haruspicine." In general, the material of the short bilinguals was extremely important for the primary processing of Etruscan inscriptions, but it is not of great value for more in-depth morphological study.

Another important group of sources for the study of the Etruscan language is formed by the glosses kept by ancient authors as well as the numerous substratum borrowings in Latin and, to a lesser extent, in the Osco-Umbrian languages.

When working with this layer of the vocabulary, the scholar is faced with various difficulties. The glosses found in ancient texts are few in number[37] (in particular, in TLE 58 glosses are taken into consideration, but here there are evident misunderstandings) and they are widely distributed semantically (the only all-embracing group consists of

---

33. The same rite is depicted on the mirror from Perusia ES 176 (fourth century BCE); the signatures read: *atlenta, meliacr, tul*[*ran*]*, aθrpa* (?).

34. The next inscription TLE 876 is sometimes mentioned among the first two, but it belongs to the other range of texts. It is made on a bronze plate. The content of this inscription is significantly different. In particular, it contains a calendar: the Ides of June (see below). The text of TLE 876, consisting of three lines, is pretty badly damaged (the endings of all three lines are missing).

35. It seems that, in this case, L = *libertus*; the main meaning of the Etruscan *lautni* "stirps."

36. However, scholars differ in the interpretation of *frontac*. Perhaps we find a similar form in the Picene *frunter* (ID 181-82). According to the most accepted view, it goes back to the Greek βροντή (cf., Mastrelli, 1976).]

37. Primarily the works of Varro (*De lingua latina*), Verrius Flaccus (*De significatu verborum*, abridged in Festus and Paulus Diaconus), Isidorus (*Etymologium*), Hesychius, some works of lesser value.

eight names for the Etruscan months; see below). The relic vocabulary, which is fairly reliably marked out in Latin, is more uniform and covers well defined areas (agriculture, some household items, the earliest components of the urban development and political system, the cult). At the same time, we have no direct evidence of its Tyrrhenian (in this case, directly Etruscan) origin. This set of lexemes stands out for its phonetic and word-formation features. For the most part, there are no parallels in the actual Etruscan texts. As for any coincidences with the pre-Greek vocabulary, they are even more scant. The principles of selection of the substratum Etruscan words were brilliantly marked by the greatest Russian expert in Latin, Tronskij, who relied primarily on the divergences with the Indo-European phonetics and the unexpected isolation of a number of lexemes in Italic (Tronskij 1953, 123-24).

Any transfer of connected Etruscan sentences in the text of other languages (primarily in Latin) is unknown. This can be explained, paradoxically, by the well-known and significant cultural role of the Etruscan language in archaic Rome. In particular, Livy says: "*habeo auctores volgo tum Romanos pueros, sicut nunc Graecis, ita Etruscis litteris erudiri solitos*" (IX, 36). It is clear that this level of language is not used for minor passages in the Latin works. The opposition of the languages is used in a monologue from the comedy of Plautus Gannon "Poenulus" in Punic (930-49, see also the translation [Schiffmann 2003, 60 et seq.]), where half of the weird, and at this stage in the text "barbaric" language, was introduced only to create a comic effect. In fact, the only reflection of the Etruscan word combination is the gloss of Festus TLE 812. For a possible interpretation, see Chapter 6: Morphology.

The existing glosses are considered in detail below in Chapter 4: The Interpretation of the Vocabulary. They were collected originally by F. Dempsterus (Dempsterus 1723-24) and today are published in the same form and quantity. Hereafter, a number of shortcomings of the existing list will be given. As far as we know, no individual publications have been undertaken in regard to them.

It should be also recalled that the glosses kept by Greek authors may be genetically heterogeneous. It should be also especially emphasized that they cannot be connected to the Etruscans with absolute certainty, as the designations Τυρσηνοί, Τυρρηνοί in the Greek sources are applicable both to the Etruscans and Tyrrhenians of Aegeida, while the name Θοῦσκοι, borrowed from Latin, was used rarely, mostly by later authors (Dioscorides, Galen, John Lydus, and some others).

Relic lexemes in Latin and Greek, as well as glosses without a sign of the Tyrrhenian origin, are significantly more numerous than the earliest glosses. All of these groups reveal a variety of similarities. Compare, for example, the Tyrrhenian root *ant-*; it is known in the "Lexicon" by Hesychius, although only two of these glosses are designated as Tyrrhenian (ἄνδας· βορέας [TLE 806] and ἄνταρ· ἀετὸς [TLE 807]).[38] Here one also should include ἄντας· πνοάς, ἄνται· ἄνεμοι and ἄντος· εὖρος. οἱ δὲ Εὐριπίδης (borrowed into Latin, the word *antemna* is a suffixal derivative of this root). This is one of those cases when we know with absolute certainty about the existence of

---

38. Compare the similarity between Latin *aquilo* and *aquila*.

derivatives of one root in the Etruscan and Aegean areas. In relation to some other Greek glosses, there is not such clarity.

The borrowings from Etruscan to Latin, as already mentioned, are primarily recognized according to the phonetic and word-formation features. The main groups of loans will be discussed in Chapter 7: Word Formation, and we shall not dwell on them here.

As noted in the introductory sections of various works on Etruscology, the first attempts at the collection of Etruscan inscriptions date back to the fifteenth century (cf., Nemirovskij 1983, 63). By the end of the nineteenth century, with a sharp increase in the number of known inscriptions and inadequacy of the existing literature (mostly fragmentary, difficult to access, and based on unreliable readings), it became necessary to produce a summarizing edition: the *Corpus Inscriptionum Etruscarum*, hereafter referred to as the CIE. The history of this fundamental edition extends over more than one hundred years. It was founded by the Berlin Academy of Sciences in 1893 under the direction of Karl Pauli (Germany) and Olaf Danielsson (Sweden). From 1902 to 1936, the edition had been continued by Danielsson and Gustavus Herbig (from 1907 to 1923, four issues of volume II were published), and Ernst Sittig (1936, the fifth edition). In 1970, another part was published by Mauro Cristofani (inscriptions from Volsinii and Caere, in addition to the inscriptions from Tarquinii number 5607-6324), and, in 1996, Cristofani, M. Pandolfini Angeletti, and G. Coppola republished the inscriptions from Latium and Campania (8601-880). Under the direction of Angeletti, new volumes were published in 1982 (10001-520, Tarquinii), 1987 (10521-943, Volsinii), and 1994 (10951-1538).

A long absence of the complete edition and a number of shortcomings in the reading of many inscriptions that have been included in early editions of the CIE[39] made it necessary to publish more concise editions containing the basic texts. Such editions were particularly appropriate because most of the famous inscriptions are extremely short, while the texts that are morphologically significant and especially interesting for the study of vocabulary can fit into a collection of a smaller size. The first attempt at such a publication was made by M. Buffa in 1935. In his book, *Nuova raccolta di iscrizioni etrusche* (further the NRIE) he included some twelve hundred inscriptions that had been already published but with revised readings or those that were difficult to access.

The exemplary collection by Pallottino, *Testimonia linguae Etruscae*, which was the second, supplemented edition published in 1968 (the first was published in 1954), has retained its great value for Etruscology. Pallotino, following Buffa, based his edition on the most important texts, but performed it at a higher analytical level and in a lesser volume, skipping some unreliable texts. However, individual inscriptions with insurmountable difficulties in the word boundary have been included in the collection as well. The anthology was published in the Latin language, which greatly facilitates its use by scholars from different countries.

It includes the text of the Zagreb book (TLE 1) and the inscriptions (TLE 2-800, 859-942), arranged on a geographical basis (the origin of the texts 725-800, 939-42 is

---

39. For example, Vetter found that, in Volume I of the CIE, 20% of the inscriptions had erroneous readings.

unknown or can be established only presumably). Under the numbers 801-858, there are given, in alphabetical order, all major Tyrrhenian glosses, provided with the indication of their origin. The bilinguals, apart from the Etruscan-Punic one, are given under the numbers 455 TLE (VCA), 462, 470-73, 500, 502, 503, 514, 521, 523, 540, 541, 545, 554, 563, 925, 926 (Cl.), 605-8 (Per.), 661, 662, 930 (Arr.), 693 (Umbria), 697 (Pisaurum). The second edition includes the most important inscriptions found in the fourteen years since the publication of the first edition, especially the inscriptions on golden plates from Pyrgi and the above-mentioned inscription TLE 876. The numbering of the texts was continued to a total of 942.

In fact, the publication by Pallottino contains almost all the texts that are interesting from a morphological point of view, which were found up to 1968. The only notable exception is the epitaph of CIE 6213, which contains important grammatical forms[40] and which has not been included in the anthology for reasons that are unclear.

In recent years, Rix undertook a new edition of the basic texts (1991) by constructing it according to a geographic and subject principle, which was reflected in the complicated nomenclature of the inscriptions (i.e., the EC are the inscriptions from Clusium, ES are the inscriptions on mirrors, etc.; all sections have separate numbering). Rix's edition has not yet received priority over the TLE. It seems that Pallottino's anthology will retain its paramount importance for a long time.

Current findings have been published in various anthologies. Among them the most important is the annual *Studi Etruschi*, which has been the central edition of Etruscologists for many decades. The publication of inscriptions in the SE was started long before the publication of the TLE and later volumes of the CIE. With reference to the texts given in the earlier editions, they usually give an issue of the journal and page. Since 1966, a separate epigraphic section, *Rivista di epigrafia etrusca*, has appeared in the annual. From that time, the publications of Etruscan inscriptions have been separated from the other Italic inscriptions (for which there is a separate section set aside, *Rivista di epigrafia italica*), and they have a clear numbering system, obligatory in reference to the REE. Sometime later, the REE became divided: the first part includes newly discovered inscriptions, the second part revised readings of the old ones. The largest revision was the publication by Cristofani in the SE edition of 1976 (187-99), where he introduced several new readings to his publication of the CIE from 1970.

"MINOR" TYRRHENIAN LANGUAGES
THE RHAETIC LANGUAGE

This language is known in about a hundred short inscriptions of the third to first centuries BCE, made with the alphabet of the "Northern Etruscan" type. Some toponyms of

---

40. Compare the text: *laris avle larisal clenar sval cn šuθi cerixunce apac atic sanišva θui cesu clavtieθurasi*; compare the translation: "*Laris (et) Aulus, L. f., vivi hoc sepulcrum fecerunt. Paterque materque defuncti (??) hic positi sunt. Claudiorum (loco)*" (Pallottino 1978, 446).

northern Italy and Switzerland originate in the Rhaetic layer. The names of some Rhaetic tribes remain to this day in their settlement areas: *Val di Non (Anauni), Val Camonica (Camunni), Val Venosta, Vintschau (Vallis Venosta, Venostes), Eisack (Isarci), Val Trompia (Trumplini)*, and others (Conway et al. 1933, vol. II: 3), as well as in Roman sources (see above the list of Pliny).

The Rhaetic inscription that is the most significant in size (if such a definition is applicable to the Rhaetic texts) and important in grammatical forms is one which comes from Val di Cembra, the inscription on a bronze situla IR 5 (CE 1). We give it in full:
(1) *lavise śeli* (2) *velχanu lup (i) nu piθiave* (3) *kusenkus trinaχe φelna vinuθalina (k)*.

The only known "Rhaetic" gloss *ploum* ("aratri genus," PID 254, from Pliny, NH, XVIII, 172), as is easily seen, comes from some Indo-European dialect (here is Russian плуг, Germanic *plōga-*, whence there is German *Pflug*, English *plow* [*plough*], etc.). The Tyrolean *plof* and Lombard *pio* act as substratum borrowings.

There are several editions of Rhaetic inscriptions. The Rhaetic section of PID (Conway et al. 1933, vol. II], should be considered out-of-date, and not just because of a certain number of unreliable readings. The fact is that the authors did not share the point of view of a kinship between Etruscan and Rhaetic, considering the latter to be an Indo-European language, so the incorrect guideline could not but affect the quality of the publication.

The publication of the Rhaetic inscriptions, answering modern requirements, was undertaken by Mancini in 1975. Because of the modest number of Rhaetic inscriptions, it was possible to not only put the publication in a regular SE volume but also to provide the articles on the most important or controversial inscriptions with the drawings. The total number has been brought to 114.

Rhaetic inscriptions have been published recently in German in a separate volume (Schumacher 1992). Since none of the publications has yet received priority, in published papers a double numbering of the inscriptions is often given using the abbreviation IR for Mancini (1975) and geographical abbreviations for Schumacher (1992). This way seems most appropriate.

THE AEGEAN-TYRRHENIAN LANGUAGE

The only reliable text in the Aegean-Tyrrhenian language is the famous double inscription of the Lemnos stele, the drawing (see Figure 9) and text of which are given in many publications (Xarsekin 1976,[1] Kretschmer 1976, Kretschmer 1942; see also Appendix 5 and our publication, Jatsemirskij 2005).

The funerary stele was discovered in 1885 by J. Cousin and F. Durbach near the village of Kaminia on the isle of Lemnos. (It is now at the National Archaeological Museum of Athens.) The monument is decorated with the image of a man with a spear, and it bears two inscriptions, on the front and side (the latter was probably made somewhat later). There is no difficulty in the reading of the text. There are some difficulties only in the numbering of lines in the center.

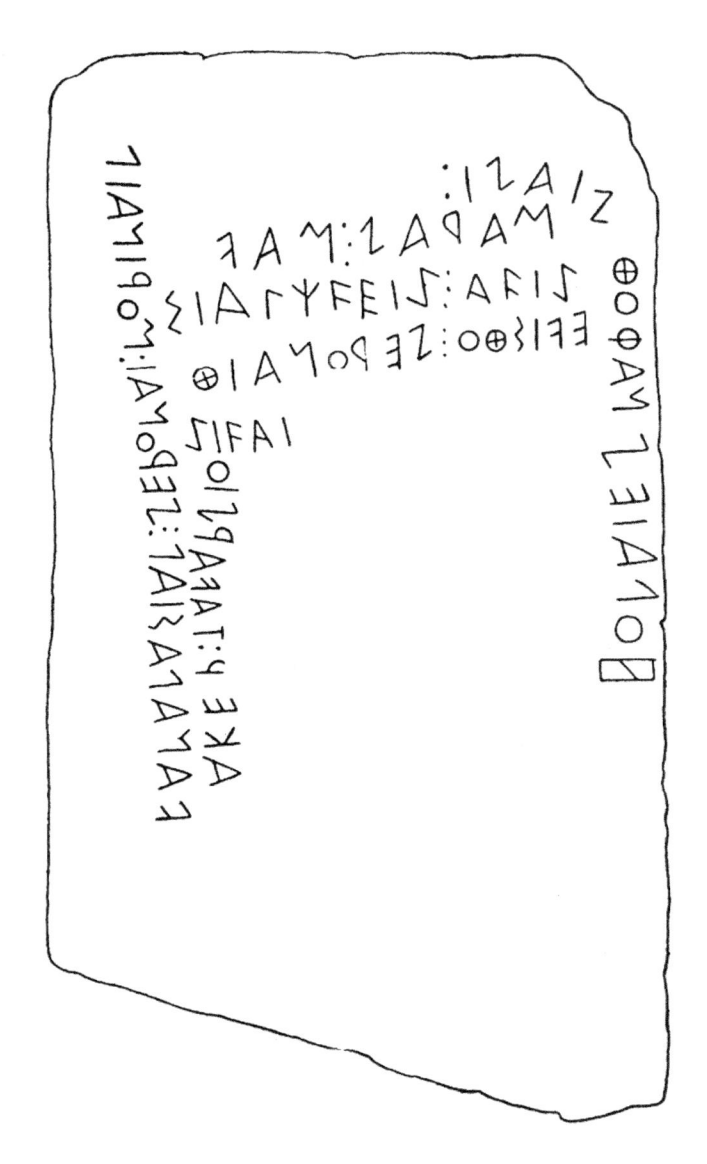

Figure 9. The Lemnos stele inscription.

Besides the stele, brief graffiti were later found on the islands of Lemnos and Imbros that are hardly analyzable. One should not attribute individual Etruscan inscriptions found in Aegeida, such as graffiti from Aegina *mi pl . . . inur* (VI in., SE 59/159), to the Aegean-Tyrrhenian language.

The Lemnian inscriptions are made with the local alphabet, being part of the group of archaic Greek variants (according to A. Schulten, it relates to the alphabet of the island of Thera [1941]). The comparison of Lemnian with other alphabets such as the Old Phrygian (W. Brandenstein) and Etruscan (C. de Simone) is less substantiated.[41] The inscriptions of individual letters are characterized by slight differences. The direction of

---

41. See the latest studies on the Lemnian alphabet (de Simone 1995; Malzahn 1999).

the writing is from right to left as well as boustrophedon. Throughout the text, word boundaries are carefully marked (denoted by two or three points in a vertical line).

The relic vocabulary that has remained from Aegean-Tyrrhenian contains mainly toponyms and proper names (including theonyms) as well as a number of nouns and occasionally other parts of speech, some of which penetrated into the Greek language, while others survive only in the glosses.

THE ETEO-CYPRIOTE LANGUAGE

The Eteo-Cypriote language is known in several inscriptions of the sixth to fifth centuries BCE, as well as by a small (compared to Italy or Aegeida) complex of pre-Greek lexemes. Eteo-Cypriote inscriptions are sharply different from the rest of the Tyrrhenian inscriptions (i.e., they are made with the syllabic writing system). The carriers of the Eteo-Cypriote language used the writing system of fifty-six characters, going back to Cypriot-Minoan[42] and, through it, to the Cretan (Minoan) writing. It will be discussed in more detail in the next chapter.

In total, fourteen texts are known. Among them, there is a small Greek-Cypriote bilingual, two parts of which do not quite match (Xarsekin 1976,[2] 255). Eteo-Cypriote texts are given in various publications. A well-established numbering system of the inscriptions has been proposed by Friedrich (1932, 50–52). The same numbering is used by Jones, who prepared a more accurate edition of the text (1950); the translation of the article by Jones (with abridgments) is available in the Russian literature (Jones 1976). For the text of the bilingual, the inscriptions KS 1–3, and the brief inscription on a vessel KS 11, see Appendix 6.

As has been mentioned, if the Eteo-Cypriote language reveals a relationship with Cypro-Minoan, the total number of texts will increase significantly.

The most famous inscription of Cypro-Minoan, a plate from Enkomi discovered in 1953,[43] includes on its front and back sides about 290 and 105 characters, respectively (not counting the word boundaries). The front side of it has been preserved rather well, while on the reverse side a fragment of the text in the center has survived. Also, there are additional inscriptions on a cylinder that was discovered there in Enkomi (1955) (about 190 characters survived, with very few of them damaged), as well as on one of the tablets found in Ugarit[44] (about 90 and 75 signs on both sides, not counting the word boundaries). For the history of syllabic writing in Cyprus, see Masson (1961).

The relic vocabulary of the Eteo-Cypriote language gives much less material than the Aegean-Tyrrhenian one. In particular, over two hundred glosses in the dictionary by Hesychius are referred to as Cypriote. The majority of them are obvious Greek dialects. We can consider quite confidently an insignificant part of these glosses as Tyrrhenian lexemes. The most impressive of them are the names of plants βουκανῆ· ("ἀνεμώνη τὸ

---

42. The number of signs in these writing systems roughly coincides (on the plate from Enkomi of 1953 there are fifty-eight various signs). For their specific similarity, see Molchanov 1992, 84.

43. See the drawing (Molchanov 1992, 83).

44. According to one of the versions, the Hurrian language may be concealed here. However, it is still necessary to check the text for the probability that it belongs to the group under study.

ἄνθος. Κύπριοι"), ἀγόρ "an eagle," a pronoun form ἰν τυίν "ἐν τούτῳ. Κύπριοι" (for detail see below), which find parallels in Etruscan and Aegean-Tyrrhenian.

THE IBERO-TYRRHENIAN (SOUTH LUSITANIAN) LANGUAGE

The inscriptions of the language or dialect of Tyrrhenian settlers in the Iberian Peninsula are very fragmentary. We know just a few funerary inscriptions with an unclear dating, that are apparently close to the dating of the inscription of the Lemnos stele, which follows from the peculiarities of the archaic alphabet. Lusitanian Tyrrhenian inscriptions have been studied in detail by Schulten. He related the beginning of the Tyrrhenian written tradition to a very early time, the turn of the ninth and eighth centuries BCE, and saw in the Lusitanian inscriptions one of the oldest Tyrrhenian inscriptions (Schulten 1941, 27). Such an early dating, in principle, may be bolstered by the assumption of a relationship with the Linear writing (for details, see below).

The Lusitanian inscriptions can give little information to scholars of the Tyrrhenian languages. All of them are very short (the largest, apparently, is inscription number 62: *ailieleier ainisa . . . anen ainalisa lusoanen saronnah konii alisio*) and uniform in content. The phrase *saronah konii* (with graphic variants), which, obviously, is to be understood as "*hic situs est*," is typical for most of these inscriptions. Several personal names are known that are close in appearance to the Etruscan. Among the other lexical parallels only *saronah* (Lemnian *śeronaiθ*) can be named, which is also grammatically identical to the form in the inscription on the stele.

All credible Lusitanian Tyrrhenian inscriptions are given in the cited paper by Schulten under their own numbering. No relic lexemes in the Ibero-Romance languages that can be reliably linked to the Tyrrhenian layer, apparently, have been revealed yet.

CHAPTER TWO NOTES

[xv] Cf., in Suetonius: "*Denique et Graecas scripsit historias, Tyrrhenicon viginti, Carchedoniacon octo. Quarum causa veteri Alexandriae Musio additum ex ipsius nomine novum; institutumque ut quotannis in altero Tyrrhenicon libri, in altero Carchedoniacon diebus statutis velut in auditorio recitarentur toti a singulis per vices*" (Claud., 42).

[xvi] In particular, in Cicero: "*Quorum alia sunt posata in monumentis et disciplina, quod Etruscorum declarant, et haruspicini et fulgurales et rituales libri, vestri etiam augurales*" [Cic. Div. I, 72]. Cf., also in Seneca ("*hoc inter nos et Tuscos, quibus summa est fulgurum persequendorum scientia, interest: nos putamus, quia nubes collisae sunt, fulmina emitti*" [Sen. Nat. II, 32, 2]) and "*Genera fulgurum tria esse ait Caecina, consiliarium, auctoritatis et quod status dicitur*" (II, 39, 1).

[xvii] "*Ortum videamus haruspicinae; sic facillume quid habeat auctoritatis judicabimus. Tages quidam dicitur in agro Tarquiniensi, cum terra araretur et sulcus altius esset impressus, exstitisse repente et eum adfatus esse qui arabat. Is autem Tages, ut in libris est Etruscorum, puerili specie dicitur visus, sed senili fuisse prudentia. Ejus adspectu cum obstipuisset bubulcus clamoremque maiorem cum admiratione edidisset, concursum esse factum, totamque brevi tempore in eum locum Etruriam convenisse. Tum illum plura locutum multis audientibus, qui omnia verba ejus exceperint litterisque mandarint. Omnem autem*

orationem fuisse eam qua haruspicinae disciplina contineretur; eam postea creuisse rebus novis cognoscendis et ad eadem illa principia referendis. Haec accepimus ab ipsis, haec scripta conseruant, hunc fontem habent disciplinae" (Cic., Div., II, 50). Cicero retells the Etruscan text (cf., ibid.: *"Vetus autem illud Catonis admodum scitum est, qui mirari se aiebat, quod non rideret haruspex, haruspicem cum vidisset"* [II, 51]).

xviii *"non Tyrrhena retro voluentem carmina frustra // indicia occultae diuum perquirere mentis"* (VI 381–82).

xix *"Purpureo aureoue colore ouis ariesue si aspergetur, principi ordinis et generis summa cum felicitate largitatem auget, genus progeniem propagat in claritate laetioremque efficit arbores quae inferum deorum auertentiumque in tutela sunt, eas infelices nominant: alternum sanguinem filicem, ficum atrum, quaeque bacam nigram nigrosque fructus ferunt, itemque acrifolium, pirum silvaticum, pruscum rubum sentesque quibus portenta prodigiaque mala comburi iubere oportet"* [De disciplina Etrusca].

xx *"Nec tamen ludorum primum initium procurandis religionibus datum aut religione animos aut corpora morbis leuauit; quin etiam, cum medios forte ludos circus Tiberi superfuso inrigatus impedisset, id uero, uelut auersis iam dis aspernantibusque placamina irae, terrorem ingentem fecit. Itaque Cn. Genucio L. Aemilio Mamerco iterum consulibus, cum piaculorum magis conquisitio animos quam corpora morbi adficerent, repetitum ex seniorum memoria dicitur pestilentiam quondam clauo ab dictatore fixo sedatam. Ea religione adductus senatus dictatorem claui figendi causa dici iussit; dictus L. Manlius Imperiosus L. Pinarium magistrum equitum dixit. Lex uetusta est, priscis litteris uerbisque scripta, ut qui praetor maximus sit idibus Septembribus clauum pangat; fixa fuit dextro lateri aedis Iouis optimi maximi, ex qua parte Mineruae templum est. Eum clauum, quia rarae per ea tempora litterae erant, notam numeri annorum fuisse ferunt eoque Mineruae templo dicatam legem quia numerus Mineruae inuentum sit. Volsiniis quoque clauos indices numeri annorum fixos in templo Nortiae, Etruscae deae, comparere diligens talium monumentorum auctor Cincius adfirmat. M. Horatius consul ea lege templum Iouis optimi maximi dedicauit anno post reges exactos; a consulibus postea ad dictatores, quia maius imperium erat, sollemne claui figendi translatum est. Intermisso deinde more digna etiam per se uisa res propter quam dictator crearetur"* (VII, 3).

Chapter 3

WRITING

The inscriptions of the languages under study are made in two fundamentally different writing systems, the first of which includes the Cretan hieroglyphs and the linear script of Crete and Cyprus (including, probably, the Cypro-Minoan stage), and the second of which is alphabetical, represented in the vast majority of known Tyrrhenian inscriptions. Also, there was a writing system on the Iberian Peninsula, which could be described as a hybrid; it will be discussed below.

The principles of working with texts of the first millennium BCE and Minoan inscriptions differ primarily in that in the first case we are dealing with alphabets, which do not provoke different interpretations, while Linear A and the Cypro-Minoan syllabary have not been fully deciphered yet. Their study is still in its infancy and is based primarily not on later Cypriote syllabary but on the facts of Linear B.

Although all the main results of the study of phonetics and morphology have been obtained through the examination of alphabetic inscriptions, the material of Linear A has also played a crucial role, becoming the basis for the hypothesis of a genetic relationship between Minoan and the Tyrrhenian group. Before that, the non-Greek inscriptions of Cyprus allowed scholars to expand the boundaries of the group under study to the east and to suggest a hypothesis on the area to which Cypro-Minoan could be related. Thus, the significance of linear inscriptions should not be underestimated, because, firstly, the range of the texts can be increased considerably (if our views on Cypro-Minoan prove to be correct, these will yield the greatest extension of texts, after the Etruscan), and, secondly, the possibilities of diachronic study of phonetics and morphology will significantly expand.[45]

---

45. Primarily phonetics; the linear syllabary is likely to have reflected quite objectively the phonetic

The writing systems relevant to our study will be characterized below primarily in accordance with chronology.

CRETAN HIEROGLYPHS

The hieroglyphics known to be the most ancient script of Crete had existed approximately from 2000 to 1700 BCE. According to paleographic features, directly reflecting the chronology, it is divided into hieroglyphic writing A and hieroglyphic writing B. The first variety, which existed from 2000 to 1900 BCE, obviously was a pictorial writing in its purest form. Owing to the extremely small number of characters and the length of the inscriptions, it is not practical to consider it here.

As for hieroglyphic writing B (from 1900 BCE), we can speak more clearly about it. Like other systems of hieroglyphic writing, it includes images of objects. A significant part of them have been clearly recognized. Subsequently, many pictorial prototypes were preserved in the signs of the linear writing system. There is no doubt that, at this stage, a partial transition to the system of syllabic readings took place.

However, there still remains the unresolved question of the principle ratio of logographic and syllabic signs in the Cretan hieroglyphics. In particular, Molchanov offered only syllabic readings for signs on the seals, although the fact is that the logograms preserved up to a much later time presumes a mixed, word-syllabic structure of the early Cretan writing. In the edition of CHIC, the signs 01–096 are given as syllabograms, and the signs 151–182 as logograms. Roughly speaking, one can distinguish "monumental" (solid figures) and "cursive" (contour picture) types, according to the peculiarities of the inscription of symbols. The first are much less common and have no parallels among the cursive ones, except in a few cases (four signs among the syllabograms and two among the logograms). In the above-mentioned edition of CHIC, it is assumed that the writing systems of Linear A and B preserved, (among the known signs, of course), thirty-nine and fifteen signs, respectively, which were derived from Cretan hieroglyphics. Having become finally obsolete by the mid-seventeenth century BCE, Cretan hieroglyphics were replaced by a simpler and more convenient linear writing system, which had directly originated from it.

On the other hand, approximately at the same time, the Phaistos disk writing was created (there are forty-five signs on the artifact itself) that can be considered a decorative version of the Cretan syllabary (see Table I). Extensive works have been written on the latter system. However, we shall not dwell on it because the Phaistos disk does not provide anything for the study of the Minoan language so far. This decorative, very elegant writing system seems to have no impact on the subsequent development of local scripts.

---

structure of the Tyrrhenian languages at an early stage of their development, similar to what we observe in Minoan preserved in the inscriptions of Linear A.

Table I. Repertoire of Phaistos signs

01		16		31		
02		17		32		
03		18		33		
04		19		34		
05		20		35		
06		21		36		
07		22		37		
08		23		38		
09		24		39		
10		25		40		
11		26		41		
12		27		42		
13		28		43		
14		29		44		
15		30		45		

LINEAR WRITING SYSTEMS

By a long-established tradition, the syllabic script of Crete, Mycenaean Greece, and Cyprus is usually called "linear." Accordingly, the oldest (Cretan) stage is called "Linear A," and the Greek version "Linear B." As for the Cypriote ones, they are called "Cypro-Minoan" and "classic Cypriote," depending on the chronology. The first three types of linear writing existed in the second millennium BCE. The classic Cypriote syllabary, after a hard-to-explain break, reappears in the middle of the first millennium BCE, then the syllabic writing turns out to be forever forgotten in southern Europe.

The story of the brilliant decipherment of Linear B, carried out by the British architect Michael Ventris in 1953, is described in detail in a number of specialized and general publications,[46] and it is unnecessary to characterize its stages, principles, and results again. This discovery, in turn, made possible a preliminary reading of the inscriptions of Linear A and Cypro-Minoan, and also the opportunity appeared for a diachronic consideration of the highly changed Cypriote script, deciphered long before Ventris.

The linear writing, compared to the pictorial, underwent a stylization and a reduction in the number of signs. Compare the following: "at the first stage, approximately from early second millennium BCE until 1650, the signs of Cretan writing were drawings of a casual life . . . Already about 1900 BCE the hieroglyphic writing began to be replaced by the linear one, originating, as it seems, as a result of schematization of pictorial drawings" (Tronskij 2004, 67).

After even a superficial acquaintance with the inscriptions of Linear A and B, one's attention is drawn to the fact that the signs of Linear B are in many cases notable for a more complex, detailed picture, although, if it is a descendant of Linear A, we would expect the opposite effect. This last finding offers hope for locating the monumental (royal or ritual) inscriptions of Linear A. Precisely because of their knowledge of them, the Achaean Greeks could have devised their complicated style of the symbols.

But if the origin of the linear writing from the pictorial has been accepted since the time of Evans' excavations, the nature of the transition from the hieroglyphic to syllabic values was unclear for a long time. It was Professor Günter Neumann who was destined to make the discovery, which has been of prime importance, not only for the history of the writing systems, but also paramount for the attribution of the Minoan loanwords in Greek and the clarification of all the major Minoan word-formation models (Neumann 1958). Neumann, considering the Linear writing sign 30 ⲯ *ni* (as a logogram it has a value of *FICus*), associated it with a gloss of Hermonax, stored in Athenaeus: "Ἑρμῶναξ δ' ἐν Γλώτταις Κρητικαῖς σύκων γένη ἀναγράφει ἀμάδεα καὶ νικύλεα" (Athen., Deipn., III, 11). It enabled him to talk about the acrophonic principle at the heart of Cretan writing (i.e., about the reading of a sign on the first syllable of the name of the object shown), and, further, to pick out a few more Cretan words in Greek. As will be shown in the chapters titled The Interpretation of the Vocabulary (Chapter 4) and Word Formation (Chapter 7), the significance of these findings for work with the Aegean vocabulary is hard to overestimate.

The current author, taking the principle marked above as a basis, considers it possible, with varying degrees of reliability, to identify acrophonic prototypes for up to twenty different characters (see Table II). Of course, their number may increase substantially.[47]

---

46. The most well-known description of this discovery was made by J. Chadwick, a friend and associate of M. Ventris (Chadwick 1958). In Russian there is an abridged translation (TDP, 105–245).

47. The following conclusions were discussed on March 22, 2006, during a conference in memory of S. A. Starostin (Moscow, Russian State University for the Humanities) but remained unpublished.

Table II. Some possible acrophonic parallels

Sign / Character	Pictorial meaning	Reading	Associated lexemes[48]	Derivatives
⊤	double axe	a	αῖρα (?)	
Ψ	reed, cane	i	ἰόβλης	
🏳	door, gate	ja	a) αἰβάλη (??) b) janua (??)	
🏺	a) basketbowl	ki	κίβισις, κυβισίς, κίββα κισσύβιον	
🍒	fruit or inflorescence	ko	a) κόμαρος b) κόρι	κορί-αμβλον, κορί-ανδρον, κορί-αννον
✢	flying swan	ku	κύδνος, κύκνος	
🐕	a) dog's head b) cat's head	ma	Μαῖρα onomatopoeic	
🐏	ram's head	me	μέθλην	
🐟	fish	mi	μύρος, μύλλος	μύρ(-)αι-να
🐂	head of the bull / bull's head	mu	onomatopoeic	
Υ	fig tree	ni		νικ-ύλ-εον
Ш ∞	hand crossed arms	no nwa	νόσ(φιν) (?)	
⌢	grassy plant or branch	pu	πύανος, κύαμος	Πυαν-όψια
Ψ	shrubs (?)	pu2	pu-ko-so, πύξος	
4	sheaf of cereal crops (??)	si	σῖτος (??)	
Υ	a stalk of sesame	sa	sa-sa-ma, σάσαμον	
7	ordinary axe	so	σοάνα	
Λ	tripod	ti	τιβήν	
Ψ	fig	tu	τῦκον	
F	rudder oar	u	ὕαξ	
2	snake	we		ἕλλ-οψ, Ἑλλ-ωτ-ίς, Ἑλλ-ώτ-ια

Linear A and B noticeably differ in the composition of characters. The situation is made significantly more difficult by the abundance of rare characters, which are complicated variants of the style of symbols and ligatures. The readings of Linear B are not fully known. There are no acceptable paleographic schemes of Linear A. If we look, for example, at the brief paleographic tables in Raison and Pope's *Corpus transnuméré du linéaire A*, we shall easily see that, in some cases, signs listed under different numbers are reduced to the same contour; thus, the number of syllabic signs and logograms cannot be estimated even approximately. The paleographic tables in Godart and Olivier's *Recueil des inscriptions en linéaire A* (V. 5, sec. XVIII–LII) are much better, but they also cannot be considered final. Including the syllabograms of Linear B, the total numeration of GO comes up to 418. Furthermore, ligatures and obscure fragments are included.

As for the uniform numbering system of signs, it is of fundamental importance for the two writing systems, since there is no point in thinking that the Greeks of the second millennium BCE could somehow supplement the writing system of Crete with new syllabic signs (but it is acceptable for ligatures and logograms). Indeed, it is impossible to assume, for example, that there was no sign number 012 ⌐ *so*, representing an axe, in Linear A. It existed already in the Cretan hieroglyphics, and, as was shown above, its reading is clearly defined as acrophonic (according to the gloss σοάνα "battle axe," stored in Hesychius). Besides, it may be that this sign simply cannot be recognized in the inscriptions of Linear A because of its rough tracing.

Another typical example is the Linear B sign number 048 ⵝ *nwa*, the image of crossed arms (with an evident parallel in number 052 ⵝ *no*); possibly in a reverse form, we find it in Linear A (⩓⩓), where it was given number 342. The image of crossed arms occurs already in the Cretan hieroglyphics.

In fact, we must assume that *all* the syllabic signs of Linear B read now must have existed in Linear A, and their apparent absence is due to the small number and length of texts.

The distinctive features of the orthography of Linear B[48] are well known, and we shall not dwell on them here. Now we only note that the existing readings of Minoan inscriptions and general theoretical considerations cause us to consider them originating directly from Linear A. These features must correspond to the facts of phonetics and morphology of the Old Cretan language.

The main syllabograms of Linear A were described by Furumark almost immediately after the discovery by Ventris (Furumark 1956). However, his work is not a decipherment in the strict sense, since he only identified the symbols, the reading of which is known from Linear B, and this reading is provisionally carried on the earlier system. Persuasive attempts to read the signs not found in Linear B, or obscure, have not been made, although the existing lexical material (the Minoan vocabulary in Greek)

---

48. The absence of differences between long and short vowels, on the one hand, and voiced, aspirate, and voiceless consonants on the other hand (except for the series *t-* and *d-* discussed in Chapter 5: Phonetics), the omission of a consonant at the end of a word, the omission of sonants and *s* in syllables like (C)VC before the next consonant (i.e., for example, the writing *pa-te* can match both πατήρ and πάντες, *a-ku-ro* ἄργυρος and ἄργυρον).

may well permit us to recognize the appropriate forms in the inscriptions of Linear A, and if unknown syllabograms are presented, to give them definite meanings.

The corpus of Linear B numbers less than a hundred known syllabic signs (numbers 001-090) and about 150 logograms (numbers 100-244).[49] Accordingly, the GO signs of Linear A are given the same numbers in case of identity, while the numbering of the unknown starts with number 301. Here are given, as coinciding with them, the signs 001-011, 013, 016, 017, 020-024, 026-031, 034, 037-041, 044- 047, 049-051, 053-061, 065-067, 069, 070, 073, 074, 076-082, 085-087, 118, 120, 122, 123, 131, 164, 171, 180, 188, 191. It will be shown below that there are obvious errors in the last table.

We should consider some specific problems in the interpretation of the syllabograms. The reading of *i* (Ψ, 028), accepted in CT, is apparently erroneous in most cases. Almost always there is an image of a hand (i.e., *no* [Ш, 052]), noticeable in the inscription. Consequently, the name of Athena *a-ta-no-*, *ja-ta-no-* ('Αθηνᾶ, Ionian 'Αθήνη, Doric 'Αθάνα and 'Αθαναία, Laconian 'Ασάνα),[50] occurring in a number of inscriptions, appeared to be unnoticed.

Let us cite a number of inscriptions containing this name. KO Za 1, the first line: *a-ta-no-?-wa-ja* (008-059-052-301-054-057); PK Za 11, the first line: *a-ta-no-?-wa-e a-di-ki-te-te* (008-059-052-301-054-038 008-007-067-004-004); AP Za 1: *ja-ta-no-?-u-ja-*[(057-059-052-301-010-057-]), etc.

It is significant that, in all cases, there appears precisely *no*, not the syllable *n* + another vowel. The next sign Я (there is also a "mirrored" variant of it) is considered not to have analogies in Linear B; in GO it is given number 301. It seems that the sound that follows the stem can help us to identify the reading of the next syllabogram. If we assume that this stem is joined with the widespread Minoan suffix -*op*- (-οπ-), having an appellative value,[51] the sign 301 should have the reading of *pV*. Linear A is known to have the signs *pa* (003), *pi* (039), *po* (011), *pu* (050), as well as *pu₂* (029); thus, only *pe* does not appear. In Linear B the latter has the contour Þ and number number 072. In our opinion, we are dealing here with the same sign. Its basic structure is a vertical line, which is joined with an arc or "corner."

Earlier we mentioned that many syllabograms of Linear B have a more complicated style (see oblique strokes in Þ); an oblique stroke in R, is likely to be parasitic (see a similar style in Western Greek, which led eventually to the appearance of Latin *R* along with Greek *P*). Another word-formation model (extremely widespread forms with the suffix -νθ-) helps us to offer a reading of another syllabogram of the Linear writing system.

---

49. A generally used system of numbering signs was adopted in Wingspread in 1961; we consider it appropriate to use only three-digit designations for the first hundred (001, 002, etc.); it can further help scholarly unification and computer processing as well as help avoid possible errors in the text composition.

50. It is unclear if there are various prefixes or the variant with a parasitic *j*- reproduced in the Minoan forms; for the root **tan*- see below.

51. The very presence of the suffix -*op* is a criterion for identifying the lexeme as Minoan; for example, the name of the island Παρθενόπη enables us to speak of παρθένος as a Minoan word; we shall consider it in detail below.

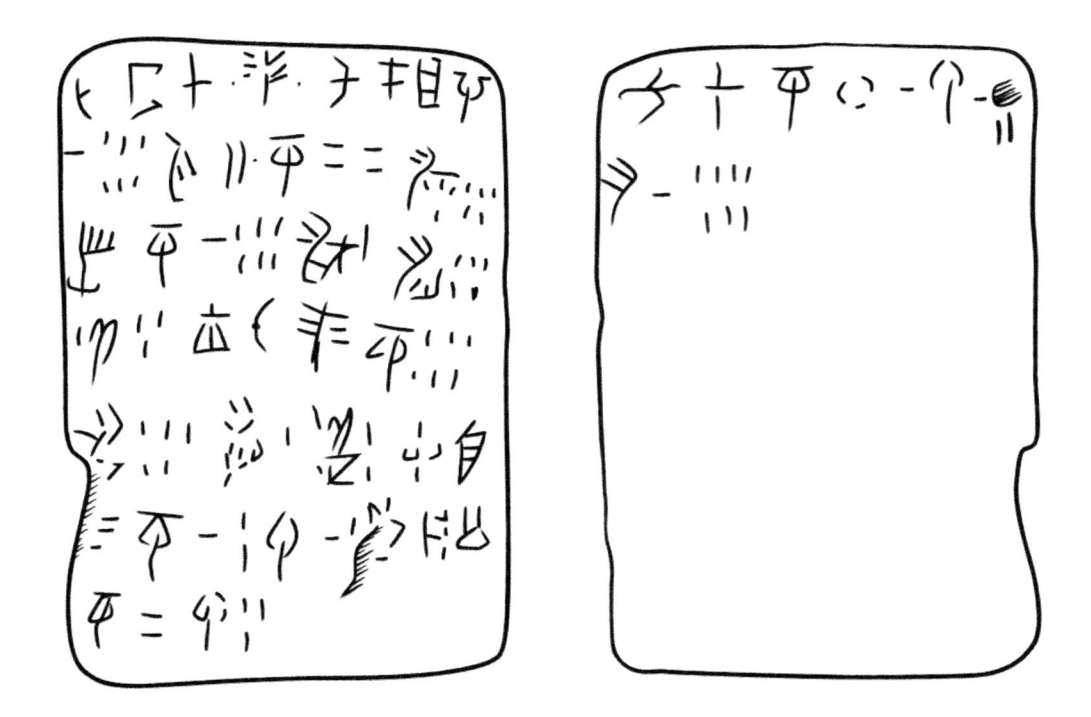

Figure 10. Tablet HT 116 from the ancient Minoan settlement at Hagia Triada.

The sign ⟨ 034, unreadable in Linear B (as is its "mirrored" version ⟩, which was given the number 035), occurs particularly in the form of *pi-034-te* from the economic inscription HT 116 (line 4, see Figure 10). Apparently, it corresponds in detail to the irregular in declension πείρινς (gen. -νθος), πείρινθος (gen. -ου) "chariot" (the development of ει from ι is supposed here). The meaning of πείρινθος, "wicker basket," was explained by Hesychius: "πείρινθος· πλέγμα, τὸ ἐπὶ τῆς ἁμάξης." It is very important that the *pi-034-te* in the inscription is followed by the logogram *GRAnum* (Ϙ, 120). Accordingly, all the combination can be understood as "five baskets of grain."

Thus, we get another sign for *ri* (along with number 053 ⟨); it can be written as *ri2* (or *ru2*). The very presence of homonymous (in our conventional reading) signs with the initial *r*- is typical. In Linear B, there are the signs 076 *ra2*, 033 *ra3* (*rai*), and 068 *ro2*. Afterward, at the stage of the Cypriote syllabary, different signs were distributed differently for the series with the initial *r* and *l* (e.g., the Cypriote sign *lo* dates back to the Cretan number 002 B *ro*). We also consider untimely the interpretations of "mirrored" versions of *f* and *g* as individual characters. "Mirrored" styles in the other cases are not particularly rare.

Another, much more risky way to clarify the readings is to find graphic correspondences between Linear A, B, and Cypro-Minoan on the one hand and the classical Cypriote writing on the other. This approach is hardly applicable even to very close languages, and here we are dealing with languages that are separated by several centuries. Moreover, the classical Cypriote writing has undergone very significant changes, both external (graphic) and internal (see, in particular, the principle of writing of final consonants and closed syllables, which will be discussed below).[52] For example, in the table from the study of Gelb (1982, 150), more than ten signs of Linear A are interpreted based on Cypriote and Cypro-Minoan in the absence of parallels from Linear B. Most parallels are unreliable, and later Cypriote paleography admits the reduction of different signs to a single type. However, one should not utterly deny the benefit of such comparisons (as auxiliary ones).

In view of the proposed revisions, Table III containing the main syllabic values of Linear A will be adopted for our discussion (the numbers of less reliable signs are given in brackets. The mark (^{cyp}) refers to the signs, the reading of which can theoretically be identified using the classical Cypriote syllabary.)

In the Cypro-Minoan script, which is a bridge between Linear A and classical Cypriote, scholars sometimes counted from fifty-eight to sixty-four syllabic signs, not counting some possible signs for numerals. Masson in her tables gives up to 114 possible variants (1974, 13–15). The presence of logograms and determinatives, which are characteristic of Linear A and B, is not obvious in Cypro-Minoan. Since the paleographic differences of the major Cypro-Minoan inscriptions are very large, we shall refrain from giving the exact number of signs. On a tablet from Enkomi, discovered in 1953, Molchanov found fifty-eight syllabograms (1992, 84). However, it is possible that, in some cases, variants of the tracing have been given as separate signs (especially for signs 17 and 18; also, signs 38 and 39, 55, and 56[53] are very similar). Although it is believed that the Cypro-Minoan script existed, as has been repeatedly stated, from the end of the sixteenth up to the mid-twelfth centuries BCE,[54] its affinity to the later Eteo-Cypriote impels us to the conclusion that the local writing tradition in Cyprus was not interrupted until the end of the fourth century BCE, when this last type of syllabic writing was finally replaced by the Greek alphabet.

Cypro-Minoan texts are by no means fully read. The cases of clear graphic coincidence with the other systems are few in number (in particular, Molchanov gives only six full equivalences between Linear A, Linear B, Cypro-Minoan, and classic Cypriote [Molchanov 1992, 84]; certainly, here we are talking about the signs that are common to all four systems, whereas there are significantly more coincidences between three or two syllabaries).

Again, it should be emphasized that the attempts at decipherment based solely on graphic similarities are methodologically unfounded. Such similarities can be elusive even in the inscriptions of closely related languages. As for the inscriptions of unrelated languages (i.e., Greek and Minoan), or probably related (Minoan and Cypro-Minoan), there the formal resemblance of syllabic signs can be considered only as an accessory factor.

---

52. Indeed, attempts to read Linear B based on the graphic Cypriote parallels have not brought any noticeable results.

53. A very interesting aspect here is that the number of signs which roughly agree with the later Cypriote signs is much smaller than in the writing systems of the Linear scripts of Aegeida. This reduction is more likely to be due to the lack of logograms than the dissimilarity of phonetics.

54. Evans, in particular, believed that it directly originates in Linear A (Pope 1976, 86).

Table III. Linear A

	a	e	i	o	u
	008	038	028	061	010
d-	001	045	007	014	051
t-	059 / 066	004	037	005	069 / 131 cyp
p-	003	072(301)	039	011	050
k-	077	044	061	070	081
q-	016	078	021	vacat	029
m-	080	013	073	317 cyp	023
n-	006	024	030	052	055
r-	060 / 076	027	053 / 302 cyp	002 / 318 cyp	026 / 034
s-	031	009	041	012	058
z-	017	074	vacat	020	079
j-	057	(046)	vacat	vacat	(065)
w-	054	075	040	vacat	vacat

Some Cypriote syllabograms, which find parallels, for example, in Linear A and B, differ in reading (cf., for example, the sign ⌀, *zo* in Cypriote and *ra2* in Linear B (number 076). Accordingly, we provisionally give the same value (i.e., *ra2*) to the syllabogram ∥ from Linear A). Another objective difficulty in working with Cypro-Minoan inscriptions is the uncertainty of even a provisional reading of some signs presented in Linear A and Cypro-Minoan because their conventional phonetic value is unknown from Linear B (as, for example, the rare sign number 312 ⌀, depicting a sword).

In general, it is possible to draw graphic analogies if coinciding readings of syllabograms of Linear B (and provisionally of Linear A) and the classical Cypriote script are known. Such a scheme makes it possible to read Cypro-Minoan (i.e., an intermediate, linking element [e.g., the sign number 067 ⌀], representing a basket, is read as *ki*, and being modified to ϒ̂, preserves this meaning in the classic Cypriote; accordingly, we can read it in the same way as in Cypro-Minoan texts). In addition, the construction of these lines matters very much to linguistic "Minoistics" because it helps link syllabic signs with Cretan hieroglyphics, which are important in identifying the acrophonic prototypes of the existing readings.

The classical Linear Cypriote writing of fifty-six syllabograms existed in the sixth to fourth centuries BCE. It was deciphered at the end of the nineteenth century by G. Smith, J. Brandis, and M. Schmidt owing to the fact that it was used mostly for the local Greek dialect and, especially, owing to the discovery of the Greco-Phoenician bilinguals. Later, as was mentioned, classical Cypriote writing was ousted by the more suitable Greek alphabet.

This script, after the manner of Cretan, has signs only for open syllables and individual vowels. It does not distinguish between voiced, unvoiced, and aspirate consonants, and it does not mark certain sounds (in particular, a single nasal consonant).[55] All these features make it somewhat difficult to read even Greek texts. What we are primarily interested in are the few local Tyrrhenian inscriptions, which are very fragmentary.

The interpretation of Eteo-Cypriote phonetics, the only Tyrrhenian language of the first millennium BCE recorded in the inscriptions of the Linear writing system, faces almost insurmountable difficulties. Even if we ignore the small number of inscriptions and their preservation, which is far from being perfect, we shall have to admit that the Cypriote script certainly did not reflect the peculiarities of the language under study as it existed with certain changes since the middle of the second millennium BCE. Accordingly, only the facts of the Cypro-Minoan language could more accurately indicate the phonetic features of the Cypriote idiom. However, as has already been mentioned, the entry of the latter into the group under study has not yet been convincingly substantiated by anyone. Furthermore, even if the latter problem is successfully solved, we shall face challenges which are fundamentally new to Etruscologists as the Tyrrhenian language of a much more ancient state will appear before us.

In any case, the interpretation of the Eteo-Cypriote and Cypro-Minoan inscriptions bring our attention to the issue of possible "pleophony" of Proto-Tyrrhenian. If the opinion of the "pleophony" of Eteo-Cypriote is not only groundless, but even absurd (as it contradicts all other Tyrrhenian languages, which are, in addition, to a large degree contemporary with Eteo-Cypriote), the supposed feature is still quite acceptable for Cypro-Minoan.

Besides, the local varieties of the alphabetic-syllabic writing system of Iberia (used mainly for non-Tyrrhenian languages, except for Ibero-Tyrrhenian [South Lusitanian]) were affected, in our view, by a linear writing system (for the development of this writing system, see Ramos 2000). Schulten has already given the Cypriote parallels ✳ *ku*, ≚ *so* for the Iberian ways of writing of *q*, *ś*; obviously, the list could be extended. In particular, the peculiar ramified sign for *i* in all the local varieties of the Iberian writing system can be explained only by the influence of a

---

55. A classical example is the spelling of the word *a-to-ro-po-se* for the Greek ἄνθρωπος.

linear writing system, which is older than the classical Cypriote syllabary (⋈ in Cypriote, but Ψ in Aegeida [number 028]). Assuming the autochthony of the Iberians, we tend to suppose that a linear writing system could have been brought to the Iberian Peninsula by the Tyrrhenians (which is consistent with the chronology of Tursha and Cypro-Minoan inscriptions). Subsequently, with the spread of the Greek or Greek-based alphabet, the local writing system was rebuilt on its base, although a number of archaic traits were retained. It should be noted that the Greek alphabetic forms penetrated to Iberia in a very archaic style. In this connection, Schulten's dating does not look too early.

The evidence for the existence of linear writing in Italy is purely hypothetical (it is based on the unverified information of the ancient tradition) and, although it apparently cannot be refuted by modern science, it does not necessarily imply the Tyrrhenian language. The references to Arcadian settlers in Latium are numerous. They are confirmed in the archaeological material and even in the vocabulary borrowed into the Latin language (this language influence can be considered proven after the works of Peruzzi [Peruzzi 1975, Peruzzi 1982; cf., the review on the latter work, Majak, 1983]). Livy and Tacitus also report on a writing system introduced by a well-known culture hero, Evander from Arcadia.[xxi] Note also the reference of the ancient historian John the Lydian (Ost., 3) to the written account of the religious doctrine, made by Tarchon prior to Evander,[xxii] but it still does not have a distinct explanation.[56] Apparently, we may agree with the following statement: "given examples . . . say that the ancient authors had some vague notions about the oldest pre-alphabetic writing" (Nemirovskij 1983: 71). Even if we assume at least a limited distribution of linear writing in Italy under the cultural influence of Arcadian settlers, it does not correspond to our information about the chronology of the Etruscans (who settled in Tuscany much later than the events mentioned). In addition, the main drawback of such hypotheses is a complete lack of the actual surviving written inscriptions. However, even the discovery of the written records of Arcadian colonists would not indicate in any way the distribution of the writing system among the peoples of Italy at that time.

In any case, the references to the existence of an archaic writing system in Italy are usually associated with the name of Evander and, in general, have no practical significance for the study of the Tyrrhenian languages. Normally these references (a relatively large number of which were preserved by ancient authors) are used by scholars of the alphabets of Italy in light of the most general concepts of the origin of the latter.

At one time, a theory was put forward (cf., Pfiffig 1969, 23) according to which the Etruscan inscriptions inherited some characteristics of a linear writing system—namely, the dot syllabic interpunctuation (in Caere, Formello, and Orvieto). (Compare such careful writings as *vel matunas larisalisa an cn śuθi ceriχunce* [TLE 51]). This point of view, with reference to Fiesel, is also given by Schulten, who associated such ways of writing with the syllabic Iberian ones (Schulten 1941, 28). As has been convincingly

---

56. Cf., the opinion of Nemirovskij: "These guesses bear no relation to Etruscans, because no author, with the exception of later Lydus, mentions Tarhunt living in the second millennium BCE" (Nemirovskij 1983, 71).

shown by Nemirovskij, the syllabic interpunctuation in Etruscan does not cover the whole area, being found only in the southern inscriptions since the sixth century BCE (i.e., it cannot be considered as a fundamental feature of the Etruscan written language in light of the genesis of the latter. Cristofani indicated that this feature is only an orthographic tradition dating back to the school of scribes in Veii (1978, 411).

On the other hand, the proposition of the principally syllabic character of Etruscan graphemes, subjected to criticism by Nemirovskij, most probably cannot be proved or disproved at present. The syllabic writings found on one of the "bucchero" vessels[57] apparently cannot be taken into consideration here, since they only list the possible combinations of sounds not bearing the traces of syllabic readings of individual graphemes. In general, we can conclude that, for the Tyrrhenian material, the problem of the development of a linear and alphabetic writing merges into one.

THE TYRRHENIAN ALPHABETIC SCRIPT

In the period from the seventh to first centuries BCE, the vast majority of the Tyrrhenian (i.e., Etruscan, Rhaetic, Lemnian, and South Lusitanian) inscriptions were made using alphabets which had some differences but were fundamentally similar. Strictly speaking, Rhaetic is a territorial branch of Etruscan, and one has to compare, in fact, two basic types, which are Etruscan and Lemnian, with extremely limited material of the latter (and some vague facts of South Lusitanian). These alphabets go back to the Greek alphabet in its very archaic form. They cannot be confidently attributed to any of the groups within the long-accepted linguistic "color" designations. Thus, the presence of the signs Φ – φ, Υ – χ prevent them from being included in the "green" alphabets (Crete, Thera, Melos), while, according to the archaic-style signs of the Lemnos stele, they are usually compared precisely with the latter. Like a part of the "blue" alphabets (Athens, Aegina, Naxos, Cnidus), they do not have "double" signs such as Ξ [ks] and Ψ [ps] (because such confluences of sounds are completely alien to the Tyrrhenian languages) but do not reveal specific coincidences.

The common features of Etruscan (along with Rhaetic), Lemnian, and Iberian-Tyrrhenian are the almost complete absence of the signs Β, Γ, Δ (except for one or two examples). In Etruscan and Rhaetic, Ο (and, of course, Ω) were not used, whereas in the inscription of the Lemnos stele there is no sign for [u], but there is only an *omicron* (both letters occur as remnants in Iberian-Tyrrhenian). However, the assertion of the complete uncertainty of the letters listed, encountered in works of a general character (cf., Bonfante 1990, 15), is wrong (at least with regard to Etruscan). The signs for voiced consonants were known in the prototype of the Etruscan alphabet and could be used later in exceptional cases (for details, see below), but they were rather quickly forgotten. Their disappearance seems to have been facilitated also by the fact that the Etruscans, unlike the Greeks, did not use a standard alphabet to designate numerals, having special characters for that.

---

57. TLE 55; here we see the prototype of the Etruscan alphabet (without 8, 8) and the syllables of the type *Ci, Ca, Cu, Ce*, but including only *c, v, z, h, θ, m, n, p, r, ś, χ, q, t.*

Table IV. The varieties of the Etruscan alphabet

Initial	Archaic 7th-5th cc.	Transitional 5th-4th cc.	Late 4th-1st cc.	Special forms	Transliteration
A	A	A	A	A	a
B	B	-	-	-	b
⅂	⅂ ⊃	>	> ⊃	-	c (= k)
⊲	⊲	-	-	-	d
⋶	⋶	⋶	⋶	⋷	e
⅂	⅂	⅂	⅂	⅃	v
I	I	‡	‡ F	‡	z
目	目	目 目	目	目	h
⊗	⊗ ⊙	⊙ ⊙	⊙ ⊙	-	θ
I	I	I	I	-	i
Ϟ	Ϟ	Ϟ	Ϟ	)I	k
⌄	⌄	⌄	⌄	⌃	l
⋈	⋈ ⋈	M	M	O ∧	m
⋎	⋎	И	И	∩	n
⊞	⊞ ⊠ ⋈	-	-	-	š
O	O	-	-	-	o
↑	↑ M	↑ M	↑ M	-	p ś q
M(⋈)	φ q	-	-	M ⋈ ⊗	r
φ q	φ q	q	Ϙ	-	
⌇	⌇ ⌇	⌇	⌇	⌇	s
↑	↑	↑ ↑	† Ϝ	↑ †	t
Υ	Υ	V	V	-	u
X	X +	-	-	-	ṣ
Φ	Φ	-	-	-	φ
Υ	Υ V	↓	↓	·│·	χ
-	8 8	8 8	8	-	f

Throughout its recorded history, Etruscan had preserved the *digamma* in its basic meaning (i.e., [w], [v]) in the form (⅂), which we observe in the archaic inscriptions of Crete and among the western forms in Boeotia. The archaic Etruscan alphabet included two additional signs for [s], š and ṣ, besides the *sigma* and *san* which had consolidated their positions.

Their contours (see Table IV) seem to find no analogies in Greek or in linear writing systems. There is a specific coincidence with Lydian, which is a sign for [f] that had both angular (earlier) and rounded styles: 8, 8, 8, 8. It is significant that this symbol does not appear early. It is absent in the ancient Etruscan inscriptions as well as in the Latin and Venetic writings that originated in Etruscan. In all these cases, for [f] the combinations *vh* and *hv* are used. These and other examples will be discussed in more detail below, when analyzing the Tyrrhenian phonetics.

On the whole, the Etruscan alphabet is the closest to the archaic alphabet of Euboea. Its development can be presented in the form of a table (see Table IV; also see the Etruscan alphabet on a vase from Viterbo [Figure 11]).

Besides the special forms given, there are a few even rarer variants. Thus, for example, in Caere for [n] and [m] the writings M and M are found, which can be viewed as symmetrically complemented ⋎ and ⋎; some graphic variants are unique: ዓ (*o*, TLE 697), ዓ (*f*, TLE 100). See also Rix (1983).

In addition, in the late Etruscan writing, ligatures that are fairly easy to understand were used to a limited extent, the most common of them being: ⋏ *al*, ⋏⋏ *ana*, ⋏⋏ *aut*, ⋏ *zn*, ⋏ *ha*, ⋑ *θe*, ⋏⋏ *ma*, ⋎ *mu*, ⋎⋎ *mut*, ⋏⋏ *nal*, ⋎ *ue*, ⋎ *ur* (Pfiffig 1969, 22).

The Etruscan alphabet has been perfectly described in the above cited work by Cristofani (1978). This study is especially important for practical training with the inscriptions, because it contains a detailed description of the local features of the writing system.

The Lemnian alphabet at present does not reveal any sort of innovations that distinguish it from the Greek environment, but the scarcity of the material makes it impossible to come to a definite conclusion about this. For a general description of the Lemnian alphabet, see also the above-mentioned separate article (Malzahn 1999).

Any scholar of the Etruscan and Italic alphabets faces the question of their correlation. Although the connection between the Etruscan and Latin writing systems is not one of the special subjects in our work, it cannot be disregarded, since it has a considerable impact on our understanding of Etruscan-Latin cultural and linguistic contacts in general. This question has provoked lengthy discussions (see also the work by Modestov [1868], anticipating many later ideas).

It sounds paradoxical, but the ancient tradition that Evander brought a writing system to Italy some time before the Trojan War is at times used to substantiate an independent (i.e., without the Etruscan participation) origin of the Latin alphabet. In principle, the interpretation of the origin of the Latin writing system is reduced to two extreme points of view—namely, the statements of the Latins borrowing the writing from the Etruscans, and, by contrast, the complete absence of the Etruscan influence on the development of the alphabet. The first point of view, that was supported, in particular, by Friedrich,[58] is, of course, closer to the truth than the second opinion, which, unfortunately, can strongly influence the Russian scientific literature, as it is consistently (though not convincingly) carried out in the works by Fedorova.[59]

It is significant that the viewpoint of the independent origin of the Oscan, Umbrian, and other Italic alphabets, as well as the North Picenian, seems not to occur in the literature. The existing statements here are quite clear.[60]

---

58. "It is accepted now to consider the Latin alphabet as a variety of Etruscan" (Friedrich 1979, 137).

59 Cf., the following: "Writing in Latium was borrowed directly from Greeks" (Fedorova 1982, 222).

60. Cf., for example, the following (on the Oscan): "The alphabet is a modification of the Etruscan one, thoroughly adapted to Oscan language peculiarities" (Tronskij 1953, 64); on the Umbrian (toward

Figure 11. The Etruscan alphabet on a vase from Viterbo, Italy.

Without dwelling on the paleographic features and issues of the origin and early history of the Latin alphabet, we should note that the evidence base of the critics of the Etruscan mediation contains three kinds of weak arguments. Thus, in the studies mentioned, the most significant features of the similarity between the Etruscan and Latin writing systems are not considered. The evidence of differences is reduced to considering the spelling of the velar (quite significant is that the last question in the 1982 edition takes

---

the description of the Iguvine tablets): "The Tables I–IV and a large part of Table V are written with a local script, going back, as nearly all other Italic alphabets, to Etruscan" (Tronskij 1953, 69; on the North Picene: "*L'alfabeto, infatti, deriva da un modello etrusco, come risulta palese dal segno per r, però presenta alcune modificazioni . . .*" (Durante 1978, 395).

up a major part of the section on the origin of the alphabet). In addition, Fedorova unconditionally accepts the extremely doubtful etymologies of Peruzzi, who traces the basic Latin terminology associated with the scribal work directly from Greek.

The weakness of these constructions is evident in two examples: the etymologization of *littera* from the Greek διφθέρα and *elementum* from the Greek ἐλέφας (gen. -αντος). In this case, Tronskij refers to *littera* as an Etruscan word (Tronskij 1953, 124) among other lexemes with *-ra* (see Chapter 7: Word-Formation). The phonetic comparison of the Latin *littera* directly with the Greek διφθέρα is questionable if we admit the affinity of these lexemes. In our opinion, it is preferable to speak again of Etruscan mediation. Here we should mention a very interesting Cypriot gloss of Hesychius "διφθεραλοφός· γραμματοδιδάσκαλος παρὰ Κυπρίοις." It seems that the terms associated with the writing system and derived from διφθέρα date back to the times of Mycenaean and Tyrrhenian antiquity[61] (cf., our assumption about Cypro-Minoan expressed above).

The relation of *elementum* to ἐλέφας is absolutely incredible, as is shown by Nemirovskij.[62] It is especially significant that Fedorova, citing the opinion of Nemirovskij of the more ancient character of Latin inscriptions in comparison to the Etruscan, not only made no attempt to overcome his harsh criticism of the views of Peruzzi, but did not even mention it. The given examples can be extended: if, in particular, we suggest after the scholar that the Latin *titulus* < Greek δέλτος (which is very likely), then it will be easy to explain the muting of an initial consonant by an intermediate Etruscan form.

Etruscan mediation can also explain another characteristic feature: the Latin naming for the letters (*be, de, em, er*, etc.) which have nothing in common with the Greek names, may originate in the Etruscan environment (Friedrich 1979, 38).

One of the scholars who has considered more carefully the correlation of the Etruscan and Latin alphabets was Cristofani. In his 1978 essay, which is still the basis for the study of the Etruscan alphabet, he proved Etruscan mediation in the formation of the Latin alphabet, explaining the discrepancies with the Etruscan by the need to adapt existing signs for dramatically different Latin phonetics.[63]

The denial of the Etruscan mediation on the ground that, in the classical texts there are no signs for *o* and for voiced *b, d, g*, is unacceptable because these letters were in the early prototype of the alphabet (it is no coincidence that Friedrich called it "Proto-Tyrrhenian"), and they are found in some inscriptions: *mazba* (TLE 160) and *frontac* (TLE 697). The attempt not to notice these signs in Etruscan, in principle, is just as absurd as the assertion about the absence in archaic Latin of the letter *z* that disappeared as a result of rhotacism but was well known to Roman antiquaries.

---

61. In the last case, we mean the time of the reference to "Tursha" and the appearance of Cypro-Minoan inscriptions.

62. "The opinion supported by E. Peruzzi . . . is unconvincing both from linguistic and historical points of view. Ivory as a material for writing was too expensive and could be used too seldom to make the corresponding word the synonym for the bases of literacy" (Nemirovskij 1983, 74).

63. "*L'operazione fonologica dei Latini, che hanno attribuito alle lettere greche non utilizzate dagli Etruschi precisi valori fonetici . . . può spiegarsi solo attraverso l'intervento greco ma l'intermediario etrusco è necessario però per spiegare il sistema di notazione delle velari*" (Cristofani 1978, 418).

One of the most striking common features in the Etruscan and Latin writing systems is the use of *hv*, *vh* (Etruscan), *vh* (Latin) to designate *f* in archaic alphabets. Later, it was precisely this designation that became simplified to F in Latin. In Latin, the most characteristic example of this is the inscription ᚠᛖᚠᚨᚲᛖᛞ (i.e., *fefaked*, "fecit") on the Praeneste fibula.[64] In general, the presence of a single variant of *vh* in Latin with the free interchange of *hv* ~ *vh* in Etruscan indicates the primary nature of the Etruscan writing, and, accordingly, the presence of borrowing in Latin.

The development of the Latin *C* in two directions (i.e., toward *C* and *G*), which has caused the speculations mentioned, agrees with the viewpoint that we share on the fact that, if there were a direct borrowing of the Greek alphabet, the Greek *gamma* would be applied to the [g]. Strictly speaking, one can postulate the borrowing not from "Proto-Tyrrhenian," in the terminology of Friedrich, but from the functional Etruscan alphabet, which actually had been used on the border of Latium, the alphabet in which some characters had already been dropped as unnecessary.

One can hardly say that the Latin alphabet had much influence on the Etruscan at a later stage. However, the expert on Etruscan culture, Emperor Claudius, who tried to introduce three new characters into the Latin alphabet,[xxiii] obviously chose for the sound [v] the reversed Etruscan *digamma* (Ⅎ). Cristofani has already expressed an opinion on it.[65] It should be noted that the "invention" of only this letter by Claudius was grounded in terms of Latin phonetics.[66]

CHAPTER THREE NOTES

[xxi] "*Evander tum ea, profugus ex Peloponneso, auctoritate magis quam imperio regebat loca, venerabilis vir miraculo litterarum, rei novae inter rudes artium homines*" (Liv., I, 7, 8).
"*At in Italia Etrusci ab Corinthio Demarato, Aborigines Arcade ab Evandro didicerunt; et forma litteris Latinis quae veterrimis Graecorum*" (Tac., Ann., XI, 14).

[xxii] "Τάρχων, ταύτῃ ἔχων τὴν προσηγορίαν, ἀνὴρ γ[έγονε μὲν] θυοσκόπος, ὡς αὐτὸς ἐπὶ τῆς γραφῆς εἰσενήνεκται, εἷς [τῶν ὑπὸ] Τυρρηνοῦ τοῦ Λυδοῦ διδαχθέντων. καὶ γὰρ δὴ τοῖς Θούσκ[ων γράμμα]σι ταῦτα δηλοῦται, οὔπω τηνικαῦτα τοῖς τόποις ἐκείνοις Εὐάνδρου τοῦ Ἀρκάδος ἐπιφανέντος. . . . Τάρχων δὲ ὁ πρεσβύτερος (γέγονε γὰρ δὴ καὶ νεώτερος, ἐπὶ τῶν Αἰνείου στρατευσαμένων χρόνων) τὸ παιδίον ἀναλαβὼν καὶ τοῖς ἱεροῖς ἐναποθέμενος τόποις ἠξίου τι παρ᾽ [αὐτοῦ] τῶν ἀπορρήτων μαθεῖν.

---

64. We reject the position on the Praeneste fibula as a fake of the nineteenth century, preventing its scientific review. It seems preferable to speak of a carefully made copy of the antique original; thus, the inscription can be considered authentic. (For more on the history of the issue, see [Fedorova 1991, 26-30]).

65. "*Il cosidetto digamma dell'alfabeto latino dell'età di Claudio non sembra comunque solo frutto dell'erudizione dell'imperatore, ma potrebbe essere anche un imprestito dell'alfabeto etrusco ancora in uso in alcune zone della Toscana*" (Cristofani 1978, 425).

66. ". . . the reform, containing along with the unnecessary for Roman writing (i.e., with the characters Ⱶ [ü] and Ↄ [ps], [bs], *S. Ya.*), offers quite a rational attempt to introduce a special sign for *v*" (Tronskij 2001, 76).

τοῦ δὲ αἰτουμένου τυχὼν βι[βλίον] ἐκ τῶν εἰρημένων συνέγραψεν, ἐν ᾧ πυνθάνεται μὲν ὁ Τάρχων τῇ τῶν Ἰταλῶν ταύτῃ τῇ συνήθει φωνῇ, ἀποκρίνεται δὲ ὁ Τάγης γράμμασιν ἀρχαίοις τε καὶ οὐ σφόδρα γνωρίμοις ἡμῖν γε ἐμμένων τῶν ἀποκρίσεων."

[xxiii] "*Quo exemplo Claudius tres litteras adiecit, quae usui imperitante eo, post oblitteratae, aspiciuntur etiam nunc in aere publico dis plebiscitis per fora ac templa fixo*" (Tac., Ann., XI, 14)

CHAPTER 4

THE INTERPRETATION OF THE VOCABULARY

The known Minoan and Tyrrhenian lexemes, as well as relicts presumably attributable to these languages, are divided into several groups. In this case, the division has not so much to do with the origin of the words or the semantic categories as with the ways and possibilities of determining whether the given words belong to the languages under study, as well as identifying their meaning (when it is a matter of words in the original texts). Since the actual Minoan vocabulary, in contrast to the diverse Tyrrhenian of the first millennium BCE, is known almost exclusively through Greek transfers (although they often find parallels in the inscriptions), it seems appropriate to consider it separately.

There are several criteria with which one can postulate a Minoan (or "Cretan," "Aegean," depending on the terminology) origin for a given word. These may be direct indications of Greek authors (i.e., glosses [very few, even in comparison with the "Tyrrhenian"]), known Minoan word formation elements, a special structure of the root, and a characteristic phonetic form of lexemes (or unexplained from Greek and, more broadly, Indo-European alternations), sometimes even just the uniqueness of individual roots in Greek, in their absence in all other branches of the Indo-European family.[67] There are a number of Greek borrowings from the languages of the Near East and Asia Minor: Sumerian, the Anatolian languages, perhaps the Hurro-Urartian, Semitic languages, and Egyptian, and, finally, the borrowings are likely to be from Minoan or some dialect unknown to us that was close to it or to these languages, especially the Semitic. The most reliable are direct parallels with the forms in Linear A inscriptions and with Tyrrhenian lexemes. However, the boundaries between all these groups are very fuzzy, and the intersections are extremely diverse.

---

67. Cf., the similar point in Tronskij concerning the pre-Indo-European loanwords in Latin (1953, 114).

1) Glosses.[68] References to the Cretan origin or peculiarities of the sounds of certain words in Greek authors are infrequent, but most of them are actually Greek (Doric) dialecticisms (i.e., it is more relevant to call them "geographic" in contrast to the ethnic references "Τυρσηνοί, Τυρρηνοί.") The Eteocretans are not mentioned in these sources at all. On the other hand, the Greek Cretan dialecticisms are also useful for studying the language of Crete, that is, for identifying the substrate phonetic influences (cf., for example, the gloss of Hesychius "λάκη· ράκη. Κρῆτες" indicating the preservation of the ancient Cretan confusion *r* : *l*, "ἄργετος· ἡ ἄρκευθος. Κρῆτες" with an interesting mix of consonants and disappearance of the diphthong, πῆριξ instead of πέρδιξ, which may indicate a Cretan affricate).

Along with the dialecticisms, there are typical forms, mainly ἅπαξ λεγόμενα, the Cretan origin of which is beyond doubt. Here are some examples that are preserved by Hesychius: ἀκακαλλίς "narcissus flower"; ἄκαρα (pl.) "thighs"; γάρσανα (pl.) "brushwood"; perhaps, ἰέττας "πατέρας. Κρῆτες. ἢ τούς ἀγρίους τράγους"; ἰόβλης "reed"; vaguely explained κάδμος ("δόρυ. λόφος. ἀσπίς. Κρῆτες"); καμάν (acc.) "field"; καρορύς, a kind of vessel; κεκῆνας (acc. pl.) "hares"; μάριν (acc.) "pig." For details, see Index.

Some glosses contain derivational elements, which in themselves indicate the Cretan or Tyrrhenian origin of the word (they will be analyzed in detail below). Compare, for example, ἄχνυλα "hazel," again in Hesychius. There is the suffix *-uR-* here that was marked out by Neumann due to the glossed (in Athenaeus) word νικύλεον and that has become one of the most notable features of the Cretan borrowings.

Finally, there are glosses that find direct parallels in the authentic inscriptions (i.e., in Linear A inscriptions, in Etruscan inscriptions, and the inscriptions in the "minor" Tyrrhenian languages). Compare, for example, "Σύρινθος, πόλις Κρήτης" in Stephen with the form *si-ru-te* from the inscriptions IO Za 2, IO Za 14; in Hesychius "τυί· ὧδε Κρῆτες" with Etruscan θ*ui* "here" or "Γελχάνος (< *Fέλχανος)· ὁ Ζεύς, παρὰ Κρησίν" with Etruscan *velχana* (source of Latin *Vulcanus*).

2) The vocabulary that is marked out by the typical affixes will not be given here, as it is described in Chapter 7: Word Formation. It should be distinguished from the set of lexemes that add the Greek endings of the first and second declension after e or i, reflecting the final vowel of the Minoan words. Indeed, such an appearance is not typical for Greek. Here are some examples: ἀκτέα "elder, *Sambucus nigra*"; ἀμάδεα (acc. pl.), a kind of fig; ἀμία, a kind of tuna; ἰτέα "willow, *Salix*"; Ἰτέα, a toponym in Attica; κιβώριον "a water lily seed pod"; κισσύβιον "bowl"; κόρσεον "tuber of water lotus"; μαλέα, μηλέα "apple tree"; μιρύκεον [Hes.] "cane, reed"; ὄσπρεον, ὄσπριον "legume"; ὄστρειον "shellfish"; περσέα, a kind of Egyptian wood; πτελέα, Mycenaean *pte-re-wa* "elm, *Ulmus campestris*." It will be shown below that similar words also penetrated into Latin from Etruscan.

---

68. As mentioned above, there are a number of glosses, undoubtedly Minoan and Tyrrhenian, not having ethnic references or references to other peoples or lands but clearly recognizable, especially by word-formation models. They will be described in other sections as they differ from the ordinary vocabulary, penetrating into Greek, in fact, only in their rarity.

3) The results of the positional analysis of Linear A inscriptions, unlike the Etruscan, are quite insignificant. For decades, often present in the numerical signs in economic inscriptions *ki-ro* "shortage, lack" and *ku-ro* "total" have remained the only known forms. The latter may be borrowed from Semitic *kl* "all" (Pope 1976, 90).

4) As for borrowings from the ancient languages of the Middle East, scholars have succeeded in marking out only a few of them. Thus, it can be argued that the word κάνναβις "hemp" (< *kunibu*)[69] is Sumerian in origin. As mentioned above, a number of words in Greek that have, according to Ernshtedt, an Egyptian origin, could have penetrated through the language of the Cretans.[70] The given words could have taken shape with typical Cretan suffixes. For example, φάρμακον with the widespread element -ακ-, μάρτυρος with υρ-; the stem of pure Egyptian ἔρπις "wine" (according to Eustathius's evidence with the reference to Lycophron)[71] may be reflected in the name of plants ἔρπυλλος (with the same -υρ-/-υλ-), ἐρπυξή (in Dioscorides), if they were used in the manufacture of some sort of wine. The stem of the word μέρμις was also present in the language of the Cretans (see Index).

In turn, on the basis of word-formation models, it can be seen that a number of Minoan words entered, for example, into the Semitic languages, but not vice versa, as it is sometimes stated in the relevant articles of Greek etymological dictionaries. Compare, for example, the uniform Cretan suffixation in the names of plants βάλσαμον, κάγκαμον, σάσαμον (here is also κάρδαμον), and irregular Semitic parallels: Classical Hebrew *bāśām*, Arabian *basām*; Akkadian *kurkānu*, Classical Hebrew *karkōm*, Arabian *kurkunr*, Akkadian *šammaššamu*, Aramaic *sūmšnā*.

5) The cases where scholars manage to find clear parallels in Linear A inscriptions to the categorematic vocabulary preserved in Greek, except for the acrophonic correspondences mentioned above, are few but extremely valuable. At present only words for household items are reliable. Thus, for decades such coincidences as κάρδοπος "trough" : HT 31 *ka-ro-pa3*, σιπύη "bread bin" : HT 8 *su-pu2-188*, κάθιδοι (apparently from Hittite *gazzi*), a kind of vessel : and HT 63 *ka-ti* have been known. Some time ago, the author of this study managed to draw parallels between the initial syllables of *a-da-ra* (the inscription on a silver female hairpin KN Zf 31) and the word ἄλαρα, ἐλάραι "spike, tip" (in Hesychius and Herodianus), as well as the beginning of the inscription on the bronze bowl KO Zf 2 *a-ra-ko-*, and the word ἄρακις "bowl" preserved in Atheneus and Hesychius.

This concludes our brief description of the Minoan lexemes, since the preponderance of the examples are given in the Index at the end of the study.

The known Tyrrhenian vocabulary also can be divided by:

---

69. At least one Sumerian stem existed also in Etruscan: *eti-*, Etruscan-Latin *Idus* with Sumerian *itu* "full moon."

70. In general, Ernshtedt takes into account 39 major supposed loans, among which he considers nine to be absolutely reliable (for the earliest stratum) (Ernstedt 1953, 201).

71. "ἔστι δὲ ἔρπις Αἰγυπτιστὶ ὁ οἶνος καθὰ καὶ ὁ Λυκόφρων οἶδεν" (I: 1633).

1) Lexemes, the meaning of which is known through the testimony of ancient writers (glosses);

2) Various forms in Tyrrhenian inscriptions, the meanings of which are established positionally (the degree of reliability of interpretation varies greatly in this case);

3) The Tyrrhenian vocabulary, which is borrowed into Latin, Greek, Umbrian, perhaps into some other languages and that finds various correspondences in the Tyrrhenian inscriptions proper;

4) Quite a large layer of lexemes in these languages which do not have written Tyrrhenian correspondences or indications on the origin but are marked out on a relatively reliable basis by the special features of phonetics and word formation;

5) Individual words, the relation of which to the Tyrrhenian languages is hypothetical but can be explained by external factors. The substantiation of a formal noncontradiction here, as above in Greek, is the isolation of a number of important lexemes.[72] At the same time, such marking out is more reliable for Latin and less for the Greek language. To this group we also may provisionally relate some of the toponyms preserved in Latin and Greek;

6) The loans into Etruscan and (to a lesser extent) into the "minor" Tyrrhenian languages from other languages. In this case, proper names are rather frequent. It is easy to see that this is the most transparent part of the well-known lexical fund. A lot of fantastic concepts of the kinship of the Tyrrhenian languages, primarily with the Indo-European languages, were built on the comparison of such loans (already graphically and/or phonetically modified) with the vocabulary of the origin languages (see, for example, the hypotheses of Georgiev [1958, 187-93]); many Greek loan words, and words that just look similar, are given, for example, in the early work of Xarsekin (1963, 28-30). Subsequently, this outstanding Russian Etruscologist completely abandoned the hypotheses of the possible relationship between Etruscan and the Indo-European languages.

Apparently, the interpretation of various Tyrrhenian words is very different in approach and reliability. In our view, at present we should not try to give the exact number of known lexemes. It may be hoped that we shall soon succeed in making a small Tyrrhenian root dictionary, but the number of derivatives of known stems will be constantly changing.

As for the glossaries that we have today, it would be more appropriate to call them word lists relating primarily to sections (1), (2), (6). They have significant drawbacks. Here are, as examples, two glossaries from Russian editions (Xarsekin 1969, 55-59; Pallottino 1976, 375-80). Xarsekin took into account 137 and Pallottino 130 lexemes and postpositive particles. The principle of their description in general is unclear. In some cases (for the most common stems), a root is given with several derivatives, while, in the other, complete forms are given. However, some paronymous words are part of different lines (for example, the adjective *spurana* "urban" in Xarsekin is given separately from *spur-*). Obviously, because of the desire to avoid any etymologization, neither scholar gives any foreign language parallels, except for the Greek words borrowed into

---

72. Cf., for example, the group of isolates with the root diphthong (the type *caussa*, *laus*) given in Chapter 5: Phonetics.

Etruscan (such as *artesi* "decoration" [< ἄρτισις], the names of vessels *aska* [< ἀσκός], *qutun* [< κώθων], etc.). The context from which certain meanings are derived is never explained (except for the Greek borrowings). Pallottino even gives the form *acale* for "June" without the gloss *Aclus*, although it is the only indication as to its meaning. The vocabulary of the "minor" Tyrrhenian languages is not included at all, even at the level of the classical parallels of the Lemnos stele inscriptions. There are practically no grammatical commentaries. There are significant differences in the interpretation of some lexemes (in addition, it should be admitted that both variants could have become obsolete to a considerable degree since the date of their publication).

However, all these features are present in comparatively new editions as well. Compare, for example, the glossary of Etruscan by Bonfante (1990, 59-62). Over 250 lexemes are taken into account here, with various derivatives of the same stem that are again given separately. The glosses are stylized into supposed Etruscan forms (!), and the vocabulary of other Tyrrhenian languages is not considered here at all. The translation is always given in brief, out of the grammatical context.

It seems to us that the preparation for compiling the dictionary of Tyrrhenian should begin with the very classification of the lexemes and clarification of the relations of the existing relicts. In the present publication, we are using not an alphabetical listing but a classification/ranging order of the description of lexical groups.

Since the object of this work is not to cover all the known Tyrrhenian vocabulary or even to conduct separate research into this subject, we deem it necessary to describe in great detail the above-mentioned groups of Tyrrhenian lexemes, because the basic argument of the study is to a large extent built on the knowledge of more or less accurate lexical meanings.[73]

1) Etruscan glosses are a rather mixed picture. The current lists of them (the majority of which are those given in TLE) go back to a very old edition by T. Dempster and contain several inaccuracies, and in this connection, we shall give them in full and thematically grouped (for example in the TLE all glosses are given [and, accordingly, numbered] in alphabetical order). The first scholars of the Etruscan glosses did a great job "sifting" the works of ancient authors, but it seems to us some lexemes have been left unnoticed in such a large corpus of material. We managed to find at least two missing glosses. Apparently, the effectiveness of such research may significantly increase when electronic editions of texts with extensive search engines are used.

In almost all glosses the grammatical characteristics, typical for Etruscan, are ignored. Commonly, Roman and Greek authors match these lexemes on the rules of their language (cf., below "ἰταλὸν τὸν ταῦρον," "a falado," etc.). Sometimes an Etruscan grammatical form is preserved but not understood, like TLE 803: "aesar ... deus vocatur." As we can see there is a plural form here (in "ἀἰσοί· θεοί" the matching is correct).

---

73. When working with Greek and Italian vocabulary, the following dictionaries were primarily used; for Greek: Dvoretskij 1958, Boisacq 1916, Frisk 1960, Liddell-Scott 1996, Woodhouse 1910; for Latin: Dvoretskij 1995, Ernout-Meillet 1951, Walde-Hofmann 1938-1956; for Oskan-Umbrian dialects: Untermann 2000.

Compare the only gloss containing a verb form, TLE 812: "arseuerse *averte ignem significat. Tuscorum enim lingua* arse *averte,* verse *ignem constat appellari.*" The conclusions, which it enables us to make, are not particularly significant for understanding the verb structure (see below), but the very important word "fire" appears here. The stem *vers-* is found in Etruscan inscriptions but in a vague context. The correlation of the same gloss with the following is completely obscure.

From the gloss TLE 857 ("*Primum agri modum fecerunt quattuor limitibus clausum . . ., plerumque centenum pedum in utraque parte [quod Graeci plethron appellant, Tusci et Umbri uorsum, nostri centenum*"]), as well as from the evidence of Varro in Res rusticae, I, 10 ("*In Campania . . .* versum *dicunt C pedes quoque* versum *quadratum*") we can see that the name of an area measurement was identical to the given word. A complete homonymy in the stem CVSSib is hardly acceptable, but the interpretation as "fire" can hardly be considered a mistake. From the context of the glosses, it was even concluded (Robertson 2006, sec. 8) that the stem *vers-* in Etruscan had the meaning of "100." However, this proposition still cannot be proven. In our view, one can assume its Italic origin (according to the mention of Campania and the Umbri, from whom it could have been borrowed by the Etruscans, if the first part of the indication "*Tusci et Umbri*" is not excessive). The use of *vers-* in Etruscan generic names also argues against the interpretation of *vers-* as the stem of the name of an area measurement.

Most verbose is the gloss of Macrobius: TLE 838 b) "Iduum *porro nomen a Tuscis, apud quos is dies Itus vocatur, sumptum est. Item autem interpretantur Iovis fiduciam . . . Iovis fiduciam Tusco nomine vocaverunt sunt qui astiment Idus ab ove Idule dictas, quam hoc nomine vocant Tusci, et omnibus Idibus Iovi immolatur a flamine. Nobis illa ratio nominis vero propior aestimetur, ut Itus vocemus diem qui dividit mensem.* Iduare *enim Etrusca lingua dividere est.*"

Compare also: TLE 838 a) "Idus *at eo quod Tisci* Itus, *vel potius quod Sabini* Idus *dicunt.*" Here an artificial "Etruscan" infinitive *iduare* "dividere" makes it impossible to come to any conclusions about the original form (in fact, it is an Asian Near East borrowing going back to Sumerian *itu* "full moon" [i.e., the "middle of the month"]).

As already mentioned, the known glosses are very heterogeneous. The most systematic is the enumeration of the eight names of the Etruscan months, preserved in a dictionary of Papias and in the Leiden *Liber glossarum*: "Aclus *Tuscorum lingua Iunius mensis dicitur*" (TLE 801); on the analogy there are the names *Velcitanus* "Martius" (TLE 856), *Cabreas* "Aprilis" (TLE 818), *Ampiles* "Majus" (TLE 805), *Aclus* "Junius" (TLE 801), *Traneus* "Julius" (TLE 854), *(H)ermius* "Augustus" (TLE 836), *Celius* "September" (TLE 824), *Xosfer* "October" (TLE 858).

The importance of these glosses can scarcely be overestimated. Almost all of them are comparable with the lexemes that occur in Etruscan texts. Due to the form *Xosfer* the interpretation of the numeral "eight" has become more certain. After all, they are important to studying the cultural traditions of the Etruscans.

Another isolated group that includes the names of several plants is preserved in the work of the physician and pharmacologist Dioscorides Pedanius. Compare these glosses: TLE 809 "σέλινον ἄγριον· οἱ δὲ βατράκιον . . . οἱ δὲ ἱπποσέλινον . . . Ῥωμαῖοι ἄπιουμ ... Θοῦσκοι ἄπιουμ ρανίνουμ"; TLE 823 "ἀμάρακον· οἱ δὲ ἀνθεμίς... Ῥωμαῖοι σῶλις ὄκουλουμ, οἱ δὲ μιλλεφόλιουμ, Θοῦσκοι καυτάμ"; TLE 825 "γεντιανή... Ῥωμαῖοι γεντιάνα, Θοῦσκοι κικένδα, οἱ δὲ κομιτιάλι˜"; TLE 830 "ὑοσκύαμος· οἱ δὲ Διὸς κύαμος... Ῥωμαῖοι ἰνσάνα... Θοῦσκοι φαβουλώνιαμ"; TLE 833 "χρυσάνθεμον ἢ χάλκας... Ῥωμαῖοι κάλθα, Θοῦσκοι γαρουλέου"; TLE 834 "δρακοντία μικρά... Ῥωμαῖοι βῆτα λεπορίνα, Θοῦσκοι γιγάρουμ"; TLE 842 "ἐρυθρόδανον· οἱ δὲ ἐρευθέδανος... Ῥωμαῖοι ροῦβια σατίβα, Θοῦσκοι λάππα μίνορ"; TLE 845 "ἀναγαλλὶς ἡ φοινικῆ... προφῆται αἷμα ὀφθαλμοῦ... Ῥωμαῖοι μάκια... Θοῦσκοι μασύτιπος"; TLE 846 "θύμος... Ῥωμαῖοι θούμουμ... Θοῦσκοι μοῦτουκα"; TLE 849 "σμῖλαξ τραχεῖα... Ῥωμαῖοι μεργίνα... Θοῦσκοι ραδία"; TLE 850 "λευκάκανθα... Ῥωμαῖοι γενικουλάτα κάρδους, Θοῦσκοι σπίνα ἄλβα"; TLE 852 "ἄσαρον· οἱ δὲ νάρδος ἀγρία, προφῆται αἷμα Ἄρεως... Ῥωμαῖοι περπρέσσαμ... Θοῦσκοι σούκινουμ"; TLE 853 "ἀναγαλλὶς ἡ κυανῆ... οἱ δὲ αἰλούρου ὀφθαλμόν... Ῥωμαῖοι μεκιατούρα, οἱ δὲ ἀντούρα, Θοῦσκοι τάντουμ."

It is easy to see that this list includes a number of Latinisms: ἄπιουμ ρανίνουμ, κομιτιάλις along with the valuable words κικένδα, φαβουλώνιαμ, ραδία and even λάππα μίνορ, as well as σπίνα ἄλβα. We have no reason to believe that these designations penetrated into the Etruscan language in the conservative phytonymic layer. Here one can assume rather the error of Dioscorides. Pallottino for some reason did not save the postscript "οἱ δὲ νάρδουμ" to the gloss σούκινουμ, which is very interesting. This name, which is present in Greek and has penetrated into Latin and the modern European languages (cf., German *Narde, Nardostachys Jatamansi*), goes back perhaps to Semitic: Classical Hebrew *nērd* and Aramaic *nirda*. We assume that Etruscan had such a designation, but the source of the borrowing is still difficult to determine. In our view, there is likely a Greek mediation here.

Thematically, this list includes another three glosses: TLE 808 "*herba quae a Graecis dicitur chamaemelon... Tusci apianam*"; TLE 813 "ἀταισόν· ἀναδενδράς. Τυρρηνοί"; TLE 826 "*nomen herbae batrachii: a Graecis dicitur batrachion, Tusci corofis (cherifis, clorisis, cloroplis* [< *χλωρόπλιον?*]), *Siculi selinon agrion, Romani apiurisum.*"

A significant part of the existing vocabulary consists of the names of different animals: TLE 806 "ἄνταρ· ἀετός, ὑπὸ Τυρρηνῶν"; TLE 807 "ἄνδας· βορέας, ὑπὸ Τυρρηνῶν"; TLE 810 "ἄρακος· ἱέραξ. Τυρρηνοί"; TLE 811 a) "τοῦτον, οἱ δ' ἐν Πιθηκούσσαις, οἳ καὶ τοὺς πιθήκους φασὶ παρὰ τοῖς Τυρρηνοῖς ἀρίμους καλεῖσθαι"; c) "ἄς· πίθηκος"; TLE 811 b) "*simiae..., quas Etruscorum lingua arimos dicunt*"[74]; TLE 820 "κάπρα· αἴξ. Τυρρηνοί"; TLE 821 "*falconis... qui Tusca lingua capys dicitur... Falco..., cui pollices pedum curvi fuerunt, quem admodum falcones aves habent, quos viros Tusci capyas vocarunt*"; TLE 827 "δάμνος· ἵππος. Τυρρηνοί"; TLE 835 "γνίς· γέρανος. Τυρρηνοί" TLE 839 "ἴταλον γὰρ Τυρσηνοὶ τὸν ταῦρον καλοῦσιν."

---

74. Perhaps, the same stem (*arim-*) is found in the TLE 150 inscription but with almost insurmountable difficulties in the word boundary.

All other glosses are not systematized at all. Moreover, in some cases they are duplicated. The Etruscan word "god" is preserved in Suetonius and Hesychius: TLE 803a "*quod* aesar *Etrusca lingua... deus vocaretur*"; TLE 804 "αἰσοί· θεοί, ὑπὸ Τυρρηνῶν."

It is common to hypothetically relate here the reference of Dion Cassius as well: TLE 803 b) "τὸ λοιπὸν πᾶν ὄνομα θεὸν (αισαρ) παρὰ τοῖς Τυρσηνοῖς νοεῖ."

The form preserved by Hesychius is not quite clear: TLE 828 "δέα· θεά, ὑπὸ Τυρρηνῶν." Apparently, one may assume that a Latin or Greek word might have penetrated into Etruscan (cf., TLE 1$^{V 20}$ *θeiviti*).[75]

The name or epithet of the Etruscan deity, corresponding to Roman Mercury, as well as a derivative term, are given by Servius: TLE 819 b) "casmillae ... *apud Tuscos* Camillum *appellari Mercurium, quo vocabulo significant deorum praeministrum... Romani quoque pueros et puellas nobiles et investes camillos et camillas appellabant, flaminicarum et flaminum praeministros.*"

The following message of Dionysius of Halicarnassus is related to that: TLE 819 a) "ὅσα δὲ παρὰ Τυρρηνοῖς ... πρότερον παρὰ Πελασγοῖς ἐτέλουν ... οἱ καλούμενοι πρὸς αὐτῶν κάδμιλοι, ταῦτα ... ὑπηρέτουν τοῖς ἱερεῦσιν οἱ λεγόμενοι νῦν ὑπὸ Ῥωμαίων κάμιλοι." In our view, here we should give the gloss "Καδμῖλος λέγεται ὁ Ἑρμῆς παρὰ τοῖς Τυρσηνοῖς," as well as the substrate name "Καδμίλος ὁ Ἑρμῆς Βοιωτικῶς" from the Scholia to Lycophron (162). However, they are absent in the TLE.

Also because of an apparent misunderstanding, the other name for the Etruscan god is not there, explained by Servius: "Mantuam *autem ideo nominatam, quod Etrusca lingua* Mantum *Ditem patrem appellant, cui cum ceteris urbibus et hanc consecravit*" (Aen., X, 198).

John the Lydian gives another name of the god with the reference to the Etruscan origin: "Ἀνύσιος δὲ ἐν τῷ περὶ μηνῶν Φεβροῦον τὸν καταχθόνιον εἶναι τῇ Θούσκων φωνῇ λέγει" (Mens., IV, 25).

In the Scholia to Lycophron there is also a name of a character that is associated with Odysseus: TLE 847 "ὁ Ὀδυσσεὺς παρὰ Τυρσηνοῖς Νάνος καλεῖται δηλοῦντος τοῦ ὀνόματος τὸν πλανήτην."

The highest (or one of the highest) Etruscan titles is present in the comments of Servius: TLE 843 "lucumones, *qui reges sunt lingua Tuscorum.*" The root from which this has been formed finds many parallels in Etruscan texts as well as in Greek and Latin transfers. They have been repeatedly mentioned in our study. The Tyrrhenian word "power/authority," which is given in the dictionary by Hesychius, might have existed in the Minoan language as well:[76] TLE 829 "δροῦνα· ἡ ἀρχή, ὑπὸ Τυρρηνῶν."

In addition, the ancient authors retained the names of some other persons. Almost all of them are names of professions, except for the word "child" given by Hesychius: TLE 802 "ἀγαλήτορα παῖδα. Τυρρηνοί"; TLE 817 "βυρρός· κάνθαρος. Τυρρηνοί";

---

75. In the combination *θeiviti faviti-c*, the appropriate translation of which is "in the temple and in the subterranean chamber of the temple" (see below *favissa*).

76. Cf., the root **tur-* "lord" (in Greek τύραννος); in Etruscan the goddess' name *turan* (and the derivative name of July *Traneus*) are derived from it.

TLE 837 a) "*quia* ister *Tusco uerbo ludio vocabatur, nomen histrionibus inditum*"; b) "*quia ludius apud eos [Tuscos]* hister *appelabatur, scaenico nomen histrionis inditum est*"; c) "*ludio Tusco verbo dicitur* histrio"; TLE 841 "lanista, *gladiator, id est carnifex, Tusca lingua appelatus, a laniando scilicet corpora*"; TLE 851 b) "subulo *dictus, quod ita dicunt tibicines Tusci: quocirca radices eius in Etruria, non Latio quaerundae*"; b) "subulo *Tusce tibicen dicitur.*"

The only glossed term of kinship is given in a Latin form: TLE 848 "(nepos) ... *Tuscis dicitur.*" We know that the word "grandchild" in Etruscan was borrowed precisely from Indo-European. It is preserved as *nefts, nefis*. The source of the borrowing is uncertain; the same stem is present in the Lemnos inscription (*ναφοθ*). It is possible that it was taken into "Proto-Tyrrhenian" before its division.

The rest of the glosses are completely different. Among them the most important lexemes are "head" and "sky": TLE 822 "cassidam *autem a Tuscis nominatam. Illi enim galeam* cassim *nominant, credo a capite*"[77]; TLE 831 "a *falado* (*falando*), quod apud Etruscos significat caelum."

The others are related to housing, clothing, and everyday life: TLE 814 "atrium *appellatum ab Atriatibus Tuscis*"; TLE 816 "baltea ... *Tuscum vocabulum*"; TLE 832 "γάπος· ὄχημα. Τυρρηνοί"; TLE 840 "laena *vestimenti genus habitu duplicis. quidam appelatam existimant Tusce, quidam Graece quam clanjda dicunt*"; TLE 844 "mantisa *additamentum dicitur lingua Tusca, quod ponderi adicitur, sed deterius ei quod sine ullo usu est*"; TLE 855 "τύρσεις γὰρ καὶ παρὰ Τυρρηνοῖς αἱ ἐντείχιοι καὶ στεγαναὶ οἰκήσεις ὀνομάζονται ὥσπερ παρ' Ἕλλησιν."

The obvious misunderstanding is the word "dawn": TLE 815 "αὐκήλως· ἕως, ὑπὸ Τυρρηνῶν." It is more likely that we are dealing here with a distorted Sabine *ausel* "sun." However, this stem has been borrowed also into Etruscan (*usil*).

As mentioned above, the vocabularies of different groups intersect in some ways. Etruscan glosses find correspondences in a variety of lexical categories (i.e., Tyrrhenian texts, loanwords into Greek and Latin, and toponyms preserved in the same languages, sometimes even in the modern substratum vocabulary).

Here are some examples of establishing the relation of glosses to lexemes from other sources. The above-mentioned word *usil* "sun" is an evident borrowing of Sabinian *ausel* (<IE *ausos + *sol) and is used in texts without the narrowing of its original meaning, displacing, accordingly, the actual Etruscan word.

On the other hand, the name of a solar deity *kauθa* (TLE 622), *caθa* (TLE 131, 719, at al.), that was established positionally, remains isolated (and therefore not very reliable) until we obtain other evidence in favor of this interpretation. Fortunately, we have such evidence: the gloss of Dioscorides καυτά(μ) (TLE 823, in a Latinized form of acc. sg.), that means "marjoram"; here the Roman name is given, literally "eye of the sun," *solis oculum* (σώλις ὄκουλουμ). The lexeme *cota*, along with the present "*occhio di sole*" is still present in Tuscany. In the absence of word formation elements, without association

---

77. It is an obvious confusion; see below the correlation between *cassis* and *galea*.

with *solis oculum*, the connection between the word "sun" and the gloss would hardly be noticed. All the subsequent conclusions are built on it.

Let us consider the Tyrrhenian root **ant-*, meaning "(north) wind" (whence is Latin *antemna* "shipyard" borrowed from Etruscan) and "eagle." It is known from the glosses of Hesychius. Although only two of these glosses are referred to as Tyrrhenian (TLE 806 "ἄνδας· βορέας" and TLE 807 "ἄνταρ· ἀετὸς"), here we should also include "ἄντας· πνοάς," "ἄνται· ἄνεμοι" and "ἄντος· εὖρος. οἱ δὲ Εὐριπίδης." The form ἄνταρ, in comparison with the rest, seems to give a derivational suffix, but there is a whole semantic series here, which goes back to Tyrrhenian.

1) We should note the similarity between Latin *Aquilo* "north wind" and *aquila* "eagle." In this case, we do not know the meaning of the stem from which the toponyms *Aquileia* (Latin), *Akudunniad* (Oscan, abl.), *Akeřuniam* (Umbrian, acc.), etc., are derived. This stem does not have a convincing Indo-European etymology.[78] On the other hand, the connection with (Eteo)Cypriote ἀγὸρυώ (in Hesychius "ἀετὸς. Κύπριοι") is more than probable. Another association occurs between *aquila*, *Aquilo* and *aquilus* "dark brown" (like in the case of the Macedonian παραός ("ἀετὸς ὑπὸΜακεδόνων"): Greek παρώας "chestnut-colored, bay," but there are no facts supporting the Tyrrhenian analogy here. In our opinion, this stem should be compared with the name *aker* of the Lemnos stele inscription, which seems to have not yet received a satisfactory interpretation. Hence, this name should be compared with Latin *Aquilius* and (in the typological sense) with Greek Ἀετίων.

Thus, we have presumably a Tyrrhenian root, which cannot be analyzed from the standpoint of word formation but can be interpreted only by analogy with the well-known stem **ant-* and miraculously survived the Cypriote glossed form.

2) The positionally established vocabulary can be related both to the most reliable layer, which is not disputed by any serious scholars (such as kinship terms occurring in short epitaphs, including those in bilinguals) and to a broad category of words for which several meanings are likely to exist. Compare the following examples: (a) *clan* "son," *seχ* "daughter," *ati* "mother," *apa* "father," *ces-* "to lie, to rest," *lup-* "to die"; (b) *snenaθ* "maidservant" ("female companion," "female friend," etc.), *sians* "copper, bronze" (based on the signatures on the relevant objects, although there may be other definitions), *nes-* "to die," and many others.

Sometimes the meaning of lexemes can be established positionally on the material of different languages, which indicates the high reliability of the result: *meθl(um)* "city" in Etruscan inscriptions and *a-na ma-to-ri*. ἡ πόλις is repeatedly mentioned in our work on the Eteo-Cypriote Greek bilingual.

---

78. It is difficult, indeed, to agree with the hypothesis of its connection with *aqua* (Pokorny 1959, s. v. $ak^w\bar{a}$-).

79. The $k : g : q^u$ correlation $k : g : q^u$ in the Tyrrhenian relicts is not something strange; as for the liquids $r : l$ may go back to the Mediterranean characteristic feature, reflected in linear writing systems (including the scripts in Cyprus), or to the Italic transitions *d* and *l*, *d* and *r*, *rs* (just like in the above mentioned toponyms). For details, see Chapter 5: Phonetics.

A special group of positionally defined lexemes consists of the signatures on objects or signatures to specific images (cf., for example, the hapax legomenon *hiuls* [probably an onomatopoetic word]), a signature to the image of the owl on the vessel (κύαθος, TLE 333), *apcar* (TLE 779), an inscription on the score board (for the second time borrowed from Greek ἄβαξ or a word of native origin; we have reasons to believe that the Greek word itself goes back to Minoan).

Even bilinguals (primarily the bilingual of Pyrgi) often do not make it possible to accurately identify the meaning of specific words, and one has to conduct additional research. Compare, for example, an adverb *snutVφ*. This lexeme occurs four times in the Zagreb Book: VI 1, 2, 4 *śnutuφ*, X 12 *snutuφ*; here it has not been interpreted in its context. We believe that it should be compared with the form *snuiaφ* from a short version of the Etruscan-Phoenician bilingual TLE 875. The analysis of the endings of both versions can be somewhat reconsidered (see also Appendix 4). First and foremost, we should admit that a single writing of *snuiaφ* in comparison with the consonant *snutuφ* is probably erroneous, that is, it contains I instead of Ͳ (i.e., by mistake, the crosspiece of the Etruscan *tau* was not fixed here).

Further, the interpretation of the end of the Phoenician version raises some objections (the variant accepted in the Russian scientific literature, beginning with the works of Xarsekin and Geltzer of the year 1965, is as follows, "(numerous, like) the years of these stars," although the word "year" does not occur here at all). The more accurate translation of it would be "(numerous, like) these stars," but this version is not quite conclusive either. In both Etruscan versions, the primary and the shorter, the pronoun is absent, while in the shorter version the word *pulumχva* "star" is followed by the final *snutaφ*.

It is known that, in the Punic dialect, at some point there was a gradual dying out of the guttural sounds that were more regularly preserved only in initial position. In turn, they are often confused: "Only in the beginning of a word in order to avoid a vowel beginning, apparently, the voiceless ligamentous ['] sounded displacing in that position the rest of ligamentous and pharyngeal sounds. Accordingly, all graphemes designating these sounds at the beginning of the word were pronounced as [']. In favor of the above, the following writings say *h* instead of ' (*hbn* instead of the expected '*bn* "stone"), ' instead of ' ('*bn* instead of '*bn*), ' instead of *ḥ* ('*mlkt* instead of *ḥmlkt*), etc. Also, see Latin and Greek writings of *Hannibal* and Ἀννίβας: instead of *ḥnbʻl* "Hannibal," as well as *Hasdrubal* and Ἀσδρούβας instead of '*zrbʻl* "Hasdrubal" (Schiffmann 2003, 25).

Thus, we assume that, in the end of the Punic inscription, one should see an erroneous spelling of ✗ *aleph* instead of O *ayin* and should read not '*l* "these," but '*l* "over, at the top." Such a reading obviates the contradiction with the lack of the pronoun in the Etruscan text and enables us to interpret the Etruscan form also as "over, at the top."

3) The group showing correspondences to Tyrrhenian inscriptions proper is adjacent to the glosses, which have Etruscan parallels (since it is not always possible to distinguish between a gloss and loanword, becoming a part of a living language; though, for example, *lucumo* "king" is nominally a gloss, we know that it was used by ancient authors while

describing the Etruscan realities; glossed *falado* (abl.) "sky" is fully consistent with a loanword *palatum* "sky," etc.).

On the other hand, the meaning of some stems in this group can be established positionally (for example, the meaning *puia* "wife" was already known from the inscriptions when attention was paid to the analogy with the Greek ὀπυίω).[80] Other typical examples are Etruscan *eleiva-*[81] : Pre-Greek ἐλαίϜα, *purt-* : πρύτανις, etc. The Latin glossed word *napurae* "*Strohseile*"[82] apparently goes back to Etruscan *naper* (Walde-Hofmann 1938–56, s. v. *napurae*). At that, the meaning of the Etruscan word can hardly be established positionally. The meaning of *cepen, cipen* "priest" which also can be reliably clarified by its position (from the text *Liber Linteus* and some epitaphs), was confirmed in Servius: "*sane sciendum* cupencum *Sabinorum lingua sacerdotem vocari, ut apud Romanos flaminem et pontificem, sacerdotem. sunt autem* cupenci *Herculis sacerdotes*" (Aen., XII, 538). Although the gloss is nominally Sabine, one should speak of the borrowing of the Etruscan term into Sabine as well as into archaic Latin.

We see that the range of the meanings of Etruscan words is very limited. The main areas of the linguistic influence were identified by Tronskij: "We do not go beyond the cult, theatre, crafts, and everyday life of lower social classes of the city. Further the Etruscan language influence penetrated only in the sixth century BCE, during the reign of Etruscan kings, while in the Republican era, it already remained in the narrow framework outlined here" (Tronskij 1953, 124). The correct selection of semantic groups can greatly facilitate the work of the scholar and improve the effectiveness, since the search for further parallels is one of the most promising issues. In general, the interpretation of such words is very reliable.

4) The identifying of lexemes in the phonetic and word formation group implies an analogy. Sometimes one word, the meaning of which is established by other sources, can be compared with a whole semantic or derivational series of the words not having the etymology in classical languages. For example, we may assume that a whole group of isolated Latin words that have the endings of the first and second declensions (more often *-a, -us,* and more rarely *-um*) after the element *-c-*[83] (Tronskij 1953, 124) (apparently the Etruscan word form ended in the above mentioned element) has an Etruscan origin. Obviously, this whole group of words, borrowed into Latin, was constructed due to the

---

80. Compare, on the other hand, an absurd comparison of this lexeme with Latin *puella* (V. Georgiev); as is known, in Latin it is a diminutive to the word *puer*, which could be used as a generic noun but only in the sense of "child" (cf., in Naevius [B.P. 29] "*Cereris Proserpina puer*," in Livius Andronicus [Od. fr. 14] "*sancta puer*").

81. This stem is most likely to be not specifically Tyrrhenian but goes back to the Minoan stratum. However, we are now talking about the interpretation of the Tyrrhenian vocabulary, and there is such a word in Etruscan.

82. See the text: "*pontifex minor ex stramentis napuras nectito, id est funiculos facito, quibus sues adnectantur*" (Fest. 165).

83. As mentioned above, the same is true for a number of Minoan loan words in Greek (cf., κόρσεον, ὄσπριον, etc.).

testimony of Varro (in Charisius [I, 77, 9]; TLE 816), who pointed out *balteus*[84] "belt, crossbelt for weapons" as an Etruscan word. Accordingly, one can also include in this category *aleae* "dice" (cf., below *aleo*), *culleus* "leather bag"[85]; *cuneus* "wedge," *hirnea* "mug; round baker's mould," *horreum* "barn, storehouse," *limeum* "celery-leaved buttercup, Ranunculus thora," *lorea*, a sort of wine, *malleus* "hammer, butt,"[86] *palea* "straw, chaff," *pilleus* "round felt cap," *puteus* "pit, underground, mine," *talea* "twig, sprout, stake," *trabea* "ceremonial cloak,"[87] *urceus* "jug" (correlates with *urna* [cf., below Tyrrhenian derivational suffix *-na*]).

Four words of this type belong to the same semantic category (i.e., they mean the components of protective arms: *galea* "helmet," *clupeus* "shield," *pluteus* "siege shield," *ocrea* "leg shields." In this case, the Etruscan words quite naturally mean objects of an older type (*galea*, a leather helmet with metal plaques, as opposed to the metal *cassis*, *clupeus*, a small round shield, in contrast to the large [approximately 120 × 80 cm.] rectangular *scutum*).

There have been attempts to interpret the facts of the lexemes in a different way. Peruzzi, considering the supposed loanwords of Mycenaean times, suggested the origin of *balteus* from the Greek παλτόν "javelin." The very etymology looks extremely far-fetched. Here, as in the analysis of some other lexemes, he postulates the vocalization of consonants (and vice versa) in some of the earliest borrowings, not explaining, however, the phonetic regularities of such a transition. Moreover, this approach deprives other listed words *-eV-* of any explanation, since one cannot find any convincing Indo-European etymology.

At the same time, Tronskij, three decades before Peruzzi, said that some words undoubtedly correlating with the Greek (ἀμόργα/*amurca*, σπυρίδα/*sporta*, πύξος/*buxus*, Πυρρὸς/*Burrus*, κυβερνᾶν/*gubernare*,' Ἀκράγας/*Agrigentum*),[88] could acquire their current appearance only in the intervening medium (i.e., he admitted an Etruscan mediation [Tronskij 1953, 128]).[89]

However, it seems to us that all of these words (of the *alea* type) penetrated into Latin from Etruscan where they apparently ended in the vowel **-e*. This type, uncharacteristic for the Latin declension, requires the change of an ending, and one such change was the addition of any endings of the first and second declensions (whence the variations in grammatical gender). Indeed, such Etruscan words as *aplustre* (see below), eventually acquired a more regular shape (*aplustria*, pl.). Even if we accept (with all the huge stretches) the Greek origin of *balteus*, we can consider the other above-mentioned words to be Etruscan, at least until one finds another more convincing etymology.

---

84. The classical etymology (Walde-Hofmann, 1938–56, s.v. *balteus*) accepts the relation to Gothic *balps* "kühn," which is not quite convincing.

85. The greatest ton is 20 amphoras or 525, 27 L.

86. A comparison with the Indo-European consonant stem is unreliable in terms of word-form structure.

87. White with purple stripes; purple for the emperors.

88. The list can be continued: δέλτος, *titulus*, etc.

89. Etruscan mediation obviously implies a later time for the borrowing. Accordingly, we, sharing the thesis about the contacts with the Arcadians and the presence of the oldest borrowings in Latin, suggest deleting the lexemes with an unclear vocalization or meaning from the list.

Accordingly, the combination *-eu-/-ea* cannot be viewed as a derivational suffix and one cannot try to find it in the Tyrrhenian texts, since the corresponding lexemes will demonstrate the final *-e* (possibly also *-i*). But we still have a special type of Latin word, which points to the Etruscan origin, or at least mediation in the process of lexical borrowing.

5) Externally explained Etruscan words are given below, mainly with reference to Tronskij (1953, 114, 117, 123–24). Independent borrowings into Latin and Greek from a common origin language are a particular variety of such words (e.g., Latin *triumphus*; *triumpe* [from a hymn of the Arval Brethren, CIL I² 2], Greek θρίαμβος [in Greek, a hymn in honor of Dionysus; a Tyrrhenian origin is very likely here]).

6) Loanwords from other languages into the Tyrrhenian languages do not imply any systematization. Chronologically, the early Middle Asian and late Greek and Latin lexemes are very clearly extracted. The latter do not cause any difficulties in identification. On the other hand, the early borrowings are quite different genetically. They change phonetically somewhat more noticeably and are identified with more difficulty, largely because the vocabulary of the origin languages is poorly known.

The Asian Middle Eastern borrowings go back to various language groups (i.e., the Hurro-Urartian and Anatolian languages, perhaps also the Semitic). It is obvious that, in the first case, the influence was quite significant. Even the Tyrrhenian numeral three, referring to a very sustainable vocabulary layer, was replaced by the *ki*, which can be confidently regarded as a Hurrian word (cf., *ki*[*g*] of the same meaning). A view has been put forward of the relationship between Etruscan *avil* "year" with Hurrian *šawali* of the same meaning (Ivanov 2008, 665), but the supposed correspondence of Hurrian *š* : Etruscan ø was not supported by other examples.[90] In addition to the vocabulary, we know some borrowed grammatical elements (the suffixes of the genitive case, adjectival formants).

Anatolian forms could have penetrated from various dialects. Their exact origin is not always obvious. These loans include Etruscan *tiv-* "moon, (calendar) month," *masn-* "deity" or "statue of a deity," the name of the prophet *Tages* (cf., Hittite *tekan*, gen. *taknaš* "earth" [one should consider his chthonic origin]). Shevoroshkin, studying the Lycian and Milyan languages in detail, points out (personal communication) a special group of parallels with these languages (cf., the following examples: *flere* "offering image" : Milyan dat. pl. *plejere*; *maru* (title): Lycian *mar-* "command"; *nunθ-* "sacrifice" : Milyan *nuni-* "bring"; *tupi* "punishment" : Milyan *tubi-* "punish," etc.).

It is difficult to identify the original language of several apparent Indo-European words. These include, in particular, *nefi-* "grandchild" (even though Lemnian *naφoθ* could have been borrowed independently), *fir-* "fire" (this word was probably borrowed into Latin for the second time (it was preserved by Festus as *exfir* "purification by fumigation").[91]

---

90. The relationship between Hurrian *šawali* and Urartian *šila*, in principle, also remains unclear. One cannot exclude that Hurrian *w* was the result of a complex splitting of the vowel of the root.

91. "*purgamentum, unde adhuc manet suffucio.*"

The borrowings from the Greek, Latin, and Umbrian languages mostly name concrete objects (cf., primarily, the Greek names of vessels) and provide little opportunity for the translation of inscriptions. More meaningful lexemes are seldom found (cf., for example, the word *claruχieś* [from Doric κλαρουχία "settlement," "community"]), which significantly facilitates the understanding of the inscription TLE 515.

The inscription on the liver of Piacenza (TLE 719) has a very interesting form *tecvm*, which requires special study. In outward appearance it has a striking resemblance to the Latin word *decumanus* (from *decumus*), which, in addition to its core meaning "decimal, tithe," means a boundary path from west to east, carried out at the foundation of a city by the Etruscan ritual (before which a priest drew a line from north to south, *cardo*, which connected him to Tin, who was in the northern part of the sky).

Stoltenberg in his time made a brilliant conjecture that the Etruscan artifact could be used to study the model of a city (Stoltenberg 1957: 98) (cf., the well-known Middle Eastern motif of the Earthly City as a reflection of the Heavenly City), and the relationship of *tecvm* with Latin *decumanus* is more than probable. We tend to assume that the fusion of the Etruscan lexeme and the pure Latin word was due to the influence of folk etymology, which connected the crossed lines with a Roman numeral X. There are no phonetic and morphological difficulties in the reconstruction of the Etruscan word **tek-um-na*, since the combinations of suffixes *-um-na* are widely known in Minoan, Etruscan, and Aegean-Tyrrhenian, and they are present in Eteo-Cypriote (see below, in Chapter 7: Word Formation). The form *tecvm* on a model of the liver may represent a variant, complicated by a suffix, as well as a reduction of **tek-um-na*.

To a lesser extent, we know other non-Latin Etruscan-Italic parallels (which is quite natural given the small number of inscriptions in these languages): *ais*, *eis* "god," Marrucini *aisos* (dat. pl), Umbrian *esono* "sacrificial offering"; *cletram* "(ritual) sedan chair," Umbrian *kletra* (here a Latin diminutive *clitellae* "pack-saddle"), etc.

It should be noted that, in some cases, by the special appearance of the loanwords, primarily from Greek into Latin, one can assume an Etruscan mediation (i.e., postulate the existence of a lexeme, which is nowhere attested). A typical example in this case is the word *groma, gruma, croma* "solar clock," whence is *gromaticus* "land surveyor" (cf., in Hyginus Gromaticus [Cons. Lim., 135], etc.). It is easy to see that it goes back to Greek γνώμων, but it could acquire the characteristic phonetic appearance only in Etruscan: cf., the dissimilation of a nasal group *aχmemrun, memrun* from Ἀγαμέμνων and Μέμνων, respectively (Rix 1984[2]: 222). Consequently, we are talking about the presence in Etruscan of the lexeme **cruma* borrowed from Greek.

Sometimes one can talk not so much of parallels as of consonances. Thus, the name of Πύργοι (whence Latin *Pyrgi*) in a pure Etruscan town (port of the city-state of Caere) is rather puzzling. Note that, at present, we are not interested in the etymology of Indo-European (but not Greek) πύργος, since the Tyrrhenian analogue is important. The clue here is the following mention in Lycophron: "Πέργη δέ μιν θανόντα Τυρσηνῶν ὄρος // ἐν Γορτυναίᾳ δέξεται πεφλεγμένον" (Alex., 805–6). As can be seen, the Tyrrhenians had a toponym sounding similar.[92] Apparently, it was reconsidered by Greeks and Romans in the folk etymology.[93]

Individual borrowings (almost all proper names) penetrated into Etruscan from other languages of Italy, which are far from being fully studied. Thus, Pfiffig gives the following examples: *mazutiu, muceti* (Celtic), *lec(u)ste/i* (Ligurian), *atru, vetu, autu, kuna, tata* (Venetic), Messapic *tasma* (< *Dazimas*), *θasta* (< *Dasta*) (Pfiffig 1969, 178).

The proposed classification is certainly rather provisional and cannot fully reflect all the peculiarities of the Tyrrhenian vocabulary, but it seems to be quite suitable for further work. What is important is the fact that, in most cases, reliable recovery of the stems are possible when their derivatives are clarified in different ways, according to the method—which can already rightfully be called complex—and such recovery is a better analysis of the Tyrrhenian language.

Here are some common stems and their derivatives:

ve/ital-: "bull, cattle": see above the gloss of Apollodorus "ἰταλὸν ... τὸν ταῦρον"; cf., in Hesychius Ἴταλος ("Ῥωμαῖος. ταῦρος") > *Italia*. The same stem is reflected in Latin *vitulus, vitellus*, Umbrian *vitluf* (acc. pl.).

On the coins of Populonia, we find the following: χa *fufluna vetalu* (TLE 379, 794); here *vetalu* cannot be regarded as a proper name, as Pallottino, for example, does in the index of TLE. This form should be translated as "money"; it is undoubtedly a typological analogy with Latin *pecunia* from *pecu* - "cattle." However, *ve/ital*- can also serve as the stem of a proper name (cf.,, Latin *Vitellius*, the name of the city of *Vetulonia*); perhaps *vi-ti-le* in the first position of the Eteo-Cypriote inscription KS 1 should be understood exactly in this way.

ner-: "water": REE 45/28 *mi neries θavhna* "I am a cup (calix) for water." With this word we should match the Greek Νηρεύς, Νηρεΐς (Νηρηΐς), the names of famous sea deities; νηρίτης (νηρείτης), the name of the sea mollusc; the toponyms such as Νήρικος are obscure. Modern Greek νερό "water" obviously goes back to the same root. The etymology of Frisk (1960, s. v. Νηρεύς], who links this group of lexemes to νηρός "frisch" (> "frisches Wasser"!), seems very far-fetched.

p:al(a): "top," "(heaven) vault," "head"; the meaning is identified by the gloss of Hesychius "φάλα· ἡ μικρὰ κάρα." It is significant that the set of lexemes, combined with the semantics of "head," is found in Aegeida. On the contrary, the meaning "sky" is so far known only in Etruscan.

We can name the derivatives: 1) *p:alanT-: "falado (falando) ... caelum" (TLE 831); Latin *Palatum* (= *falado*), *Palatium*; 2) *p:ul-um-: pulumχva* (TLE 874, 875, Pyr.), *fulumχva* (TLE 570, P.) "stars" (= Punic *h-kkbm* in TLE 874; here is the generic name

---

92. Their presence in Cortona, a Cretan city, is attested not only here; the very name Γόρτυν = Etruscan *curtun*, Latin *Cortona* (cf., also Tyrrhenian Λάρισσα; the earlier Ἑλλωτίς: "Γόρτυν ... ἐκαλεῖτο δὲ καὶ Λάρισσα. πρότερον γὰρ ἐκαλεῖτο Ἑλλωτίς" [in Stephen] goes back to Minoan).

93. Both considered roots are likely to be loans in the Tyrrhenian languages as well (cf., Hittite *parku-* "high," *park-* "to rise above," Urartian *burgana* "Palast, Feste," Aramaic *burgu* "Burg," Hittite *gurta-* "Burg, Festung").

pulena (TLE 131 and others). The **p:al-um-* > *p:ul-um-* harmonization indicates, apparently, a very early formation. Faliscan-Latin *Falerii* < **Falesii̯*, *Falisci* is not clear (Giacomelli 1978: 509). A number of other lexemes containing *fal-* (TLE 2[22], C. *falau*, TLE 992, V.-Cl.-Ar. *falica*, TLE 887, Tarq. *faluθras*) should not necessarily be associated with this root. Only the forms *falaś*, *falzati* (TLE 570) can be related to the name of the sky (it is possible that we are dealing here with the name of the month).[94]

In pre-Greek, a whole group of words is related to this stem: φαλακρός, φάλανθος "bald, bald-headed," φαληρίς, φάλαρις "coot" (*Fulica atra*), φάλος "the cone of the helmet," φάλαρα, a part of the helmet (cheek pieces); in Hesychius "Φάλακρον· ἀκροτήριον Ἴδης" and "τρυφάλεια· ἡ τρεῖς κεφαλὰς ἔχουσα" (in the explanation to φάλος).

According to Frisk (1960, s. v. φαλός), this group of lexemes should be compared with φαλός "white." However, in our view, this explanation is far less probable than a semantic relation to the concepts of "top" > "head."

purt:(-): title (≈ dux?). In Etruscan inscriptions we find *purθ-* (TLE 87, Tarq., 465, 501 Cl.), *eprtn-* (TLE 171, 195, 896, Tarq., 233, Vols., 463, 464, Cl.); the derivative *purtśvana* (TLE 324, Volc.) > Latin *Porsenna* (*ts > Latin *s*, with the loss of semivowel *i̯*); a similar mistake was made by Roman historians in the interpretation of an Oscan title *meddix* as the name "Mettius" (in particular, in Livy, I, 23–28). Concerning the inversion in *eprθ-*: cf., *eslz* < *zalz, a peculiar phonetic development in *purutn* (TLE 1[II 3], VII[9]), compare examples of the use of it: *cepen tenu eprtnevc eslz te(nu)* (TLE 171) "served as a priest, twice held the post of a prytanis"; *ziχnu cezpz purtśvana θunz* (TLE 324, Volc.) "eight times was a zilc and once a prytanis"; *zilcti purtśvavcti* (TLE 325, Volc.) "in the capacity of a zilc and prytanis." This word has penetrated into Greek (cf., πρύτανις [with an inversion?], with quite a wide meaning, which is not the same, in particular, in different places. Frisk (1960, s. v. πρύτανις) also points to a connection with Etruscan and Aegean.[95] Perhaps the root of the word was borrowed in Asia Minor (cf., Lycian *epriti* "governor," Hattic *puri* "master"). We may hope that, in the future, it will be possible to describe in this way, or even more thoroughly, some part of the preserved Minoan and Tyrrhenian vocabulary.

---

94. It is possible that *θunχulθe falaś* "in the first (day of the month) *f.*"; *falzati* is also a locative form.

95. "*Mit dem etruskischen Beamtentitel purθne, eprθni zusammenhängend, gehört* πρύτανις *unzweifelhaft zum kleinasiat.-ägäischen Bestandteil der griech. staatsrechtlichen Terminologie.*"

CHAPTER 5

PHONETICS

The study of the phonetic system of the Minoan and the Tyrrhenian languages, like any other extinct groups of which only certain terms have been described, logically implies some difficulties. In the absence of even superficial descriptions of the pronunciation of at least some phonemes (which are sometimes available for the study of other languages), one has to obtain all the information in an indirect way, through the analysis of dialect-related alternations within the Minoan and the Tyrrhenian inscriptions written at different times, as well as varied correspondences with the vocabulary of the languages with which the Minoan, Etruscan, and related languages were in contact in historic times. In principle, the effectiveness of this approach is due to a number of inscriptions and foreign-language parallels, as well as the presence or absence of languages having a more or less close relationship with those under consideration.

It is easy to see that many of the above sources (glosses, loanwords, toponyms) are available only for the phonetic and partly morphological (in matters of word formation) studies, as well as for comparison with the substratum vocabulary of Mediterranean Europe. In fact, the phonetic and phonological analysis should be given a privileged position, since in many cases it is the only study to which the Minoan and the Tyrrhenian forms are subject. In addition, sometimes phonetic features are the only criteria that enable us to distinguish the Minoan and the Tyrrhenian lexemes in a heterogeneous pre-Indo-European layer.

At the present stage, the reconstruction of the phonetics and phonology, especially for Minoan, is moving forward more slowly than the study of the grammatical structure, where success is also limited. Analysis of the Minoan phonetic features is particularly difficult because of the nature of linear writing, which makes it practically impossible to mark alternations and diachronic changes, and, only in exceptional cases, allows the identification of dialectal features. As far as Etruscology is concerned, it should be noted that the characteristic features of the phonetic sections of summarizing works here are descriptive, relying on the Indo-European forms that have crept into the Etruscan language and, often, the substitution of phonetic analysis of the constructions or even a simple listing of graphics features. It is quite obvious that the primary analysis of Indo-European words having been altered according to Tyrrhenian linguistic laws, is the most simplistic and also unreliable form of work. Since the Tyrrhenian and Indo-European languages are unrelated, one cannot find regular phonetic correspondences, and the Tyrrhenian language phonology is fundamentally different from the Indo-European; all the major deviations from the Tyrrhenian correspondences and oppositions being reconstructed are observed in that very part of the vocabulary.

A few more reliable facts of Etruscan phonetics are found mainly in specialized articles, which almost never cover a significant number of phonemes (cf., Bonfante 1968, 1974, 1983; Maggiani 1987–88). In many papers, very weak or faulty constructions of the past are replicated. They are the basis for some of the conclusions of grammar and vocabulary, which, as will be shown below, do not meet modern standards of linguistics. The analysis of the Tyrrhenian sound system is one of the major elements for proving our schemes and lexical interpretations.

It is difficult to overestimate the actual value of the reconstruction of the Minoan and Tyrrhenian phonological system. The revealed regularities make it possible not only to clarify a number of grammatical categories and raise to a new level the work with the vocabulary, but also to make possible an objective comparison of the languages under study with other language groups.

THE MINOAN LANGUAGE

Vowels

Judging by the repertoire of the symbols of linear writing known to us there were five simple vowels in Minoan: *a, e, i, o, u*. The specific features of the linear writing styles and Greek transfers can also aid us in making a preliminary conclusion about the presence of diphthongs as well.

We do not have any reason to talk about the difference in Minoan of long and short vowels. In the reliable Greek transfers words with long vowels are very rare (κρώβυλος, Κυδωνία, σαγήνη, τήβεννα), while in other cases the Minoan origin of substratum words may be questioned (ἦνοψ, μῶλυ, πώλυπος, χηραμός, etc.). It can be assumed that the lengthening for one reason or another took place in Greek (cf., Πηνελόπα αλονγ with Πενελόπα, ᾽Αθηνᾶ with Ἴτανος).

Judging by the majority of the Greek transfers, stress in the Minoan language could fall on the root syllable. The alternations of vowels are quite diverse, but it is not possible at present to make significant conclusions because of their disjunction. We can outline, for example, the alternations *a - o* (σκάλοψ, but σκόλοψ, σκολόπαξ), *e - i* (δέπας along with Mycenaean *di-pa-*, probably, σέσυφος : Σίσυφος) and some others.

The most typical is the alternation of *u ~ i*, already noted by Ventris and Chadwick and reflected in a variety of Greek transfers (Αἴσυμνος : αἴσιμος, μύλλον, μύρος, but LA, LB 073 ⍦ *mi*, τόρδυλον : τόρδιλον (compare below the suffix -υρ- and other common suffixes), but here, in fact, a glide is reflected. The desire to avoid the discordant alternative vowel υ-υ led to the emergence of parallel spellings: μιστύλη and μυστίλη, Σύρινθος, and Σίρυνθος. The author of this study tends to assume that this phenomenon could even be the substrate for the Greek language, where in ancient times **u* transformed into a narrow *υ*, and in the Medieval and modern language it finally merged with ι. By analogy with the facts of the Tyrrhenian languages of the first millennium BCE, we can assume that these alternations did not have any grammatical function.

One cannot speak of diphthongs with a high degree of certainty. Indeed, combinations, such as *a-e, a-u, e-u, o-u*, occur at the juncture of syllables in Linear A inscriptions but to prove a diphthongal nature of such combinations is hardly possible. There are reliable Greek transfers, but they are very few in number (for example, the toponyms Αἴσυμνος, Αἰσύμη with Etruscan *ais* "god"; *aisuna* "sacrificial offering"). In most cases, we are dealing with diphthongization which occurred already in Greek: pejrin~, pejrinqo~ with *pi-ri⍺(n)-te* (HT 116), Seilhn3~ with Silhn3~, perhaps, here is πείρινθος. The diphthong *au* was supposed to exist in Minoan, but in the most reliable transfers it is tightened (Λίκυμνα along with **λαυκ-* "to reign," Etruscan *lauχumneti* "in [the royal] palace"; probably the phenomenon itself goes back to Minoan [see the variant *ku-do-ni*]).

Consonants

As can be seen from the repertoire of well-known Linear A and Linear B[96] characters, in the language of Crete there are nine basic consonant phonemes - *p, t, d, k, m, n, r, s, z* and two semivowel phonemes - *j* and *w*. Some syllables that begin with *p-, t-* and *r-*, coinciding in the provisional Mycenaeanological reading, may be indicated by different signs. There is no doubt that they contained different phonemes in the Minoan language; as far as the Greeks are concerned, for them this distinction lost its meaning. In addition, there were a number of labialized consonants. We know four syllables *qV-* (in Linear B also 032 *qo*) from Linear A, and from Linear B also we know signs for *dwe* (071), *dwo* (090), *twe* (087), *two* (091) and *nwa* (048, the image of crossed hands, that has something in common with 052 *no*). Consequently, *q* shifted to *b* (cf., Βελεμίνα in Pausanias and *qe-de-mi-nu* in the inscription MA 1; we should probably also include here βασιλεύς "king"; cf., Mycenaean *qa-si-re-u*) and may also be *p*. As for the destiny of the other labialized elements, it is obscure.

It is well known that, in the linear writing system, there was no difference for the voiced, voiceless, and aspirates, and the Greeks, who did not introduce new syllabograms into the writing, retained this system, although it did not fit for Greek with its fundamental

---

96. Cf., Table III.

difference of these three series. However, one should not think that Minoan had no "opposed to one another" series of consonants, though they were designated in the same way in the writing, since in Greek transfers of Cretan words the aspirates and voiceless are scarcely less common than the simple voiceless.

Based on the Tyrrhenian material, described in detail below, we concluded that in the Tyrrhenian languages of the first millennium BCE there were two series of consonants which can be provisionally called "strong" and "weak." Over time, the first found a tendency to turn into aspirates (in the texts and loanwords), and the second into voiced (in loanwords).

Assuming that the Minoan language was akin to the Tyrrhenian, we believe it is possible to preliminarily extend the scheme also to it. The only exception (externally) is a set of syllabic signs with the initial *d-*, which the Greeks used regularly for their native δ. With regard to the language of Crete, one should consider it a special phoneme, which is viewed through two series of alternations. On the one hand, we know that the Greeks used syllables of *rV-* type to designate their original l, signs for which were absent in the linear script (*do-e-ro* = δοῦλος); however, along with it in a number of words the writing of δ- corresponds to the reading of λ, with the most striking example here of the Cretan word λαβύρινθος (cf., *da-pu-ri-to-*). Thus, it is possible that in Minoan there was a particular phoneme, the intermediate between *d* and *l*, which is characteristic for the various languages.[97] For their native λ the Greeks never used *d-*.

In the system of sonants, no alterations of Cretan *m-*, *n-* and their Greek reflections were attested, except in cases of nasal weakening before the next consonant (for example, the suffix -υμβ- can take the form of -υβ-).

As for the situation with *r-*, it is somewhat more complicated. First, it is certain that some of the signs (due to *ra2, ra3, ro2, ri2*) hide very special phonemes, and secondly, in the Tyrrhenian languages of the first millennium BCE *r* and *l* are never mixed (in fact, one cannot assume that a single phoneme **R* once differentiated into two distinct phonemes). We tend to think that in the language of Crete there were phonemes *r* and *l*, but they did not differ in writing to express the force of the features of pronunciation; perhaps they also could be perceived as "strong" and "weak," with no written distinction being made between them. Their close pronunciation also influenced the later Greek dialect of Crete (cf., in Hesychius "λάκη· ράκη. Κρῆτες").

The features of the reflection of Cretan *z* in Greek are unclear; *w* is restored indirectly because of the disappearance of the *digamma*, *s* is reflected on a regular basis (there is also a parasitic variant [cf., for example, μήρινθος - σμήρινθος along with Greek σμικρός - μικρός, στέγος - τέγος]).

As for the semivowel *j*, it could turn into ζ, at least in some cases. Thus, we know the root of plant names ζιζ-, with reliable Cretan suffixes (these forms are discussed in Chapter 7: Word Formation): compare forms ζιζουλά "millet," ζιζάνιον "darnel, cockle," ζίζυφον "*Rhamnus jujube*," in the Latin language the last substratum word is

---

97. Cf., in dialectal-archaic Latin: *dingua ~ lingua, odor ~ olere, sedeo ~ solium, con-silium, dacruma ~ lacrima* (with Greek δάκρυ); and Ὀδυσσεύς ~ Ὀλυσσεύς, whence is Latin *Ulixes*, at al. Also, the evolution of *d > l* is a classifying indication of the Eastern Iranian languages.

preserved as *jujuba*. Also, Cretan mediation can explain a phonetic appearance considered to be borrowed from the Egyptian word ζῦθος "beer" (Ernstedt 1953: 27) from the Egyptian name for the barley *jt*, Coptic ⲉⲓⲟⲩⲧ, ⲉⲓⲱⲧ.

It seems that, in Minoan, there were also several affricates, which in Greek transfers exist as groups ρ + consonant. The combination of ρδ occurs more often than others in the examples so far found (see the widespread stem καρδ-, κορδύλος "newt," πέρδιξ "partridge," the gloss of Dioscorides τόρδυλον / τόρδιλον "*Seseli*" gives "*Tordylium officinale*," and suffixed derivatives, which will be discussed in Chapter 7: Word Formation, the glosses of Hesychius κικίρδης "fig" and the name of the fish σαπέρδης). There are also groups ρσ (the Cretan gloss of Hesychius γάρσανον "brushwood," κόρσεον "tuber of water lotus," the names Περσεύς, Περσεφόνη (Περσέφασσα, Φερσέφασσα), the name of the tree περσέα) and ργ (γόργυρα "dungeon, prison," σαργάνη "cord," σαργός, a species of fish). Some other options are not ruled out (e.g., παρθένος).

In the inscriptions using syllabic writing, these special sounds were reflected in different ways: if in Linear A, they always seem to have been reproduced through the signs of *rV* type in our provisional reading (*ka-ro-pa₃* in the plate HT 31 with Greek κάρδοπος "trough"), in Linear B the affricate "unfolded," and *r* was omitted as a general rule for the sonants before a consonant (*ka-da-mi-ja* along with κάρδαμον).

One special pronunciation, which goes back to the supposed affricates, remained in Crete until later times; the gloss of Hesychius ("πέρδιξ· πῆριξ. Κρῆτες") shows that the "group" ρδ is implemented as one sound. The appearance of a shivering faint concurrent sound under the influence of the Cretan substratum occurred in the native Greek words as well; see again in Hesychius τρέ ("σέ. Κρῆτες") instead of the expected Dorian τέ.

THE TYRRHENIAN LANGUAGES OF THE FIRST MILLENNIUM BCE

Vowels

It is also very difficult to analyze the vowel system of the Tyrrhenian languages. Vowel phonemes in these languages, primarily known in Etruscan, are very unstable. There are examples of a great variety of their substitutions and alternations. They are often weakened until they completely disappear (in particular this applies to vowel phonemes at the end of a word-form). On the other hand, there are certain combinations of vowels, sometimes quite complex (up to three phonemes), in which one can see diphthongs (and the presence of semivowels in the confluence of three vowels). In turn, in the diphthongal combinations as well one can find rotations and different (including dialectally conditioned) cases of simplification.

In Etruscological studies, it is usually stated that in the Etruscan and Rhaetic languages there are the vowels *a, i, e, u*, as well as combinations that should be considered diphthongs (it concerns mostly Etruscan): *ai, au (av), ei, eu (ev), ui*, and simple vowels *a, i, e, o* and the expected diphthongs *ai, ei* in Aegean-Tyrrhenian. It should be mentioned in advance that we cannot yet classify Etruscan diphthongs as phonological or phonetic. Since reliable oppositions, based on the contrast of vowels with the corresponding diphthongs, have not been found, the second variant is preferred.

In favor of the diphthongal character of Etruscan combinations is the fact that, in Latin loanwords and in glosses of Roman authors, they are also categorized as diphthongs (*aisar* : *aesar*, *ceicna* : *Caecina*, etc.). More complex combinations consisting of three vowels usually contain *i* (cf., common name *seiantial*, TLE 35 *vipiiennas*, TLE 87 *ziiace*, etc.), which, apparently, must be understood as a semivowel [j] (see below).

At the most superficial acquaintance with the Tyrrhenian written inscriptions, one may notice the absence of the vowel *o* in Etruscan and Rhaetic, and *u* in the Lemnos stele inscription, despite the fact that υ occurs regularly in the Aegean-Tyrrhenian relic vocabulary; accordingly, Latin *o* and Greek o, ω, and in most cases, υ are also transmitted in the Etruscan inscriptions through *u* (cf., *pultuce*, later *pulutuce*[98] [REE 42/146, Rus.], *from Greek* Πολυδεύκης). It is natural that the stem of the Aegean-Tyrrhenian word *morinail* "a Myrinian, a citizen of Myrina" corresponds to the name of the city Μύρινα, Μυρίνη, etc.

However, the difference between the vowels *u* and *o* is preserved in South Lusitanian inscriptions, too short for serious analysis and, more importantly, it is well preserved in the inscriptions of the Eteo-Cypriote language. It seems that the asymmetric four-membered systems of phonemes go back to the five-membered, still attested in Minoan, and were differently formed in different areas—through the merger of *i* and *u*, with the preservation of *o* in Aegeida, and through the merger of *u* and *o*, with the preservation of *i* in Italy; while in the periphery (in Cyprus and Lusitania) the five-phonemed model remained.

It is possible that later in Etruscan *o* and *u* could act as allophones of one phoneme, and contrasts between them did not exist. In addition, differences in pronunciation—but not the status of the phonemes—may be dialectal in nature. In literary Latin and short Etruscan-Latin bilinguals, Latin *o* often corresponds to Etruscan *u* (cf., the names *Volcii*, *Volsinii*, common *petru* : Latin ***PEDROS*** (TLE 542), *hanusa* (CIE 1296) : Latin ***HANNOSSA*** (CIE 1295), etc.). It is unclear whether the old phonemes reflect these differences or already show the secondary allophones of late Etruscan.

In the dictionary entry of Etruscan forms, one should only use the grapheme *u* at present. The reconstruction of *o is possible only through the parallels of Minoan and Eteo-Cypriote, but they are still too few in number (in particular, we can restore this vowel in the adjective and possessive suffix through the form *a-ra-to-va-na-ka-so-ko-o-se* (KS 11), while in Etruscan we find -*uc*, -*uχ*). In addition, sometimes Eteo-Cypriote *o* is equivalent to other Etruscan and Aegean-Tyrrhenian phonemes or even a zero sound (cf., Etruscan-Tyrrhenian *aker*, Umbrian [from Etruscan] *akeř*-with Eteo-Cypriote ἀγόρ "eagle," Etruscan *meθl* with Eteo-Cypriote *ma-to-ri* "city").

---

98. Cases of broadening the stem at the expense of the vowels are not rare. Other examples will be given below.

As has already been mentioned, the vowels in Etruscan very often vary (it is particularly well exemplified in the common proper names and the main verb forms) (cf., such variations as *ramaθa ~ rameθa ~ ramuθa ~ ramθa; amuce ~ amce; turuce ~ turice ~ turce* and many others; it is not necessary to repeat the examples available in sufficient quantities in many other works. In addition, obvious cases of harmonization (distant assimilation) of vowels have been attested: *cluθumusta* (Κλυταιμήστρα), *fuflunsul, fuśunuś*, etc. (as can be seen, mostly with the sound *u*). In the Lemnos stele inscription only the alternation *sialχveiś-sialχviś* is known, but here, in regard to a very ancient (sixth century BCE) text of such a limited size, it is impossible to make definite conclusions.

Some variations in the writings of vowels may reflect different trends in the designation of a reduced, neutral vowel, the existence of which in Etruscan is quite possible, especially at the later stage. However, such frequency in writing, which may reflect attempts to designate a neutral sound, has not been found.

The most typical process of Etruscan vocalism is, therefore, a frequent reduction of the vowels, especially at the end of words.[99] Often, the words which had several syllables in the past are reduced over time to the monosyllabic, and, at the end of words, hard-to-pronounce clusters of consonants appear. Thus, the transition of the possessive form of the name *titeleś* into *titleś* and, further, in *titlś* has been attested. Forms such as *tivr* "months," *menrva* "Minerva," *masn* "deity" or "a deity's statue," *heχśθ* "do," the names *arnθ* (from *arunθ*), *larθ*, giving a specific phonetic color to a text, are very common.

It is believed that such a reduction of vowels, regularly occurring in both the Tyrrhenian words themselves and in borrowed words, can be explained by the existence of a stress or a simple rise of the tone on the first syllable in Etruscan (Tronskij 1953, 86), which first led to the weakening and then to the complete disappearance of many vowels at the end of words and the emergence of clusters of consonants.

However, in foreign language transfers of the Tyrrhenian lexemes, there is, though rarely, a reduction of the first vowel.[100] Clusters of consonants (not necessarily containing a sonant) are sometimes found at the beginning of words in Etruscan inscriptions. In addition, in the substratum words and glosses preserved in the Greek texts, the stress can also vary, although the picture here is probably somewhat distorted by the later revisions (such as those in the Tyrrhenian glosses in the dictionary of Hesychius). One cannot completely ignore these designations. Apparently, if the words with the stress (or the rise of tone) on the first syllable were the majority in the Tyrrhenian languages, other variants were known as well. It is possible that rare cases of the use of long vowels in the Greek transfers can indicate stress placement in the word.

It seems to us that, at present, we can speak of the existence of the stress on the second syllable as well. Other opinions are hardly provable (including the fact that all the

---

99. Rix assumes that Etruscan roots must end in a vowel, which is restored before suffixal elements. However, in the last case, we see combinations which are too varied to make a judgment on such a process (Rix, 1984^2, 215).

100. Cf., the glosses δροῦνα, *Traneus*, etc.

reliable Tyrrhenian roots consist of one or two syllables; to talk about the possibility of shifting the stress on the suffixed elements in longer word forms would be premature).

Like the Minoan, neither Etruscan nor other Tyrrhenian languages give us any reason to suppose the existence of differentiation of long and short vowels. Common in the Italic languages, a trend to a graphical doubling of the vowel to indicate length (from non-Indo-European writing marked in the inscription of Novilara [PID 345][101] *gaares*), is not attested anywhere in the Etruscan and Rhaetic texts. In the Greek glosses, Etruscan vowels are reproduced almost exclusively by the short form (among the writings of long vowels one should remember the gloss of Hesychius TLE 802 ἀγαλήτορα). The Greek digraph ου in the late period only serves to indicate the [u] without any connection to the length (cf., the transfer of Latin *sōlis ocŭlŭm* as σώλις ὄκουλουμ in the gloss TLE 823. Long vowels rarely occur in pre-Greek words that can be linked to the Tyrrhenian vocabulary (cf., for example, the toponym Ὑττηνία, discussed in detail in our work below).

In turn, the Greek and Latin long and short vowels are not differentiated in the Etruscan transfers; although, according to Rix's point of view (1984², 216), the long vowels in the borrowed words are not subject to reduction, he does not give sound examples (if such forms as *telmun* < Τελᾰμών, correspond to the Rix's explanation, it is easy to find opposite examples as well [cf., *clutmstra* < Κλυταιμήστρα, with the reduction of the stressed long, etc.]).

One can conclude with complete certainty that the variation of root vowels in Etruscan and other Tyrrhenian languages are purely phonetic; any attempts to ground them in morphological alternation (cf., *clen* "di *clan*" [Rix 1984,² 227]) are totally arbitrary. No single trustworthy example showing that Tyrrhenian languages at some period of their history developed the system of morphologically or lexically meaningful vowel alternation has been found. That sharply opposes them to Indo-European languages in the surroundings of which they existed for a long period of time.

The character of vowel reduction makes it possible to notice one more quite interesting regularity: one can suppose that, alongside the stressed vowels, those which had morphological value were not reduced. Accordingly, proceeding only from the phonetic appearance of the word, one can mark out some formants.

Etruscan diphthongs are of special interest. With a certain confidence one can speak about the existence of diphthongs *ai, au* (αυ), *ei, eu* (ευ), possibly, also *ui* which appears significantly less frequently (similar combinations in the word endings hardly can be considered as diphthongal); in the inscriptions root diphthongs occur everywhere.

Normally Etruscan diphthongs *ai, au* clearly correspond to Latin *ae, au* (*ais-* : *aesar*, *laive* : *laevus*, *aule* : *Aulus*, etc.). Variants of other correspondences are caused properly by the simplification of diphthongs in Etruscan (cf., below with an example of the root *lauc-/luc-*, etc.). It is very characteristic that Etruscan diphthongs occur almost exclusively in the first root syllable (examples, such as *matausnal* [CIE 1160], are very rare). It is possible that the syllable containing a diphthong was stressed. Words with a diphthong

---

101. For the language of the inscription of Novilara (Northern Picenian), see Durante 1978.

in the second and third (??) syllable are just as rare as the supposed stress on the second syllable.

The overwhelming majority of words with the final combinations V+*i* corresponds to feminine proper and generic names, where *-i* is a feminine marker. Accordingly, one cannot speak about the diphthongs here. (See below about this element in detail.)

Although we cannot explain the cause of the spread of diphthongs precisely in the initial syllable, this fact itself is quite important and can be used for ascertaining Tyrrhenian borrowings in other languages.

One can suppose that the appearance of the diphthong *au* (and in some other cases also *ae* < Etruscan *ai*) in the root syllable testifies to the Etruscan origin of separate lexemes, particularly if they are isolated or have strictly specialized meaning. For example, in Latin there exists the isolated word *lautia* (from older *dautia*, *pluralia tantum*), with the narrow meaning of "maintenance of ambassadors and high-ranking visitors." Probably, Latin *lautus* and *laus* and Gen. *laudis* (voiced) also should be included here. In the absence of an Indo-European etymology, comparable (but not deduced within Latin) meaning and considerable external resemblance, it is possible to suppose precisely an Etruscan origin for them.

In addition, *caussa*, *laurus* (cf., also Minoan or Aegean-Tyrrhenian toponym Λαύρειον in Attica), *fauces*, *caelum*, etc. should be included. Sometimes after being borrowed into Latin, they preserve their morphological meaning (cf., *caupo* "innkeeper" in Chapter 6: Morphology. It was the premier expert in Latin, Prof. I. M. Tronskij (1953, 114) who drew attention to their non-Indo-European appearance. Among the Etruscan glosses preserved in Greek sources, the name of "marjoram" καυτά(μ) (TLE 823) also belongs to this type.

The hypothetical separation of Etruscan borrowings is confirmed by clear examples. For one, the name *Aulus* certainly originates from Etruscan, where it is very widespread. Some names, preserved in Latin sources but not having penetrated into living speech, also date from Etruscan (cf., for example, *Lausus* [son of Mezentius],[102] Etruscan *lavsieś* (TLE 679), and also Rhaetic *lavisiel* (IR 103).

The root of the Latin word for "heaven," *caelum*, as well as the similar in meaning *palatum* "palate," *palatium* "arch," "chamber" (see above), is borrowed from Etruscan (cf., the names *cailinal* (CIE 45) and particularly the inscription on the mirror (CIE 10854, fourth to third centuries BCE), which is identical to the Latin transfer *Caele Vibenna*. One can easily see that the name of a Roman hill, *Caelius*, was formed from the same root. It is also present in Faliscan (cf., the proper name *CAILIO*, later *CELIO*).

The Latin *taurus*, Oscan *taurom* (Acc. Sg.), Umbrian *turuf* (Acc. Pl.), and Greek ταῦρος may belong to a similar type. In Etruscan, we have the unclear forms θ*aura* (TLE 419, 570), θ*aure* (TLE 619), θ*auruś* (TLE 621), the name θ*evruchnas* (TLE 13) and a particularly interesting form θ*evrumines*, the name of the Minotaur above his image on the mirror (TLE 755). The other personages of the myth are also depicted there: Minos and Ariadna (*mine* and *aria*θ*a* respectively). The fact that the components of the name

---

102. In Roman mythology, the king of Caere, killed, according to one version, by Aeneas, to another by Ascanius (Liv., Verg.).

are joined in the inverted order, characteristic of Etruscan (*mines* can be interpreted as an independent possessive form), indicates, it seems, the independent borrowing of a Cretan theme without Greek mediation. A generic name, formed from the stem *mine*, is also known in Etruscan: *minate*[103] (CIE 1899, Cl., REE 50/40, Vet., etc.). In addition, if it were a case of borrowing the Greek ταῦρος, the phonetic appearance of *θevru* would be quite unexpected.

Correlation of the Etruscan word *θevru* and the root spread, not only in Greek and Italic, but also in other branches of the Indo-European family, is unclear. Probably it dates to a non-Indo-European Mediterranean source, from which it penetrated into European languages (it does not occur in Indo-Iranian and other Eastern branches). In summary, it is evident that one can find a number of similar loanwords based on phonetic appearance alone.

Etruscan diphthongs display the types of alternation similar to those from simple vowels. Alternation *ai : ei* is common (cf., *aiser : eiser* "gods" and other cases). It is probable that Etruscan-Latin bilingual TLE 470: *leucle φisis lavtni* : *L. PHISIUS L. LAUCL* and the root *θaur- : θevr-* given above, may be other examples showing the possibility of an *au : eu* alternation.

The diphthong *eu* is observed in the name of Clusium. This Latin name of this city originates from the Etruscan variant with a diphthong (cf., *cleusin-*, *clevsina-* [TLE 138, 233, 488, etc.]). It is evident that, having penetrated into the Latin language at an early stage, this root contained precisely the diphthong, which was later monophthongized according to the rules of Latin phonetic evolution (cf., *Leucesie* [in the Hymn of Salii], *Loucanam* [CIL I^2 7], *Lucius*). As an Etruscan generic name, it possibly indicates men who were Clusians by birth (it appears in Tarquinii, Volsinii, Caere, but is not seen in such quantity in Clusium; however, it cannot be excluded that *cleus-* should be examined as an independent nominal stem, presented, besides the other cases, in the name of the city). As a designation of the city this root appears, for example, in the epitaph from Volsinii TLE 233: *clevsinslθ zilaχnve* "was a *zilc* in Clusium" (where *-θ* is a locative formant).

Besides the alternations, different reflexes of the diphthongs *au, ai*, which are of dialectal character, can be seen. The easiest way to see the evolution of the diphthong *au* is to examine two widespread roots: *lautn-* "emancipated slave; stirps" and *lauc-/lauχ-* with the meaning "to rule, to reign." In the example of *lauc-*, one can quite clearly see the preservation of the diphthong in the northern areas of Tuscany and its contraction in southern ones. Thus, we know the forms *lauχme* (TLE 440, *Lucignanello*), *laucanias* (TLE 534, Cl.), *lavcisla* (TLE 681, Faes.), *laucis* (TLE 682, Faes.), *lauχusieś* (TLE 918, Volat.) etc.; the form *lauχumneti*, which should be translated as "in the royal palace," appears in *Liber Linteus* (TLE 1)$^{IX\,γ2}$. On the other hand, in the southern areas, this diphthong is contracted into *u* (cf., the verb *lucairce* "ruled" [TLE 131. Tarq.], the names *lucini* [TLE 291, Vols.], *luχrias* [TLE 563, Cl.], *lucer* [TLE 119, Tarq.]). We can observe the same evolution in the name of the town Λοκροί (in

---

103. Cf., below the suffix *-te*.

Bruttium), etc. The last nominal forms, apparently, are identical to the name of the Roman tribe *Luceres*. We should remember that, according to Varro (lL, V, 55), all three names of the Roman tribes had an Etruscan origin. Evidently, the exact southern form penetrated into Rome in the term *lucumo*, designating the Etruscan kings (see below); it seems that here the Etruscan *lucumu* (CIE 5617, Hort.) was the source. The form *laχumni* (NRIE 451, Per.) is quite interesting. It seems to be the only attested example of a transition from *au* into *a* in the given root.

In the stem *lautn-* two reflexes of the same diphthong are found, *u* and *a*. The distribution of all three variants is somewhat different from that which we observe for the root *lauc-*. The primary form, *lautn-*, occurs many times and in many places. Along with it, we have the contracted forms *lutni*, *lutnit/θa*, occurring in Clusium (TLE 528, CIE 4790), Perusia (TLE 589) and Umbria (TLE 690), and *latni* in Saena (TLE 443), Clusium (CIE 248, 2326, 3125), Perusia (TLE 588, CIE 4028, 4091, 4093), Cortona (TLE 637, REE 54/5). The complex splintering of a diphthong also exists in the case of *lavutn* (TLE 880, Tarq.). One can adduce some other examples with an analogous transformation of the diphthong, although less widespread (cf., for example, the frequently observed name *raufi-ś* [CIE 3482, etc., Per.], *RAUFIA* [TLE 561, Cl.] : *rafi-s* [CIE 3481 etc.; ibid.]).

On the whole, one can outline a quite complex picture: the transformation of *au* into *u* is spread in southern Tuscany, but also takes place further to the northwest and takes in the territory of Clusium. In northern areas, the diphthong *au* mostly remains, but in the northwest, it tends to transform into *a*, and such forms also appear in Clusium. It seems to us that the main types of its evolution were the transformation into *u* in the south and into *a* in the north, but in the area of Clusium (and, possibly, Perusia) the whole picture was somewhat changed because of the Umbrian substratum and/or contacts with Umbria (we should remember that Umbrian monophthongized all old diphthongs, particularly *au* transformed into *o*). It is possible that it is because of this that *au* sometimes appears as *u* in this very region. One cannot exclude a similar two-way influence in southern areas, bordering upon Latium. In dialectal "rural" Latin monophthongization of *au* into *o* had taken place long before this phenomenon became widespread (Tronskij 2001, 81).

The evolution of the root "to be" that appears as *am-* in Etruscan is not absolutely clear (its past tense *amce* belongs to the most frequently seen Etruscan grammatical forms). In the inscriptions of the Lemnian stele we find the form *aomai* "was" (*-ai* is the only past tense suffix attested in Aegean-Tyrrhenian). But the very wide distribution of the root *am-* in Etruscan along with the entire absence of the variant of **aum-* prevents us from reconstruction of the diphthong in the common Tyrrhenian root. The diphthong in Aegean-Tyrrhenian is probably the result of an independent evolution.

The diphthong *ai* transforms into *ei* in most cases (cf., *aisar* : *eiser*, etc.). The fact that this transition is not attested in Latin transfers can probably be explained by the peculiarity of the classical Latin phonetic system, where the diphthong *ei* is absent (*aesar*, *Caecina* along with Etruscan *ceicna* appears everywhere, while *caicna* is a far rarer form, cf., CIE 5039). Other variants of the evolution of this diphthong are found in infrequent but quite interesting examples. The diphthong *ai* in the borrowed Latin name *cnaive*

(TLE 14, REE 42/301), from archaic Latin *Gnaivos* "Gnaeus," contracts into *e: cneve* (CIE 4306, 4376, Per., TLE 300, Volc.). In the scholias to Virgil (Aen., 10, 183), the transition of *ai* into *i* is also attested. So, for the city of Caere (Latin *Caere*; the earlier form of this name should be reconstructed as **Kais[V]ra*) the variant *Cisra,* is used. It was analyzed by C. de Simone (de Simone 1976, 177): "*Flaccus primo Etruscarum: Agylla, inquit, ab Etruscis [conditoribus sci]licet nominata est Cisra.*" Thereby, the Punic form *kyšry* in the bilingual TLE 874, admitting both readings, also can be reconstructed as **Kisra/e*.

An attempt has been made to describe the evolution of this name in dialectological terms, based on preservation of the sound *z/s* or its absence (de Simone 1978, 174). Accordingly, the Etruscan forms *ceizra* (CIE 10789–91, Vols.), *CEZRTLE* (CIE 4825, Cl.), etc., belong to the first group, Latin *Caere, Caerites*, Etruscan χ*eritne* (CIE 1506, 3064, Cl.), etc., to the second. But here the evolution of the diphthong is ignored. It seems that there are not enough given examples to outline the dialectal differences.

Consonants

Tyrrhenian consonants of the first millennium BCE appear as an isolated phonetic system, remaining strictly separated from the closest linguistic environment. Usually, in works devoted to the Etruscan language, the authors note the main feature of Etruscan writing—the absence of the signs for the voiced consonants in the available inscriptions (as in Linear writing) and the evolution of voiceless ones, which tend to transform into the aspirates; the inscription of the Lemnian stele and Rhaetic inscriptions show the same features[104]; similar phenomena also are attested in some Faliscan writings, but here it is entirely explained through Etruscan influence, but only in graphical form (cf., *LECET* (LF 75) "legit, *CUPA* (LF 144) cubat, *ARCENTELOM*, and some others elsewhere).

The description of Etruscan consonants in most generalized works is superficial [cf., Pallottino 1976, 364; Bonfante 1990, 18]; actually, only the absence of voiced consonants and the weak opposition of voiceless and aspirates are postulated, whereas if one considers the relatively long time of the existence of Etruscan inscriptions, it is necessary to admit that the character of Etruscan consonants might have undergone serious changes. For example, the absence of the signs for voiced sounds does not mean that they could not exist in later pronunciation but that the traditional graphic was preserved; the thought of the evolution of voiceless into aspirates appears to be quite valuable under more careful analysis.

In contrast to vowels, which are analyzed mainly by the alternations in Etruscan texts, reconstruction of consonantism is deeply dependant on comparing Tyrrhenian writings with the loanwords, firstly in Latin, glosses and the transfers of the Etruscan words in bilinguals. Moreover, borrowings play the main role for the earlier periods, while for the later (third to second centuries BCE) the value of epigraphic variants increases. The

---

104. Voiced sounds are found in a non-Indo-European language, attested in the inscription from Novilara (PID 343) and usually called "North Picenian"; the singular coincidences with Etruscan that it shows can be explained as lexical borrowings.

question of glosses is more complicated, because the time of their fixation is not evident. Greek glosses and transfers or relic lexica are also of some value, but the phonetic evolution is more obscured. It is quite natural that the character of Etruscan writing itself should reflect the earlier consonant system, and its analysis would not be precise for the later stage. Below we shall discuss two main stages of consonant evolution, considering the archaic borrowings into Latin (as *populus, urbs*(?), *palatum*, but not *flexuntes*!) in the earlier stage, and solving separately the questions of glosses and epigraphy.

Thus, the most typical feature is the total absence of the signs for voiced plosive consonants in Etruscan texts, and corresponding sounds seldom appear even in Latin borrowings or Tyrrhenian glosses and are relatively numerous only in bilinguals (cf., also [Talocchini-Giacomelli 1966, 239–57]). The only more or less reliable case of using the voiced sound χλ;η properly in an Etruscan text is the word *mazba-* in the inscription from Tarquinii TLE 160. Because it is, undoubtedly, a borrowing of Phoenician (Punic) *mzbh* "altar," the reading *mazba-* is preferable to *mazfa-* as was offered earlier (CIE 10447, NRIE 736). The voiced *b, d, g*, as was shown, never appeared in the inscription of the Lemnian stele and Rhaetic inscriptions.

The Latin transfers of Greek words seem to be somewhat more exact than the Greek ones because of the character of the Greek phonetic system itself. If we consider, for example, the correspondence of Latin *triumphus* and Greek θρίαμβος, we can explain the voicing in the Greek word by the position after the nasal sonant, as in Modern αντί (andi), δεν ξέρω (ðen ́gzero). The Latin variant is evidently closer to the prototype, especially in the form *triumpe* (from the Hymn of the Arvalian brethren). Sometimes the voiceless can also remain in the position after the nasal (cf., Greek ἄμπελος "grapes, vine"). In our opinion, this word, which does not have an Indo-European etymology, is comparable to the gloss TLE 805 *Ampiles* "Majus." (The meanings of the words do not contradict each other: it seems that the name of the month is connected with the character of agricultural works (cf., the toponym Ἄμπελος, preserved in Chalcidice).

In Latin transfers, the oldest supposed Etruscan borrowings can contain the voiced, but it seems that here also the voicing does not reflect an Etruscan sound (cf., *urbs*, gen. sg. *urbis*, the analogical influence of *orbis* is quite possible: the phonetic appearance of *urbs* itself is rather uncommon). In other cases, when we are faced with the voiced plosive consonants in Etruscan words (cf., *subulo, Vibenna*), occurring in Latin texts, they usually belong to the later period when their character changed in Etruscan itself, and Etruscan writings with the voiceless (*suplu* [TLE 237][TLE 237], *vipiiennas* [TLE 35]), apparently, did not reflect real pronunciation. It can be seen particularly clearly in the corpus of brief bilinguals (cf., below).

It may seem that plosive consonants in all the oldest loanwords from Tyrrhenian languages or transitions of Tyrrhenian words in foreign texts date from the simple voiceless. Then one should suppose that, at some period of the existence of the Etruscan (or common Tyrrhenian) language, both voiced and aspirates were absent in its consonantism, or they could act as the allophones of the voiceless, and there was no minimal phonetic opposition. One should make the reservation that, even if the system once existed, it began to collapse before the appearance of the earliest inscriptions. Aspirates (primarily *θ*) are attested in texts which are quite early. For some of the very early words (as, for example, the female name *ramaθa, ramθa*) variants with the simple voiceless instead of the aspirate are either unknown or are singular; the very writing *ramta* is found, apparently, only once (REE 41/166, Al.). Accordingly, it has been accepted that, at the early stage of the Etruscan languages, voiceless *p, t, c* (in archaic orthography *k*, occasionally also *q*), aspirates *φ* (a quite rare letter, found only in the inscriptions from the seventh to fifth centuries BCE), *θ*, and *χ* existed. The question about this group is the most complex.

Besides these, the following groups of consonants are accepted with some reservations: sibilants: *s* (with the variants *ś, ṣ, š*), *z*, labial *f*, labiovelar: voiceless $^*q^v$, aspirate $χ^v$; sonants: liquid *l*, flapped *r*, nasal *m* and *n*, aspiration *h*; semivowels: [w], [j].

The graphical variants *q, ṣ*, and *š* that evidently did not reflect any phonetic variants and were conditioned only by the peculiarities of the alphabet, disappear approximately in the fifth century BCE. The grapheme *k* residually appeared later but was steadily replaced by *c*, with the exception of the northern areas of Tuscany (and also in Rhaetia). Thus, from the earliest stage, the differentiation of voiceless and aspirates was apparent, and, in late Etruscan inscriptions, voiceless steadily concede their place to corresponding aspirates (so, the locative formant *-ti* gradually took the appearance *-θi*, the noun *atre* changed into *aθre*, the name of the city *pupluna* "Populonia" into *fufluna*.

This phenomenon, apparently, is reflected in the phonetic features of modern Tuscan dialects of the Italian language ("gorgia toscana"), for which, as is known, Etruscan acts as a substratum. So, depending on the area, voiceless occlusives in intervocalic position acquire an aspiration, and aspirates are reduced to complete elision (cf., such transitions as $[k^h] > [χ] > [h]$; $[p^h] > [χ] > [h]$; $[t^h] > [χ] > [h]$; cf., [amiho] "friend," [tenehe] "you keep" [Čelyševa 2001, 126]).

Especially interesting is the fact that this phenomenon has not affected the Aretian patois of the Tuscan area. In ancient times, apparently it was the Umbrians who settled there, and, accordingly, the influence of the substratum was different. It has also been attested that Tuscan spirantization takes place in the midst of the word and does not touch initial consonants (cf., Devine 1974). This, in some degree, supported the attempts to explain even Etruscan spirantization as a phenomenon, conditioned only positionally.

However, this process was prolonged and rather complicated. In some degree, it depended on the phonetic environment (cf., for example, the form *vaχr* (TLE $1^{VII\ 8}$, 570^{a2}) along with the more often observed *vacl, vacil*. The appearance of the uncommon ending *-χe* in the verb *ziχuχe* can be explained by incontiguous assimilation. But voiceless and aspirates often are close in position within the same inscription (*ramaθas mi tutinas* [TLE 73], and many others), a n d voiced and voiceless (in Latin transfers) even in the same word (*TIDI* [CIE 819] along with Etruscan *titi*).

Rix once assumed that the development of each from three plosive consonants could go into two directions (i.e., to the type of aspirate or voiced [Rix 1984^2, 219; cf., Maggiani 1987–88, 202; Boisson 1989–90, 176]) but did not define correctly enough the positional terms for different variants. We shall return to his schemes below. In any case, if we agree with such explanations, it must be admitted that the differences between $χ : g, f(φ)$

: *b*, *θ* : *d* will remain purely phonetic, positionally conditioned, while phonologically these sounds will be neutral, since the pairs *χ* : *g*, *f*(*φ*) : *b*, *θ* : *d* would not form any minimal oppositions. If one accepts this point of view, it would be reasonable to introduce the term of "archiphoneme" (i.e., *K, *P, *T), but we shall abstain from using this term. The curious idea of aspirated variants as primary ones (Devine 1974), in spite of seeming differences, dates from the same scheme. It is based on the quantitative predominance of aspirated forms (i.e., it ignores the chronology; later inscriptions are considerably more numerous). Appropriately, this version did not meet with warm support.

Firstly, we should examine in detail the different cases of changes of Etruscan plosive consonants (in the order of *c*, *p*, *θ*). The consonant *c* (*k*), which occurred throughout the whole period during which Etruscan was inscribed, was naturally reflected as *c* in older inscriptions and in the majority of later borrowings in Latin (cf., the names *Caecina* [*caicna, ceicna*], *Larcius*, *Maecenas* [CIE 8384 : LF 129 *MACENA*]).[105] A little-known name of the "eighth" Roman hill *Cespius* (Varro, lL V, 65), *Cispius* (the name of one of the Esquiline peaks [along with *Oppius*] from the list of Festus, preserved among the other extractions from Verrius Flaccus)[106] originates from the Etruscan root *cezp* "eight," and, apparently, correctly reflects an Etruscan numeral.

In turn, not only Latin *c* but also *g* in Etruscan are transferred with *c*: *cae, caia* "Gaius, Gaia," *macstrev* (TLE 195) "magister," etc. Greek *γ* is also reflected with *c*: *meliacr* "Μελέαγρος." Interestingly, sometimes in Etruscan we find *c* in a position where historically an aspirate occurred: *antrumacia* (CIE 1738, Cl.) along with Greek Ἀνδρομάχη, *cerun* (CIE 5366, Tarq.) : Greek Χάρων (but in TLE 884, 885 *χarun*).

In what follows, *c* can turn into *χ* in different (if not all) positions. Let us consider some examples. In the beginning of the word; *ca* (demonstrative pronoun) ~ *χa* (TLE 794), *χalχas* "Κάλχας," *Caerites* (and the others, see above) : *χeritne* (CIE 1506, 3064), *ciem* (TLE 1$^{IX\,γ2,\,X\,2}$, 166) : *χiem* (TLE 570, if it is exactly the same word).[107] As a whole, the change of *c* into *χ* in the beginning of the word is the rarest (cf., the evolution in two positions in *χuliχna* [TLE 12] and partial aspiration in *culiχna* [TLE 3]; such a distribution reminds one of the peculiarity of Tuscan phonetic development, mentioned above) and may be partially of dialectal character.[108]

---

105. The inscription is made with the Faliscan alphabet, dating to the fourth century BCE; the variant *macena* should be evidently explained as a particular case of Faliscan monophthongization *ai* > *a*, while usually *ai* > *e* (Giacomelli 1978: 514).

106. The whole list is the following: *Palatium, Velia, Fagutal, Subura, Cermalus, Oppius, Caelius, Cispius*. The names *Palatium, Velia, Caelius* are obviously Etruscan. *Fagutal* should be compared with the nominal root, appearing in *facual* (CIE 3907), *facui* (CIE 4035), etc.; to other forms, *Subura* and *Oppius*, could correspond to *sup-nai* (REE 42/319), *sup-ri* (TLE 398) and *uples* (TLE 193), *ufleś* (CIE 4492); *u* < *au*? (cf., CIE 4063 *aufleś*). A parallel for *Cermalus* (Germalus) is lacking; according to Varro, *Germalus* "*a germanis Romulo et Remo*" (vulgar etymology).

107. Where *ci* "three," *-em* formant with subtractive meaning, see in the next chapter.

108. In particular, western or southwestern, drawn toward the seaside. For example, *χa* appears only on Populonian coins *χurvar* in the bilingual from Pyrgi (TLE 874), *χuliχna* in Campania.

In the middle of the word between vowels: *zicu* (TLE 472) – *ziχu* (TLE 601), *ziχuχe* (TLE 27, 278, 570), etc.; here also the variant of the verbal ending *-χe* along with the more widespread *-ce* (cf., below).

In the middle of the word after the consonant: *alqu* (TLE 160) : *alχu* (TLE $2^{10,\ 18}$); *velc-* (here also *Velcitanus* "Martius" (TLE 856); cf., Latin *Vulcanus* and the name of the Etruscan city *Volcii*) : *velχ-* (this noun stem is found everywhere in Etruscan inscriptions, it also occurs in Rhaetic (cf., IR 5, CE 1 *velχanu*), etc.

In the middle of the word before the consonant: *vacl* (which often occurs in *Liber Linteus*) : *vaχr* (TLE $1^{VII\ 8}$, $570^{a\ 2}$); *ectur* : *eχtur* from Greek Ἕκτωρ; *elacsantre* : *elaχsantre* from Greek Ἀλέξανδρος; *aχmemrun* Greek Ἀγαμέμνων (signatures for the images on mirrors are given).

In the middle of the word between consonants (a quite rare type, originating as a result of vowel reduction): *χurcles* (Ἡρακλῆς, TLE 165) : *χurχles* (TLE 166).

At the end of the word: *zilc* : *zilχ*; *marunuc* (SE 52/13) : *marunuχ* (TLE 137, 165, 234); *ziχ* (TLE 131) along with *zicu*, mentioned above (cf., the construction *mlaχ mlakas* [TLE 864]).

Can one define the conditions leading to the change of *c* into *χ*? The case of alternations such as *vacl* : *vaχr* makes us think that under the influence of some sounds (subsequent *r* in the given example) the changes into an aspirate could be hastened; the same can be said about the final position (*mlaχ mlakas*). As was mentioned above, the appearance of *χ* in the verbal ending *ziχuχe* can be explained as a harmonization; it is possible, that harmonization can occur in such forms as *χalχas* along with Greek Κάλχας, *χurχles*; cf., also the characteristic phonetic appearance of the demon's name *tuχulχa* (CIE 5375).

However, if one operates only with positional variants, the picture as a whole would be unclear. In later inscriptions in many positions, where *χ* could be expected, *c* is stably preserved. One of the most characteristic examples is the root *lar-*, found in a great number of inscriptions. It is often extended with the element *-c-*, which never appears as **larχ-*. In this case, one can suppose only that *c*, found in the position after *r*, could remain or undergo other changes (cf., below *tarc/q-* : *tarχ-*). One cannot define the most common regularities based only on position; in this case we would have to limit ourselves to a description of numerous separate variants; moreover, they can be complicated with regional dialects.

Besides the transformation into aspirates, there took place a completely different process, to wit, voicing in some positions (from third to second centuries BCE). Because of the peculiarities of Etruscan writing with its absence of letters for the voiced, it can be observed using the material of Etruscan-Latin bilinguals and Latinized forms.

Let us look at the following Latinized names: *GREBO* (CIE 6118, 6190, Caere) and the quite widespread Etruscan *crepu*, *MAGILI* (CIE 6024–26, 6029, Caere) along with Etruscan *maci* (CIE 309, 4735); *GARGOSSA* (CIE 1955, Cl.) and Etruscan *carcu-*; *LARGE* (CIE 2108, Cl.) the above mentioned stem *larc-* (here also Latin *Largius* along with the earlier variant *Larcius*). Undoubtedly, the character of Etruscan *c* has changed in these examples. In this case, what is important for us is not the character of *c*, *g* itself, but the fact that this sound developed in a direction different from χ. Lacking any precise data about the pronunciation of *c* and *g*, we cannot speak about voicing with certainty, but we shall use this slightly conditional term as the simplest and most convenient. One should pay attention to the fact that *g* appears in the first place in such positions, where it does not change into χ.[109]

It is most important to notice the following: in the lexemes known to us, confusion between χ and [g] is never observed in any position. In that case, if some stem or morphological element includes an aspirate, the voiced cannot appear, and, on the contrary, where we can see the voicing, one cannot find any example with an aspirate (as in the given stem *larc-*:*LARG-*). Accordingly, one should distinguish either the conditions of the development of *c* into χ and into [g], or the character of the original sound. It is easier to analyze the transformation into χ, because it is shown in proper Etruscan inscriptions. On the other hand, Latinized forms with *g* are enough to examine the voicing (and to consider it as belonging to a later period?).

If one accepts Rix's opinion about the development in two different directions (1984^2, 219), it could be concluded that *c* becomes voiced in initial position, after *r*, and beside *i, e*; the last formulation seems to be more correct than "before *i, e*" (cf., below our observations on other consonants [b] and [d]). If one wants to speak about the influence of *i, e* on voicing, the results of this influence are not clear enough. An absence of such voicing (cf., CIE 928, 930 *PACIN[N]AL*) could be explained unless we are dealing with dialectal features (but even the last example is given from the inscriptions of Clusium, where, taking into account their great number, one can find various phonetic changes which are needed in the current discussion).

On the assumption of all discussed above, we can draw the following conclusion: the changes of *c* into χ or [g], even if they were not shared in time (which is unlikely), cannot be explained only positionally. On the other hand, based on the alternations *c* : χ and *c* : [g], conclusions can be reached on lexical and morphological distinctions. These conclusions may promote the finding of related stems which are already phonetically changed and clarification of some grammatical features (cf., below the alternations of verbal endings *-ce* and *-χe*). Actually, any attempt to contrast any forms with lexical or grammatical meaning only by the "voiceless-aspirate" alternation should be considered ungrounded.

According to Rix, *c* in some positions could develop into an affricate, like *c* before *e, i, ae* in late Latin. This affricate is supposedly written through *s*, *ś* (1984^2: 219). But he does not give clear examples of the correlation between *c* and *s*. We also have not succeeded in finding them. It is possible that the interchange of verbal morphological elements or word formation suffixes containing *c* and *s* could be taken for such a correlation. As a whole, the opinion about that *c* developing into an affricate is not confirmed, although it should not be absolutely excluded, especially as a dialectal feature. Simple voicing of *c* at the later stage would remain the main explanation of its change. It

---

109. If one tries to explain it positionally, after *r*, sometimes in the initial position: *GARGOSSA* : *carcu-*; on the other hand (cf., *CORSDLE* [CIE 2058, Cl.] : *curstli* [CIE 2059] and some other examples). But this cannot explain such cases as *MAGILI*.

is also difficult to judge if the sound [k] was preserved then or had to change in some way.

The voiceless consonant *p* underwent changes at different times, similar to those which we have observed with *c*. In the oldest Latin loanwords and transfers it was preserved: *populus* (here also the name of the city *Populonia*; voicing in *Publius*, *publicus* took place in Latin),[110] *palatum*, *Palatium*, "name" *Porsenna*, etc. As in the example of *c – g*, borrowed words, containing *b*, are written through *p* in Etruscan; cf., the widespread name *fapi* (Latin *Fabius*), etc; in turn, the aspirate in the borrowings can be reflected as a simple voiceless: *pisice* from Greek. φυσικός, apparently, with the meaning "doctor" (TLE 609, Per.; the inscription comes from a later period).

Evidently, the sound marked as *p*, following a common tendency, changed into φ, but φ disappears quite early, so we have few such correspondences: *persona* : φ*ersu* (TLE 80), *papanaia* (TLE 484) : φ*apenaš* (TLE 65). Along with it, there are more regular alternations *p* : *f* (in archaic graphics *vh*, *hv*): *puplun-* : *fuflun-* (a widespread nominal stem), *pulumχva* (TLE 874, 875) : *fulumχva* (TLE 570) "stars." Such alternations are typical for the inscriptions from Clusium, Perusia, and Tarquinii (de Simone 1975, 125). It is quite difficult to define the character of Etruscan *f*. It seems that it changed considerably over time (cf., below). We distinguish φ, *f*, developed from *p*, and labial or labiodental *f*, showing other alternations. But while analyzing the change from *p* into φ and *f*, we will examine φ and *f* as the same phoneme. Thus, *p* changes into the aspirate in different positions.

In the beginning of the word: *persona* – φ*ersu*, *pulumχva* : *fulumχva*, φ*ersipnai* (TLE 5365) along with Greek Περσεφόνη.[111] It seems that the most widespread stem with this evolution is *puplu(n)-*;[112] in Etruscan it is presented in the name *fuflun-* (TLE 719, etc.) and the city name Populonia, in particular, on the coins from this city (third century BCE) (cf., χ*a fufluna vetalu* [TLE 379, 794], etc.). The form *pufluna* on one coin (ET NU 30) is quite interesting. It shows that the phonetic spirantization really became slower in the initial position.

An extremely important gloss TLE 831 *falado* demonstrates that, by the later period, the identity of this word and the earlier borrowing *palatum* had not been perceptible, apparently because of phonetic changes. It is possible that the names *Falerii* < *Falesii*, *Falisci*, with the analogous phonetic change belong to the same stem (Giacomelli 1978, 509).

In the middle of the word before the vowel: *apuna* (TLE 94, etc.) : *afuna* (TLE 570, etc.); *apa* "father" (CIE 6213, etc.), possibly, also *aper* (TLE $2^{14, 21, 42, 59}$), *aperu-cen* (TLE 572) "forefathers": *a*φ*ers* (TLE 363), *afrs* (TLE 359) (cf., below θ*ufulθaś*) (TLE 557).

In the middle of the word before the consonant: repeatedly cited stem *puplun-* : *fuflun-*; θ*apna* "bowl" (TLE $1^{X\ 22}$, 375 etc.) : θ*ahvna* (TLE 64), θ*avhna* (REE 45/28), θ*afna* (TLE 341 etc.); θ*uplθal* (TLE 477), θ*uplθaś* (TLE 654) : θ*ufltas* (TLE 149, 719 etc.).

---

110. Cf., *Publicola* along with the earlier *Poplicola*.
111. Although this Minoan word could appear as Φερσέφασσα in Greek.
112. The meaning "populus" for this stem has not been observed in Etruscan texts yet.

In the middle of the word after the consonant: the name *alp* (TLE 719) : *alfa* (TLE 584), *alfi* (TLE 581).

In the middle of the word between the consonants: *alpnas* (TLE 740 etc.) : *alfnal* (TLE 448 etc.).

In the end of the word the alternation *p* : *φ*, *f* has not yet been observed, because we lack clear examples with a final *p*. Moreover, *p* and *φ*, *f* do not appear in known morphological elements.

The aspirate *f*, developed from *p*, sometimes shows a tendency to further changes, to wit, an evolution into *v* and *h*. The correlation between *f* : *v* and *f* : *h* will be analyzed below. Here we shall give only the examples with *v*, *h* dating to the time of *p*. The proper name *puluni-ce* (CIE 5254, Volc., fourth cent.), *pulni-ce* (AG., tab. 16, 68, Per., fifth cent.), containing an aspirate in most cases (TLE 662, Arr. *fulni* : *FOLNIUS*, TLE 401, Volat. *fulnei*, TLE 749, orig. inc. *fulnial*, etc.), appears as *Volnius* in Varro (lL, V, 55). The noun *θapna*, *θavhna* "bowl," given above, once appears as *θavna* (CIE 8834, Camp.). In the bilingual from Pyrgi (TLE 874), the name of October, examined above, underwent the most extensive changes: *χurvar*, where not only the change *p* > *f* > *v*, is attested, but also a replacement of *s* with *r* (for detail, see below). There are some examples of the development of *p* > *f* > *h*: *θapna* > *θavhna* > *θahna* (REE 52/72, Caere); *capati-neś* (CIE 862) > *cafate* > *cahati-* (cf., *sehtumial* (CIE 4287) : Latin *Septimius* (development through an intermediate form *seftumi*).

Proceeding from the spread of forms with *v*, one can suppose that the further change *f* > *v* (*f* from *p*) has a dialectal character (southwestern dialecticism?); appropriately, in the Latin transfers (in this case in Varro's work), southern forms would prevail (as was shown with the example of *luc-* from *lauc-*).

In the later period *p*, as well as *c*, often becomes voiced; *b* appears in Latin transfers. Moreover, if one examines separate examples, it is possible to list mutually exclusive conditions about the positions where voicing takes place. It is necessary to analyze a great number of forms. It seems that the most reliable cases of voicing are observed in the position near to *i*, *e*, especially after *i*: *vipi* with numerous derivatives (TLE 584, etc.), Latin *Vibius*, *VIBIES* (CIE 2209); *vipiiennas* (TLE 35, Veii), Latin *Vibenna*, *trepi* : *TREBI* (TLE 541, Cl.). Writing *vipies* (CIE 10803, REE 42/213) along with *vipiś* (TLE 518, etc.) and particularly the form *vipiiennas* suggest that the combination *-p-(i)i-* is used to mark [bi] or simple [b]. Apparently, *vipiienna-* precisely corresponds to Latin *Vibenna*. Palatalization of many consonants before *i* is not only widespread in different languages but is also confirmed by Etruscan examples with *c*, *p*, *t* (*θ*); the *ex facto* ungrounded appearance of *i* and the combination of a few vowels is quite explicable with this process. It is especially clear in the case of *t* (*θ*) (cf., below). On the other hand, there is the above given name *GREBO* (CIE 6118) along with the often seen *crepu*, where voicing takes place without the influence of *i* (cf., also the gloss TLE 851 *subulo* "tibicen," Etruscan *suplu* (TLE 237, 362), *TLABONIA* (CIE 1772), *tlapu*.

As in the case of *c*, *p* can become voiced in the initial position: *BARNAES* (CIE 987, Cl.) along with *parna* (CIE 594, Cl.). We have a few reliable examples of this sort. In other cases, *p* is preserved in the beginning of the word (cf., the names *PERGOMSNA* [CIE 935], *PACIN[N]AL* [CIE 928, 930] given above). Accordingly, if one proceeds only from the position of the consonant, voicing can be interpreted here only as a dialecticism. As was shown above, the transition *c* > *g* in an initial position is also present in the inscriptions from Clusium, though it appears in an entirely different region, in Caere.

The Latin transfer of an Etruscan name *papasa* (CIE 2951, 2952; REE 48/61, 62 etc., all the examples are taken from the inscriptions of Clusium) is one of the most characteristic cases of apparent voicing. In the inscription CIE 832, it looks like *PABASSA*. Unfortunately, we do not have any such examples from the whole territory of Tuscany, and here, as in most cases, there is no opportunity to draw conclusions about the dialectal features of different regions, because we do not have the possibility of differentiating more dialectal variants. If one presupposes dialectal peculiarities specifically, we should point out a tendency of voicing initial *c* and *p* in the greater part of the Clusium area and preservation of voiceless in other places (where, in turn, intervocalic also can remain unvoiced [cf., *PACIN(N)AL*]). Any attempt to explain voicing or aspiration positionally is again shown to be unfounded, even if one makes the assumption of dialectal features.

In the correlation of voiceless *p*, aspirated *f* (φ) and voiced *b*, the same feature can be observed, as in the case of *c*, χ, *g*: only the evolution into an aspirate or voiced; *f* (φ) and *b* are never mixed, as χ (< *c*) with *g* (< *c*), which is confirmed by well-known stems. For example, the root of the name *crep-*, where one can see voicing (*GREBO*), never looks like *cref-*. The quite widespread root *capr-* (TLE 428, Volat., CIE 5674, Hort., CIE 5204, Vols., etc.) does not appear as *cafr-*, along with the Latin form with voicing *Cabreas* ("Aprilis," TLE 818), etc. It is obvious that there is no way to interpret *f* (φ) and *b* as the variants of archiphoneme *P*.

In principle, it is possible to find some correspondences between Etruscan *f* and voiced *b* in other languages. But it seems that they reflect only an evolution *p* > *f*, which took place in accordance with a common tendency in the words borrowed into Etruscan. In turn, Etruscan *p*, reconstructed from the earlier period, would be only a reflection of voiced *b* from the source language, as will be seen in many examples. As one such imaginary example, one can suggest the stem *brVnd/t-*, widespread in Italy (cf., the name *Brundisium*, Messapic βρένδον "deer," Venetic *Brenta*, etc.). It is obvious, that in Etruscan this stem should appear as *prVnt-*, in the sequel *p* > *f*; possibly, we also see it in the title *netśvis trvtnut frontac* (TLE 697, in Latin version *HARUSPEX FULGURIATOR*) and Picenian *frunter* (ID 181-82). According to another point of view, it originates in Greek βροντή (Mastrelli 1976) (that does not change the picture of phonetic development). However, Latin *frons, ntis* and *frons, ndis* can date from the same stem which is present in Venetic and Messapic but seems Etruscan in phonetic appearance.

As a whole, the distribution of aspirated and voiced here, as in the case of χ, *g*, evidently depends on the character of the initial sounds. But in order to make some conclusions one must also analyze the reflections of *t*.

The evolution of *t* is distinguished for having the greatest complexity; this consonant in different times appears in the most numerous reflections, including dialectal ones. The consonant *t* often appears in Etruscan borrowings into Latin and pre-Greek words, which can be reasonably connected with a Tyrrhenian substratum. Some examples were given above, and we shall not repeat them again. In these early borrowings this sound appears almost exclusively as simple voiceless *t* or τ, respectively, and only on rare occasions appears as q in Greek, which, however, does not change the whole picture (see above). In those cases, when simple *t* never appears in some root, it can be reconstructed indirectly. For example, the adverb θ*ui* "here," known from a great number of inscriptions, never contains voiceless *t*, but dialectal (Lesbos, Crete, Cyprus) Greek forms, which are, in our view, loanwords from Tyrrhenian, contain not the aspirate, but the simple occlusive: they are Hesychius's glosses τυ-δε, τυί, ἰν τυίν (see Chapter 6: Morphology). One of the most widespread feminine names, θ*ana*, it seems, remains in its archaic appearance not only in compounded *tancvil*, but also in singular cases (TLE 749, orig. inc.), cf., θ*ankviluš* (TLE 766), θ*anaχvilus* (TLE 876), etc.; also see below θρίαμβος, etc. But in all such cases we have enough material to reconstruct *t.

As in the cases of *c* and *p*, analyzed above, the earliest and the most widespread type of change of *t* is its development into an aspirate θ. We can observe it in different positions, but the distribution here is very uneven, we have singular cases in the middle of the word close to a consonant and dozens of examples with θ in final position (due to the exceptional extent of some names); one should analyze the main forms. In the beginning of the word: *tanasar* (TLE 82, 83) : θ*anasa* (TLE 541); given above the nominal root *tan-* : θ*an-*, etc. In the middle of the word: *atial* (TLE 266, 752) : *a*θ*is* (TLE 100), *a*θ*ialisa* (TLE 656); widespread *ram(a)*θ*a* along with *ramta* (REE 41/166, Al.); *a*θ*re* (TLE 1$^{XII\ 11}$) along with Latin *atrium*. Here is also the locative formant *-ti* : *-*θ*i*, etc. At the end of the word, the development *t* > θ can be seen many times in the most widespread names *arnt* : *arn*θ, *lart* : *lar*θ, and in some other cases.

In the inscription of the Lemnian stele, we have the form ναφοθ "grandson," which corresponds to Etruscan *nefts* (in different variants, TLE 131 etc.; usage of this stem as an Indo-European borrowing[113] is not regulated, in contrast to *tetals* "granddaughter" and *papacs, papals* "grandson," these words, it seems, should be interpreted as primordial but dating from the nursery language). Apparently, the Lemnian form shows that a similar process took place in Aegean-Tyrrhenian.

As can be seen, there are no positional limitations for the evolution of *t* > θ, but, by all appearances, further changes could partly depend on the phonetic environment (cf., below the correlation between *-te/-ti* and *-*θ*ui*).

Judging by the Latin forms *ARNTHAL* (CIE 832, *Montepulciano*), *ARNTHEAL* (CIE 561, Cl.), *LARTHI* (CIE 987, Cl.), *LARTHIA* (REE 59/32, *Mont.*), *SETHRE* (CIE 708, *Mont.*), *THANNA* (CIE 956, 2882, Cl.), *THANIA* (CIE 873, 874, Cl.), etc.,[114] θ designated an aspirate precisely, but this sound could subsequently develop in different directions. In the inscriptions from the neighborhood of Clusium we find at least two cases of the appearance of φ instead of the expected θ: *arn*φ (CIE 598 add.), φ*ania* (CIE

---

113. Cf., Latin *nepos*, Gen. *nepotis*, I..-Ir. **napat-*.
114. Far more rarely with simple *t* (cf., CIE 2182 *TANA*).

2872) (Maggiani 1987-88, 199). Here one can presuppose only that θ developed into an interdental, which, for absence of a corresponding grapheme, was written as φ; further we suggest using þ in phonetic transcriptions to avoid mixing with an aspirate. However, judging by the minimal number of corresponding records one can suppose that the evolution into an interdental was not very widespread.

The development t/θ > χ in some examples is quite interesting: *meχl* (TLE 87), *meχlum* (TLE 233) "town" along with widespread *met/θl-*, *met/θlum-*, Eteo-Cypriote *ma-to-ri*. Here one can hardly speak about a local dialect; the inscription TLE 87 comes from Tarquinii, TLE 233 from Volsinii. A similar phenomenon can be seen in the bilingual from Pyrgi TLE 874, where we have the combination *meχ θuta* (= Oscan *meddix tuticus*).

Singular examples of simplification of θ to an aspirate *h* are also known: cf., *hui* "here" instead of *θui* (TLE 510, Cl., rec.).

As far as can be observed in existing examples, more often θ changes into an affricate, which might possibly be further simplified. The widespread use of the stems *arat/θ-*, *arnt/θ-*, *lart/θ-*, which could form both male and female names (from the stem *arat-* a patrimonial name with the suffix *-na* is also known [cf., TLE 243 *araθena-s*] allows us to recall many such examples; let us examine the most characteristic. Nominal stem *araθ-* in some cases appears as *araz-*: *araziia* (TLE 24, R.), *araz* (REE 47/29, R.), *arznal* (TLE 570, 602, Per., 880, Tarq.), *arzneal* (TLE 566, Per.), etc.

The stems *arnt-* and *lart-* often transform into *arnz-*, *larz-* accordingly (cf., the forms *arnziu* [TLE 588, Per.], *arnza* [CIE 5277, Volc., IV; 4894, Cl., rec.], *arnzaś* [NRIE 641, Pop., IV-III], *arnzial* [REE 40/8, Per., rec.]; *larza* [TLE 324, Volc.; CIE 5613, Hort.; REE 48/96, Rus.], *larzl* [TLE 713, 714, *Sp.*; REE 46/137, Tarq.], *larziia* [SE 33, 532, Caere], *larzile* [CIE 1458, Cl.]), and many others. One should note that some inscriptions, containing the given forms (in particular, both inscriptions from Rome), belong to an earlier period, sixth to fifth centuries BCE (i.e., the change t/θ > z took place long before the voicing of *c*, *p*, *t*).

The interpretation of *z* as an affricate [tˢ] in the given stems seems to be the most probable. Apparently, it developed through the intermediate stage of a palatalized [t']. It can be easily seen that *t* changes into *z* before *i*, and *z* in some cases corresponds to the combination *ti*; apparently, the forms *larza* and *lart/θia*, *arnza* and *arnt/θia* are identical. Accordingly, in cases with the usage of the combination *ti* one can presuppose that it, in fact, was already pronounced as [tˢ] or, at least, as [t'], when the writing with *z* was only a particular tendency.

The name *araz* in the Roman inscription REE 47/29 is the most difficult to understand, because it corresponds to the masculine form *arat/θ* (cf., the text: *araz silqetenas spurianas*; it can be seen that the forms with *-na*, used in the genitive, belong exclusively to the masculine gender because feminine forms add *-i*, as shown in the examples above). The appearance of *z* can be explained either as a reflex of the final stem vowel *i* (which is less probable, because the masculine form *arat/θi-* was never attested), or as a result of the fact that pronunciation with an affricate spread to an original form by analogy with the feminine forms and indirect cases, where the transition into an affricate took place. However, one can suppose that in individual cases (for the first time, with the name *araz*) the letter *z* was used to designate the interdental *þ* (in consideration of the fact that writing with *φ* had a limited character). As a whole, the interpretation of a sound (or sounds) written with *z* for the first time is complicated because of the difficulties in understanding the presence of a sibilant *z* at this early stage of Etruscan writing.

It seems to be quite possible that the voiceless *t* already had a tendency to the transformation into *z*, before its transition into an aspirate *θ*. On the other hand, regular alternations of a later *θ* and *z* show the possibility of transformation into an affricate also in later times. In any case, an aspirate *θ* and its variant due to the position [t^s] cannot have phonemic differences.

It is doubtful whether we could accept the scheme, offered by Rix (1984^2, 219). Although he presupposed the transition [t] > [t'], he saw the further development of this sound into [þ] and [s], without giving any regularities of one or another transition, and interpreted *θ* only as [þ]. The fact that the transition [θ] > [þ], as was shown, was of a limited character, and *θ* in general designated the simple aspirate, was not taken into account

The point of a development of *t/θ* > *s* is even less conclusive. It is possible that Rix relied on the "alternation" in nominal stems *lart/θ* : *lar(i)s-* and *vVlt/θ-* : *vVls-* (evidently, one can find similar examples), but it is necessary to take into account that the roots of these names are *lar-* and *vVl-*, and the variants *lart/θ*, *lar(i)s-*, *lar(i)c-* and *vVlt/θ-* (cf., the widespread name *velθina*), *vVlc/χ-* (cf., also widespread *velχ-*, Latin *Vulcanus, Volcii*) are formed later with the different suffixal elements (which are common for both roots), so there are no phonemic correspondences *t/θ* : *s* here. We allow the possibility of a further simplification of the sound designated through *z*, but the existence of [t^s] itself at a certain stage seems to be the most probable.

The reflection of Greek d in some names in Etruscan is a similar (nevertheless a particular) case. One should cite two basic examples, *ziumiθe* (CIE 10412, third century BCE) and *arχaze* (CIE 10913, third to fourth centuries BCE). The writings given reflect the Greek forms Διομήδης and Ἀρκάδιος accordingly (Bonfante 1968, 57). It is quite typical that *z* appears only before *i* and is never attested while transcribing any other Greek names (one should hardly analyze the possibility of borrowing of a dialectal Greek word with the alternation Δ : Ζ). The author, who devoted a separate paper to the interpretation of the Etruscan letter *z*, presupposes that it can both designate an interdental (like English *th* in *think*) and an affricate [t^s], and insists on the absence of its voiced correlate [d^z] (Bonfante 1968, 58). However, taking into account that, in the third century BCE, voiced consonants had already appeared in Etruscan, there is nothing improbable in the fact that voiced affricates could exist too. We find it conceivable that, at the time being talked about, a voiced affricate could exist in Etruscan, at least as an allophone of [t^s].

Cases of an apparent voicing of *t* > *d* are more complicated than those we had observed above for *c* and *p*. In Latin writings, *d* appears in different positions and quite irregularly. Even the simplest cases when *t* is voiced before *i* show quite strange confusions (cf., CIE 819 *TIDI URINATIAL*, where *t* may become voiced or not in similar positions). Voicing is not attested in the inscriptions CIE 2882 (*TITIA*), CIE 2860 (*TITE*), etc. Reflexes of *t/θ*, attested in a few variants due to a widespread use of some names, are characterized by a special complicacy: *TANA* (CIE 2182), *DANA* (CIE 819), *THAN(N)A* (TLE 551, CIE 956, etc.): Etruscan *θana*; *LARDIA* (CIE 1068): Etruscan *larθia* (TLE 1144 *LARTIA*); *THOCERONIA* (CIE 715) : Etruscan *θucerna* (TLE 546, CIE 2335, etc.); the list may be continued. The Etruscan word *lautnita* "freedwoman," appearing both with simple *t* and aspirate *θ* (*lautniθa*), is presented in the form *LAUTNIDA* in the inscription TLE 542. For the first time, one should pay attention to the fact that, in cases of "voicing," *d* often appears in Latin writings in positions where in Etruscan an aspirate *θ* prevails or is at least possible. As was shown above, in cases with *c* and *p*, the evolution was possible either into an aspirate or into a voiced, and no confusion is observed there.

From our point of view, the appearance of voiced *d* in Latin transfers does not reflect so precisely the character of the Etruscan sound, as happens with *c* and *p*. By all appearances, it was caused by the peculiarities of Latin phonetics proper. The aspirates *ch* and *ph* were used in Latin to a limited extent (though they seldom penetrated into colloquial speech), but *t*, it seems, was never pronounced in Latin with the aspiration. This fact, along with the variants of writing *T, TH, D*, shows that in a number of cases these designations were a substitution of the uncharacteristic for Latin sound *θ*, but not a voiced *d*. As can be seen *TANA, THANNA, DANA* correspond to Etruscan *θana*, *LARDIA* (CIE 1068) to *larθia*, *ARNTHEAL* (CIE 561) to *arnθ(e)al*, etc. As a result, the known cases of true voicing can easily be marked out due to an absence of Etruscan forms containing an aspirate, because the same regularity must take place as in the evolution of *c, p*: it could transform either into a voiced or into an aspirate. Thereby, in cases with *TIDI* (CIE 819) : Etruscan *titi*, *SPEDO* (CIE 713 etc.) : Etruscan *spitu* we are dealing with the voiced consonant (the variants *tiθi, *spiθu are unknown).

In spite of the fact that the evolution of Etruscan *t was complicated by the appearance of interdental [þ], affricate [tˢ] and, possibly, [dᶻ], designated through *z*, the principle division of the aspirates and voiced remained. As a natural result, we do not observe the confusion of [tˢ] : *d* (in the given examples containing the voiced *d* the variants *tiz-, *spiz-, etc., are absent). Indirectly it indicates that the affricate [tˢ] developed not from the simple *t* but from the aspirate *θ*. The process of voicing took place later when the transition *t* > *θ* and possibly also *θ* > *z* had been completed. As in the cases analyzed above, we are dealing with two lines of correspondences, which are not caused positionally. In turn, the alternations *t* : [d] and *t* : *θ* : [tˢ], and also dialectal *φ* [þ], *h* do not show the appearance of new lexical and grammatical oppositions.

The given considerations about the occlusives and their reflections showing two independent ways of development, made us considerably change and supplement the existing (relatively recognized) picture. The unreliability of constructions explaining the changes of simple consonants in one or another direction due to a position in the word and phonetic environment, force us to entirely reject the "positional" approach for reconstructing the Etruscan phonological system as a whole, having admitted its certain utility for explaining a number of dialecticisms. As was shown, positional variants are too diverse and contradictory to become the basis of an integrated system. With some effort, one can find here an explanation for varied hypotheses. The clearly seen differentiation of the reflections of Etruscan consonants, which never mix, can be the only point of support here.

In our opinion, there were two series of phonemes in Etruscan. We shall mark them as "strong" and "weak." Corresponding phonemes are indiscernible in simple voiceless writings of *c* (*k*, *q*), *p*, *t* in earlier Etruscan inscriptions, and it tells us that, in this period, none of these series were close to phonetically voiced ones. As a result, the letters *b*, *d*, *g*, which existed in the prototype of the Etruscan alphabet, in the course of time became completely forgotten.

In what follows, we offer to transcribe the strong Etruscan consonants in this way: *k:*, *p:*, *t:*. It seems to be excessive to introduce special marks for weak ones. With regard to late Etruscan, it is also reasonable to use the common signs for aspirates and voiced (φ [*f*], χ, θ and *b*, *g*, *d*). For those cases when any alternations are absent and it is impossible to define the status of the source phoneme, we offer to use capital letters in the transcription: *K*, *P*, *T*. Proceeding from the phonetic universals and some observations of Tyrrhenian lexemes, it is possible to presuppose that the strong consonants exhibited a tendency to change into aspirates and the weak ones into voiced. It seems that the first type of change took place appreciably earlier, which is shown by the alternations in the Etruscan writings themselves, but the definition of the phonetic status of separate letters at some stage is not important in the main. It is paramount that, having introduced a new opposition in the sequel, we shall be able to etymologize Tyrrhenian stems with a higher degree of trustworthiness and, perhaps, differentiate the elements which are similar in graphics.

As can easily be seen, the main difficulty for further reconstruction is that, because of the absence of the signs for the voiced in Etruscan writing, material for the comparison of weak consonants is limited mostly by relatively late borrowings into Latin, Latinized forms, and glosses. However, there are two circumstances that help to overcome this difficulty to a considerable degree. Firstly, if some stem or morphological element appears many times in the inscriptions chronologically remote, or at least at the later stage of Etruscan, and the consonants it is composed of never change into the aspirates, we can speak of its weak nature with a high degree of confidence. As an example, we can give the rather widespread terms of relationship *clan* "son" and *puia* "wife," which, in the TLE collection, appear about 70 and 30 times respectively. The total absence of writings with χ or φ (*f*) make us suppose that here we have weak consonants, which subsequently became voiced. Secondly, the widespread use of aspiration and the absence of evident positional limits for this change make verisimilar the supposition that most or even all writings with voiceless may already hide voiced consonants. In any case, if one agrees to see weak consonants in such writings, only the variations in how to define their phonetic status are possible (here we can also deal with the allophones). Phonologically the pairs *k* - *g*, *p* - *b*, *t* - *d* would remain neutral, as the pairs *k:* - χ, *p:* - φ (*f*), *t:* - θ.

The presence of an opposition of strong and weak consonants, exposed in the cases of the pairs *k: - k, p: - p, t: - t*, make us think about the possibility of such opposition in the other groups of consonants, particularly, sibilants and sonants. Here the situation is somewhat complicated by a lesser amount of material for the comparison, but for the first time by the absence of evident changes in writing, which are widely attested for *k > χ, p > f, t > θ*. Below we shall try to summarize the existing material.

Both correspondences of Tyrrhenian strong and weak consonants in the foreign borrowings and Tyrrhenian reflections of different loanwords (primarily from Latin) are notable for higher complicacy. Some Tyrrhenian-Greek parallels were given above, but since Greek reflections are noted for distorting Tyrrhenian phonetics, we have to operate mainly with Tyrrhenian glosses and the most evident coincidences. For example, from the Aegean-Tyrrhenian toponym Ὑττηνία,[115] it may follow that the reduplication ττ in the Greek transfer is a specific reflection of a strong Tyrrhenian consonant *t:*.

Judging by some Tyrrhenian stems and Latin transfers, in Etruscan, as well as in Aegean-Tyrrhenian, there existed a labiovelar consonant $χ^v$, apparently, developed from $*q^v$. Here, as in the cases with $*k:$, $*p:$, $*t:$, the alteration of a voiced and an aspirate does not reflect phonemic differences. We have four[116] more or less reliable cases of the appearance of this sound in Etruscan and one in Aegean-Tyrrhenian. Probably, the number of examples may increase, primarily owing to the revelation of new forms where the labiovelar was changed into simple χ. The existence of a labiovelar is the most conclusive for the widespread nominal root $*tarχ^v$-: Latin *Tarquinia, Tarquinius, TARQUITI* (CIE 5910); the labial element often remains in Etruscan: *tarχvetena-s* (CIE 4922), *tarχunies* (TLE 300) but shows a tendency to disruption: *tarχis* (TLE 665), etc. It is absent in the available transfers of the place name "Tarquinii": *tarχnalθ(i)* (TLE 131, 174). In the Latin forms *Tarpeia, Tarpeius*, this root is presented in an Oscan-Umbrian phonetic appearance, with the phonetic development $*q^u > p$, characteristic for these languages. It is evident that these forms penetrated from the Sabinian dialect.

Labiovelar was also presented in the end of the words with the suffix *-aχ* marking tens (see below). Although this sound did not remain in Etruscan, the form *śiaχvis* "sixty" is known in the Lemnian inscription, which proves its existence. It is obvious that, in the given examples, labiovelar was appropriately simplified in the end of the word (similarly to Latin *neque : nec*), and does not reappear even before the suffixal elements with an initial vowel. It is also necessary to mention here the forms *haχ* and *hiχvetra* from the Zagreb book ("ten," see below). As can be seen, the labial adjunct is lost in the end of the word but remains before the vowel and pronominal enclitic *-tr-*. Preservation of the labial sound here may also indicate the relative antiquity of the text kept in the Zagreb book, or, at least, in some parts of it.

The correlation between *maχ* "five" and *muvaχ* "fifty" presupposes that one should reconstruct the root $*maχ^v$-. Subsequently, $χ^v$ was changed depending on its position in a word. It is possible that the form *muχ* in the inscription TLE 157 (Tarq.) also goes back

---

115. The structure of this word **hut:ena* "(group of) four" is explained below.
116. Here we are talking about the roots but not the derivatives as a whole.

to this root, but the context of this short inscription, which also contains abbreviations, remains unclear. It is most likely to mark out the labiovelar sound in the suffix of the collective plural -χva.

The combination χv, which might be used for marking the labiovelar, is also known in Rhaetic (cf., IR 83 *iskesaχviliske*), but any convincing examples are absent (in the given example even the word-boundary is unclear).

The principle for choosing the grapheme for *k (in Etruscan for *k: and *k), common for Latin, Faliscan, and Etruscan, is well known. It consists in using k before a, q before o, u (in Etruscan, of course, only before u), c before e, i and consonants. The form *kacriqu* (CIE 10159, Tarq., eighth century BCE) is a typical example of such a distribution. It is possible that, in Etruscan, this principle was determined by including the character of labiovelars. On the other hand, the writing of q before u in Etruscan usually is a purely graphical feature, which does not show the labial character of the corresponding sound at all. It can be seen that writing with q in Latin showed incomparably greater steadiness than with k, because the phonetic differentiation k : c was minimal. On the contrary, in Etruscan q disappears earlier while k and c both remain, and it indicates the early simplification of the labiovelar (in the Faliscan inscription c also appears in the position of the labiovelar under the influence of Etruscan: -*CUE* [in several examples], *CUICTO* [LF 144]). Such alternations in writing, as θ*ankviluš* (TLE 766) : *tancvil* (TLE 749) and some others possibly indicate it could be divided into two independent sounds (see below).

Thus, one can conclude that the evolution of the labiovelar went in two directions, which are its simplification into occlusive and its decomposition into two components, k/c and v. The second variant is virtually unprovable now, because we can say nothing about forms like *cver,* if they contained the labiovelar or if such a combination of consonants was secondary. On the other hand, the most widespread root with the labiovelar, *$*tarq^v$-/$*tarχ^v$-*, is usually simplified to *tarc/χ-*. Along with it, the labiovelar gradually changed from the voiceless to the aspirate, similar to the strong consonants *$*k:$, $*p:$, $*t:$, and there was also no opposition between the variants k^v and $χ^v$. In the etymological transcription, we offer to mark this sound as $*q:^v$.

As the labiovelar shows a tendency to develop into an aspirate, drawing it closer to the strong consonants, and any phonetic system tends to symmetry, one can presuppose the existence of a weak consonant, which had a labial adjunct. By analogy with the simple consonants *k, *p, *t it should, apparently, develop in the direction of [g^u]. Although we have not yet found traces of this sound, the methods for detecting it can be laid down. As in the cases with weak *k, *p, *t, the preservation of the group cv or c and total absence of writings with an aspirate χ could be the criteria here.

On the other hand, one should try to find parallels with the Italic languages. In the correlation of Etruscan writing with cv, c with an initial v in Latin transfer (as it is known, Italic $*g^w$- > Latin v-) or Oscan-Umbrian b (Italic $*g^w$ > Oscan-Umbrian b) can indicate a weak labialized sound.

Rix's supposition that some other consonants, including f (along with the main labial f), also could appear in the labialized variant, are almost speculative, because it is not grounded in reliable cases of writing for the group *fv. In particular, his reconstruction of the name *cafate* as *kaf^{u}ate* (Rix 1984²: 221) is not proved in any way (therefore, such forms as *capati-* (CIE 862), showing that this stem originally contained *p*, but not *f*, are ignored here).

The sound [f], which apparently was of a labial character at the earlier stage, in archaic orthography is written through the combinations *vh* or *hv*: *vhelequ* (TLE 56, Caere), *vhlakunaie* (TLE 429, V.-C.-A.), *hvuluves* (TLE 41), *hvlaveš* (REE 57/45, Caere), etc., where, as can be seen, the semivowel *v* and aspiration *h* are used, and such a combination, it seems, must reflect a labial sound. As in Etruscan, in Latin in the earliest times *f* could be written as *vh*: *vhevhaked* (fibula from Praeneste CIL I² 3) *feked* (in the so-called "Duenos inscription," CIL I² 4), classical *fecit*. One can perceive in it not only Etruscan-Latin interaction, but also similar phonetic features. Analogous writing also occurs in Umbrian. Subsequently, the sound [f] was written using the letter 8, 8; it seems that, because of the specificity of this sound, the letter marking it was an innovation in Etruscan writing and does not date from any West Greek grapheme (although it is known in the Lydian alphabet).

Further evolution of Etruscan *f* is not very clear. In the first place, it was complicated by the appearance of (< *p*). In later inscriptions, the transformation of *f* into the aspiration *h* takes place (cf., a widespread variant *hasti* [in the inscriptions of Clusium, Perusia, and Cortona] for a well-known feminine name *fasti*). We should mention that in Volsinii, where the name *fasti* also occurs, the variant *hasti* has not yet been found. The transformation *f* > *h* could take place not only in the beginning, but also in the middle of the word: *mehnatial* (CIE 4180, Per.), *mehnateś* (CIE 3888, Per.) : *mefanateś* (TLE 630, Cort.); *cahatial* : *CAFATIA* (TLE 605, Per.), here also *cafate* (CIE 4106, Per.), etc.

Echoes of this process, it seems, became apparent in Latin and the dialects close to it (cf., Sabinian *fasena* along with Latin *harena*; Etruscan *huze-* [REE 46/102, Caere et al.] : Latin *Fusius*). Such confusion is especially frequent in Faliscan: *FOIED* : Latin *hodie*; *HIRMIO* (LF 61), *HIRMIA* (LF 66) : *FIRMIO* (LF 71), *FIRMIA* (LF 143); *HILEO* (LF 96) : *filia*; *FE* (LF 72, 123) : *hic*. The forms with *f*, which arose under the influence of Etruscan, sometimes penetrated into archaic Latin: *fostis* instead of *hostis*, the pairs *fircus* – *hircus*, *Foratia* – *Horatia*, etc. Sometimes they supplanted primordial Latin variants: *fel* instead of **hel* (Greek χόλος) (Tronskij 2001: 138). The already expressed opinion that the confusion of *f* : *h* in Latin (including the dialect of Praeneste), Faliscan, and Sabinian (i.e., the languages which were in direct contact with Etruscan), can be entirely expected with an Etruscan influence (Giacomelli 1978, 515), seems to fully correspond to the facts. However, such a transformation also exists in other languages of the Romance area, where the substratum was completely different (i.e., Etruscan influence must be excluded in Spanish and Gascon, such as Spanish *hijo* (< *FILIU*) "son," *hacer* (< *FACERE*) "to make"; Gascon *hada* (< *FADA*) "fairy," *hilu* (< *FILU*) "thread."

The alternations which have been analyzed, as well as the writings *vh* and *hv*, indicate the labial character of Etruscan *f*, at least at the earlier period. In Latin in the archaic period, *f* was also labial, as can be seen in such forms as *COMFLUONT* (CIL I² 584), classical *confluent*. At the earlier stage, apparently, Etruscan and Latin *f* fully corresponded to each other, which was reflected in the borrowings of that time (for example, the name *fapi*: Latin *Fabius*). Further, when the character of *f* in Etruscan changed, in Latin the letter *f* was still used to transcribe Etruscan words. Evidently, with the lapse of time, the difference between *f* and *h* in Etruscan was entirely lost, which was reflected in the writings where *f* occurs in positions where its appearance was impossible from the etymological point of view: the form *ferclite* in the short bilingual from Perusia TLE 500 is the most typical of such examples (corresponds to Latin *HER[.] CLIT*).

The evolution *f* > *v* and *f* > *h* (see above) is quite difficult to understand. Different transformations rather reflect local dialects. We did not succeed in finding cases of the evolution of labial *f* proper into *v* (though the alternation in the name *avle* : *afle* requires special analysis). Known examples concern only *f*, originating from *p*. It seems that, in the process of time, the latter coincided with the labial *f* (the letter 8 (*f*) supplanted φ which became unnecessary). Apparently, the confusion of *f*: *v* chronologically applies to a somewhat earlier period than the transition *f* > *h*. When this transformation had happened, and *f* (< *p*) and *f*/*vh* had coincided, the development of *f* (< *p*) went in the same way, and we have examples of the evolution *p* > *f* > *h* (cf., above the form θ*ahna* (REE 52/72, Caere) from the word θ*apna*, and the evolution *capati-neś* (CIE 862) > *cafate* > *cahati-*).

The aspiration *h*, as we suppose, shows a considerable resemblance with Latin *h* in its development. In the transfers of names, including those exotic for Etruscan, as *hanipalus-cle* in TLE 890 (Pfiffig 1967), it fully corresponds to Latin. It seems that this sound weakened very early. In Etruscan inscriptions, we meet it only in the initial position, and in the few borrowings in Latin it is reflected in the same place: *harena*, the first element of a composite *haru-spex*, etc. Judging by the name Ὑττηνία, in Greek words dating from the Tyrrhenian stratum, Tyrrhenian is reflected as a rough breathing. In those cases when Etruscan aspiration appears in the middle of the word, it either goes back to *f* (*cahatial, mehnatial*) or is preserved after the act of combining words (cf., the compound pronominal form *cehen* [TLE 619, 621], occurring in the area of Perusia, along with *hen* [TLE 570]). Besides, *h* disappears in cases of earlier word combinations. The root *halχ* "ten" loses *h* in the forms for Etruscan tens (cf., below the forms *cealχ-, cialχ-, muvalχ-, śealχ-* [Lemnian *śialχv-*], *śemφalχ-, cezpalχ-*).

Clear cases of the omission of *h* in writing are unknown with the exception of *alχu* (TLE 2[10, 18]), *alχuv-aisera* (TLE 939). Evidently, this orthography was kept as traditional. It seems quite probable that the early weakening and disappearance of Latin *h*, almost never pronounced in the classical period (Tronskij 2001: 57), can be connected directly to the influence of the Etruscan language.

The question about the affricate [tˢ], partly touched upon above, is quite difficult. It is not known if it appears as a result of the evolution of *t*/θ or could initially exist as an independent phoneme. Quite often the names or, for example, widespread titles *zilc, zilaθ* are transcribed through [tˢ] in European and Russian studies, but such *a priori* judgment seems to be unprovable for the present (and, more likely, refutable). Really, we cannot check this reading using Latin transfers, even if [tˢ] existed as an independent phoneme, in Latin it should be transcribed through *s*, we believe. As evident parallels, one can adduce names of cities: Latin *Cisra, Volsinii* along with Etruscan *keizra, velzna*, and also Latin *Pansa* with Etruscan *panza* (CIE 2915, etc.), *VENSIUS* : *venzile* in the bilingual TLE 473, etc. Thereby, we do not have a sufficient foundation to read Etruscan *zeta* as [t^s] but not [z].[117]

While analyzing Etruscan sibilants, one should first decide which phonetic differences are covered under the writings of *s, ś, š, ṣ,* and *z*. As was said above, *š* and *ṣ* disappear very early, and it is senseless to try to find any phonetic opposition here. The Etruscan letters *ś* and *s* alternate regularly (which is especially noticeable in a genitive suffix), sometimes even in the same inscription and, apparently, different writings also do not reflect any real opposition. Such alternations often appear in this research, so there is no necessity to dwell on them again. From our point of view, the preference for which variant to choose depended on graphics, similarly to Greek *s* and *ς*. There was a general tendency to the predominance of writing with *s* in the southern areas of Tuscany and with *ś* in the northern, but there also existed a great multitude of local peculiarities. For example, in the area of Tarquinii, *s* often stands in an initial or a final position and *ś* in the middle in the same inscription. Such alternations, as well as many others, show that a single scribal tradition never existed in Tuscany.

The question of the correlation between *ś, s,* and *z* is more complicated. The grapheme *z*, which is usually transcribed as [z] or [t^s] while reading names and place names, as was said above, sometimes appears in the position where one could expect *s* or *ś*. So, we see such forms as *cealχuz* (TLE 1$^{X\,2}$) along with *cealχus* (TLE 1$^{IX\,\gamma 2}$), *cealχuś* (TLE 1$^{XII\,12}$), *cialχuś* (TLE 1$^{XII\,50}$), etc., *zuθina* (TLE 69, along with widespread *suθi, suθina*), the name *zerturi* (CIE 4355, Per.) : *sertur, serθur* (Latin *Sertorius*), *zerapiu* (TLE 475) : Greek Σέραπις, *zpurana* (TLE 421, along with *spur-* "town," *spurana* "urban," here also the frequently occurring name *spuri(a)na* and some others (cf., also the numeral *śar-* "twelve" in the text of the Zagreb mummy and *-zar-* in the compound *huθzars* (TLE 191), *zeriś* in the inscription TLE 380. The Etruscan form *CEZAR(T)LE* (CIE 708, 709), dating from the stem **kaisVr-*, analyzed above, which also appears in the name *Cisra – Caere*, demonstrates an earlier voicing of intervocalic *-s-*. It should be noted that the inscription is written with the Latin alphabet.

The opposite process (i.e., the use of *ś* or *s* in the place of *z*) is rarely observed. As a natural result of the almost entire absence of Latinized parallels, it is hard to define the character of Etruscan *s/ś* and *z* (as is well known, *z* had disappeared in the Latin alphabet when the intervocalic sibilants had changed into *r* and was reconstructed later, being used almost exclusively in words of Greek origin [Tronskij 2001: 73]). We have succeeded in finding only one reliable nominal stem, where Etruscan *z* is also transcribed through *z* in Latin: *Mezentius* along with Etruscan *mezenties* (REE 56/73, Caere). The letter *z* never appears in Etruscan glosses, saved by Roman authors. The traditional writing of *-ss-* in archaic orthography, used for voiceless, shows the corresponding pronunciation in such Etruscan words as *PABASSA* (TLE 832),

---

117. On the other hand, we should take into account the earlier reading of Greek Z.

mantis(s)a (TLE 844), *favis(s)ae, caussa*, etc. (It can be easily seen that, in all these words, we are dealing with the same Etruscan suffix). In Latin transfers, *s* is preserved in suffixal elements (cf., *PEDROS* [TLE 542] and many others). Actually, we can operate almost exclusively with orthographical alternations, but they are quite rare and monotonous.

It is not excluded that, in the course of time, phonetic differences between *z* and *ś/s* became obliterated, but we are to ascertain in which direction their development went. Early on it was an unvoicing of *z* rather than voicing of *ś/s*. A comparison between *z* and *ś/s* is also complicated because of the presence of the grapheme *z*, dissembling an affricate described above. We rarely find forms showing phonemic differences between *z* and *ś/s* (i.e., lexical pairs) where the differentiation between voiced and voiceless can be demonstrated. As an example, one can adduce the nominal root *silqetenas* (REE 47/29), sometimes erroneously understood as a derivative of the title *zilc* (in fact, this root must be compared with non-Indo-European "rural" lexica: *silicia, siligo, siliqua*; here also Σιλακηνοί [Strabo XVI, 1, 18], *Seligius* [cf., REE 29/47]). But, because the presence of the affricate in the title is still possible, we cannot oppose **silVk-* to **zil-Vk:-*, **zil-Vt:-* by the category of voicing.

It seems that, in some period of the history of the Etruscan language, the unvoicing of *z* took place, which caused some confusion in orthography. The well-known Faliscan word using *z*, *ZENATUO* (LF 59), which could appear only under the influence of Etruscan, definitely shows that *z* could cover a voiceless sound (i.e., the phonetic difference between *s* and *z* was lost). It is doubtful whether one can suppose that, in the words historically containing [z], this writing was preserved by tradition so strictly that we do not have any variants with *s* instead of *z*. But, even if we are dealing with an affricate as the main sound, designated as *zeta*, one cannot deny that, at the earlier period, *z* could also mark [z] besides an affricate, because in the opposite case the appearance of *z* in the position of *s* would be absolutely impossible.

We do not yet have any grounds to correlate an existing opposition of *s* : *z* with the distribution of strong and weak consonants, which is evident for many of the consonants analyzed above. In addition, if one accepts that the distribution *s* : *z* corresponds to such opposition, it would follow that it is the only case of such distribution of strong and weak consonants in archaic orthography (with the exception of isolated *n:* and *n*), which is unlikely.

New voicing of *s*, if it took place in the later period (apparently, such forms as *CEZAR-* indicate just that), cannot be considered in the context of the distribution of *s* : *z*. In contrast to the latter, it cannot be phonologized. Therefore, the only option is that it would be reflected in orthography.

Some Etruscan forms are most uncommon. It seems that they underwent changes similar to Latin and Umbrian rhotacism (i.e., the development *s* > *r* in intervocalic position in both languages and also in final position in Umbrian. Thus, in a group of funeral inscriptions of the same kin from Perusia, the forms *navesi* (CIE 3896), *navesial* (CIE 3892, 3894) are there along with *naverial* (CIE 3893, 3895). The same stem is also present in the inscriptions from Volsinii: *nevrnies* (CIE 5050), *naveries* (CIE 5198).

Besides this most striking example, rhotacism can be observed in at least two more stems. One must draw attention to the name *helverial* (CIE 3965–67), because *r* does not belong to the stem, which can be seen from the structure of the kin name *helvi-na-ti* (REE 44/42, Vols.). With the suffix *-na-* and a similar nominal formant unknown, there is nothing else to do but presuppose that *r* appeared as a result of rhotacism from the genitive suffix, which, in this case, is used in combination with another suffix, *-al*, often collocating with it. The form in the bilingual from Pyrgi χ*urvar* (from χ*osfer*) also cannot be explained by anything except a similar process.

Of course, the given examples do not permit us to speak about any widespread rhotacism in Etruscan. The large majority of words with intervocalic *s*, especially in the genitive suffix, remain for the whole history of the Etruscan written language. From our perspective, such a phenomenon at the periphery of the Etruscan area was caused by the interaction with Italic languages, to wit, Umbrian (in the area of Perusia and Volsinii) and Latin (Pyrgi-Caere).

We have no data about the existence of "swish" sounds in Etruscan or any other Tyrrhenian language. A supposition about reading the Etruscan *ś* (M) as *sh* in English *shin* (Bonfante 1990, 14) is not confirmed by any examples.

There were four sonants in the Tyrrhenian languages: *l, m, n,* and *r*. We have some reasons to presuppose that they could have syllabic and nonsyllabic variants (particularly, Rix held such an opinion [Rix 1984^2, 216]), but, in most cases, it is not possible to speak about this category with confidence. It seems that all sonants could act as syllabic (only the situation with *m* is questionable). Nearly all such examples, with the exception of the words which can be understood as abbreviations and evidently mistaken writings, are provided by the pronouns: compare numerous forms such as *clθ, cn, cnl, cr, tn, tr*. On the other hand, one can presuppose that these words do not have semantic, phrasal stress (they are often used as enclitics), and vowels had been lost there before the writing appeared.

Etruscan sonants *l, r,* and *m* are notable for their greater stability. We did not manage to find clear examples of their alternations or dropping. Tyrrhenian sonants *l, r,* and *m* do not display any alternation in Etruscan texts nor in Latin borrowings. The continually registered Minoan alternations *r - l* and *l - d*, also reflected in some parts of the Latin vocabulary (a few archaisms and Sabinisms) do not occur in proper Etruscan texts and are caused by the influence of other languages in foreign transfers.[118] In Etruscan inscriptions, sonants are never reduplicated graphically.

There are singular cases of dissimilation of a nasal group. Thus, the Greek names Ἀγαμέμνων and Μέμνων appear as *aχmemrun* and *memrun* correspondingly (Rix 1984^2: 222). The analogous evolution of sonants can be observed in the Latin words *groma* and *creper*, passed from Greek through Etruscan (γνώμων, κνέφας).

The situation with the sonant **N* is somewhat more difficult. One should analyze two aspects of its development: the graphical gemination of *n* in Latin transfers and singular Etruscan inscriptions, and cases of its visible dropping in a few Etruscan writings. Cases of variation of simple and reduplicated *n* can be observed in a substantial part of Etruscan lexemes (mostly in kin names) in Latin sources. Usually the studies mention an

---

118. Rare alternations such as *cuchnial* (TLE 126, Tarq. etc.) : *cucrina-θur* (TLE 635, Cort.) are unclear; it is possible that here we are dealing with different word-formational suffixes.

Etruscan origin of the suffixes -*na*, -*ina* (-*inna*), -*ena* (-*enna*), -*eno*- (-*enno*-), in detail examined below (cf., Tronskij 1953, 124), but the cases of gemmination of *n* are never explained. Obviously, orthographical variants were consolidated inconsistently, in fact, randomly (cf., below the borrowings of such a type). It is quite important to note that Latin transfers show reduplication when it is not possible to observe it using Etruscan orthography (such a possibility is provided primarily by brief bilinguals: cf., *THANNA* [CIE 956] along with the widespread Etruscan name θ*ana*, *HANNOSSA* – *hanusa* [CIE 1295-96]), etc.

On the other hand, one can find cases of the dropping of the grapheme *n* in the lexica borrowed from Etruscan. But it seems this sound originally was present in the stem. The primary example would be the word *palatum* (TLE 831 *falado*), described in detail above. It also has the orthographical variant *falando*. The presupposed Etruscisms *hirudo* and *hirundo* most likely have the same origin. Also, in Latin they differ in meaning (just *n* falls in one case). It is possible that one should add the variant *arut* (REE 49/38), Faliscan *ARUTE* (LF 129) without a nasal along with the name *ar(u)nt:*- found everywhere. Such a peculiarity of orthography, close to the Latin principal of omission of *n* before *s*,[119] is evidently caused by the weakening of *n* before the consonant, which is known from different languages of the world.

It is possible that the mentioned variations are directly bound with one of the main conclusions of the chapter, notably with the question of strong and weak consonants in the Tyrrhenian languages. If we accept that the existing cases of reduplication of *n* in Latin transfers reflect a strong consonant, it will be seen that, in many (or most) cases, simple *n* in Etruscan texts marked the strong sound with minimal tendencies to orthographical gemmination. In addition, it may seem that in the case of *n* (in contrast to *k: - k, p: - p, t: - t*), there was practically no orthographical difference between strong and weak. But, from our point of view, this may clarify the situation.

Apparently, the omission of *n* in writing indicates the weak sonant, which could possibly change into a nasal overtone of a preceding vowel. Such an *n* was optionally reflected in Latin transfers, because in Latin proper the tendencies to nasalization were minimal. In fact, weak *n* in Etruscan writing (at least at the later stage of its development) makes phonetic reconstruction slightly more complicated, but, in some cases, we can overcome the difficulties due to the presence of foreign transfers.

One can affirm with certainty that the semivowels *v* [w] and [j] (written using *i*) also existed in Etruscan. The fact that, in some cases, *v* should be understood as a semivowel is confirmed by numerous alternations in diphthongs like *lauciś-/lavcis-, eterau-/eterav-, lautn-/lavtn-*, and confusion in writing in such forms as *arvn*θ*e* (TLE 277). In Latin, in the pre-classical and classical periods, *v* also resembled English [w] rather than the later occlusive (and in some Italian dialects similar pronunciation continues to this day), and such parallels between Latin and Etruscan as *Aulus* : *aule/avle* confirm our treatment of the Etruscan sound as [w].

---

119. Cf., *COSOL* (from which the abbreviation *cos*, stable even in the Empire epoch) "consul," *CESOR* (CIL I^2 8) "censor."

In some cases, *v* quite unexpectedly appears after *u* in different positions (cf., *aχuv* [TLE 939, orig. inc], etc.). It is possible that, here, some kind of diphthongal splitting takes place, but it is more probable that this sound is parasitic. In such a quality, *v* often appears in Etruscan inscriptions both after vowels and consonants. It can be observed in some examples from Chapter 6: Morphology.

The semivowel [j] is seen mainly as a component of the diphthongs *ai, ei*, possibly also *ui*, and in the combinations of type *-aie*, occurring in the final position of some names (cf., *vhlakunaie* given above), and other similar clusters of vowels. Such a [j] also is more likely to be parasitic, and it appears in relatively late inscriptions. Separation of this sound is grounded more by language universals than proven facts but seems to be quite acceptable.

In the inscription of the Lemnian stele, a similar sound, apparently, occurs in diphthongal combination: in verbal suffix *ai* and in the name *holaieś* (evidently non-Tyrrhenian; though the name *Ὀλαίης is not known in Greek, its Greek origin seems to be more verisimilar).

The results of our studies of Tyrrhenian consonantism, based primarily on Etruscan material, are represented in Table V.

Table V. Etruscan consonants

Phonemes		Earlier period		Later period	
		Phonetic meaning	Orthography	Phonetic meaning	Orthography
Occlusive	*k	k	k, c, q	k, g	c, k, **g**
	*k:	k:, χ	k, c, q, χ	χ	χ, c, k, **x**
	*t	t	t	t, d	t, **d**
	*t:	t, θ	t, θ	θ t^s(i) *p* *χ* *h*	θ, t, **d**, **th** ti, θi, z φ χ h
	*p	p	p	p, b	p, **b**
	*p:	p:, φ	p, φ	φ, f	φ, f
Labial	*f	f	hv, vh	^{h}	h, f
				w	w
Aspirated	*h	h	h	h, ø	h, f, ø
Labio-velar	*k^w	k^w	kv, cv (??)	k^w, g^w	cv, c, **b** (??)
	*k:^{w}	k:^{w}, χ^w χ	kv, cv, χv χ	χ^w χ w	χv, **qu**, **p** χ v
Sibilants	*s	s	s, ś, š, ş	s	s, ś, z, s-, **-s,** **-ss-**
				r	r
	*z	z	z	z, s	z, s, **s**, **z**
Affricate (?)	*t^s	t^s	z, s	t^s, d^z (?)	z, s, **s**
Sonants	*r	r	r	r	r
	*l	l	l	l	l
	*m	m	m	m	m
	*n	n	n, ø (?)	n, ø (?)	n, ø, **n** (?)
	*n:	n:	n	n	n, -nn-, **-nn-**
Semivowels	*w	w	v, u	w, v (?)	v, u
	*j	j	i	j	I

Etruscan dialecticisms are given in *italics*; Latin and Faliscan transfers in bold (not for all sounds but only where they give additional information); b and p as labiovelar mean Oscan-Umbrian phonetic appearance; mark (?) refers only to the last sound or grapheme.

CHAPTER 6

MORPHOLOGY[120]

MORPHEME STRUCTURE

All the morphemes of the Minoan and Tyrrhenian languages can be divided into two groups: primary (categorematic) and syntactic. Their structures are quite different, so identification of the root and suffixal elements in Minoan and Tyrrhenian words do not pose significant difficulties.

Consonant endings of root morphemes are a fundamental feature of all the languages being analyzed. Only five reliable exceptions from this rule have been attested yet (all from Etruscan; a pronoun *tV-* is also found in the inscription of the Lemnos stele): first person sg. personal pronoun *mi*, demonstrative pronouns *tV-* and *kV-*, and also numerals *ki* "3," *sa* "6" (numeral *θun* "1" sometimes loses its final *-n*, but this sound is always reconstructed before word-formational and morphological suffixes as in below *θun-s, θun-em, θun-ur, θun-χ*). We suppose that the numerals "3" and "6" were borrowed (*ki* displays indubitable resemblance with Hurrian *kig* "3" (and also with the Basque form *hirur*), while *sa* resembles more an Indo-European type. Thereby, the roots of type CV are now limited to these three oldest pronouns.

The other root morphemes are generally divided into one- and two-syllable units. The simplest one-syllable morphemes are represented by the types VC and CVC (Minoan *ἀμ- in ἄμυλος "pie made of a good flour"; *ϝελλ- "snake," *κορ- "top, head" [?], *μαρ- "swine," *νικ- "fig," Etruscan *al-* "to be granted," *am-* "to be," *ar-* "to become,"

---

120. According to considerations explained above, the conclusions given here are founded almost exclusively on the material of the languages of the first millennium BCE. Minoan parallels are singular, nevertheless they are quite tempting as they always have special emphasis on them.

ap- "father," *at-* "mother," *cer-* "to be placed," *mar-* "to rule," *mul-* "to be dedicated," *seχ* "daughter," *θun* "1").

The type CVC in Tyrrhenian can become more complicated by sonants *m, n, l, r* and sibilants *s, z,* taking on the appearance of CVC₁C, CC₁VC and CC₁VC₁C, where C₁ is a sibilant or a sonant (*cezp* "8," *nunθ-* "to be made a sacrifice," *clan* "son," *sval-* "to live," *frVnT-* "lightning" [?]). By analogy, one can suppose also the type VC₁C, but the existing examples are insecure (so, Minoan *αρτ- "bread" can contain not only the combination SC but also a specific phoneme; the Etruscan *alp-* "donation" is likely to be not an independent root but a suffixal derivation of *al-*; and the form *ailf* [TLE 234] is absolutely mysterious; in addition, it has something in common with the root *alf-* "white," which is borrowed from Umbrian, etc.).

The simple types VC and CVC can contain diphthongs (Minoan *ka-u-d-* place name root, Minoan and Etruscan *ais* "god," *lauk:-* "to reign," Etruscan *keiz-ra* "Caere" (the name of the city), *fraus* "lie" [in the Latin borrowing, presumably from Etruscan], etc.). As was shown above, root diphthongs are quite typical for Minoan and Tyrrhenian languages.

Bisyllabic roots are incommensurably rarer than the monosyllabic type, especially in the Tyrrhenian languages. Accordingly, here it is also more difficult to mark out possible variants containing sonants, sibilants, and diphthongs. One can outline two main types: VCVC and CVCVC (Minoan *αμαρ-, plant name, *αταλ- "plum," Tyrrhenian *aKas-* "to make" [?], *aKVr* "eagle"). From the second type, the most reliable are: Minoan *penel-*[121] (?), Etruscan *tVvVr-* "to establish," *ve/ital-* "bull." As an example of the root with sonant, one can adduce *amPVl-* "sun, spring." Minoan examples are far less reliable, because they can reflect a variant with a vocalic prefix.

The lengthening of the root in Minoan can happen due to its partial reduplication: compare ἀκακαλλίς "narcissus flower" (in Hesychius "ἄνθος ναρκίσσου. Κρῆτες") along with Ἀκάλλη (the name of Minos's daughter) and ἄκαρα (nom. pl.) "foot," "thigh" (in Hesychius "τὰ σκέλη. Κρῆτες"); μαίκυλον along with μιμαίκυλον "fruit of the strawberry tree." In the theonym (?) (*j*)*a-sa-sa-ra*, it is possible that both partial reduplication and prefixation are reflected. On the other hand, *ais* "god" can appear with *i* not being reflected in Linear writing.

Another type of reduplication can be observed in the derivatives of two roots: *γαλ- and *μαρ- (cf., also in Chapter 7: Word Formation). The root *γαλ- in its pure type can be found in the form ἄγλις "clove of garlic" (with metathesis), and with suffixation in the plant name γάλινθος preserved by Hesychius. In addition, one should note the reduplication of the initial consonant in γέλγις (gen. -ιθος, -ιδος), also with the meaning "clove of garlic." In the same way, from the root *μαρ- (cf., in Doric μαρύομαι) suffixal μήρινθος "threads, rope, cord" and reduplicated μέρμις (gen. also -ιθος, -ιδος) forms with the same meaning are made. One might propose that the reduplication caused the transformation of the root vowel: α > ε. Thereby, Ernschedt's supposition about the borrowing from Egyptian (1953, 51) is not confirmed. If the resemblance with

---

121. Πηνελόπη.

Coptic ⲙⲁⲣⲙⲏⲧⲉ "a thing girt about the middle (?), belt" is not accidental, the direction of the borrowing must be the opposite. It also leads us to think that some other words with ιθος- genitive (including ὄρνις) date from Minoan, too. This suffix may be just a variant of -νθ- with a weakened nasal.

Minoan and Tyrrhenian syntactic morphemes, to which belong word-formational and morphological suffixes and postpositions, are distinguished by their brevity and simplicity. Three-phoneme syntactic morphemes, it seems, occur on rare occasions (cf., Minoan -υ(μ)β-), in contrast to combinations like *CC, *VV; actually, all the suffixes appear as V, C, VC or CV. Here we would abstain from giving examples, because all understandable syntactic morphemes are analyzed in the previous and following chapters.

Sometimes in the Etruscological literature, supposed three-phoneme suffixes are given, but these examples are extremely unreliable (so, the allative suffix appears first as -ri, and -e-ri, evidently, acts as a combination with a connecting vowel). The "suffix" -θur is actually a plural form ending in -te. The collective noun suffix -χva contains labiovelar [χᵛ] (i.e., one consonant [in detail see below], etc.).

Since root morphemes are quite short and the length of the syntactic never exceeds the bounds of a syllable, in complex Etruscan forms it is quite easy to mark out their components (only the attribution of a connective vowel presupposes some difficulties.) Compare the following examples: in *lauχ-um-ne-θi* "in the royal palace," where the root is *lauχ-* "to reign," *-um(-)* and *-ne(-)* act as widespread word-formation suffixes,[122] *-θi* a locative suffix. The form *θun-χ-er-ś* "the first (gen. pl.)" contains the root *θun* "one," the suffix of ordinal numeral *-χ* (an adjective originally), plural suffix (-[V]r) and genitive suffix (-ś).

GENERAL INFORMATION ABOUT MORPHOLOGY

The Tyrrhenian languages are all agglutinative. Apparently, one can presuppose the same for Minoan. The forms presented in Tyrrhenian inscriptions can be subdivided into inflected and uninflected. Such a division approximately corresponds to the division into categorematic and syntactic words. The border between categorematic and syntactic words is not insuperable, because fossilized derivative forms can move into the category of uninflected.

The distribution of the inflected words as parts of speech is based on the set of grammatical categories, inherent in these words. Inflected words formally differ from the uninflected only in their morphemic and grammatical structure. Any word form includes the root which adds different affixes (possibly, it is better to say "suffix" and "infixes"; in Minoan there are also widespread prefixation and partial reduplication of the root). All the nuances of word-formational and grammatical meanings are reproduced by the instrumentality of these exact affixes. In earlier Etruscan case forms we can occasionally

---

122. *-ne* is a reduced or dialectal variant of *-na*.

also find circumfixes—archaic constructions using them are preserved only in the sacral style inscriptions.

Currently one can ascertain that grammatically meaningful phonetic alternations in Tyrrhenian languages are totally absent, and there are also no grounds to speak about them with regard to Minoan. The languages of the first millennium BCE also did not use prefixation at all. Only singular cases of word-compounding are known (except for complex numerals where it is implemented regularly).

By all appearances, periphrastic grammatical forms are not found in any Tyrrhenian inscription.[123] Stable syntactic constructions with some specific meaning have not been found either. Really, one cannot easily classify such singular repetitive forms as *mlaχ mlakas* or *mini-pi ca-pi*.

In compliance with the general tendencies in development of the agglutinative languages, any Tyrrhenian grammatical element expresses only one grammatical meaning. Even such an affix as the archaic feminine genitive formant *-a*, which would seem to combine two functions (i.e., gender and case), is not, in fact, close to an inflectional element because it is added to the forms which already have the feminine suffix, that is, such a feature can be understood as a result of distribution of the originally neutral genitive suffixes for different stem categories.[124] A similar distribution can be observed among the plural formants, which also indicate animate and inanimate nouns. One can say that the Tyrrhenian languages of the first millennium BCE are characterized by a moderate degree of synthesis: along with the whole absence of prefixes, no more than four (or possibly five) elements are counted in well-understood suffixal chains (with the exception of pronominal enclitics).

It is hardly possible to give the exact number of suffixal elements now with a high degree of reliability. Not less than fourteen nominal and sixteen verbal suffixes (nonmetering word-formational) can be analyzed in Etruscan. Some of them are common.[125]

The forms adding pronominal enclitics are notable for their greater complexity (in structure, but not in interpretation). The larger part of them belongs to the Zagreb texts, which somewhat complicates understanding their lexical meanings.

Since Etruscan is preserved for the most part in Tyrrhenian inscriptions and remains the only Tyrrhenian language present for a long period of time, it is only here where one can observe diachronic changes of some grammatical facts. Etruscan grammatical constructions are characterized by different degrees of stability. For example, turns of speech expressing belonging did not seriously change during the whole period of Tyrrhenian writing, while the differences of archaic and later verbal constructions are rather noticeable.

---

123. The verbal construction from the inscription TLE 135 is the sole possible "pretender." It will be analyzed below in Chapter 6, Verb section.

124. In the genitive feminine form *lartia* and some others there are two independent indicators: the feminine suffix *-i*, appearing also in the nominative case, and the genitive suffix *-a*.

125. We do not count complex forms; for example, the formants *-pi*, *-s*, *-l* are included here as opposed to combinations *pul*, *peś*.

In the category of inflected words, one can delimit two main classes: nominal and verbal, based on different suffixation. Derivative nouns and verbs are marked out more clearly than simple roots, which in the case of the absence of grammatical suffixes can be recognized by the known lexical meanings of syntactic function (i.e., simple nominal and verbal roots do not differ formally). Thus, the root *ziχ-* "to write" can form both verbs and nouns. Personal forms *ziχunce* "(he) wrote" (trans.) and *ziχuχe* "is written" are known when the unmarked root *ziχ* itself is translated as "book" (cf., *ziχ neθsra-c acasce* "composed haruspicinal book" [TLE 131]). Simple verbal roots also act as imperatives (*tur* "give" sg. or pl.), which is quite common.

The distinction between verbs and nouns is also drawn in the main word-formational models. Thus, the stems complicated with the suffix *-na* can act only as nominal forms (it is one of the most evident layers of relic Tyrrhenian lexica both in Latin and Aegean substrata), but, for example, stems with the suffixes *-m* and *-r* can act both as nominal and verbal: *pulum* "star," *serθur* proper name (Latin *Sertorius*), but *lucumu* "ruling," *lucairce* "ruled." For more detail, see Chapter 7: Word Formation.

The nominal class is distinguished by the categories of number, case, animateness or inanimateness, and relicts of gender. Singular forms are never marked while plurals are formed with different suffixes. Number and case, in compliance with the agglutinative structure, are expressed with different suffixes, and the plural suffix precedes the case formant (cf., *ais-er-as* genitive plural "[of] gods"). Plural suffixes, in fact, express the meaning of plurality and animateness at the same time. In singular forms, the last category seems to be reflected only in archaisms containing a gender indicator.

It is difficult to distinguish adjectives within the nominal class. The situation is complicated by the fact that adjectives are not found among Etruscan glosses, and those which can be observed in relic lexica belong to the same types which can be observed in Etruscan texts. Actually, all Etruscan adjectives having trustworthy translations (*spurana* "urban," *suθina* "funeral," *rasnal* "Etruscan," coming primarily from the epitaphs) are mostly derivatives from known nominal roots and thus cannot be distinguished from genitive forms. Simple qualitative adjectives are almost unknown. As reliable examples, one may list only the lexemes *hamφe* "right" and *laive* "left" (the last from Latin *laevus*), ascertained recently (Gianecchini 1996). It is possible that we can mark out the simple root meaning "white": *cerussa* "lead white,"[126] borrowed in Latin. It can be seen that the word is formed similarly to reliable Etruscisms such as *mantissa* and *favissa* (see below). However, it could be formed in Etruscan from a Greek root. There are no data about the degrees of comparison. The existing supposition (Pfiffig 1969, 100) is not grounded enough.

There are no special markers for numerals. The numerals, showing different ways of forming complicated stems, add the same suffixes as the other nominal parts of speech. By all appearances, the only exception known for certain is a "subtraction" suffix *-em*, which appears in complex numerals with the second component "seven," "eight," "nine." See below about the ways of forming such numerals. On the whole, the

---

126. Despite the traditional etymology (Walde-Hofmann 1938–1956, s. v. *cerussa*) from Greek *κηρόεσσα* "wächsern" and κηρός "wax"; the resemblance with "*mantissa*" type is ignored there.

Etruscan system of numeration can be characterized as tenfold with traces of twelvefold (relics of a twentyfold system are minimal if they exist at all).

Clarification of the structure of Tyrrhenian verbs seems to be even more tightly bound to Etruscan data than the other main grammatical categories. While Etruscan verbs are quite diverse, the Rhaetic material is extremely limited and does not show any substantial differences from Etruscan. There are only nine verbal forms (divided into two types) attested in Aegean-Tyrrhenian, South Lusitanian forms are singular, and there are no more than one to two forms presumably marked out in Eteo-Cypriote. In turn, it may call into question our understanding of the system as a whole and unfounded conclusions about the subtle nuances of meaning for some ill-understood formants.

In Etruscan, as in the other Tyrrhenian languages, we can mark out finitary, participial (quite diverse), imperative, optative, and gerundive verbal forms. Finitary forms as a statement of action are opposed to imperative, optative, and gerundive (inducement to action). In turn, all of them are opposed to participial, marking agent or state (cf., part. I Etruscan *svalas* "living, alive," *zilaχnθas* "who was *zilc*," Aegean-Tyrrhenian *maraś* "ruling," part. II *tevaraθ* "observing," and many others). Also, some finitary forms (med.-pass.) have been substantiated with the lapse of time: Etruscan *lupu* "died," *alqu* "was donated," but *zicu* "writing" was already usually "scribe" in translations (= Latin *Scribonius*), *pleku* "rider," etc.

Undoubtedly, the number and characteristics of these categories must be defined more exactly in the future. There are also a number of forms for which no satisfactory explanations have yet been offered. The most widespread types for which there is not a plausible interpretation at the present time are forms ending in *-a*, constructed both from simple roots (*am-a* (TLE $1^{X\ 9,\ 14}$, 570) from *am-* "to be") and roots marked with different suffixes such as *nunθ-en-a* from *nunθ-* "to make a sacrifice, be sacrificed" (cf., below *muluvana*).

Finitary and participial forms have such categories as voice (closely bound with transitivity and intransitivity), and tense and/or aspect. They do not have gender distinctions. Known finitary forms do not differ in number and, probably, person. The forms being substantivized which can be declined (in cognomens for the first time) are likely to have the category of number (one can presuppose the presence of the forms ending *-u-r*). Some derivatives of such forms regularly appear in plural (the type ending *-u-te*, which looks like *-u-θur* in plural, but this transformation does not differ from nominal derivatives). Participial forms have the categories of voice, time, or aspect and do not differ in gender. Imperative forms probably express tense or aspect and do not have the category of number. Gerundive is presented by the forms derived from simple roots using the directive postposition *-(e)ri*. Concerning the possibility of its further morphological changes nothing is known (most likely, the form is invariable), but the syntactic function is explained quite satisfactorily. In their mood, all known finitary forms are sharply opposed to optative and imperative. It seems that the gerundive is close to the latter. All the reliably interpreted finitary forms are of indicative meaning.

All these word classes can be contrasted with uninflected forms. Analysis of the latter presupposes greater difficulties. Syntactic words are known only from Etruscan.[127] In most inscriptions, they are present in minimal quantity and are hardly understood.

There are singular conjunctions and particles. Prepositions most likely do not exist as a special word class, and postpositions are practically indistinguishable from case formants. They can be written both as a single word (as postfixes or even infixes) and separately (including prepositions).

The term "uninflected" would be quite conditional, at least because in the texts that have not been interpreted, we can find examples of their grammatical modifications (for example, along with the well-known syntactic word *nac* there exists an unclear derivative *nacar* [in the severely damaged inscription TLE 878], formally similar to plurals ending in -[V]r). The conjectured postposition *pi* "to, for" is likely to be bound with the variants *pul*, *epl*, and *peś* "from, out" (the latter, apparently, only in Tavola Cortonensis). In principle, these forms remind one of the common suffixal genitive.

Copulative conjunctions are the most transparent. They are postpositive *-c* (syntactically close to Latin *-que*; as Shevoroshkin states, it is likely to be borrowed from Lydian), and *etnam* "also" (*-tnam* as an enclitic). There are also the known particles *-m* "and, while, whereas" (shows the opposition), *ic* "as," "and." It seems that *e-ki* in Eteo-Cypriote inscriptions (KS 1, 2) corresponds to it. There exists also the derivative *iχ-nac* "because." About the conjunction *et/θ* see below.

The derivative adverb *θui* "here" is known for certain. Suggestions about the adverbs *matam*, *matan* "above" or "before," *nac* "so, then" (according to a not very reliable translation in Pallottino's glossary) is hypothetical. Their interpretation is built only on syntactical positions. As was said above, we have no foundation for talking about prepositions as a special part of speech (cf., the interpretation of *ceχa*). All the more or less reliable elements (as *pul*, for example) follow the word which they determine.

Previously, I expressed the opinion that the spread of the postpositions (which are not very substantial) in Italic languages (in Latin only *cum* with personal pronouns: *mecum*, etc.; in Oscan and Umbrian somewhat wider, such as Oscan *húrtín kerííín* "in horto Cereali" in Tavola di Agnone, etc.) can be connected precisely with the influence of Etruscan (Jatsemirskij 2006, 149).

NOUNS

Gender

The category of gender in Etruscan, and, it seems, in other Tyrrhenian languages, is hardly ever expressed morphologically with the exception of rare archaisms and some forms of female proper and patrimonial names. However, Pfiffig's (1969, 73) wording (with the reference to [Fiesel 1922]) about the whole absence of grammatical gender

---

127. In principal, one can try to find them in Eteo-Cypriote inscriptions (based on some external features), but their interpretation has not been very effective yet.

seems to be too strict. The relics of gender in Etruscan are quite recognizable (Pfiffig himself writes about the ways of forming female name variants [Pfiffig 1969, 74]).

In some cases, gender distinction is based on lexical difference (nevertheless it can also combine with suffixal indicator): *apa* "father," *ati* "mother," *clan* "son," *seχ* "daughter."

The suffix *-i* is the only reliable (relict) formant of feminine nouns. Among the common (animate) nouns, it can be marked out in the word *ati* "mother." It is also present in the theonym *uni* "Iuno" and in a number of female names, both independent and derivative (i.e., having masculine parallels): *fasti* (with the variant *hasti*), *larti*, *arnθi*, *araθi*, etc. Foreign names can also be formed with this suffix: *elinai* "Ἑλένα," *φersipnai* (CIE 5365) "Περσεφόνη," although it is not an invariable rule (such variants, as *elina*, are quite common).

One can also concede that infrequent but steady lexemes preserving *-i* over all periods of the existing Etruscan inscriptions also are feminine (cf., for example, *neri* "water," *suθi* "grave," *celi* "September").[128] However, formal labeling of such lexemes as belonging to some grammatical gender is conditional and wholly hypothetical. At least in Latin transfers, gender characteristics are entirely ignored. By all appearances, forms like *ati*, *fasti*, etc., can be considered as fossilized.

During the later period, the suffix *-i* is productive only in forming patrimonial names, which are quite reliable owing to parallel writings with masculine ones (cf., TLE 98: *ramθa matulnai seχ marces matulnas* . . . "Ramtha Matulna, daughter of Marcus Matulna . . ."; the analogical in structure TLE 127: *larθi spantui larces spantus seχ*, etc.) It is significant that the feminine patrimonial names ending in *-i* are often preserved unmarked in the positions where the masculine words require the genitive suffix *-as*. Indirectly, it can be a reflection of the extinction of grammatical gender as a whole.

One can suppose that some forms ending in *-i* in the inscriptions of Linear A (they are quite numerous) reflect the same suffix (cf., *ka-u-do-ni* – *ku-do-ni* again), but it is scarcely provable now.

I do not exclude that the suffix *-t/θa*, occurring, in particular, in the feminine parallel *lautni-θa* to the masculine form *lautni* "family member, offspring" or "freedman" and in what seems to be the most widespread female name *ramθa* can be considered a gender indicator. It seems that the name *ramθa* has not been offered any other trustworthy variants of subdivision yet. The interpretation of *lautniθa* is complicated by the vagueness both of the morphological appearance of the masculine (!) *lautni* and the origin of the very root.[129] An external similarity with this element can be found, for example, in the

---

128. See the gloss TLE 824 "*Celius*."

129. G. Devoto (1970) suggested that these Etruscan words go back to Indo-European **leudh-*, but he unfairly calls the root **laut-* reconstructed by him "proto-Latin." As is well known, Indo-European **-dh-* > proto-Italic **-þ-* > Latin *-b-*, Oscan-Umbrian, Faliscan *-f-* (cf., Latin *luber/liber*, Pelignian *loufir*, Faliscan *loferta* "liberta" along with the earlier form *loifirta* [LF 73], *loifirtato* "libertatis" [LF 25]). On the other hand, sometimes in Italic we can mark **-t-* < Indo-European **-dh-* (cf., Siculan λίτρα and Latin *libra*, Αἴτνη and *aedes*). Thereby, if we consider Etruscan *laut-* as originating from the very root, we can presuppose that *laut-* is a borrowing from proto-Italic, with the reflex *-t-* for **-þ-* (which is unlikely

name *crisiθa* (ES 378, etc.) from Greek Χρυσηΐς (cf., *elina* : *elina-i*), but the reflection of a Greek stem (gen. ΐδος, etc.) seems to be more probable here.

It seems that an archaic feminine genitive suffix *-a*, later replaced by standard *-al* and *-as*, was the only case formant maintaining the gender differentiation (see below).

The vast majority of Tyrrhenian lexemes do not display any word formational or morphological model or peculiarities of usage that would allow us to talk about the category of gender. This is reflected also in the appearance of Tyrrhenian words borrowed in other languages (primarily in Greek and Latin). It is easy to notice that the choice of gender here is quite unconditioned. It can be observed especially clearly in the word endings *-ea*, *-eus*, *-eum* and -ιον, -εον and derivatives, formed with the widespread Tyrrhenian suffix *-na* (with phonetic variants). Thus, in Latin and Greek, they give the masculine, feminine, and (less frequent) neuter nouns. For more detail, see Chapter 7: Word Formation.

Pre-Greek toponyms, dating from the Tyrrhenian stratum, usually belong to the feminine gender (cf., Cretan Λάρυμνα, Λίκυμνα, Ρίθυμνα, Ριθυμνία [Etruscan *ritumena-s*, CIE 4950], etc.) It can possibly be bound to the proper Greek tendency. On the other hand, words containing the same suffixes may belong to the masculine gender, if we consider masculine deities or heroes (cf., Hesychius "Γελχάνος· ὁ Ζεὺς παρὰ Κρησίν" along with Etruscan *velχana*, Latin *Vulcanus*), "Ἐλύμνιος· Ποσειδῶν ἐν Λέσβῳ καὶ νῆσος τῆς Εὐβοίας" (along with Etruscan *velimna*).[130] The form *aper* "parents" or "forefathers" may indicate that the masculine root was used in generalized forms.

As one can judge by the well understood Etruscan materials, Tyrrhenian languages possessed a distinctive feature different from the gender one, to wit, an opposition between animate and inanimate nouns (or the nouns belonging to "superior" and "inferior" classes, if we use the term, accepted for some other languages, for example, Dravidian). Such differentiation is shown by the method of forming plurals (any attempts to find similar indicators for singular forms were not crowned with success). The suffix *-(V)r*[131] forms animate plurals: *ais-er* "gods," *ap-er* "forefathers," *clen-ar* "sons," *huś-ur* "children," *papals-er* "grandchildren," *tusurθ-ir* "spouses." There is also *tiv-r* "months" (one should remember that the same root is present in the name of the moon deity). Possibly, the form *mesnamer* (TLE 366) with its supposed meaning of "sculptures of gods" (cf., in Chapter 7: Word Formation) also finds itself here. Its context is unclear.

On the other hand, the suffixes *-a* and *-l* combine with inanimate nouns: *mursl* "sarcophagi," *cleva*, possibly the plural marking "yearly nails" (from Latin *clavus*), and *tartiria*, a kind of sacrificial offering. The formant of collective plural *-χva* is usually used with inanimate nouns: *flerχva* "donations," and so on, but it is known also in

---

chronologically) or it comes from some peripheral dialect where the transition *-dh- > -t-, close to Siculan, took place (cf., an interesting example in Latin where we also find -t- < *-dh-: *rutilus* from *raudhros and -il-, along with *ruber*, *robus* [dialectal vocalism], *rufus* [dialectal consonantism]).

130. Where *digamma* has dropped in Greek Ἐλύμνιος, see above.

131. One can suggest that *-ur* is the oldest vocal variant for the suffix; it may be confirmed by the forms of disjunctive numerals (see below). Whereas *u* in *θun-ur* can be explained by the harmonization (from *θun* "one"), the vowel in *zel-ur* evidently seems to be unmodified.

combinations with animate nouns. As a matter of fact, the supposition about the existence of a collective plural is based on some peculiarities in the usage of the forms ending with -χva. Thus, in the inscription TLE 194 the suffix -χva is added to the well-known title: *maru-χva*, which primordially indicates the category of animate.

The peculiarities in usage of case suffixes, which are usually given in a single list, also show the same differentiation. As will be shown below, it concerns dative, locative in instrumental cases, and also a directive case different from standard dative.

Grammatical exceptions are rarely observed here. The word *nap-er* (in Latin preserved by Festus in the form *napurae* "Strohseile") may possibly contain a plural suffix, but the element *-r-* may be also word formational.[132] Similar examples have not been found so far.

It is doubtful whether the subdivision of nouns into animate and inanimate can be disputed now. It seems that the acceptance of such opposition can be conducive both to further specification of lexical meanings and uniform grammatical description.

Number

The category of number supposedly contains three grammemes: singular, plural, and collective plural. Materially it is witnessed among the nouns, possibly pronouns, and certain forms of numerals (notably, distributive). Plurals and collective plurals are always marked. Plurals, formed with the suffixes *-(V)r,*[133] *-a, -l,* and *-χva*, given above, had been identified due to the combinations with the numerals positionally (cf., kinship terms), and also by foreign parallels. Sometimes there are two or even three criteria. Compare the following examples: (a) with the numerals *ki aiser* "three gods" (TLE 719), *huśur maχ acnanas* "who has left five children" (TLE 887), *papalser acnanasa VI* "who has left six grandchildren" (TLE 169), *tivrs śas* "of three months" (TLE 181), *murśl XX* "20 ossuaria" (TLE 135), *ci tartiria* "three . . ." (TLE 2^3), etc.; (b) positionally, *laris avle larisal clenar* "Laris (and) Aulus, Laris" sons" (CIE 6213), (TLE 587), etc.; (c) by foreign transfers, compare above *aesar* "deus" instead of "dei" (TLE 803), and grammatically correct form "ἄϊσοι· θεοί" (TLE 804), preserved by Hesychius (cf., also *pulumχva*).

The accepted opinion is that the suffix -χva (with the unclear, probably only phonetically changed variant -χve) forms collective plurals for nouns. Examples of usage that we have seem to confirm such a proposition: the quite reliable forms *pulumχva* (TLE 874), *fulumχva* (TLE 570) "stars," *flerχva* "donations" (TLE 1$^{VIII\ 3,\ IX\ 16}$) are known

---

132. The root **naP-* "plant; bush" is attested in Etruscan (including Tuscan substratum) and Aegean areas (cf., Aegean-Tyrrhenian νάπα, νάπη, νάπος (Gen. -εος) "woody valley," Latin *nepeta* "catswort"; Modern Tuscan *nepa* "greenweed"; the form *nap-ti* (Loc.) in the text of the Zagreb book (TLE 1$^{X\ y5}$) apparently should be translated as "in (the sacred) grove."

133. One should avoid mixing the plural formant with the similar word-formational suffix (not only Etruscan): *lucer* (TLE 119)—personal name from (lauk:-) "to rule," *tular* (from Umbrian) "border, limit" (TLE 632, etc.) (cf., *tulerase* "defined" [TLE 874], etc.). In the combination with *-na* (Etruscan θucerna [TLE 546, etc.]) the same suffix appears in some borrowings in Latin (see below).

to us. In the bilingual from Pyrgi TLE 874, the word *pulumχva* corresponds to Punic *h-kkbm*, which, however, does not reject the meaning of collectivity, because collective plurals are absent in Phoenician (including its later dialect, Punic). The form *culścva* (TLE 1$^{VIII\,2}$) designated the group of deities (we find the same root in the name *culsan-*). Ivanov is of the opinion that the Etruscan collective suffix can be compared with Abkhazian *-ҡa* with the same meaning (Ivanov 2008, 666), that is, one can allow that it was borrowed from the Middle East or Asia Minor.

The word *avil* "year," while joining case suffixes (in contrast to wholly unchangeable *ril*, usually translated as "age" or "at the age"),[134] is always used in the singular form:[135] *maχ cezpalχ avil svalce* "lived 85 years" (TLE 94), *avils huθs muvalχls lupu* "dead at the age of 54" (TLE 142), *avls XXII* (TLE 907), etc. We find the same in the inscription of the Lemnian Stele: *śivai aviś sialχviś* "lived 60 years." It is significant that, in its independent usage, this word can join the collective numeral suffix: *avil-χva-l* (TLE 875).[136]

The plural form *caperχva* "cups" (TLE 1$^{VII\,10}$) may be the most mysterious. The suffix *-r* seems to be word formational here (cf., TLE 1$^{VI\,6}$ *caper*). The form *huθcva* (TLE 131) designates, it seems, a kind of stone construction or simply boundary stones. The forms *maθcva* (TLE 1$^{X\,9,\,17}$), *sulχva* (TLE 1$^{X\,27}$), and some others are unclear.

The methods of forming plurals for most suffixal derivatives have not been clarified yet, or we just have a few examples (particularly, among the forms marked with the suffix *-na* where the plural with *-l* may possibly be hidden only in the city names *tarχna-l-* "Tarquinii," *velzna-l-* "Volsinii").

The "well-known" and often cited "suffix" *-θur*, supposedly designating some communities, must be classified with the components (cf., also in Chapter 7: Word Formation). It seems that it also contains the plural formant *-(V)r*.

Usually it is considered that a suffix *-θur* existed in Etruscan that formed the meaning of belonging,[137] as though this opinion is supported by the well-known examples *velθinaθuraś* (TLE 570) "member of the family Velthina," *clavtieθurasi* (CIE 6213) "in (the burial vault of) Claudii." The form *paχaθuras*, from the interesting epitaph TLE 190, belongs to the same type. The combination *maru paχaθuras* (from the nominal stem **paχa-* "Bacchus") agrees with the *maru* and, in principle, must mean a bacchantus, a priest who was responsible for ceremonies in honor of Bacchus. One should also include the form *ceχasieθur* (in the badly preserved inscription TLE 90), from a quite widespread stem, and an interesting inscription TLE 635 *heva vipiθur cucrinaθur cainal*.

---

134. The supposition about *ril* as a fossilized genitive form with *-l* contradicts the root structure CVC; it can be accepted only if we admit the evolution **ril-l> ril*.

135. If there is no parallel homophonic plural form *avil* from * *avil-l*.

136. This inscription is a "summary" of the bilingual from Pyrgi TLE 874. The distribution *aviχval – pulumχva* corresponds to Punic *wšnt l'mš 'lm bbty šnt km hkkbm 'l* lit. "(may) the years of the deity in this sanctuary be as (numerous) as the stars above (us)."

137. According to the definition by Pallottino, "*appartenenza specialmente a collettività*" (Pallottino 1978, 453). Pfiffig gives "*Kollegialnomina . . .-Genosse, . . .-Genossenschaft*" (Pfiffig 1969, 166).

From our point of view, the interpretation of -θur- as some suffix of belonging has an imprint of morphological uncertainty. In actual fact, reliable forms ending with -θur (but not only the indirect case -θur-as) designating a concrete person are unknown. By the peculiarities of their structure and usage, they coincide with the plural indirect case forms ais-er-as "of gods," clen-ar-as-i "to the sons." It seems that such are just the plurals of well-known nouns (mostly names) ending with -(na)-te (cf., also in Chapter 7: Word Formation; see the type -te, -na-te, -te-na, in Latin *Mevanates*). Pfiffig approximated the solution of these forms, as he believed that forming plurals was one of the functions of -θur[138] for the words ending with -na, but he disregarded the ties with the forms ending with -na-te. From the phonetic point of view, fricativization $t > θ$ can be explained as a substitutive phenomenon, conditional on the elision of e before another vowel: -θ"-ur < *-te-ur. On the other hand, a confusion between -te and -θ in such cases may obscure the differentiation with the element -θ, usually considered as one of the participial formants (cf., in the glossary by Pallottino tesin-θ "trustee"). The plural genitive klanturus we also find in Rhaetic (IR 99, PU 1) (cf., the Etruscan name clante/i).

Morphologically, such combinations as maru paχaθuras correspond to the Latin genetivus partitivus or the genitive in its simplest function of possession. The existing translation becomes more logical with the acceptance of such a word form structure.

The most reliable proof of our interpretation is provided by the epitaph TLE 176. Here we read: nerinai ravnθu avils ril LIIX at[l] cravzaθuras velθurs hθal-c "N. R. (died) at the age 58, mother of Veltur and (from the kin) *Cravzate." As can be seen, the standard genitive of two proper names in the same syntactic function agrees with the genitive of a patrimonial name.

The conclusion about the character of the forms with -θur(-), made by me during a study of the cited inscriptions, was confirmed during an analysis of the text of the Tabula Cortonensis (see in Chapter 2: Sources and in Appendix 3). This text is rich in numeral forms: "12" occurs twice, "two" and "six" occur once each. In addition, there is also a numeric record where the first component is not fully clear (most likely, IIII "four"). They allow us to make some quite interesting observations. In the beginning of the inscription we read: [1]et pétruiś sceveś ...[2] cen[ ]u ténθurś sar cus[3]uθuraś, in the following context: "let Petru Sceve and 12 executors from the kin Cusu accomplish ..." (unfortunately, the semantic verb is damaged and does not lend itself to translation; however, the grammatical form is clear: the ending -u remains). Here, as can easily be observed, the forms with -θur(a)ś are used in an intensive function.

One should especially emphasize the fact that the form ténθur(ś), in spite of an external likeness to the form analyzed above, is made in a different way. Here -θ- is a participial formant, which is followed by the same plural suffix (see below). See the combination [3]ténθur[4]sa, here the numeral "six," combining with the nominative case, clearly shows the plural for "six executors."

---

138. "-θur *wird zur Bildung des Plurals der GN auf* -na *verwendet*" (Pfiffig 1969, 166).

CASE

The ways of expressing case relationship in Etruscan and other Tyrrhenian languages are understood very unevenly. Such are the peculiarities of the inscriptions that the suffixes most clear to us are those that express belonging, direct and indirect cases of the personal 1st sg. pronoun, etc. The least understandable are the combinations with pronominal enclitics, most of which are presented in the Zagreb book (i.e., the text which contains far more complicated constructions than the short inscriptions).

In consideration of the long history of Etruscan writing, one should speak about the appreciable changes of case constructions. With a large measure of probability, we can also conclude that pronominal forms remained more archaic. Different ways of expressing the relationship between subject and object have been noted in Etruscan inscriptions. We can say that, over the course of time, the grammatical system of this language has undergone visible changes. The inscriptions of Eteo-Cypriote are much poorer, so they do not allow marking any similar process. Aegean Tyrrhenian cannot be analyzed in a diacritical way at all.

While describing Etruscan morphology, one cannot pass over the question of possible grammatically meaningful vocalic alternation. Many papers repeat the point of view according to which in Etruscan there was a category close to Indo-European ablaut (it seems to us that it was initially suggested by scholars who tried to ground a hypothesis of the Indo-European origin of Etruscan or who worked mostly with classical languages). It is also contrary to a general theoretic base: the agglutinative character of Tyrrhenian languages. However, such constructions rely on a very limited number of examples. Let us analyze the most typical. The correlation among *clan* "son" : *clenś* "of son (gen.)" (TLE 580): *clenar* "sons" is a classical base for various conjectures (cf., *clen ceχa* in TLE 652, 737). Here, it might seem, one could presuppose the combination of an indirect form with a postposition ("filii gratia" according to Rix [1984^2, 226]), but in the well-known inscription TLE 570, line a12, we can read: *clen θunχulθe*. As is seen, any other grammatical elements are absent here.[139] However, in the cited Rix work, the form *clen* is shown as an ablative.

One can think that such alternations may be connected, for example, with the change of stress (it might be laid on morphological elements and the root vowel might be weakened) (maybe *e* and *i* hide a reduced vowel?), but *clan* will remain a unique root, and its features should not be extended to other Tyrrhenian lexemes. Other examples of such "morphological" alternations are absolutely insignificant. If we followed the logic of ablaut adherents, we could give, for example, an imaginary correlation *ais* "god" with *eiser* "gods," but the variants with *a*- in plural (TLE 359 *aiseras*, etc.) or *e*- in singular (TLE $1^{X\,10}$ *eis*) would be easily found. The genitive form from *seχ* "daughter" (*seχi-s*, in contrast to *ati-al* from *ati*) sometimes acts as one more

---

139. We must be careful with the interpretation of *ceχa* as a syntactic word: verbal forms *ceχane* (TLE $1^{VII\,7}$), *ceχase* (TLE 101), deverbative noun *ceχasieθur* (TLE 90), gerundive *ceχaneri* (TLE 90, 126) are formed from the same root. The only conceivable explanation here is a change of a nominal root into an improper postposition.

piece of "evidence" of fusion in Etruscan. Unfortunately, this root is not only somewhat rarer than *clan* but is also far poorer in its paradigm, which, in turn, promotes some speculations. Such a conclusion could make some sense if there existed any evidence about a final vowel in the root *$se\chi$-. But such evidence is totally absent: in TLE 15 (!) cases of usage of *s/śeç/χ* and two of genitive *seχis* are taken into account. It is impossible to understand how the inflection of *ati* and *seχ* can be opposed based on such examples. The vowel *i* in *ati* is a feminine marker, though it is fossilized, but in *seχ-i-s*, it is most likely a connecting vowel, because the point about the final stem vowel has not been confirmed. Thereby, while analyzing Tyrrhenian material, we should abstain from using such Indo-European categories.

Pfiffig once presupposed that borrowed lexemes were indeclinable in Etruscan (1969: 76). Such an assumption seems to be unconvincing. As can be easily seen, known loanwords basically designate objects or substances (e.g., *qutun*, *vinum*), which are used in a nominative or accusative meaning. On the contrary, the form *claruχies* (TLE 515),[140] which is borrowed κλαρουχία "community, settlement" in the Doric variant (Ionic would give κληρ-) is an unquestionable genitive, showing possession. The vessel name *pruχ-ś* (TLE 1$^{IV\ 22}$), proper name *sispe-ś* (CIE 5373, from Σίσυφος) and some others borrowed from Greek are known in genitive form. As regards other case forms, they cannot be easily found because of context peculiarities.

The case relationship in Tyrrhenian languages can be expressed by means of: (1) indicators that express the relationship between subject and object; (2) genitive suffixes *-(V)s*, *-(V)l* and their combinations[141]; (3) dative, locative, and instrumental formants *-e*, *-i*, and their combinations with different genitive forms; (4) agglutinative elements, possibly originating from postpositions (or directly postpositions which were written as a solid word with the stem or complicated word form): *-in*, *-a*, *-θi*, *-ri*; and (5) pronominal enclitics.

The indicators from group (4) are highly specialized by their value. In contrast, *-e*, *-i* express quite diverse meanings. Genitive forms also can sometimes be used as allative or locative, which, it seems, is conditional on simplification of the combinations of *-e*, *-i* with *-Vs*, *-Vl* (cf., TLE 156: *itun turuce venel atelinas tinas cliniiaras* "V. A. brought this [as a donation] to the sons of Tin") (i.e., Dioscuri), where we find *clinii-ar-as* instead of expected *clin-ar-as-i*[142] (cf., *clenaraśi* in TLE 619). Pronominal enclitics can cover a wide range of meanings.

One of the most typical features of Etruscan (and other Tyrrhenian languages as well) is a so-called "redetermination" (the term was proposed by Pallottino) of affixes, which consists of an overwrite of two or more suffixal elements often having similar meaning and developing some new shades of meaning. Compare, for example, *vel avleś* "Vel (son)

---

140. Cf., the: *tular hilar nesl ein ser vl remzna clan-c au latini cesu claruχieś*.

141. According to the Rix schemes, "ablative" and "emphatic genitive" have the same meanings in Etruscan (Rix 1984^2, 223); from our point of view, existing syntactic constructions do not allow us to make such a conclusion.

142. It is possible that we have an engraver's mistake in the inscription; on the other hand, is not the inversion of the suffix *-i* also possible?

of Aulus" and *veluś avleśla* "of Vel (son) of Aulus." Etruscan redetermination in such quality has been brilliantly explained by Tronskij. For example, the combination *trepi θanχvil vipenas arnθal arnθialisla puia* would be translated into Latin in the following way: *Tanaquil Trebia Arruntis Vibennae Arruntis f(ilii) uxor* (Tronskij 1953, 86). Some scholars, particularly Rix, suggest analyzing such combinations as new independent case formants. This proposition may be justified for those cases where the reduplicated suffix does not form a secondary attribute.[143] However, it seems that, structurally, such combinations do not differ from any other suffixal chains, typical for Etruscan as an agglutinative language (cf., the form with different suffixes: *clavtie-θur-as-i* "in the burial vault of Claudii" [CIE 6213], where *-as-* is a genitive suffix, *-i* forms a locative case; see above about *-θ-ur*). For the present we analyze, in fact, the origin of complicated forms almost without the possibility of explaining the shades of meaning which could appear there.

The most trustworthy Etruscan nouns, usually translated as nominative or accusative forms, have a zero suffix. Sometimes marking out some formants (for example, *-s*) as indicators of the animate form is suggested, but such schemes are based on isolated examples, which are not numerous and are unconvincing as a whole. Pfiffig believed in the possible existence of both marked and unmarked accusatives in Etruscan (Pfiffig 1969, 74), but one should rather speak of a gradual supplanting of the marked accusative by the simple stem acting in both functions.

The most reliable marked accusative form is the pronoun *mini* "me" (appearing also as *mine*, *mene*).[144] Pronominal demonstrative forms *cn*, *tn*, and some others are not suffixal. Here we face sonantic extension of the stem. They act in both case functions. On the other hand, it would be premature to speak about a common scheme of forming accusatives, because only one case is known in Etruscan where *-ni* is added to the nominal stem. There also exist some forms which are similar externally (cf., the epitaph of Laris Pulena from Tarquinii (TLE 131): *tarχnalθ spureni lucairce* "ruled (the) city in Tarquinii." The form *capeni* (TLE $1^{X\,2}$) also may be accusative; the meaning of the lexeme is "vessel, cup" (cf., the plural forms above). One should also mention the form *velznani* on the gold coin (NRIE 453–54), presumably from Volsinii. But the usage of the accusative is quite uncommon here. *Lesuni* (TLE 426) is unclear. The form *versni* (TLE 395), externally identical, is a patrimonial name, mounted with the feminine suffix.

By analogy with the Etruscan forms, one can presuppose that the accusative suffix in Aegean-Tyrrhenian appeared as *-on* (the Etruscan suffix *-ni* also serves for forming transitive verbs from intransitive stems, and *-on-* has the same function in the Stele inscription, which could also combine these two meanings). One cannot exclude the possibility that the Minoan nominal (which can be seen by the suffix -vθ-) form *a-si-da(n)-to-no* from the inscription ARKH 2 contains the accusative suffix exactly. If this

---

143. The development of Etruscology shows that some earlier conclusions which had been under criticism have been brilliantly confirmed later. An aspiration for unreasonably complicating the paradigm has not proved its value, whereas the older point about the redetermination remained viable while analyzing Tyrrhenian grammar.

144. Along with it, the form *mene* in the inscription TLE 359 is not pronominal but seems to be constructed from the verbal root *men-* "*bringen*" (Pfiffig 1969, 29).

supposition is correct, it would appear that the given formant differed in Etruscan and Aegean from the earliest times, which would somewhat change our notions about the closeness of the Tyrrhenian languages of the first millennium BCE. The usage of *-no* after a logogram *VIR* and before the number 3 (case formant?) in tablet HT 11 is also exceptionally interesting, whereas the form *tu-me-no* from the inscription PK Za 8, should be compared rather with the Lycian toponym Τύμηνα, preserved by Stephanus.

The question of the suffix *-ś* remains one of the most debatable for Aegean-Tyrrhenian. Different scholars believe it to be a nominative formant, marker of animateness, etc. This element allegedly occurs in the name *holaieś*, the title *maraś* and the word *aviś* "year" (Etruscan *avil*). If such an indicator really existed, it, of course, could not be recognized in Hellenized lexica, where it would join with final Greek ς. The extraction of this suffix is based on the external difference from the Etruscan title *maru* (Umbrian *maru*, Latin *Maro*). The present title can possibly be a borrowing from Indo-European (a similar root exists in German, Celtic, Thracian, and some other branches of the Indo-European family), but here it is mounted according to Tyrrhenian structure. (It will be shown below that *maru* is a substantivized verbal form, and *maraś* is a participle, which has an analogue in Etruscan).

The name *holaieś*, in principle, may be Greek. The root of the word *aviś* probably should be reconstructed as **av-* (with different suffixation in Etruscan and Aegean-Tyrrhenian). In the nominative form *ναφοθ* there is nothing similar to the suffix *-ś*, as in Etruscan nominative as well. Thereby, postulating such a suffix does not seem grounded yet.

Compare the examples of usage of the marked and unmarked nominative and accusative forms in Etruscan and other Tyrrhenian languages. In Etruscan: *laris avle larisal clenar sval cn śuθi ceriχunce* (CIE 6213) "Laris (and) Aulus, sons of Laris, built this sepulcher while alive"; *lris pulenas . . . ziχ neθsrac acasce* (TLE 131) "Laris Pulena . . . composed (the) haruspicinal book"; *arnt χurcles . . . zilc parχis amce marunuχ spurana cepen tenu* (TLE 165) "Arnth Churcle . . . was (a) plebeian (?) *zilc*, held (the) post of urban *maro* (and)"; *larθi petrui larθial sentinateś puia ame* (TLE 469) "Larthi Petru (who) is (a) wife of Larth Sentinate" (*am-e* is a present form of the verb "to be"; see below).

In Aegean-Tyrrhenian: *śivai aviś siaχχviś maraś-m aviś aomai* "lived 60 years, was (a) *maro* (for a) year"; Rhaetic examples are not very reliable. The construction "*-(k)u . . . -s-i/-l-e*" (see below) occurs there more often.

Since nominative and accusative cases of nouns almost never differ in a formal way, we should try to find other means to express the relationship between subject, object, and, probably, subject of an acquired state in the Tyrrhenian languages. The delimitation of subject and object can be partly based on the word order, but it never was especially difficult in Etruscan. As will be shown below, the morphological structure of Tyrrhenian verbs allowed them to correctly express different relationships without using special accusative forms. This grammatical category becomes quite rare and later becomes apparent only in pronouns, which are more archaic.

Different variants of the genitive are the most frequent among the case forms occurring in Tyrrhenian texts, which is natural because this case expresses possessive meaning, as, for example, in terms of relationship or on different objects—property or donations of various people. It seems that attested formants greatly differ in their origin.

The element *in* is one of the oldest variants, and we should examine it at greater length. Pfiffig already believed that *in* was one of the oldest genitive suffixes and could combine with indeclinable nouns (Pfiffig 1969, 80, etc.). Here he was guided mostly by the forms *in crapśti* "des Crapśti" and *in culścva* "der Culśe," where an evident inaccuracy crept in. It is easy to notice that the deity name *crapśti* (from the root, which is also present in Umbrian *Grabovie*, an epithet of Mars and Jupiter) is feminine (cf., the usage of the suffix *-te/-ti*). We have no reason to ascribe it as indeclinable, because genitive forms of the same type are also attested (cf., proper name *clanti-ś*) (TLE 924), etc. Likewise, the collective plural *culś-cva* is not indeclinable (cf., the genitive *avil-χva-l*).

The formant *in* could also appear as a postposition. The form of the theonym *tin-ś-in* would be the most typical example here. One should analyze the fragment *eslem zaθrumiś acale* ("eighteenth of June") *tinśin śarve*... (TLE $1^{VI\ 14}$). Unfortunately, subsequent lexemes are most unclear. *Śarve* can be compared either with the term *śarvena-* "body of twelve" (TLE 170), or with *śar* "twelve" (see below), and, in Pallottino's index, it is interpreted even as a proper name. However, the context is more likely to show the direction of the activity; it is written about the oblations to Tin.

We can adduce some examples of an archaic genitive. The name of the solar deity, *kauθa*, along with standard forms *caθas* (TLE 131), *caθs* (TLE 190), *cauθas* (TLE 359^a), once (TLE $1^{X\ 18}$) is attested in genitive *caθin*. The name of the dawn goddess in genitive appears as *θesn-in* (TLE $1^{IV\ 16}$) along with *θesn-s* (TLE $1^{XI\ 11}$). Two lexemes meaning "fire," presumably Tyrrhenian and borrowed from an Indo-European source, appear as *versin* (TLE $1^{III\ 15}$) and *firin* (TLE $1^{VII\ 7,\ 9,\ 20,\ 22}$); the word "community," borrowed from Oscan-Umbrian *tutin* (TLE $1^{VII\ 8}$); the word *favi-* (its derivative is present in Latin *favissa* "subterranean room of the temple") forms the genitive in the same way: *favin* (TLE $1^{XI\ 20}$).

One can suppose that the form *puiian* (TLE 2^{19}) is also the result of the phonetic development of the archaic genitive (< *puiain* from *puia* "wife"). From the word ending with *-in* but lacking reliable translations we should cite TLE $1^{X\ γ2}$, 100 *cesasin*, TLE 99 *calusin*, TLE $1^{XI\ 3,\ 7}$ *hantin* (cf., TLE $1^{III\ 23}$ *hante*), TLE $1^{VI\ 5}$ *θaχśin*, TLE $1^{IX\ γ2}$ *θaχsein*, TLE $1^{V\ 2,\ IX\ 1,\ 9}$ *lecin*, TLE $1^{X\ 5}$ *nuθin*, TLE $1^{XII\ 2}$ *hinθθin*. The word *mutin* (TLE $1^{III\ 14}$) also is not quite clear (cf., the personal verbal form *mutince* [TLE $1^{IV\ 5,\ 18}$]).

With regard to the later period, we incline to the interpretation of *in* as a formant of the allative case (especially because examples of the usage of *-eri* with animate were found nowhere; see below). This function does not annul the genitive meaning. So far as we assume the borrowed status of the suffixes *-s*, *-l* (it will be discussed below), the reduction of function of *in* (it really can be understood as primordial) and its evolution into the allative is a natural result. In addition, such differentiation of "functions" could be simply based on the ascription to Etruscan of features that are peculiar to our translation and not having a practical application for the description of Etruscan grammar.

The formant *in* also appears in Rhaetic (cf., SZ 16 *apan-in*, etc.). This formant can be used while forming more complex grammatical elements and forms. We can analyze the ones listed in the publication of TLE.

In the Zagreb book (XI γ3), the form *inin-c* is attested (in an unclear context). I am inclined to believe it is an intensifying reduplication rather than an analogue of "redetermination." On the other hand, we find an example of redetermination using *in* in the lead tablet from Monte Pitti (TLE 380): *ins* from **in-s*, followed by the unclear form *semutin*, which, in turn, contains the same indicator appearing as a circumfix. It is also possible that *ins* is combined with the preceding genitive *ceś zeriś* "of fifteen." In the same tablet, the combination *in-pa* occurs twice (cf., an obscure formant *pV-* above).

The combination *in-pe-in* with the same element *pV-* in inscription TLE 27 is the most complex. Unfortunately, the context is not clear here because of the difficulties with word division in the preceding line *alespuraθevnalθia* (while we have an obvious beginning *mi aliqu auvilesi* "I was brought by Aulus." In the rest of the inscription, only the present form *al-e* (cf., TLE 1$^{III\ 17,\ IV\ 4,\ VIII\ γ21}$, 331) and the root *spur-* "city" can be attested.

The form *klan-in-ś-l* from the well-known root *klan* "son" is also quite interesting. The context of the short inscription TLE 668 (made on a statuette) *mi klaninśl* may seem to show a proper name (in addition, we know the names *clante*, *clanti* from Etruscan and Rhaetic). One may suppose that *in* acts here in a word formational function (as *-s* and *-l* could be used, especially the latter), while *-ś(-)l* shows the case relationship.

In the archaic period, a case suffix *-a* was joined to proper feminine names: compare TLE 695 *mi malena larθia puruhenas* "I (am a) mirror of Lathia Puruhena," and *mi tafina lazia*[145] *vilianas* "I (am a) cup of *Latrhia Viliana" (TLE 30). Here also the inscription TLE 243 is close in its structure: *mi araθia araθenas*, and, in the inscription TLE 154, the suffix occurs also in the patrimonial name: *mi larθa ṣarṣinaia*.

We concede that this suffix could also form the plurals for some names. The form in the inscription TLE 939 of uncertain origin is especially important here. In this inscription of a "bucchero" type vessel, there occurs a combination *alχuvaisera*, which should be subdivided as *alχuv aisera*. As can be seen, this plural differs from *ais-er-as* (wrong word division is also improbable; next follows *turannuve*, which is clearly read) from the Zagreb book, and, in principal, can be understood as a feminine genitive form **ais-er-a* "of goddesses." In later periods, the current suffixes *-as*, *-al* are applied to feminine names, and we are faced with them in the overwhelming majority of inscriptions.

These genitive suffixes in the Tyrrhenian languages can be presented as the following:
    a. in Etruscan *-s*, *-sa*, *-ś*, *-śa*, *-Vl*, *-l*, *-la*;
    b. in Aegean-Tyrrhenian *-ś*, *-śi* (?), *-al*, *-il*;
    c. in Rhaetic *-ś*, *-s*, *-l*;

---

145. It seems that we have a carver's mistake here; one should reconstruct the form **larzia*.

    d. in South Lusitanian *-isa, -al-*;
    e. in Eteo-Cypriote **-s*.[146]

A separate substantial article by Rix deals with the Etruscan genitive with *-s* (1987–88).

The principles used for choosing among the articles (for the first time, between *-Vs* and *-Vl*) for the proper form are not always understandable and were not common for a long period when the Etruscan inscriptions were created. Maybe it makes sense to use marks like «Genitive-1» and «Genitive-2» for a more accurate description, but such numeration, of course, would be unconditioned. One cannot exclude that there was a tendency to use *-as* mainly with the masculine forms and *-al* with feminine, but it never became a general rule. Only in patrimonial names was *-as* strictly kept (cf., the examples of using genitive in the other languages: Eteo-Cypriote *ta ve-ta-re-se* "it (is a vessel) of *Vetarius" (an inscription KS 11)[147]; South Lusitanian *ain-isa*, but *ain-al-isa* (with redetermination, an inscription number 62 according to Schulten); Aegean Tyrrhenian form *vanalasial*.

The typical genitive construction *mlaχ mlakas* found on several votive objects can hardly be translated word for word, but it has analogues in Greek, Latin, and Faliscan (Agostiniani 1981).

Sometimes the morphological appearance of genitive forms (and many others as well) can be obscured because of the parasitic phonemes: compare *flenzneves*[148] (TLE 100) along with *flenzna* (twice, in the same inscription) instead of expected **flenzna-s*.

The problem of the origin of the formants *-Vs*, *-Vl* may be bound with a hypothetical "Asia Minor" sprachbund, or language union (Shevoroshkin, personal communication). Thus, the first formant can be compared with Hittite genitive *-aš* (sg., pl.), seldom *-s* (sg.) (Friedrich 2001, 58). The tie with Hurrian ergative *-s* and Urartian *-še* is less probable (D'jakonov 1961, 385; Melikišvili 1964, 32). The second element finds some parallels in forming adjectives (see Chapter 7: Word Formation).

Genitive forms with *-s* and nonstandard vocalism (cf., TLE 323 *veluis tuteis θanχviluisc turialsc*), as was proposed long ago, might have arisen under the influence of Latin inclination ("die Endung *-is* ist ja direkt lateinisch" (Cortsen 1935, 151]). Case suffixes *-e*, *-i* in Etruscan form, it seems, have the widest range of meaning. In Rhaetic and Aegean, fewer variants can be observed, which is connected with the scantiness of the material. Both in Etruscan and Aegean-Tyrrhenian the suffixes *-e*, *-I* often combine with *-as*, *-al*, and sometimes in such forms where the usage of the genitive suffix itself is not always understandable and may seem excessive at that. Compare Etruscan constructions *mi mulu laricesi... clinsi velθurusi* "I was brought by *Laricus, son of Velthur" (TLE 32), *mi araθiale ziχuχe* "I was painted by Arathius" (TLE 278), *mi mulu kaviiesi* "I was brought by *Cavius" (TLE 153), etc., Lemnian *φokia-śi-al-e* "to (man of)

---

146. U (*-se*) in writing, as in Greek words ending with *-ς*.
147. The Etruscan aspect of this name is especially characteristic (cf., *vetru* [TLE 690] and [*Mamurrius*] *Veturius*, the name of the smith who made *ancilia* and Latin cognomen [particularly, *Veturia*, mother of Cn. Marcius Coriolanus]).
148. There is an evidently erroneous "correction" in TLE: *fleśzneves* instead of CIE 5407 *flenzneves*. We can suppose the letter M instead of ϒ, but the form *flenzna* shows the latter variant.

Phocaea." On the other hand, there also occur simpler combinations: *zilci velusi hulχniesi*"(under the governing of) *zilc* Velus *Hulchnius" (TLE 91) (cf., a simple form in TC *zilci larθal cusuś titnal*). We have no foundations to divide *-e* and *-i* on any basis other than phonetic development. Both elements can form dative-allative, locative, and instrumental cases (cf., also a separate study on this question [de Simone 1996]).

Typical examples of usage of this case form are found where a recipient is meant: *mi aranθ ramuθasi vestricinala muluvanice* (TLE 868, buc.) "I was given by Aranth to Ramtha *V."; *mi atianaia aχapri alice venelisi* (TLE 49) "I was brought by A. (from the kin) Atiana to Venelus," etc. The alternation *-e* : *-i* – is a reliable example of a phonetic variation under the influence of the environment. It is common to Etruscan, Rhaetic, and Aegean-Tyrrhenian to put the suffix *-e* after *-l* and *-i* after *-s*: Etruscan *larθiale hulχniesi* (TLE 84), etc.; in the inscription of the Lemnian stele *holaieś-i φokiaśial-e* "to Holaies, Phocaean"; in Rhaetic: *auzile eluku* "was brought by A." (IR 29, SZ 30); . . . *ku φeluriesi φelvinuale* "was . . . -ed by *Phelurus *Phelvina" (IR 1, NO 3).

The widespread Etruscan adverb *θui* "here," found in the epitaphs, is possibly a fossilized locative with *-i* from the pronominal root *tV-. It is also present in Aegeida (cf., Hesychius's glosses [1] "τυί· ὧδε. Κρῆτες"; [2] "τῦδε· ἐνταῦθα. Αἰολεῖς.") In an Eteo-Cypriote gloss, it keeps its pronominal meaning: "ἰν τυίν· ἐν τούτῳ. Κύπριοι."

Besides the suffixes *-e*, *-i*, which were forming locative and dative-allative cases already in the oldest inscriptions, there were also indicators in Etruscan which were simpler and more concrete in meaning to express similar case relationships, *-t/θi* and *-(e)ri*. One can suppose that they, as *in* as well, date from once independent auxiliary words (postpositions). In other Tyrrhenian languages, *-(e)ri* and *in* have not been found yet. The presence of [-t:i] is quite probable.

The locative case with [-t:i], appearing as *-ti*, *-θi*, in later inscriptions also *-θ*, occurs mainly in such combinations as "lies in the grave," "in this coffin," etc., and does not provide special difficulties for translation. We shall give some examples: *θui clθi muθniaθi* "here, in this coffin" (TLE 93), *celati cesu* "lies in the tomb" (TLE 105, etc.), *śuθiti, śuθiθ* "in the grave," *paχanati* "in the board of Bacchus" (TLE 137). Reliable plural locative forms are provided by the place names: *tarχnalθ(i)* "in Tarquinii" from the epitaphs TLE 131, 174, *velclθi* "in Volcii" (Latin *Volcii*) in TLE 327, 336. The inscription CIE 10803 is damaged: . . . *ina vipies veθus velznalθr*: it contains the form "in Volsinii."

Pronominal forms connecting the locative suffix [-t:i] after the genitive one are also known: *-s*, *-l*: TLE 630 *tuśti θui hupnineθi arnt mefanateś veliak hapisnei* "here, in this tomb, Arnth Mefanas and Velia Hapisne"; TLE 135 *calti śuθiti* "in this grave," etc.). We have no trustworthy cases using the forms ending *-ti*, *-θi*, *-θ* in any meaning other than locative.

Evidently, this suffix can be registered also in Eteo-Cypriote (cf., the forms *mu-no-ti* [twice], *ja-no-ti* [KS 1], *a-no-ti ta-so-ti* [KS 3], *ka-i-li-po-ti* [KS 11]; possibly, in some other words where the reading is not absolutely clear). The combination *a-no-ti ta-so-ti* seems to be agreed on. It is characteristic that any case forms from *an*, with the exception of nominative, are unknown in Etruscan. It seems that in the form *ka-i-li-po-ti* one can observe a typical Etruscan root *kail- "heaven,"[149] but its interpretation is complicated because we do not know any word formational suffix containing *P, *φ, *f in Etruscan (we can adduce only *snutuφ* with the presumptive meaning "top, head").

The suffix [-t:i] can combine with -*Vl* and -*Vs*, but the reliable examples show genitive rather than adjective meaning of the latter: *unialθi* "in (the sanctuary) of Juno," where *uni* is a proper name, -*al* shows the belonging, and -*θi* is locative. Apparently, the form *tin-s-θ* on the bronze liver model (sector c1) is identical in structure.

The same, it seems, can be ascribed to quite late (third to second centuries BCE) inscriptions on sacrificial objects (cf., *vipa luncane patna velsnalθi* [CIE 10768]). The latter form, if it, of course, does not coincide with *velznalθi*, can be translated as "in (the tomb of the kin) Velzna" (if we understand the suffix as genitive after the form ending with -*na*).

The formant -(*e*)*ri*, possibly once existing as an allative postposition or something close to it, could also join verbal stems in Etruscan, forming a gerundive (Pallottino 1976, 369, etc.); for detail, see below. It is typical that it was used far less frequently than the suffixes -*e* and -*i* and, in contrast to them, could not join proper names (at least, such forms have not been attested yet). It appears that it is in favor of the fact that only animate stems join -(*e*)*ri*. Such forms are absent in Rhaetic and Aegean-Tyrrhenian (here we should remember the brevity of the inscriptions).

The most reliable examples of using a dative-allative case with -(*e*)*ri* are attested in the Zagreb mummy text, including a repeated phrase: *śacnicleri cilθl śpureri meθlumeri-c enaś*. It seems to us that this combination designates the governing body in the name of which the text was written. The words *śpur*- and *meθlum*- usually are translated closely as "city, town,"[150] but the combination makes us differentiate them in meaning, roughly translating the phrase as "for the city and state." The construction itself, from our point of view, can be compared with Latin terms like *tres viri rei publicae constituendae*. Thereby, we can translate the whole combination as "the body for conducting rites for the city and the state."

In some other cases, while the forms with -(*e*)*ri* are used, we cannot be sure about the part of speech to which the formant is joined (cf., the title *zilχ ceχaneri* in the inscription TLE 126; apparently, the second form shows the duties of an official, but it is difficult to decide whether it is from the nominal or verbal root).

As opposed to suffixes -*e*, -*i*, -*θi* or *in* the formant -(*e*)*ri* never joins the genitive -*as*, -*al*. The peculiarities in usage of the latter elements brought us to the conclusion that they were connected with inanimate nouns, but, if in the case of -*ti*/-*θi*, it does not require any special explanations (locative forms can hardly be found among the inanimate), the usage -(*e*)*ri* can be analyzed in the inscriptions. We see that it is connected only with inanimate. Animate nouns stably join -*i*/-*e*. The results, both accepted before and suggested by me, are generalized in Table VI.[151]

---

149. Compare the derivatives in Chapter 5: Phonetics.
150. About the forms *meθlum* and *meθl* see below in Chapter 7: Word Formation.
151. Of course, unreliable forms are not given here.

Table VI. Nominal declension

	Animate	
Case	Singular ∅	Plural -Vr, Coll. -χva
Nom. ∅	ais, clan, Vel, Mefana-te	ais-ar, clen-ar Cucrina-θ-ur (tenθ-ur), maru-χva
Gen. (archaic) -in	Tin-ś-in in Crapśti (Raet. Apan-in?)	in Culś-cva
Gen. I -(V)s	clen-ś, Marce-s, Patrucle-s (Ae.-Tyrr. Φoke-s, Raet. Pianu-s Et.-Cypr. Ve-ta-re-se, S. Lus. Ain-isa)	ais-er-as Cusuθ-ur-as (Raet. Klant-ur-us)
Gen. II -(V)l	Arnθ-al, Maris-l pui-l (?)	?
Gen. III -(V)s-(V)l, -(V)l-(V)s	Vel-us-la, Neθun-s-l (Ae.-Tyrr. Vanala-si-al(?), S. Lus. Ain-al-isa)	?
Gen. (fem.) -a	Larθi-a	ais-er-a (?)
Dat.-Instr. I -e, -i	zilc-i, cepen-e (Ae.-Tyrr. Holaieś-i)	nap-er-i (?)
Dat.-Instr. IIa -(V)s-i	Vel-us-i (Raet. Φeluri-es-i)	clen-ar-aś-i
Dat.-Instr. IIb -(V)l-e	Araθi-al-e (Ae.-Tyrr. Φokia-śi-al-e, Raet. Φelvinu-al-e)	?
Acc. -ni	*X-ni?	?
	Inanimate	
Case	Singular -∅	Plural -χva, -l, -a
Nom. -∅	pulum, avil murs, aisu-na	pulum-χva murs-l tartiri-a (?)
Gen. (archaic)	vers-in	?
Gen. I -s	avil-s, meθlum-es	?
Gen. II -(V)l	aisuna-l spur-al (?)	avil-χva-l
Acc. -∅, -ni	= Nom.; (spure-ni**)	= Nom.;
Loc. -θi	suθi-θ(i), nap-ti (E.-Cypr. ta-so-ti, mu-no-ti, ja-no-ti?)	Tarχna-l-θi (?)
Allat. -eri	meθlum-eri, spur-eri	?

We find this Etruscan element in the combinations *pul, epl*, the latter with a prothetic vowel, typical for Etruscan (cf., Pallottino's glossary, etc.), and also *peś*. From the formal point of view, these postpositions can be described as compound, with the indirect case formants *-l, -s*. However, the forms we know are used in some quite obscure fragments (cf., for example, the following: *cerine pul alumnaθ pul . . . meθlumθ pul* (TLE 131[6, 7]); TLE 570[8, 11-12] *enesci epl, cenu epl*; other examples are unreliable. As can be seen, no meaning of these forms joining a postposition are known for certain. The form *cerine* is verbal (see below), *pul* is most likely to be construed with the word *alumnaθ* (twice). In addition, we have a word division in all cases.

PRONOUNS

Tyrrhenian pronouns occur in the texts but can be analyzed only unevenly. By their meaning they can be subdivided into personal and demonstrative, morphologically into independent and enclitic. Enclitic forms for personal pronouns have not been attested yet. Demonstrative enclitic pronouns, it seems, could also be used as possessive.

Among the personal pronouns we know the nominative and accusative cases for the first-person sg. "I, me," *mi* and *mini* correspondingly, again only from Etruscan. An externally similar form *menu* in the archaic inscription TLE 408 is verbal (see below). Furthermore, an accusative *mini*, which is the only known indirect form for personal pronouns, can add more formants, presumably postpositions (at least *-pi*).[152] In a number of examples, the first sg. pronoun shows us a specific phonetic development: it occurs as *ni* (TLE 2, 24, 246, 710), and with a preposition *ni-pe* (TLE 18).

Stylistic reduplication, which does not influence its translation, is also known: *mi vefarśii()naia mi ramθas* (TLE 163) "I (am a cup) of Ramtha V."

Some time ago, a hypothesis about the possible detection of the second person sg./pl. pronoun was suggested (Rix 1991), but from our perspective, it is not grounded enough. Rix once conjectured that the forms *un, une* are nominative and dative singular correspondingly and *unu* is one of the plural case forms. It is characteristic that all forms noted (with a single exception) are found in obscure fragments of the Zagreb book: *un* (seven times) and *une* (twice). It is not fully clear what is meant in the case with *unu*, because in this fragment the reading *unuθ* is more probable (TLE 1[X 13]). Only once the form *une* is attested outside of the Zagreb text (TLE 213, see below), and it casts doubt on the reliability of such an interpretation as a whole. There are also some other difficulties. If we accept Rix's opinions, we would not find any suppletion in forming singulars and plurals, which can be expected by linguistic universals, and would have to explain the suffix *-u*, nowhere else confirmed in declension. What is most important, we are faced with the form *unχva* (TLE 1[XII 6]). As was shown above, mainly collective plurals for inanimate are formed with the help of the suffix (there are only two well attested examples with animate), and it weakens the point about a personal pronoun as a whole.

---

152. However, this postposition also could be added to *mi*.

Proper possessive pronouns are absent in the texts or have not been identified yet. It is known for certain that the genitive forms from the root *tV-* were used as possessive for the third sg. (We can observe the same in the inscription of the Lemnian stele.) The paradigm of demonstrative pronouns (which have, therewith, enclitic variants) is understood less fully than the one for nouns. It is still possible that, at the later stage of the development of Etruscan, only pronouns kept special accusative forms.

The pronoun *an*, acting as demonstrative in Eteo-Cypriote (*a-na*), could be used as relative in Etruscan (most likely only for animate, but without gender): TLE 131 *lris pulenas . . . an cn ziχ neθśrac acasce* "Laris Pulena . . . who composed haruspicinal book") and TLE 321 *θanχvil tarnai an fartnaχe* "Thanchvil Tarnai. She donated" (Pfiffig 1969: 75). Any examples of its declension have not been attested.

From these pronouns one should distinguish reduplicated forms sometimes occurring in more complex texts, as *an-an-c* (TLE 1$^{XIV\ 14,\ X\ 11}$), probably, with an intensifying meaning: *cn-ti-cn-θ* "(exactly) in this . . ." (TLE 1$^{VII\ 19,\ XI\ 5}$) (cf., also three-part [?] pronoun *ca-ti-ca* (TLE 1$^{VI\ 15}$). Morphological elements of some complex pronouns can be analyzed with greater difficulty. Compare the forms *cehen, ceiθim* (in the first case with unclear *hen*), which could also be used independently (TLE 570$^{a\ 5,\ 14}$), and, in the second, with possible locative (*-θi*), joining a particle *-m* "and, but").

If the form *en* (TLE 40, 483) is pronominal, it is not clear whether it could be independent or just a phonetic variant of *an*. In the text of the Zagreb book, we find the form *enaś* not less than 16 times, but the formant *-aś* itself may hide both genitive and participle. Sometimes the form *enaś* is compared with the genitive formant *in*, which is an evident confusion (Pfiffig 1969, 105).

Besides *mini*, the following forms (with graphical or phonetic variants) of indirect cases are known among the pronouns: *cś, clz, clθ, clθi, eclθi, ecnas, tei, teiś* (*tiś*), and some others.

As an example of a description of pronominal declension, we would adduce a well-known scheme (Pfiffig 1969, 109), our Table VII. It can be characterized as debatable.[153]

Pronominal enclitics are formed both from simple roots *-tV-, -kV-* and roots extended with sonants: *-cl-, -cn-, -tl-, -tr-, -tn-*. In the most evident cases, they have a genitive meaning. Enclitic genitive, it seems, may form both secondary attributes and be used for substitution of common suffixal forms with *-(V)s, -(V)l*. In the epitaphs, which are grammatically the simplest, such forms occur very seldom. Evidently, they were typical for more expressive constructions. Detailed schemes of their declension (particularly those by Rix) are unconvincing in larger part.[154]

---

153. Particularly, presumable plural forms, having no analogues in nominal declension, are not reliable. A pronominal character of the forms *ei, ein* still does not seem provable.

154. From our point of view, excessive exactness of definitions, not reflecting the modern level of understanding (quite approximate) of Tyrrhenian texts, is a general shortcoming of such schemes. Really, it is hard to ground, for example, the distinctions between *cś* and *-cś, -cla* and *-cle, calθi* and *clθi* (Rix 1984^2, 229) by the peculiarities of their usage in the obscure passages of the Zagreb text.

Table VII. Pronominal declension (according to Pfiffig)

	Sing.		Plur.		Sg. Pl.
1. Nom.-Akk.	ca	Ta	cei	tei	ei
2. Gen.	cla	(-)tla	clal		
3. def. Akk.	c(e)n	tn	cnl		ein
4. Lok.	clθi		ceiθi		
	calti		caiti		
5. Mod.	(-)cle	(-)tle			

Forms with pronominal enclitics are known only from Etruscan texts. They are absent in the inscription of the Lemnian stele, and it has not been possible to say anything definite about Rhaetic and Eteo-Cypriote.

Furthermore, a number of such nouns passed through Latin and Greek (see below in Chapter 7: Word Formation). Enclitic forms in the texts are analyzable only positionally (cf., such forms as a secondary genitive *velθuruscles* [TLE 245], locative *municlet/θ* [TLE 99, 570], allative *śacnicleri* [TLE 1, eight times], etc.). In a single case, it seems a secondary genitive arose from the archaic form with *-in* (cf., *θapintaiś* and *θapintaś* [both in the inscription TLE 380]; evidently, it remained owing to the stability of wording in the sacral style.)

Compare the main enclitics from the root *c(S)-*: *-ca, -cś, -cn, -cla, -cleri*, and *t(S)-*: *-ta, -tś, -tn, -tla, -tra, -tnes, -treś*, etc. They join both nominal (*śpures-treś*) and verbal stems (*teśam-itn*), and there can be more than one enclitic (*śacni-cś-treś*). The verbal stem *śacni-* in *Liber Linteus* forms the following words: *śacni-cla, śacni-cleri, śacni-cn, śacni-cś-treś, śacni-tle, śacni-tn*. According to Xarsekin (1969, 56) (cf., also Pallottino 1976, 376), such enclitics are close to the definite article, which does not explain the peculiarities of double attributes or usage of verbal derivatives. In such cases, it is preferable to speak about substantivization. Besides that, the widespread use of pronominal enclitics enables us to make the accusative case more precise when they provide the only distinction (cf., the combinations *aθemeiś-caś* [genitive] and *aθemei-can* [accusative; both in TLE 878]).

Indeed, in some cases, the augments like *-cla, -cles, -treś*, etc., can be understood as articles (cf., the form *vipinaltra* in the inscription TLE 398 or *śpurestreś* in TLE 1), but, in most cases, they obviously have another meaning. If we consider the inscription TLE 245 (*mi larθia hulχenas velθuruscles*) in detail, we shall see that both parts of the feminine name are used in genitive (as it expresses the meaning of possession), when the masculine name *velθur-* is complicated with a single genitive formant and pronominal form *-cles*, where the same case suffix is also present. Here, one should probably draw an analogy with secondary attributes like *larθ-al-s*. In the given example, it expresses the kinship of *L. H.*, a daughter or wife of Velthur. Thereby, by means of pronominal enclitics, such nuances of meaning could be expressed which were usually formed by combination of different affixes. In addition, enclitics, it seems, could also express adjective meaning (cf., TLE 619 [θaure] lautneścle "family (tomb?)" from lautni- "stirps" [Pallottino 1979, 436]).

Only on rare occasions, relying on single sure forms, can one explain the sense of the whole phrase containing pronouns. The inscription on a ritual donation (bronze bird statuette) TLE 398 can serve as one such example: fl supri manince vipinaltra ulχnisla[155] clz tatanuś, "(by it) honored the Manes F. S. (fl, an abbreviation for fulni[156] (from the kin) Vibenna (from the kin) H.,[157] (the wife?) of T." Most such constructions occur in the text of the Zagreb book and have not become clearly translatable yet. Nevertheless, it is possible to make some conclusions.

An often-repeated combination śacnicleri cilθl śpureri meθlumeric enaś is the most significant. We may conventionally translate it as "(the body) which (exists) for (conducting) religious rites in/for the city and the state." It can be seen that the nouns and complex form śacnicleri both have the same formant of dative-directional case (-eri). The stem śacni- itself is obviously verbal. It occurs not only in the ritual text being analyzed but also in the inscriptions TLE 85, 205 (where it does not add special formants). It seems to us that, in this example, the pronominal enclitic -cl- substantivizes the verbal stem, which is more logical if we take into account the quite insignificant number of Etruscan word formational models and the absence of formal indications to distinguish nominal and verbal stems.

It is most likely that, also in many other cases, pronominal augments not only make grammar forms more concrete, but, in the first place, show the nominal character of such lexemes, formed from verbal stems. As can be seen in the example of śacni-ćś-treś (also in TLE 1), such substantivized forms could add (by means of pronouns) several case formants, which is typical for nouns as a whole.

It seems that the group of Latin and Greek words (including fenestra "window," which has been an etymological riddle for a long time, λεπαστή "cup," etc.), originate in Tyrrhenian forms, compounded with pronominal enclitics. For these and other possible interpretations, see Chapter 7: Word Formation.

Since Etruscan existed longer than any other Tyrrhenian language, and the inscriptions of an earlier stage (Minoan) are less understood, the Etruscan data still serve as the foundation of our knowledge about the diachronic development of the family. Relying on them, one can make a preliminary conclusion about a tendency to form a common indirect case, and its meaning could be easily defined by different agglutinative formants. The loss of the marked direct object in this scheme is still to be explained. Analysis of verbal structures would play an important role here.

---

155. Evidently, identical to hulχena- with the loss of aspiration.
156. Here also fuluna, Etruscan-Latin Fullonius, Umbrian Fulunie.
157. The appearance of two equally formed patrimonial names, with the enclitics of direct (-tra) and suffix of indirect (-la) cases, can be understood as a secondary attribute indicative of adrogation.

NUMERALS[158]

The system of Etruscan numerals is restored exclusively on materials of proper Etruscan texts. Comparisons with the data of other languages are very rare. In languages related to Etruscan, we have only one reliable form *śialχveiś* "sixty" (Stele of Lemnos).[159] In spite of some questions concerning origin, formation, and principles of coordination of simple and compounded numerals, it is necessary to underline that this part of speech is known to us well enough. Etruscan numerals are identified in various types of artifacts. A special place among them belongs to dice found in 1848 in Toscanella (TLE 197) with the sign meanings from one to six.[160] They caused a breakthrough in the interpretation of the simple numerals, carried out basically on a method of positional statistics.

The rate of appearance of different numerals, as well as the amount of derivative forms, are far from being equivalent. Some simple numerals and their derivatives are found tens of times whereas, for example, the stem of the word *nurφ* "nine" appears only once, at that, in a derivative adverb. Numeric signs are considerably more frequent. The following figures are known to us: I = 1, Λ = 5,[161] X = 10, ↑ = 50,[162] ✕ = 100, Δ = 500, ⊗ = 1000, ⊛ = 10000; fraction Ϲ = 1/2 occurs on coins (Pfiffig 1969, 130). The likeness between Etruscan and Lycian figures was proved by Ivanov (1980, 20, et seq.).

Since Etruscan numerals are used mostly in epitaphs, numbers exceeding the duration of human life are unknown to us. The sequence of simple cardinal numbers *tu(n), θu(n)* "1," *zal* "2," *ki, ci (χi?)* "3," *hut, huθ* "4," *maχ* "5," *śa, sa* "6," *śemφ* "7," *cezp* "8," *nurφ* "9," for the first six numbers had been established for the first time by Stoltenberg (1943, 234) (cf., Pallottino 1976, 368; Xarsekin 1969, 44; Pallottino 1978, 454), and, despite a number of later hypotheses (cf., Xarsekin 1964, 60-61, etc.), is mostly, if not completely, corroborated.[163] The present system was essentially strengthened after the discovery of the famous Etruscan-Phoenician bilingual from Pyrgi, in which Punic combination *šnt šlš III* "three years" corresponds to Etruscan *ki avil* (cf., Pallottino 1978, 445).

It is important to note that the criticism of the interpretation mentioned above was carried out primarily by scholars trying to etymologize Etruscan numerals based on

---

158. The conclusions expounded below in their main part were discussed at the conference *in memoriam* of V. M. Illich-Svitych (Moscow, Oct. 17–18, 2004) and then formulated in my article (Jatsemirskij 2007, 2008). The most extensive additions are the statement about the character of *sar* "twelve" (as a plural from *sa* "six") and supposition about the forms "ninety" and "two hundred."

159. In pure theory one can suppose, for example, that the form *tu*, which opens the Eteo-Cypriote inscription KS 3, is a numeral "one," but we have no reliable confirmation for it.

160. It should be noted that the Greek order of inscribing the numbers is not followed here (it required that the sum of opposite numbers was equal to seven (i.e., 1 : 6, 2 : 5, 3 : 4). Slotti counted five ways of inscribing numbers, then the prevalent order was identified as 1 : 2, 3 : 4, 5 : 6 (Xarsekin 1964: 50). On the dice from Toscanella, the numbers are inscribed in the following order: 2 : 5, 1 : 3, 4 : 6.

161. It can be seen that the sign is created with the same principle as Latin V (i.e., the half of x).

162. Also partitioned sign 8 "one hundred."

163. See the survey of the main points of view in Pfiffig: *maχ, ci, θu, huθ, śa, zal* (G. Devoto), *maχ, θu, ci, śa, huθ, zal* (E. Goldmann), *maχ, θu, zal, huθ, ci, śa, cezp, semφ, muv* (F. Ribezzo), *maχ, zal, ci, śa, θu, huθ, semφ, cezp, nurφ* (A. Trombetti), etc. (Pfiffig 1969, 124).

hypotheses concerning external relations of the Etruscan language particularly by Georgiev, who insisted on the Indo-European character of Etruscan, and, accordingly, would ignore many Etruscan materials. Today, such constructions cannot be perceived seriously anymore.[164]

Obviously, most disputes were caused by the problem of interpretation of *huθ* and *śa*. Scholars ascribed to them either the meanings "four" and "six" or vice versa (in particular, Pfiffig holds the opinion about *śa* "four" and *huθ* "six" [Pfiffig 1969, 123]; sometimes such an attribution appears even in recent works [Bonfante 1990, 22]). The meaning of *huθ* "four" should not be called into question anymore. Here we follow the classical analogy of the pre-Hellenic (apparently, Tyrrhenian) placename Ὑττηνία, corresponding to Greek "τετράπολις," "Τετράπτολις" (four Attic cities, i.e., Οἰνόη, Μαραθών, Προβάλινθος, and Τρικόρυθος, to which Stephan the Byzantine[165] testifies; probably, the name of the Lycian town Ὕτεννα [Steph., Ethnica, s. v. Ὕτεννα] and the derivative Ὑτεννεύς [ibid.], Ὑτεννέων [Herod., III, 90] for its inhabitants are identical to it). The given placename cannot be divided into two stems (in Tyrrhenian languages, the root **tVn-* meaning "city" or "settlement" is the only such one known; besides, compounds appear very seldom). As far as the structure is concerned, this form should go back to the Tyrrhenian noun **hutena* "four" with word-formation suffix *-na* (cf., below *śarvena, zelarvena*).

Usage of the same numeral in two toponyms, very distant from one another, can bear a relation to social structure, common in Tyrrhenian antiquity. Thus, Virgil describes the organization of his hometown Mantua in the following way (X, 201): "*Mantua dives avis, sed non genus omnibus unum: // gens illi triplex, populi sub gente quaterni, // ipsa caput populis, Tusco de sanguine vires.*"

Servius's comment is especially interesting here: "The fact is that in Mantua people were divided into three tribes, and each from them, in its turn, was divided into *four* (my emphasis) curias, and there was a lucumo as a head of each."[xxiv] It can be seen that the division both into four and into twelve was quite important for this community.

Next, relying on the bilingual TLE 925 *senti vilinal*: SENTIA SEXT[I] F[ILIA], the supposition has been suggested that the root *vil-* once had had the meaning "six" (Robertson 2006, 7–8) and then was supplanted by the form *sa*, but, judging by the other bilinguals, Etruscan *nomina* were never literally translated into Latin. Here we may be dealing with a phonetic alternation in the nominal root *vel-*.

The other frequently challenged interpretation was *cezp* "eight." One available interpretation is first of all supported by the gloss TLE 858 *Xosfer* "October"), the root

---

164. The scheme of Georgiev can be shown as an amusing example: *maχ* – 1, *sa* – 2, *huθ* – 3, *θu* – 4, *ci* – 5, *zal* – 6, *śemφ* – 7, *θun* – 8, *muv, nurφ* – 9 (Georgiev 1958, 192). As can be seen, there are no right variants for the first numerals from 1 to 6. Phonetic variants *θun* and *θu* are taken as different numerals, as in the case with *maχ* and *muv* (cf., below *muvalχ-*). The "identity" of *muv* and *nurφ* is not explained, and *cezp* is not analyzed at all.

165. "Τετράπολις τῆς Ἀττικῆς, ἔχουσα δήμους καὶ πόλεις τέτταρας, Οἰνόην Προβάλινθον Τρικόρυνθον Μαραθῶνα. Ἀνδροτίων δὲ Τετραπόλιδός φησι διὰ τοῦ δ' αὕτη πρότερον ἐκαλεῖτο Ὑττηνία" (Steph., Ethnica, s. v. Τετράπολις).

of which should be restored as *Chosf- (the mixture of Latin *x* [ks] and Etruscan χ is quite natural, taking into account the absence of a corresponding grapheme in Latin writing). As one can see, the name structurally coincides with Latin *October*. It is important to note the shift from *c* and *p* to the corresponding aspirates. Besides, Varro and other authors kept the name of the "eighth" Roman hill *Cespius, Cispius* (one of the tops of the *Esquiliae* hill, along with *Oppius*).

Among the numerals from one to nine, the forms *ki* "three" and *sa* "six" attract our attention because of their uncommon structure: with the exception of pronouns, they are the single categorematic words with well-known meanings that have a CV root structure. I am inclined to believe that these numerals may be borrowed. The form *ki* is comparable with hypothetical "Proto-North-Caucasian" *qo/kig, Basque *hirur*, and especially Hurrian *kig* "three." The idea of borrowing from the area of Asia Minor seems to be quite probable. The form *sa* can be compared both with Hurrian *šeže*, Basque *sei* and with common Indo-European (dialect Greek [Boeotian] ἔξ, Latin *sex*, Gothic *saíhs*, etc.).

About the interpretation of the numeral "ten," see below. Other tens in the Etruscan language (except for *zaθr-, zaθr-um* "twenty") are formed from simple numerals by adding the element -*alχ*- (as also in Aegea-Tyrrhenian *sialχveiś* "sixty"). Such compounded forms were not attested except for the root *huθ* "four." It seems that I succeeded in finding the derivative from *nurφ* "nine" (see below), a unique form, because such a long duration of life is not attested in the epitaphs. The meaning of the forms *zaθr-iś* (gen.), *zaθrum* "twenty" is confirmed by calendar dates in the text of the Zagreb ritual. It need not be explained that, after the identification of the meaning "thirty" in date designations, the other form, *zaθrum*, could only mean "twenty." The form *zaθrum* itself is derivative. It is compounded with the well-known word-formational suffix -*um* (see Chapter 7: Word Formation). *Zaθr*- occurs only once in a short inscription TLE 921.

Other tens, mostly showing age in the epitaphs, are easily recognizable in spite of some phonetic variations: *cealχ-, cialχ-* "thirty"; *muvalχ-* "fifty"; *śealχ-* (Lemnian *śialχv-*) "sixty"; *śemφalχ-* "seventy"; *cezpalχ-* "eighty." The root *maχ-/muv-* apparently underwent serious phonetic changes. Obviously, it was tied to various types of development of labiovelar *χv, which, as was shown above, should be restored in the present root (with the further transformations -χv > -χ at the end of the word and -χv- > -v- before a vowel (as in *muvalχ-*). The numeral "hundred" has not been identified yet (see above the supposition about the root *vers-/vors-*), and that is quite natural, since we would say again that we usually find the numerals designating age in epitaphs. Hopefully, in due course, it will be recognized in the ritual text of the Zagreb mummy, though the basic part of the lexicon used there is not clear to us.

Usage of simple numerals in epitaphs is absolutely clear (cf., TLE 143 *avils huθs lupu* "died [at the age] of four years"; TLE 193 *avils śas amce* "was [of the age] of six)." The inscription TLE 181, containing an indication about the age, is especially interesting: *avils XX tivrs śas* "(died at the age) of 20 years (and) six months"; it is more proof of the interpretation of *sa* as "six." Nowhere else do we find a specification up to the months, and it is far more logical for six months exactly, if we accept that the year consists of twelve months. And we know that the Etruscan calendar, brought into Rome by Numa Pompilius, contained twelve months exactly.[166]

Compounded numerals could be formed in at least two ways. Double-digit numbers with the second element from one up to five or six were formed by adding a simple number before ten: *maχ cezpalχ avil svalce* "has lived 85 years" (TLE 94). Such constructions, not complicated by suffixal parameters, are rare enough. More often both components have genitive suffixes, and, if for the first numeral suffix -s is used, for the next (except for the word *zaθrum* "twenty") two suffixes, both *-l* and *-s* are used. The numeral *zal* "two" has a specific genitive form, *esals*.

Compare the following examples: TLE 1VIII 3 *celi huθis zaθrumś* "on 24th of September"; TLE 142 *avils huθs muvalχls lupu* "has died at 54 years"; TLE 324 *lupu avils esals cezpalχals* "has died at 82 years."

Another method of forming compounded numerals was used in numbers with the second element 7, 8, 9 (there is nothing certain to say about 6). Here, 3, 2, or 1 accordingly were subtracted from the nearest greater ten, and this subtraction was formed by a suffix *-em* (derivatives of the numeral two, as well as those in other cases, are formed from a stem *esl-*). Typologically, such forms are similar to Latin *duo-de-viginti*, *un-de-viginti* where preposition *de* is used for subtraction.

Consider the following examples: TLE 134 *θunem muvalχls lupu* "has died at 49 years"; TLE 192 *θunem zaθrums* "at 19 (years)"; TLE 1$^{VI\ 14}$ *eslem zaθrumiś acale* "on 18th of June"; TLE 1$^{X\ 2}$ *ciem cealχuz* "27," etc.

When the compounded numerals are designated with figures, their order corresponds to the common one used for subtraction: XIIXX (CIE 5834; one should take into account the direction of writing, from right to left) = *eslem cialχ*, to wit, "twenty-eight" (Pfiffig 1969, 130).

Besides genitive forms of simple numerals, a derivative with dative-allative case postposition is also known: *hut-eri* (TLE 1$^{X\ 14}$). Little is known about ordinal numerals. Besides the base *θunχ-* "first," occurring in several texts, a reliable case of the use of an ordinal numeral may be seen in an archaic inscription from Pyrgi TLE 876. The form *θunχ-* (TLE 100 *θunχum*) contains a relatively rare Etruscan adjective suffix *-uc, -uχ* (cf., *marunuχ* [TLE 137, 165, 234] "related to *marones*") that combines with various suffixes: *θunχeiś* (TLE 1$^{VI\ 7}$) plural genitive (cf., also compound *θunχule* [TLE 1$^{XII\ 3}$]), *θunχulθe*, *θunχulθl* (TLE 570). Another form, *θunśna* (TLE 1$^{VI\ 13}$), is not clear. In the above-mentioned inscription from Pyrgi we read: *hutila tina etiasas acalia* "the fourth day (from) June's *Idus*."[167] Apparently, the numeral is formed by a standard genitive (adjective) suffix *-l(a)*. It is possible that the combination *hutila tina* is a genitive formed by the feminine type. Some have expressed the opinion that the form *zaθrumsne* (TLE 1VI 9) also represents an ordinal numeral (cf., Xarsekin 1969, 44). However, the context in which it is found indicates instead a cardinal numeral: *zaθrumsne lusaś fler hamφisca*

---

166. "*Omnium primum ad cursus lunae in duodecim menses discribit annum*" (Liv., I, 19).
167. Compare above Macrobius" gloss TLE 838b.

θezeri laiviśca lustreś "one shall put twenty gifts both at the right side and at the left side."[168]

Adverbial numerals in Etruscan are formed by the suffix -zi, known also as -z and -ze, -za (?). Compare the following combinations: TLE 99 cizi zilaχnce meθlum nurφzi canθce "three times was a z., ruled the city nine times ..."; TLE 136 eslz zilaχnθas "was a z. twice"; TLE 171 eslz tenu "held a post twice ..."; TLE 324 ziχnu cezpz ... purtśvana θunz "was a z. eight times ... once (held a post) of p.," etc.

Pfifig has brilliantly defined the combination *LXXXez* from the inscription TLE 359[a] as a mixed writing for the adverbial numeral (1969, 128). One can, with confidence, reconstruct the form *cezpalχez, "achtzigmal."[169] The forms tuśurθi (TLE 586), tuśurθii (TLE 627), "spouse," tusurθir (TLE 587) "spouses," which clearly is a calque of Latin *con-sors, con-sortis*, provide a unique case of participation of numerals in a composition. Besides these forms, some individual distributive numerals are known that have been formed by the familiar plural suffix -r: tunur "singuli" and zelur "bini" (both in the inscription TLE 619).

In the interpretation of Etruscan numerals, detection of the numeral "ten" has been one of the key problems for a long time. The ambiguity of such an important form is a serious lack of clarity in the existing model of the Etruscan numerals. At the same time, considering the significant amount of known Etruscan texts and the substantial size of some of them, such as the Zagreb text or Capuano tile (TLE 2), it seems quite probable that the numeral ten is allocated among the already known word forms, whereas the most frequently accepted point of view is not convincing enough for us.

It has been stated that the compounded form huθzar-s from epitaph TLE 191, which specifies the age of the deceased person (*avils huθzars* [i.e., has died in the age of] *x* years) can serve as a key to the solution (Xarsekin 1964, 60). Taking into account the fact that the compounded numerals in which the second component was a number from one up to five or six were formed in the Etruscan language by putting a simple numeral before ten, a similar pattern was ascribed to huθzars, and it was judged that zar means "ten" (this opinion was first stated by Cortsen [1932, 59]). Consequently, the form huθzars was understood as "fourteen" (or "sixteen," if one accepts huθ as "six").[170]

---

168. Here only the meaning of *lus-* is unclear. However, the translation "side, edge" seems to be quite probable; -treś in the second position is a pronominal enclitic, so the forms are equivalent for the expression of belonging; -ca = Latin -que.

169. It is not a unique example of writing combining letters with figures (cf., the inscription TLE 506 *mi śuθi lartia(l) larkien[a]ś IIIrve ver ...*, which clearly has something in common with CIE 2143 *L. Volusius. C. L. [ibertus] Philerotis IIIvir* [ibid., 130]).

170. According to Nemirovskij's point of view, the form huθzars, meaning "sixteen," is formed also by a principle of subtraction, and -zar- is understood as a variant of zaθrum "twenty" at that (Nemirovskij 1983, 93). Such an explanation seems to be completely unsatisfactory for several reasons. Firstly, a comparison of -zar- and zaθrum is too hypothetical from the phonetic point of view (other cases of simplification zaθrum to zar are unknown). At the same time, the connection between -zar- and śar- is not taken into account, so the difference between *ciem zaθrums* "seventeen" and *ciś śariś* is ignored. Secondly, the suffix of subtraction -em is lacking here. At last, when Nemirovskij ascribes to huθzar- the meaning

In addition, a connection between -*zar*- and *śar*- was identified (TLE 1[VIII 1], in a combination *ciś śariś* [Xarsekin 1964, 60], which, accordingly, was understood as "of the thirteenth" [genitive case]). With insignificant phonetic changes (in the variant *ceś zeriś*), the same combination appears twice in a large inscription from Monte Pitti (TLE 380[6,9] *tabella defixionis*). However, it is not possible today to translate this inscription. In our opinion, the word *zar* in the brief inscription TLE 295 also can be interpreted as a numeral, but the context here is rather complex for understanding (*cvl alile hermu zar*).

In the above treatment of *zar* as "ten," we have to consider, first of all, the fact that *zar* has nothing in common with the well-known suffix of tens -*alχ*-. It would be more logical to assume that -*alχ*- is based on the numeral meaning "ten." Besides, one has to pay attention to the phonetic similarity not only between *zar* and *zaθrum*, but also between *zar* and *zal* "two," and if a connection between numerals ten and twenty or twenty and two is obvious, it is rather inconvenient to explain a connection between ten and two. The search for a lexeme that can be interpreted as a numeral and tied to the element -*alχ*- has led us to some results. So, the form *halχ* (TLE 24, 14) was found, as well as forms *halχza* (TLE 1[X 21]), *halχze* (TLE 1[X γ2]), and also *hilχvetra* (TLE 1[VI 2], with a well-known pronominal enclitic). In our opinion, the form *halχ* cannot be divided into components, since, having separated -*alχ*, one is left with a simple aspiration *h*- as the first root, which is almost incredible. One may propose that *halχ* precisely designates the numeral "ten." The loss of aspirate *h*- in compounded forms is not difficult to explain. However, in order to prove our assumption, it is necessary to consider how appropriate forms are used in their context.

In the Capuano inscription, the word *halχ* is used in the following context: *ci tartiria cim cleva acasri halχ tei vacil*. Apparently, the numeral "three" is used here twice. A gerund with -*ri* is formed from a stem *acas*- ("to make, suggest, endow"). Evidently, it is proposed here to perform some action, and certain cult objects (*tartiria, cleva, vacil*) in plural are listed. If one excludes the gerund *acasri* and pronoun *tei*, one may assume that *halχ* refers to the noun *vacil* (cf., above plurals with -*l* and TLE 228 *vaci*). In another fragment of the same Capuano text, *halχ* is connected with the form *aper* "ancestors" in which, as can be seen, the basic Etruscan plural suffix -*r* is used.

In the Zagreb book, two forms from the root *halχ* are present that include the element -*za/-ze*. Though the context in which the word *halχze* is used is completely unclear, the other form appears in the same fragment with numerals one, two, three: *zal eśic ci halχza θu eśic zal*. Unfortunately, it is very difficult to interpret *eśic*. Nevertheless, a connection between some simple numerals is evident here: *2 eśic 3 . . . 1 eśic 2*. The use of the given form in this particular context presupposes its adverbial character. Variability of vowels in similar positions, as well as their loss, is an exceedingly widespread phenomenon in Etruscan. Therefore, one can suggest that the suffix appearing as -*zi*, -*z* in adverbs known before may also appear as -*za/-ze*.

"sixteen," he contradicts his own opinion that *huθ* means "six" but not "four," so, having accepted *huθ* "six" we should again receive "fourteen" after subtraction.

Thus, it is possible to consider with a certain amount of confidence the form *halχ* as a numeral, and its meaning "ten" seems to be the most probable. This conclusion is corroborated not only by the phonetic similarity of *halχ* and *-alχ-* and by the usage of *halχ*, but also by the function of the well-known adverbial suffix.

Apparently, this root, with some phonetically explicable variants, is present in a certain Etruscan patrimonial name: *hulχenas* (TLE 245), *hulχuniesi* (TLE 90), *hulχniesi* (TLE 84, 91). It seems we should interpret it as **Decimius*. It is difficult to tell whether the present root is identical to the infrequent form *alχu* (TLE 210, 18, 939). The combination with plural *aiser(a)* in this inscription TLE 939 can well specify a numeral. On the other hand, it is more difficult to explain the stable element *-u* as well as fluctuations in spelling (with *h* and without it) in one and the same text.

Accepting the meaning of *halχ* as "ten," we are compelled to search for a new explanation of *zar-/śar-*. The presence of only two compounded numerals from this root, as mentioned above *ciś śariś* (with a variant *ceś zeriś*) and *huθzars*, as well as the phonetic similarity of the first element *zar*, *zaθrum*, and *zal*, forces us to assume the meaning "twelve" for *zar* and to explain the forms compounded with it as relics of a duodecimal notation. This system, uncharacteristic for Indo-European languages, had influence on the Roman world: the "monetary weight system was based on duodecimal system of notation, possibly borrowed from Etruscans" (Tronskij 2001, 409). Identification of numerals compounded with twelve is also supported by historical and cultural data, especially by the unique importance of this number in Etruria.

The roots *śar-* and *zar-* are united by a common phonetic feature: a rather rare Etruscan alternation $z \sim ś$ (i.e., *zal* ~ *esl-* "two" and *śar* ~ *zar-* "twelve"). Identification of a special lexeme for twelve is also supported by historical and cultural facts, especially the importance of this number in Etruria. Some other forms containing *zVr-* (TLE 1IX 1, 8 *zarve*, TLE 1V 2, 22, VII 21, IX 1, 8 *zeri*, etc.), do not provide, it seems, the bases for comparison with *śar* ~ *zar* "twelve." It is significant that spelling with *z* for *śar* ~ *zar-* "twelve" is not found in *Liber Linteus*.

If we divert our attention away from the external similarity with *zal-* "two" and proceed from a morphological analysis, it turns out that *śar-* "twelve" is most likely to be a plural with *-r* from the root *śa* "six." It is known that the mentioned suffix was used while forming distributive numerals, but this fact cannot be given as a reason against our interpretation. One can speak with great confidence about the considerable age of the form *śar-* "twelve." It seems that it originated from an earlier stage than Etruscan, whereas the less important distributive forms can be far younger (and maybe even originated under the influence of Latin). The combination of numerals itself or the genetic relationship between simple and "geminized" numerals occurs in various languages of the world, which is not something unique from a typological point of view.[171]

---

171. Compare French *quatre-vingt(s)* "eighty" as a result of the multiplication of 4×20 or the pairs *pitö* "one" : *puta* "two," *mi* "three" : *mu* "six," *jö* "four" : *ja* "eight" in Old Japanese, *kum* "three" : *kud* "six" in Mari (Syrom'atnikov 2002, 79).

Table VIII. Etruscan numerals

	Cardinal	Ordinal	Distributive	Adverbs
1	θu(n)	θunχ	θun-ur	θun-z
2	zal		zel-ur	esl-śi
3	ciθunχ			ci-zi
4	huθ	–	–	–
5	maχ	–	–	–
6	sa	–	–	–
7	semφ	–	–	–
8	cezp	–	–	cezpz
9	nurφ	–	–	nurφ-zi
10	halχ	(hulχena?)	–	–
11	?	–	–	–
12	s/za-r	–	–	–
13	*θun-zar	–	–	–
14	*esl-zar	–	–	–
15	ci(s)-sar	–	–	–
16	huθ-zar	–	–	–
17	ci-em zaθrum	–	–	–
18	esl-em zaθrum	–	–	–
19	θun-em zaθrum	–	–	–
20	zaθr(um)	zaθrums-ne ?	–	–
21	*θun zaθrum	–	–	–
22	*esl/zal zaθrum or **sarzlχ	–	–	–
23	*ci zaθrum	–	–	–
24	huθ zaθrum	–	–	–
25	*maχ zaθrum	–	–	–
26	*sa zaθrum	–	–	–
27	ci-em cialχ	–	–	–
28	esl-em cialχ	–	–	–
29	θun-em cialχ	–	–	–
30	cialχ	–	–	–
40	*huθalχ	–	–	–
50	muvalχ	–	–	–
60	sealχ, Aeg.-Tyrr. sialχv	–	–	–
70	semφalχ	–	–	–
80	cezpalχ	–	–	*cezpalχez
90	–	nuzlχ-ne ?	–	–
100	–	–	–	–
200	–	zatlχ-ne ?	–	–

If we add up either *ci* or *huθ* and *zar* by the general rule, we receive "fifteen" and "sixteen" correspondingly. It is obvious that an identification of any compounded form containing *zar* with the first component more than four (for example, *maχ* "five") would invalidate our point of view, because any such addition would result in a numerical value higher than "sixteen" (in our example with *maχ* "seventeen"), whereas the known regular forms are produced by the principle of subtraction.[172] Nevertheless, such compounded numerals are unknown. In any case, even if they will be found, they could not be used against the interpretation of *halχ* as "ten."

A purposeful search for compounded forms which include -(a)*lχ*- had some more interesting consequences. In the text of the Zagreb book, the form *nuzlχne* appears three times (IV 6, 18, VIII 13). In the last case, it is close to *zatlχne*, and the identity of morphological elements makes it possible to define them as homogeneous parts of the sentence. The very context is most interesting: *ruzi nuzlχne zati zatlχne*. It is possible that here we are faced with a rhythmical structure of the fragment (cf., above, in Chapter 2: Sources). Judging by grammatical indicators, *ruzi* correlates with *zati* and *nuzlχne* with *zatlχne*. At the same time, *zati* is unlikely to be bound with *zatlχne* etymologically, just as *ruzi*, being consonant to *nuzlχne*, is of a different root. With a certain degree of confidence, we can presuppose that *nuz-lχ-ne* is a derivative from the numeral "ninety" (from *nurφ* "nine"), formed by the type of *zaθrums-ne* (TLE 1$^{VI\,9}$). Apparently, it is the only form in the texts known at present that can have such a meaning. The probability of finding the numeral "ninety" in epitaphs is negligibly small.

The interpretation of *nuz-lχ-* also makes us analyze the hapax legomenon *zatlχ-ne* more fixedly. The rare element -*lχ*- quite definitely shows the connection with *haχl* "ten," but after the detection of "ninety" we have only one gap in the line of tens: "forty," but *zatlχ-ne* absolutely will not do for it. Here one could expect *huθalχ* or a plural from *zaθr*- "twenty" (along with *sa-r* "twelve") or even an isolated word (such as Russian сорок),[173] which had replaced the oldest четыре десяте).

The only realistic equivalence for *zatlχ*- among the numerals can be found with *zaθr*- "twenty," and it leads us to a formal conclusion about the meaning of *zat-lχ-* as "two hundred" (20×10). Such a formation is not impossible in principle. It again can be connected with a monetary weight system.[174]

It can easily be seen that it is impossible to speak not only about some specific closeness but even elementary superficial likeness, both in roots and in principles of forming compounded numerals. The table can only confirm our supposition about "three" and "six" as the roots, borrowed from Hurrian (or a language close to it).

---

172. That is, *ciemzaθrms* "seventeen" (TLE 166), *eslem zaθrumiś* "eighteen" (TLE 1$^{VII\,4}$), *θunem zaθrums* "nineteen" (TLE 192).

173. Probably, from Turkic languages (cf., Turkish *kirk* "forty," etc.).

174. Cf., Latin *denarius* from the distributive numeral *deni* "in tens" (i.e., ten *asses*; later 1 *denarius* = 16 *asses*). The gold coin *aureus* originally was equal to 250 *asses* (100 *sestertii*). In principle, the Etruscan form could reflect a similar system: 1x = 10y = 200z. Typologically, also compare Scandinavian 1 *timbr* "40 skins," 1 *serkr* = 5 *timbr* (i.e., "200 skins").

Table IX. Examples of comparison with Etruscan numerals[175, 176]

	Etruscan	Hurrian	Basque
1	θu(n)	šukki, šuga	bat
2	zal-/esl-	šin(a)	bi(ga)
3	ki	kig(a)	hiru(r)
4	huθ	tumni	lau(r)
5	maχˇ	nariy(a)	bost/bortz
6	sa	šeže	sei
7	semφ	šindi	zazpi
8	cezp	kira/i	zortzi
9	nurφ	tamri/a	bederatzi
10	halχ	eman	hamar
11	?	–	hamaika
12	sa-r	–	hamabi
13	*θu(n)-sar	kigman(i) (30)	hamahiru(r)
14	*esl-sar	šinašinda	hamalau(r)
15	ci(s)-sar	–	hamabost/bortz
16	huθ-zar	–	hamasei
17	ki-em zaθrum	šindeman(i) (70)	hamazazpi
18	esl-em zaθrum	kir(e)man (80)	hemezortzi
19	θun-em zaθrum	–	hemeretzi
20	zaθr(um)	–	hogei/hogoi
30	ki-alχ	–	hogeitahamar
40	huθ-alχ	–	berrogei
50	muv-alχ	–	berrogeitahamar
60	se-alχ	–	hirurogei
70	semφ-alχ	–	hirurogeitahamar
80	cezp-alχ	–	laurogei
90	*nuz-lχ	–	laurogeitahamar
100	?	–	ehun
200	zatlχ (?)	–	berrehun

---

175. By (Gernot 2004, 115).
176. By (Hualde de Urbina 2003, 127).

The context in which the last two forms with -*ḳ-ne* are used is unclear. On the other hand, there also exists the form *sarzḳ* from the inscription TLE 426, which is absolutely mysterious. It stands in the second position after the name *larθi*. If it really is a numeral and defines the age, it can be interpreted only as "twenty-two" (12+10), the more so because the lines 21-23 and 31-33 are unknown to us. The system of known numerals is presented in Table VIII.

In comparing Etruscan numerals with the forms from some other isolated languages, different conceptions about genetic relationship have been suggested. It is not possible to describe them all here. For example, we would compare numerals from Etruscan, Hurrian, and Basque (the relationship between the last cannot be excluded because they may be congeneric with the hypothetical North Caucasian group), in Table IX.

VERBS
GENERAL INFORMATION

The Tyrrhenian verb, as with any other part of speech, does not have a unanimous description in the literature. Its basic categories have been differently interpreted by scholars (cf., in particular, the widespread opinion about the absence of the category of tense[177]; sometimes quite exotic terms are proposed instead, such as "aspects" by Pallottino[178] [1936, 54]).

The following description seems preferable to us: the Tyrrhenian verb can be defined as a part of speech which discerns the categories of tense or aspect, mood, and transitivity/intransitivity closely bound with voice and reflexivity, possibly person, and case (in participles). It is also quite probable that there are some other categories not yet attested. It is possible to separate verbal forms only by lexical meaning: a simple root does not have formal indications and can be used independently. Cases of independent usage are different. We find it in the imperative function and also as an adverbial modifier: *laris avle larisal clenar* <u>*sval*</u> *cn šuθi ceriχunce* (CIE 6213) "Laris (and) Aulus (the) sons of Laris, built this tomb while <u>alive</u>"; *tur heχśθ vinum* <u>*trin*</u> *flere neθunśl* "give, put wine with a prayer (as a) donation for Neptune" (TLE 1$^{IX, 6-7}$). However, in the second example, the first type of usage (i.e., imperative) is also possible.

All the rest of the paradigm known to us is formed by the use of various suffixes, partly in common with nominal ones. It would be premature to speak about periphrastic forms.

A simple verbal root, in compliance with the basic characteristics of the Tyrrhenian languages, can appear as VC (*am-, ar-, uT-*), CVC (*kes-, lup-, mul*), CVC₁C (*nunt:-, p:urt:-*) or CC₁VC (*sval-, p:lek:-*). Derivative stems are formed by means of some morphemes of the type VC. Among them, the suffixes *-in-* and *-ik:-* are interpreted most

---

177. "*Das etr. Verbum ist kein 'Zeitwort' in unsern Sinn*" (Pfiffig 1969, 130).
178. The very "aspects" are offered: I - indicative, imperative; II - deverbative nouns; III - gerund, participles; IV - passive forms; V - perfect.

reliably. In our opinion, they form the inchoative and causative meanings correspondingly (*cer-in-* "arise, get up" and *cer-iχ-* "set up, make stand" from *cer-* "be set [stood]"). Derivative stems with *-Vr-*, *-Vt-*, and possibly some others are also known. Their interpretation is complicated by their utmost rarity (cf., below *ces-eθ-c-e* from a damaged inscription TLE 85). The role of these suffixes is not obvious even when the meaning of the wordform is clearly known (cf., Etruscan *luc-a-ir-c-e* "ruled," possibly, Aegean-Tyrrhenian *tov-er-on-ai* "set (if **TVvVr-* is not an indivisible root).

It seems that, among the main verbal categories, the most general meaning is inherent in tense/mood. The others find a use in closer limits, occurring in different groups of forms. Thus, it makes sense to speak about mood only with regard to personal forms, about case to participial, etc. The system of tenses will be analyzed in detail below.

Now (based only on the Etruscan data), one can for convenience mark out the indicative mood and a group of hortative forms: imperative, optative, and gerundive.[179] The forms that can express imperative and optative are quite diverse. The far more numerous indicative forms, according to their use in reliable contexts, are appropriate only in such translations. However, we should understand that many characteristics can change considerably.

The category of person is a serious problem for scholars. Even if we describe the forms ending with *-e* and *-u* as "personal" and translate them as such, a difference among proper personal indices cannot be observed.

Although it is acceptable to translate the overwhelming majority of known verbs as third person sg. (i.e., "built," "devoted," "died," "held a position," etc., in combinations, definitely showing one person, mainly in epitaphs), the presence of the forms corresponding to first sg. and third pl. cannot be disputed today. Below is an example of the first sg. (see TLE 213) and third pl.: *arnθ larθ velimnaś arzneal*[80] *husiur suθi acil hece* (TLE 566) "Arnth (and) Larth Velimna, A.'s children, the tomb . . . constructed"[181]; *laris avle larisal clenar sval cn šuθi ceriχunce* (CIE 6213) "Laris (and) Aulus, Laris's sons, built this tomb while alive." As can be seen, the suffix *-e*, understood as a personal ending, is common for all the forms given. Accordingly, it is not possible to speak about further personal differentiation, at least for half of the paradigm.

Analogous usage can be seen among mediopassive forms: in the inscription TLE 515 *vl remzna clan-c au latini cesu* "Velia Remzna and (her) *or* Velus Remzna and (his) son, Aulus Latini, lie (here)" along with widespread *cesu* in cases where one person is meant. On the other hand, it is possible that the choice of tense suffix could be tied with personal differences (in past tenses).

The category of mood in Etruscan and other Tyrrhenian languages is not fully understood. The known model includes an opposition of active and mediopassive forms, which differ if the action is turned (medium) or not (active) to the subject.

---

179. According to Pfiffig "necessitative" (Pfiffig 1969, 142).

180. Seems to be an erroneous writing instead of **arnzeal*.

181. Asyndetic combinations of two nouns (mainly two brothers' names) can be presented as a common epigraphic feature of ancient Italy (for example, Latin inscription CIL I^2 61, widely known because of the fact that it may contain a dual (with *-o*) form: *Q. K. CESTIO Q. F. HERCOLE DONV [d]EDERO*: "Quintus (and) Kaeso Cestii, Quintus' sons, brought as a donation for Hercules."

It is believed among some scholars that the opposition between the moods is based on two ending series. Such a point of view is to be rejected. A theory about the opposition between "active" (*-ce*) and "passive" (*-χe*) forms (grounded mainly on the form *ziχuχe* "was written") was introduced by de Simone (1970) and supported by Cristofani (1973). Later Pallottino supported it, too (1979, 435). Rix, who also accepted such a distribution, translated the form *vatieχe* in the bilingual from Pyrgi as "*sono stati consecrati*" (Rix 1984², 229). However, this word does not find a clear Punic parallel. Positionally, it may even correspond to a dative form *l-rbt* "to a mistress."

Besides *ziχuχe*, there are some other forms with *-χe*, which are understood quite clearly. In particular, the word *menaχe* from the verb *men-* "to be brought" belongs to them (TLE 282, 652, 896). The form *farθnaχe* (TLE 321, 323, 344) is of a similar meaning.

Taking into account that *χ* and *c* in the forms given are the reflections of strong *k:* and do not have any phonemic differences, one should admit that their alternation cannot be the basis for any morphological distribution. Furthermore, such an explanation touches upon only one tense form without taking into account such types as *-e*, *-s-e*, *-u*, etc., and so cannot be considered explicit. Besides some stretches in peculiarities of usage, such a model faces the objection of a theoretical character: if we accepted *ziχuce* and *ziχuχe* as "*ha scritto*" and "*è stato scritto*," we would get *inflectional endings* indicating both tense and mood, which is absolutely unfounded for agglutinative Etruscan forms.

At last, long after this hypothesis had been proposed, *Tabula Cortonensis* was found, in which (line 8) we can see a combination *cén zic ziχuχe*, literally "wrote this text," with a number of names. Here the verb is combined with a pronominal object and so may be understood as active.

However, suppositions about possible mood indicators do not confine themselves to this one distribution. Cortsen (1935, 102) and then Pfiffig (1969, 148) put forward a hypothesis that there existed a mediopassive mood in Etruscan formed with the suffix *-in-*. We should analyze the verbs containing this element in detail. The root *cer-*, which can join the formants that have not been mentioned yet, is especially important.

The conclusion about mediopassive was made by Pfiffig based on the form *cerine* (cf., TLE 1[VII 11-12] (*enac*) *usil cerine*. When the translation *usil* "sun" (< Sabinian *ausel*) and forms of *ceriχunce* type with the meaning "set up, made stand" are clear, one can assume here the context "when (the) sun rises." Another tense type is also possible: "rose," and the inscription TLE 315 *eca śuθi-c velus ezpus clensi cerine* may be evidence of it. It can be translated as "and this tomb of Velus Ezpu is set by (his) son."

However, for such an important category as mediopassive, there are no more examples given. This almost singular root is obviously not enough to postulate one more structure. It wittingly cannot be compared with the well-known word forms with *-c-e* and *-s-e*. In addition, the stem of *ceriχunce* is formed with the suffix *-(i)χ(u)-*, and it is evident that *ceriχunce* and *ceriχu* have active and passive meanings correspondingly. Judging by Etruscan and Rhaetic data, mood difference was expressed with the help of endings (*-e* for active and *-u* for mediopassive). Along with it, there also existed a differentiation between transitive and intransitive forms.

It follows from Etruscan and Lemnian materials that the category of transitivity was inherent in different verbs by their lexical meaning or could be changed while adding the formant *-ni-* (sometimes simplified to *-n-* phonetically) to a simple stem with intransitive, medial meaning. It should be noted that this formant spread in Etruscan more widely in a later period, which could be connected with the decay of mediopassive forms with *-u*. The latter remained appreciably longer in Rhaetic, which corresponds with typical linguistic processes. (Etruscan, as central, was the source of innovations while peripheral Rhaetic preserved more archaisms.)

I had made a preliminary conclusion about the transitive formant while working with the inscription of the Lemnos stele (Jatsemirkij 2001, 118), which was then supplemented with the point about its common origin with the accusative formant *-ni*, well known from Etruscan (Jatsemirkij 2006, 204). The conclusion about the genetic relationship between these formants also clarifies the fact that the unmarked direct object is used with verbs containing *-ni-*. Compare the following examples: *am-* "to be," *ar-* "to be, to stay," *ziv-* "to live," etc., always with medial meaning; *al-* "to bring, to devote," *tur-* "to donate" (probably from Greek δωρ-); *lauk:-* "to rule"; *tulVr-* "to determine, to assign," always with active meaning (mainly they combine with the direct object). On the other hand, compare the roots that can change mood and become transitive: *mi mulu* "I am devoted" : *mini muluvanice* "(he/she/they) devoted me," *mi araθiale ziχuχe* "I was painted by Arathius," *ziχunce* "(he) painted," etc.

SYSTEM OF TENSES[182]

For the Tyrrhenian languages one should, apparently, distinguish two main tenses: present (or present-future, unmarked stem) and past (marked stem). Special future forms from marked stems have not yet been uncovered. The relative diversity of past formants may possibly reflect different types and allow us to describe them in the course of time, but for now we cannot definitely speak about their distinctions (for example, find an analog of Latin *plusquamperfectum* or the difference between momentary or prolonged action).

As was said above, the simple unmarked root can act as an imperative (cf., *tur* "give"),[183] which is quite common in different languages, but its main function is forming the present tense. While being added to the simple root, different suffixes and their combinations generate personal, impersonal (participles and gerundive), and main hortative forms. Personal (finite) forms are constructed by joining universal suffixes *-e* (accusative) and *-u* (mediopassive) to a simple stem.

---

182. We shall label such groups of forms as "tenses" for convenience and brevity. Such a definition does not contradict translations in known contexts, but one should remember that these groups can be aspectual.

183. Such forms as *hara*, with the conjectural translation "kill" or "strike" (TLE 490, an inscription on the missile weapon), could hardly be added here. We know that the roots in Minoan and Etruscan have consonant finals.

The most reliable present forms are obviously derived from the root *am-* "to be" (cf., the inscription TLE 213 *turis mi une ame* "I am (a) . . . donation," where *ame* is a linking verb "am").[184] Also compare the inscription TLE 469: *larθi petrui larθial sentinateś puia ame* "Larthi Petru (who) is (a) wife of Larth Sentinate," so the linking verb with *-e* may correspond at least to the first and third sg., which is analogous to past forms.

The usage of the form *leine* (TLE 394) in the context of *ril XLII* ("at the age of 42") is obscure. Usually this root is given the meaning "to die," and the appearance of the present tense here is hard to explain. One can presuppose, for example, the meaning "to live in the past" or "to live in another world."

The *repinθi*, appearing in the Zagreb book three times (TLE 1$^{II\,7,\,V\,5,\,12}$), is absolutely unclear. That is another case where one may postulate the relationship between verbal and nominal formants (with locative suffix *-t:i* in a given example), but its meaning when used with a verb remains unknown.

Two forms, *θapintaiś* and *θapintaś*, externally similar to the verbs with *-in-*, for example, understood as verbal by Pfiffig (1969: 142), are preferable to be considered as combinations with enclitics, as was shown above.

We are inclined to describe another suffix *-ik:-* as causative: the syntax of forms *ceriχu, ceriχunce*, cited repeatedly, may show this meaning rather than "*Faktitiv*" (*ceriχu-* "*machen lassen*") per Pfiffig (1969, 136).

Mediopassive forms with *-u-* ending in Etruscan (among the other Tyrrhenian languages it is noticeable, it seems, in Rhaetic, but may be found also in Minoan), reflects the fact the action is reflexive, inverted into a subject (*mul-u* "to be brought") or action described by a wittingly intransitive verb (*θui ces-u* "here lies/rests"). At the present, examples with *-e* and mediopassive forms with *-u* known to us are constructed from a limited number of roots/stems, but they occur quite often.[185] Compare the typical usage of the simple forms with *-u*: *mi mulu X-e/i* "I am devoted by X.": *mi mulu kaviieśi* (TLE 153) "I am devoted by Cavius"; *nomen auctoris* here is used in an indirect case (dative-instrumental), personal pronoun (subject) in direct. On the whole, the verb *mulu* appears very often and does not give rise to doubt in translation (cf., the similar inscription *mi mulu licineśi velχainaśi* (TLE 866) "I am devoted by Licinius Velchana," etc.). Another widespread form is *lupu*, usually translated as "dead" (TLE 98, 99, 108, and many others). Compare also the funeral inscription TLE 135, where the phrase *śuθi zivas ceriχu* "(who) built a tomb (for himself) while alive" appears. Here the suffix *-u* is also joined to a present stem. This phrase itself, in spite of grammatical differences, inevitable for unrelated languages, comes to full agreement with the Italic tradition (Latin *vivus* [*sibi*] *fecit*).

In the inscription from Volaterrae (Volterra) TLE 408, one can read: *menu turu vepet . . . ś* "(I) am brought, donated. . . ." It seems that here we find a line of synonyms, also typical for Latin dedications (cf., the type "*datum, donatum, dedicatum*," etc.). About similar synonymy in Latin, see also (Tronskij 1953, 139).

---

184. See above about the possible interpretation of *une*.
185. So, *cesu* appears in TLE eleven times, *mulu* nine times.

As has already been said, later the *-u-* type falls into decay (firstly in the past tense paradigm, see below), being preserved mainly in fossilized formulas like *θui ces-u*. On the other hand, the suffix *-u* stabilizes as a formant of a name of action or state (including the names of actor and instrument). Such forms with *-u* are the most numerous. Furthermore, in that precise state, they quite often appear in Etruscan cognomina,[186] and, due to that fact, were understood quite early while studying epitaphs.

A classical example of usage of the *-u-* forms in a new meaning is the cognomen *zicu* in the bilingual TLE 472, where it corresponds to Latin *Scribonius*. In a dedication ScAnt, 1, 422 the same form is somewhat changed because of the vowel harmonization: *zuqu* (Veii, sixth century BCE). The title *maru*, preserved in Latin as a cognomen in the family of Vergilii (*Maro*), Etruscan by origin, is an analogous derivative[187] (cf., below Aegean-Tyrrhenian *maraś* and Etruscan *marvas*). It also possibly occurs in the Sicilian inscriptions PID II 447, III 30 in an unclear context.

The southern (with a change *au > u*, Ager Hortanus) word *lucumu* (CIE 5617) is formed from the root **lauk:-* "to rule," complicated with a well-known word-formational suffix *-um-* (see below). Obviously, this exact word, being a *nomen auctoris*, was the basis for the Latin transfer *lucumo* "king."[188]

In principle, such forms once and for all lost personal shades of meaning and became closer to participles (cf., above the usage of *lupu* and *ceriχu* in the past tense context; while being substantivized, they can join the suffix **-te*, which forms the plural *-θ-ur* by the common rule).

In such a way, we can reconstruct the stem **plek(u)-* from Latin *flexuntes* and *flexumines* (with the changes *p > f* and *k > χ*). It can be seen that this stem coincides precisely with the form of the Etruscan cognomen *plecu-s* (TLE 136, Tarq.) and, possibly, occurs in the inscription CIE 8679 in the word *plekuiiunas* (if we need not accept the reading *plenuiiunas* as it is proposed in REE 63/49). Although we do not know the exact meaning of Etruscan *plecu*, one can suppose a translation of "horseman," "warrior," etc., morphologically having defined *-u* as a suffix of *nomen auctoris* (in this very case, of a cognomen).[189]

The category of number in "pure," not substantivized, forms with *-u* is not expressed, as in the verbs with *-e* as well (cf., CIE 6213 *apa-c atic* [. . .] *θui cesu* "father and mother . . . lie/rest here." The substantivized word *maru* also forms the collective plural *maru-χva* (TLE 194).

---

186. For details, see Rix 1963, which has a special focus on this aspect of Etruscan names.

187. This word also acts as a proper name, in particular, a teacher and companion of young Bacchus is so named (at Ennius).

188. According to Servius's gloss TLE 843 "lucumones" cited above.

189. As is known, this historical term is used for horsemen in active service (later *trossuli*). This word also occurs as *flexumines*, and the alternation of the suffixes indicates the stem **flex(u)-*. Vulgar etymology, recounted by Servius (". . . *"flectere" autem verbo antiquo usus est: nam equites apud veteres flexuntae vocabantur, sicut ait Varro rerum humanarum*" (Aen., IX, 603), of course, cannot be taken into account here. Some difficulty occurs with the interpretation of *x*, because the combinations *ks, cs* are practically never found in the middle of a word, if one discounts the distorted Greek name *elacsantre* Ἀλέξανδρος. From our point of view, in the Latin transfer the same mistake has been made as in the gloss *Xosfer* (TLE 858), analyzed above, where the Etruscan letter *χ* is confused with Latin *x* [ks].

With the loss of the old medial meaning, there appeared the means to join the suffix *-u* after the transitive indicator. Singular such examples are known, as *zil(a)χ-n-u* (TLE 133, 169, 324, 325), with the formant *-n-* (the translation "who ruled" [part.] is appropriate here). A number of Etruscan *nomina auctoris* with *-u* passed through the Latin lexicon, having formed there a solitary type of borrowing with final *-o* (the phonetic correlation is identical with that between *maru* : *Maro*). Compare the following words: *aleo* "gambler" (*aleae* "dice"), *caupo* "innkeeper" (cf., Etruscan *caupnal* [CIE 224], *caupis* [CIE 2034], here also Etruscan-Latin *Coponius*), *fullo* "fuller, launderer" (cf., TLE 638 *cure fulu* [oss., Cort.], TLE 415 *aule cesu vipinal fulu*, here also Umbrian *Fulonie* "Fullonii"), *lanio* "butcher," *leno* "mediator, procurer," *opilio* (*upilio*) "herdsman, shepherd" (here also the Etruscan name *ufle*, *ufli* : Latin *Opillus*, Oscan *Uplis*), *tiro* "recruit," *vespillo* (with a variant *vispillo*) "member of funeral service" (cf., *arnθintur vespu* [REE 45/22, Volcii]). The glosses 837 *histrio* "ludio" and *subulo* TLE 851 "tibicen" are formed in the same way as these words.

Most of these borrowings were pointed out by Tronskij (1953, 124). The word *balatro*[190] "fool, talker," included by him in this line, belongs to another word-formational type (see below). The stem of the word *tocullio* "money-lender," seems to be borrowed from Greek τόκος "harvest" > "income, interest" and formed with the same Etruscan suffix as *opilio* and *vespillo*.[191]

The structure of the form φersu (TLE 80, signature for a man wearing a mask) is also not fully clear. It is significant that the noun *persona* properly, borrowed in Latin, is formed with the suffix *-na*. This word has been given quite a strange interpretation by Heurgon, who compared it with the goddess's name φersipnei (CIE 5091) "Περσεφόνη" (Heurgon 1961, 265). Subsequently, it was supported by Nemirovskij when he was elaborating on his statement about religious perfomance φersu (Nemirovskij 1983, 225).

From our point of view, a comparison between φersu and φersipnei does not have any foundation. A word-formational suffix like *-P- is unknown in the Tyrrhenian languages, but we would have to postulate its existence even if we detach conjectural *-nV* from the word form. The form φersipnei reminds one rather of irregular transfers like *elina*, *elinai*, *elinei*, and certainly goes back directly to the Aegean region (i.e., Minoan). The ties between the man wearing a mask and the goddess of the underground kingdom are not confirmed by anything in either Greek or Etruscan traditions. The morphological correlation between the signature φersu and suffixal derivative *persona* lead us to a quite definite solution: *persona*, the mask as an attribute of a ritual player, commonly formed by the suffix *-u*.

It seems that the rare (preserved by Festus) word for an instrument with *-u* is a term *tolenno* "sweep, shadoof"; perhaps also *odo* (*udo*), a kind of felt footwear.

---

190. The connection of this word with Greek βάραθρον (cf., Walde-Hofmann 1938–1956, s. v. *balatro*) is absolutely improbable semantically. Greek βάραθρος appears in its abusive meaning late and is a derivative from βάραθρον "pit, hole, quagmire" (i.e., βάραθρος "worthy to be thrown down into abyss").

191. A direct borrowing from Greek (Walde-Hofmann 1938–1956, s. v. *tocullio*) is absolutely unlikely, being based on the form *τοκυλλίων, nowhere attested.

Present participles in the Tyrrhenian languages are formed using two main suffixes: -*as* and -*(a)θ*. They are known to us basically from Etruscan, and, to a lesser degree, from Rhaetic, Aegean-Tyrrhenian, and, maybe, South Lusitanian (only the forms with a suffix -*ah* are found in the latter; this suffix may be understood as a reflection of -*[a]θ]*).[192] For convenience of description, we would conditionally name them as part. I, II). Semantic differences between them are unknown: the frequency of -*as*- forms is noticeably higher.

Present participles with -*as* (part. I) in Etruscan are relatively infrequent when compared with their analogues in the past (see below). However, cases of the usage of participles from well-known roots/stems allow us to speak about this category quite definitively. The widespread forms ziv-*as* "living, alive" and sval-*as*, with the same meaning, are especially important. In the inscription TLE 171 (*avle aleθnas . . . zilaχ . . . spureθi apasi svalas marunuχva cepen tenu . . .*), where most of the lexemes are understandable, the participial form should be translated precisely in the present tense, because it is constructed in such a way as to express the fact that the buried person, Aulus Alethna, held some positions (of a priest, *cepen*, and took part in the collegium of *marones*).

We also know the reliable participial form, complicated with the case suffix -*i*. So, in the damaged epitaph from Tarquinii TLE 173, participle *sval-as-i* combines with the form *clen-ś-i* "to son" or "by son."

With a certain degree of confidence, one can suppose that the Aegean-Tyrrhenian form *maraś* (in the inscription of the Lemnian stele), formed from the same root as Etruscan *maru*, is a participle with -*as*, identical with Etruscan. We should especially emphasize the fact that the participle with -*as* from this root seemingly occurs in Etruscan. In the inscription TLE 73, the combination *spural marvas* goes after the name (then the inscription comes abruptly to an end). The inserted -*v*- is most likely to be a parasitic sound similar to that in *muluvanice* and other forms, but it may also appear as the tense formant (see below).

Another form, part. II with -*(a)θ*, occurs very seldom in Etruscan. In all reliable cases, it is a *nomen auctoris*: *snen-aθ* "maidservant,"[193] *tes-in-θ* (TLE 227) from *tes-* "to place, set" (with the same extension as *cer-in-e*), which is sometimes given the not very accurate translation "trustee"[194]; *trin-θ* (TLE 1[VII 4]) from *trin-* "to pray" or "to call." The form *tevar-aθ* (TLE 81), usually translated as "judge," literally, it seems to mean "setting" > "determining" (cf, below Aegean-Tyrrhenian *tover-on-ai* "set up"). Evidently, this suffix is identical with Aegean-Tyrrhenian -*θ*, which will be discussed below (the latter is known only in the past tense).

Besides these forms, I suggest an infinitive from the unmarked stem (i.e., the stem of the present tense), based on some linguistic regularities.

So, one can suppose that the forms with -*ni* (identical with the accusative suffix), constructed from verbal stems, are examples of the Etruscan infinitive. It is not excluded

---

192. Compare above a similar occurrence in Etruscan: dialectal *hui* instead of *θui* "here."
193. Signature on a mirror (TLE 691).
194. We would suggest the translation "keeper."

that such a formation is conditional on the prolonged interaction with Indo-European languages, where the formants of the accusative case and indefinite mood are often the same (more exactly, infinitives usually date from the fossilized cases of deverbal nouns [cf., Italic *-om, Oscan *ezum*, Umbrian *erom* "esse," Oscan *deikum* "dicere," Avestan [hvaryān] "to eat," etc.). Such forms are known to us from Etruscan texts, as *mulveni* (TLE 359, 878), *θuruni* (TLE 570^{b17}), *peθereni* (TLE 1$^{VI\ 4,\ X\ 2,\ 4,\ XI\ 8}$), etc. Assignment to one or another part of speech is unclear for *capeni* (TLE 1$^{X\ 2}$), *ceχani* (TLE 90), *mlaθcemarni* (TLE 359^{a}), where different word divisions are possible (*mlaθ-cemarni* or *mlaθce-marni*),[195] *muśni* (TLE 646), *uχulni* (TLE 407). In the other Tyrrhenian languages, similar forms of the infinitive have not yet been found.

The past tense is formed by joining suffixes -*k:*- (Etruscan, Rhaetic, probably Eteo-Cypriote); -*s*-, -*v*- (Etruscan); -*ai*(-) (Aegean-Tyrrhenian, possibly, here also South Lusitanian -*a*-) to a simple or marked stem. In turn, they join suffixes of personal or participial forms. Aegean-Tyrrhenian personal forms end with the suffix -*ai* properly, which is quite uncommon. Possibly, here the liaison of tense suffix with a vocalic personal indicator (close to Etruscan-Rhaetic -*e*) took place.

A large number of finitary forms in Etruscan are complicated with the suffix -*k*-, -*c*-, -*χ*- < *k:*, and these forms are usually marked as "perfect" in the literature (e.g., Pallottino 1976: 369). Such a designation is quite conditional at least because of the fact that, in most reliable cases, these verbs express past momentary action (closer to Greek aorist). Compare the usage of such forms: *mini muluvanice* "dedicated me"; *avils LX lupuce* "died at the age of 60" (TLE 172); *mini urθanike aranθur* "(brothers)[196] *Aranthii* shaped[197] me" (TLE 764), and many others. Also compare above *ziχ neθsrac acasce* "composed haruspicinal book." The term "perfect," obviously, should be left only for concise grammar description.

Pfiffig used the term "preterite," in this very case "weak," because he treated (unreasonably) the present tense forms with -*e* as a "strong preterite" (he postulated their identity with -*ai*- verbs from the inscription of the Lemnian stele [1969: 138-41]). The distinction between "strong" and "weak" forms is weak itself, because it is manifestly evoked by Indo-European grammar and is alien to agglutinative languages of which the Tyrrhenian group is one.

Sometimes for the verbs with -*k:*- analogies with Greek past forms (type ἔθηκε, δέδωχε [Pallottino 1979, 434]) were suggested. These comparisons, going back to the time of unsuccessful attempts to ground an Indo-European origin of Tyrrhenian languages, have now lost any practical support.

A few analogous verbs are found in Rhaetic (cf., *trin-a-χ-e* [IR 5, CE 1]), derived from a root *trin-* "to pray, call" known in Etruscan (cf., TLE 1$^{III\ 18}$ *trin-c-e*, TLE 1$^{VII\ 6}$ *trin-t-aśa*,

---

195. The latter is preferable, because it allows finding "perfect" with -*c-e* and correlating the second component with the verbal root *mar-*.

196. Here we are dealing with a standard plural form of the name *ar(a)nθ*. Morphologically, as has been shown, the form *ur-θa-ni-k-e* can also express plural.

197. Cf., *urna*, *urceus* in the next chapter.

etc.), *zin-a-χ-e* (IR 14, SZ 1) along with Etruscan *zineke* (TLE 859), *zinace* (TLE 27, 28, 49), without a clear translation.

It is tempting to see a similar form in Eteo-Cypriote: *pa-ku-ke* (KS 3). It is characteristic for this word to be put after the name *ta-le-ja* (< Τάλλιας), used in the direct case. It seems that we find the same verbal root in the Etruscan form *φeχ-u-c-u* in TLE 194[198]; here, as in Eteo-Cypriote, we find the tense (aspect) class with *-k:-*. However, the inscription which opens quite traditionally also contains the absolutely unclear forms *tarils cepta*. We do not know which action of a buried man is mentioned in the final part of the inscription.[199] In any case, now only the form *pa-ku-ke* can claim to be called an Eteo-Cypriote verb. It is especially interesting that the remote Cypriote form appears to be closer to Etruscan and Rhaetic than to Aegean-Tyrrhenian. It again shows the importance of studying the Cypriote material.

Let us analyze some constructions containing intransitive verbs with *-k:-e* that are generally used and mostly accessible for translation. The vessel inscription TLE 278 (seventh to fifth centuries BCE): *mi araθiale ziχuχe* "I was painted by Arath." Here the personal pronoun *mi* "I" is used in the direct case, and *nomen agentis* is complicated not only with genitive suffix *-al* but also dative-instrumental suffix *-e*. We conclude that the form *ziχuχe* is of passive meaning; TLE 570: *ca ceχa ziχuχe*. Unfortunately, the context is not very clear here because of the serious damage to the inscription, but the direct case of the pronoun *ca* is evident and *ziχuχe* can be translated in the passive, because some inscription or artifact was written or painted by somebody.

On the other hand, there are other quite numerous forms, including ones from well-known stems (sometimes the number of their derivatives can reach five or six; the derivatives of the root *mulu-* are used especially often). We should cite the most typical examples containing the transitive indicator: TLE 34: *mini muluvanice avile vipiennas* "Aulus Vibenna dedicated me"; TLE 36: *mine mulvanice karcuna tulumneś* "Karkuna Tulumniu dedicated me"; REE 40/30: *mi larθia θarnies muluvuneke* "Larthis Tharnia dedicated me"; TLE 57: *mini mulvanice mamarce velχanaś* "Mamercus Vulchanus dedicated me"; the constructions with *muluvanice* (with some graphical or phonetic variants) yield only perhaps to ones with *lupu(-c-e)* in distribution and may serve as a good key to translation of the whole inscription; TLE 764: *mini urθanike aranθur* "(brothers) *Aranthii* shaped[200] me" (vessel inscription).

One can see that, in every example that has been analyzed, *nomen agentis* is used in direct case and the personal pronoun "me," which is the object, in indirect (accusative). Accordingly, we translate the verb in active voice in all cases.

As has already been said, the forms with the transitive suffix did not spread in Etruscan texts at once. In some older inscriptions, the verbs do not join *-ni-*, being used

---

198. Compare the full text: *atnas vel larθal clan svalce avil LXIII zilaθ maruχva tarils cepta φeχucu*.

199. If we concede that there was a word division in *tarils*, we should not exclude that the form could be connected with *ril* "age," but there is no numeral showing it. However, the meaning "for life, lifelong" is acceptable. Moreover, any numeral would add nothing to our understanding of the verb not knowing *cepta*. The connection of the latter with *cep-ar* and, above all, *cep-en* is quite confident, but the exact lexical meaning is unknown.

200. We understand *ur-* as "clay," similar to the Greek verb κεραμεύω.

in standard constructions with the forms in accusative (in particular, with the pronoun *mini*) for all that: *mini alice velθur* "Velthur donated" (TLE 43, the inscription on an archaic vessel). Considering that the same suffix acts both as transitive indicator and accusative case suffix, this way to express grammatical meaning (its single usage) does not seem to be unusual.

For some verbs, including *-c-e-* forms, there are different forms known, both with and without the transitive suffix *-n(i)-*. In principle, one can suppose that, originally, this suffix was rather optional but became more widespread with the lapse of time. Compare typical examples: *ziχunce* (TLE 2) along with *ziχuχe*, *ceriχunce* (TLE 51, 880, 882) and *ceriχu* (TLE 135) "who has built" (part.), *zilaχnce* (TLE 99) and *zilaχce* (TLE 182) "ruled," "exercised direction of *zilc*," *θezince* "made a sacrifice" (?) (in the Zagreb text [cf., ibid.. *θezeri*]). Of course, the difference cannot be phonetic here. The transitivity of the verbs with *-ni-* is confirmed by context in most cases. As was said, the transitive indicator *-n-* can be found in the participle *zilaχ-n-θas* (TLE 92, 135) "who ruled," in the form *acna-n-asa* "who left," etc. As one can see, the suffix *-n(i)-* makes the verb transitive in meaning; the verbal root itself more often is of reflexive or passive meaning. In the translation of the Etruscan prophecy of Vegoia into Latin, the passive form prevails. It seems that it can fully reflect the original morphology and syntax.[xxv]

Thus, the system that has been analyzed had been finally formed by the late Etruscan period. Although archaic inscriptions as a whole yield to late ones in quantity, some of the archaic ones contain verbal constructions which show us that the way to express transitivity, discussed above, had not taken shape as early. Compare some of these inscriptions: *mi aranθ ramuθasi vestricinala muluvanice* (TLE 868); *mi θancvilus kanzina venel muluvace* (REE 56/42, seventh century BCE); *mi hamφinasi avhircinesi muluvana* (REE 52/15, seventh century BCE).

In the inscription TLE 868 "Aranth brought me to Ramth V." *mi*, as we see, is used as a direct object. It is evident that the suffix *-ni-* in verbal form is sufficient to express the transitivity. Along with it, the name of the vessel grantor (*aranθ*) is also used in direct case, and the recipient"s name is formed with a complex dative-directive suffix *-s-i*. The structure of the inscription REE 56/42 is the most peculiar. There are no indications of transitive action at all (that is, of course, if *muluvace* is not a mistaken writing; other similar examples are completely unknown). In this case, the sense becomes clear owing only to the lexical meaning of the words.

The form *muluvana* in REE 52/15 is unclear. One can try to find the transitive suffix *-n(i)-* and the ill understood verbal element *-a* in it or make a supposition about a nominal form with *-na*. However, the combination of the direct case *mi* and the case with *-si* for *nomen agentis* is quite standard.

Some past tense verbs with *-k:-e-*, joining the suffix *-in-*, which we define as inchoative, are also known (cf., *θez-in-c-e* [TLE 1$^{IV\,3,\,IX\,2}$] "brought, donated," *ut-in-c-e* [TLE 1$^{II\,9}$] with an unclear meaning). By all appearances, we can also include *man-in-c-e* (see below).

Some finite forms (the verb *lucairce* is especially revealing) are unclear from the positions of word formation. Nevertheless, their meaning is known to us. Here one can include the existence of the verbal suffix *-Vr-*, but its meaning can only be conjectured.

Compare a damaged inscription TLE 85 . . . *inas sacni θui ceseθce* along with *cesu* "lies, rests." On the basis of the given verbal form, Pfiffig made a conclusion about the causative suffix *-eθ-* (*ces-* "liegen," *ces-eθ-* "ligen machen, legen," *ces-eθ-ce* "er legte" [Pfiffig 1969: 143]). However, because the suffix *-eθ-* is unique, and the context is unclear as a whole (the translation "founded a sanctuary here," "treasure is placed here" is also acceptable), this version does not seem grounded enough.

All the mediopassive verbs in the past known to us are formed with the suffix *-k:-*. Verbs with *-u* in Etruscan belong to a few morphological units for which it is possible to observe chronological changes applying to formation and peculiarities in usage. In the archaic period, past forms with *-u* were used, it seems, more widely than finite ones with *-k:-e*, which sometimes are presented as the most widespread. So far as these forms were used as a part of the reflexive-passive construction, their decay and replacement with the *-k:-e-* verbs should apparently be connected with the spread of a new way of expressing the relationship between subject and object—namely, verbs marked with the transitive indicator *-ni-*. Compare the following examples: *mi aliqu auvilesi* (TLE 27, C.) "I was brought by Aulus"; *mi spuriesi teiθurnasi aliqu* (TLE 940, orig. inc.) "I was brought by Spurius Teithurnus"; *mi zinaku larθuzale kuleniesi* (REE 40/1 Faes., seventh century BCE) "I was . . . -ed by Larth Kulenius," *vhelequ* (TLE 56) in an unclear context, etc. On the other hand, the tense (aspect) indicator *-k:-* in the given context, apparently, was not of paramount importance, because, it appears from the examples being analyzed, that the action described has a shade of the result, or even state, applying to the present. It is quite natural that, by the late Etruscan period, such forms had disappeared by degrees, and we find the forms with *-u* only in the present tense.

In Rhaetic inscriptions, chronologically coincident with late Etruscan, this type remained predominant: compare such forms as *eluku* (IR 25, SZ 12; IR 29, SZ 30), etc. The inscription on a bronze shield IR 1, NO 3 fully corresponds to archaic Etruscan ones in its structure: *u--ku φeluriesi φelvinuale*.

The form *a-ja-ku* (if the word division is made correctly) in the final part of the Minoan inscription from Mauro-Spelio is of exceptional importance. It is easily seen that it can fully correspond to Etruscan mediopassive in the past (the root itself is possibly borrowed from Luwian *aya-* "to make"). The syllable *mu* (= Etruscan *mi*?) precedes the form *a-ja-ku*, so even the construction "I was made" is probable here.

Verbs with final *-s-e* belong to another tense (aspect) group of finite forms. In some cases, they were given the name "aorist," not less conventional than "perfect" for *-c-e-* type. The most reliable among these forms is *tulerase* "(he) defined" (TLE 874), clarified due to a borrowed Umbrian[201] lexeme *tular* "confines, limit," known from the inscriptions on boundary stones (TLE 632 *tular rasnal* "*fines populi*," etc.). The meaning of the forms *apirase* (TLE 2), *fanuśe* (TLE 1[X 23]), *θentmase* (TLE 381), etc., is unclear. Most mistakes in the interpretation of such forms are conditioned on the unwarranted mixing of these forms with participles marked with the suffix *-as(a)*. While the forms with *-s* and *-sa* freely alternate in the same context (which is especially clearly seen in the

---

201. Compare Umbrian *tuder* "finem" with dialectal change $d > l$ (nom. pl. *tuderor*, acc. pl *tudero*, *tuderato est* "finitum ibit"); here also Latin *tundo* (*tutudi*, *tu*[*n*]*sum*) "to hew from stone."

group of funeral inscriptions from Tarquinii, containing the participles *acnanas* [TLE 887-9], *acnanasa* [TLE 169, 170] with the meaning "who left [children]"), the alternation between *-as(a)* and *-s-e* is never observed. Compare TLE 887 *spitus larθ larθal svalce LXIII huśur maχ acnanas manim arce* "Larth Spitu (son) of Larth, lived 63 (years), having left 5 children, died" (I give this translation because I assume the literal meaning "became [on of] *Manes*").[202] Any alternation between these forms and verbs with *-s-e* has never been found. In this specific case, we are dealing with different grammatical categories.

Verbs with *-s-e*, not numerous as a whole, do not have a reliable interpretation in a number of inscriptions and can be marked out quite conditionally. For example, the epitaph TLE 101: *laris pumpus arnθal clan ceχase* "Laris Pumpu, son of Arnth, . . ." Here one can speak about the form *ceχase* as a verb with certainty ("built," "set," or something close). Any other "pretenders" are absolutely absent, but its lexical meaning is troublesome.[203]

One should mention that, although finite forms with *-c-e* and *-s-e* are seldom found in the same syntagma, participles with *-s(a)* can occur close to both of them. When the reliable alternations are so few, peculiarities in the usage of finite *-c-e* and *-s-e-* forms do not allow us to describe the nuances of meaning. It is quite probable that *-s-e-* forms reflect local dialecticism or morphological archaism. For example, in a quite early (fifth century BCE) inscription from Pyrgi TLE 875, all the finite forms are represented by the type with *-s-e*, whereas the verbs with *-c-e* occur not once. In the bilingual TLE 874, both types of forms occur. Therefore, we cannot suggest any morphological distribution between the tense (aspect) indicators *-c-* and *-s-* at the present time.

It is possible that a singular Etruscan gloss (by Festus) indicating a verb belongs to the same type (*-s-e*): *arse verse* "*averte ignem*" (TLE 812), with the explanation of the meaning of both elements: *arse* - "*averte*" and *verse* "*ignem*," which was analyzed above. However, this form still remains isolated. It may reflect a distorted stem or Etruscan category unknown to us.

---

202. This root, which is reflected in Latin *Manes* and *Mania* (the mother of *Lares* [cf., Etruscan *Lasa*]) in Etruscan occurs quite often. The Latin particle proper allows us to interpret its meaning. Other attempts to find an etymology failed (so, according to a remark by Nemirovskij, one cannot take into account the vulgar etymological connection between *manus* "good" and the name of the souls by which the Romans were inspired with awe (Nemirovskij 1983, 186]). Most Etruscan examples are difficult to understand because of an unusual word formation (TLE 730 *mani*, 184 *mania*, 887 *maniim*, 169, 891 *manim*). The context in which the form *manimeri* (TLE 170) is used is not clear, because we cannot say with certainty if it is a directive case of a noun or a gerundive. The verbal form *manince* on a bronze bird statuette (TLE 398) we should evidently understand in the context as "honored *Manes*," (i.e., "devoted to ancestors"). It seems that the name of the other world deity, *Mantus* (corresponding to Roman *Dis Pater*, Father Dis; see above), preserved by Servius, should be included here, too. It was also preserved in the name of Mantua (de Simone 1992). It is possible that only in the form *man* (TLE 359[a,b], 579) do we deal with the pure root.

203. Versions suggested by Xarsekin (*ceχa* "higher, superior") and Pallottino (*ceχase* understood as the term for a magistrate's post) are not very probable; they contradict the syntax of the inscription.

By analogy with *-kː-u-* verbs, one can admit the existence of past mediopassive forms with *-s-u* in Etruscan, but the great rarity of verbs *-s-e* and relative sparsity even of mediopassive *-kː-u-* verbs minimize the probability of revealing such forms.

The rarest past tense formant in Etruscan is the suffix -*v*-. It is presented in the inscription TLE 233 in only two certain forms: *zilaχ-n-v-e* "was a *zilc*," *ten-v-e* "held a position." In the inscription TLE 939, the form *turannuve*, which can be translated with certainty as "reigned," appears three times (the stem itself, presented in Greek τύραννος, goes back, as was mentioned, to Minoan). It is most probable that the suffix -*v*- is a rare dialecticism (the inscription TLE 233 comes from the area of Volsinii, the origin of TLE 939 is unknown). One cannot exclude the possibility that we find the same tense suffix in the participial form *marvas* from the inscription TLE 732, given above.

Aegean-Tyrrhenian verbal forms, known to us only from the inscription of the Lemnian stele and ending with -*ai*, are formed from five roots. Altogether, seven finite forms can be counted: *śer-on-ai* "buried," *śiv-ai* (three times) "lived," *aom-ai, ar-ai* "was," and *tover-on-ai* "set up (a monument)." One can postulate that the suffix -*on*-, with which transitive verbs (*śer-on-ai, tover-on-ai*) are formed, is remotely related to Etruscan -*ni*-. Known Tyrrhenian past participles are formed with fewer suffixes than the finite verbs.

In Etruscan and, by all appearances, in Rhaetic, past participles are also found ending with -*as(a)*. The inclusion of another affix was also possible (cf., for example, the Etruscan form *zilaχ-n-θ-as* "who was *zilc*," occurring twice [TLE 92, 136]), where the transitive suffix -*n*- again goes between the tense character and participial formant. It seems that only once do we see the formation of a participle with -*as(a)* from the same root in both tenses: *sval-as* and *sval-θ-as* "living" and "who lived" correspondingly. The typical case of the usage of such a form, . . . *avil svalθas LXXXII* (TLE 126) shows us the past tense or perfective aspect exactly: "who lived 82 years." Often found in funeral inscriptions, the participle *ten-θ-as* is also preferably translated in the past tense, "who held a position." A similar participle, but with the inclusion of parasitic -*v*-, is *nesiθvas* (TLE 138) with the quite certain meaning "dead."[204]

In Aegean-Tyrrhenian and possibly South Lusitanian, only one participial form is presented in phonetically close variants. The known Aegean-Tyrrhenian participle of the past tense (or perfective aspect) is formed with the same tense (aspect) character -*ai* (*śeron-ai-θ* "buried"), as all the other verbal forms, presented in the inscription of the Stele, and proper participial suffix -*θ*.[205] The meaning *śeronaiθ* "buried" is clear not only from the context but also due to comparison with analogous forms in South Lusitanian inscriptions. Thus, the forms *saronah* (seven times), also *saronnah* and *zaronah* (once each) were found there by Schulten with the following adverb *konii, konθi*,[206] for which

---

204. An epitaph of a woman, which contains the combination *avils cis muvalχls* "(at the age) of 53 years" after *nesiθvas*.

205. It seems that its external likeness with the locative suffix -*θ(i)* brought Pfiffig to the paradoxical conclusion that *śeron*- was a place name (Pfiffig 1969, 139).

206. In principle, Lusitanian forms can be explained as locative, formed by the elements -*i* and -*θi* from the pronominal root *c(S)*-.

the meaning "here" is postulated (i.e., *saronah konii* "*hic situs est*"), and also the unclear derivatives *śarunθoa*, *saroθo* (Schulten 1941, 20). In Etruscan past participles, the element *-θ* has not been attested yet. However, present tense forms with this suffix are quite rare, too.

HORTATIVE FORMS

Tyrrhenian hortative forms, known only from Etruscan, are formed from unmarked stems, so they can be formally rated to the present tense paradigm. However, we shall analyze them separately for the convenience of explanation.

The imperative (as, in principle, other forms) is known mostly from the text of the Zagreb book. The usage of the simple root in such a function is not called into question (Pfiffig 1969, 134). With a certain degree of confidence, one also can include in this type forms which are complicated with the inchoative suffix *-in(-)* (cf., *θezin* (TLE 1$^{\text{VIII 16}}$), and, maybe, some other verbs.

Besides that, it is often thought that the imperative (with the exception of those cases when it coincides with a simple stem) can be formed with the suffix *-θ*, homophonic to the participial one (*ar-θ* "be," *heχ-ś-θ* "put," *trin-θ* "pray") (Pallottino 1979, 454, etc.). Pfiffig marked such imperatives as "weak" (1969, 137). Compare above the examples of their usage: *tur heχśθ vinum trin flere neθunśl* "give, put the wine while praying (as a donation) for Neptune" (IX, 6-7). It is not known for sure how the suffix *-θ* changes the meaning of the word, but it seems that this element itself helped us to uncover a new verb category.

In the text of the Zagreb book, some derivatives with *-en* are formed with the help of the suffix *-θ* to which a meaning close to hortative (*nunθ-en* : *nunθ-en-θ*, etc.) can be attributed. The widespread root *cer-* with the meaning "to stand, to make stand" helped us to understand their meaning. Twice in the text (VII, 9, 21), the derivative form *ceren* is combined with the word "priest": *cepen ceren* and *ceren cepen*. Actually, only an optative can be presupposed here, although we do not know the character of the action: "let the priest stand" or "let the priest set up." As can be seen, the form correlates with the singular. One can accordingly conjecture about a plural meaning for the suffix *-θ*, but we cannot speak about it with certainty because of the absence of such differentiation in the other verbal categories. To the root *cer-* itself we shall return again.

Gerundive forms are mostly provided by the text of the Zagreb mummy, too. Compare the typical examples of how it is used: *celi huθiś zaθrumiś flerχva neθunśl śucri θezeri-c* "on 24th of September (one) should *declare and make a sacrifice for Neptune" (VIII, 3-4); *cntnam θesan fler veiveś θezeri etnam aisna . . . iχ huθiś zaθrumiś* (XI, 14) "and in the same morning a sacrifice for Veiovis should be made, as on 24th." We should also adduce the forms TLE 1$^{\text{V 22}}$ *eluri* (along with TLE 1$^{\text{XII 52}}$ *eluce*), TLE 2 *faniri*, TLE 75 *pateri* (along with TLE 107), but their lexical meaning is not always clear (it is possible that, in the first case, we are dealing with a variant of the root *al-*).

Table X. Known paradigm of Tyrrhenian verbs[207]

		Finite forms		Non-finite forms	
		Act. -e	Med.-Pass. -u	Part. I -(a)s(a)	Part. II -(a)t:
Present	ø	am-e *Inchoat.* cer-in-e, fer-in-e	lup-u, ces-u, ten-u *Inchoat. (?)* lup-in-u (Rhaet.) *Trans.* zilaχ-n-u *Caus.* cer-iχ-u *N. Agentis* Zic-u, mar-u	sval-as, teśam-sa, marv-as, mar-aś (Ae.-Tyrr.)	snen-aθ, tevar-aθ *Inchoat.* tes-in-θ
Past	-k:	am-c-e, lupu-c-e, trin-c-e, pa-ku-ke (Et.-Cypr.), ziχu-χ-e, trina-χ-e (Rhaet.) *Inchoat.* man-in-c-e *Trans.* muluva-ni-c-e *Caus. Trans.* cer-iχ-un-c-e	al-q-u, φeχu-c-u, elu-k-u (Rhaet.), upi-k-u (Rhaet.)	–	–
	-s	tulera-s-e alśa-s-e	?	–	–
	-v	ten-v-e, turannu-v-e *Trans.* zilaχ-n-v-e	?	–	–
	-e		-u	-(a)s(a)	
	-t:	–	–	sval-θ-as *Trans.* zilaχ-n-θ-as	?
Past	-ai	aom-ai, śiv-ai, *Trans.* śer-on-ai, tover-on-ai	–	?	*Trans.* śer-on-ai-θ, saron(n)ah (S. Lus.)
"Infinitive" (transitive) -ni					
mulve-ni, θuru-ni, peθere-ni					
Hortative forms					
Imperative Sg. -ø, Pl. -θ		Optative Sg. -en, Pl. -en-θ		Gerundive -eri	
tur heχs-θ, trin-θ		cer-en nunθ-en-θ		nunθ-eri, θez-eri	

---

207. Etruscan forms are not marked specially. The formant is known from Aegean-Tyrrhenian and South Lusitanian.

For a certain number of the forms with -(e)ri, it has not been defined yet to which part of speech they belong (cf., TLE 75 *leiθrmeri*, TLE [IIV 4, 17] *meleri*, TLE 426 *muceri*, TLE 860 *tenateri*, etc.). The forms like *śacni-cl-eri* should be understood as substantivized (with an enclitic *-cla* translated in accordance: "for consecration"). Conclusions about the Etruscan verbal system in comparison to other Tyrrhenian forms are presented in Table X.

CONJECTURAL PERIPHRASTIC FORMS

Complex verbal forms in Etruscan have not been clearly revealed yet. As was shown, almost the only possible "pretender" here is the inscription TLE 135. We should cite it in full: *camnas larθ larθal*ś *atnal-c clan an śuθi lavtni zivas ceriχu teśamsa śuθiθ atiśrr-c escuna calti śuθiθi munθ zivas murśl XX*. The beginning of the inscription is absolutely transparent ("Larth Camna, son of Larth and Atna, this family tomb alive. . ."). Then there occur certain difficulties.

Pfiffig offered for *ceriχu teśamsa* the explanation "ordered that it should be built." Generally speaking, the conglomeration of participial forms (*teśamsa* is, of course, the same participle as *acnanasa* "(who) left") looks rather strange (roughly, as "living, having ordered [that] [it should) be built"). But even this does not constitute the main complication. We should also look at the end where a single word is unclear: *escuna*. Thus, *śuθiθ atiśrr-c*[208] "in the atrium of a tomb," *calti śuθiθi* "in this tomb," *munθ* religious term, probably comparable with *mundus* (a hole which was thought to bind the earth and underworld), *zivas* again "living, alive," *murśl XX* "20 vessels." It is clear that the deceased also had time to place there some religious vessels, but the verb which must describe the act (if we accept Pfiffig's conclusion) is absent. Such a verb (more precisely, participle) with the meaning "who had placed" could be *teśamsa* (a substantivized form from the bilingual TLE 874 confirms our opinion),[209] so any formal binding of this form to *ceriχu* is very disputable. From the formal point of view, there is no antagonism, because *ceriχu*, as was shown, does not need any more special forms (if it is used in the context of "who built").

Among the syntactic words that could combine with the verb, it is certainly now possible to include *et/θ*. This presumable conjunction can be used both in preposition and postposition to the verb. The rupture of the construction is also acceptable. The most prominent example of its usage seems to originate from TC: [1] *et pétruiś sceveś* . . . [(2)]*cen*[ ]*u* "let Petru Sceve (and the members of *Cusu*) perform . . ." Unfortunately, we do not know any suffixal elements (if they existed) preceding the *-u*. In the inscription from San Manno TLE 619, *eθ* also precedes the mediopassive form: *eθ fanu*. In the other cases, it is not possible to confirm such grammatical agreement, since *eθ* is also used with some other forms, particularly, with the gerundive: *nunθeri eθ* (TLE 2[12]). The

---

208. With a probable mistake of the carver.
209. In the Punic parallel for *teśiameitale* "(in the day) of burial" (i.e., "placement in the tomb").

clear context in TC, likewise the main meaning of a gerundive, quite definitely point to *eθ* as a conjunction, which expressed a hortative meaning.

The examples of which we can be more or less confident that they could express a negative meaning seem to be the forms *nunar* in TLE 13 (*θupes fuluśla mi ei min[i]-pi capi mi nunar θevruchnas*) and *ei*, found quite often (TLE 1, several times, 2^{13}, 12, 13, etc.). We analyzed above a complex possessive (?) construction *mini-pi* on the example of the inscription TLE 12. It is possible that here we should find an opposition: "I am a cup for (. . .), but not for *θ*." In such a case, the form *nunar* could easily be a product of the composition of a negation **nun* with the root *ar-* "to be, to become" (i.e., typologically similar to Old Church Slavonic нестъ). In its turn, in most cases when *ei* is used, the context is absolutely unclear (cf., TLE 157 *muχ ara an eiseθasri*).

CHAPTER SIX NOTES

[xxiv] "*quia Mantua tres habuit populi tribus, quae in quaternas curias dividebantur: et singuli singuli lucumones imperabant, quos tota in Tuscia duodecim fuisse manifestum est, ex quibus unus omnibus praeerat.*"

[xxv] "*Cum autem Juppiter terram Etruriae sibi iudicavit, constituit iussitque metiri campos signarique agros. Sciens hominum avaritiam vel terrenam cupidinem, terminis omnia scita esse voluit [. . .]. Sed qui contigerit moveritque, possessionem promovendo suam, alterius minuendo, ob hoc scelus damnabitur a diis. Si servi faciant, domino mutabantur in deterius. Sed si conscentia dominica fiet, celerius domus extirpabitur, gensque eius omnis interiet. Motores autem pessimis morbis et vulneribus officientur membrisque suis debilitabuntur. Multae dissensiones in populo. Fieri haec scitote, cum talia scelera committuntur.*"

CHAPTER 7

WORD FORMATION

GENERAL CHARACTERISTICS

Issues of proper word formation both in Minoan and Etruscan, along with the other Tyrrhenian languages to some degree, are known quite well (and for Minoan, as was shown, this category has been the most complete during our studies). For quite a long time now, typical word formation models have allowed scholars to single out Minoan and Tyrrhenian lexemes. For the research of relic lexica (mainly passed through Greek and Latin), word-formational features are paramount. At the same time, there are some difficulties with the morphological interpretation of exact forms. This is explained by the fact that, even if the lexical meaning of the borrowings are clearly known to us, for certain words in the inscriptions, we have to confine ourselves to general semantics (for example, the derivative of the Etruscan root *ziχ*- "to write" [see above], *ziχina* can have the meaning "inscription," "inscribed," "bookish," etc.; the pure root *ziχ* has the independent meaning "book," and it complicates the interpretation of *ziχina*). In relation to Minoan texts (i.e., the inscriptions of Linear A), the number of identified word-formational elements is even more embarrassing because of the peculiarities of the Linear writing itself. We know few reliable parallels, so convincing conclusions can in practice only be made when corresponding roots or full words are known from the Greek transfers. Rare and, at times, single formants are the burning issue for all the languages being analyzed. So, for example, we suggest singling out the suffix -ρδ- in Minoan on the basis of the alternations which can be observed for the root of plant names **kik-*: in Hesychius the word for "fig" is given: κικίρδης, and along with it the forms κεικύνη : *ki-ki-na* and κικένδα (Etruscan gloss given above) are known to us. This, in its turn, allows us to ascribe to the Minoan language the name of a fish, also preserved by Hesychius: σαπέρδης,[210] and to link the latter with σηπία. It is possible that the word for (supposedly)

---

210. "ὄνομα ἰχθύος. οἱ δὲ ταρίχου εἶδος. ἄλλοι ὑπὸ Ποντικῶν τὸν κορακίνον ἰχθύν."

a wild pear (*Pirus salicifolia*) ἄχερδος also belongs to this type. I have not succeeded in finding any similar examples. Our hope of finding them in the inscriptions of Linear A is not great, either. As was shown above, a special Minoan phoneme is hidden here, and the reconstruction of this suffix in some case where *rV* is used can hardly be conclusive.

The cases when some suffixes are used in Tyrrhenian inscriptions are also singular. Compare, for example, (*ziχ*) *neθśra* "haruspicinal (book)" (TLE 131) and *netśvis* "foreteller, haruspex" (TLE 524, 697). The root itself is also presented in pre-Greek νηδύς "stomach, entrails" (i.e., meaning fortune-telling with internal organs). This example can be correlated with some Latin words with -*ra* of an unclear origin, such as *acerra*, whereas the epigraphic correspondences are unreliable.

Actually, scholars have learned rather to recognize Minoan and Tyrrhenian lexemes than to draw a distinction between the meanings. However, an analysis of the stems which appear often or are unquestionable for other reasons can throw light not only on the principles of word formation of the languages under study but also on the meaning of certain affixes.

In Minoan and Tyrrhenian lexemes, the main morphological and word-formational function belongs to suffixal elements, which are quite numerous and are often easily combined among themselves. Prefixation, not observed in the materials of any analyzed language from the first millennium BCE, had also been quite widespread in Minoan. The alternation of different suffixes joining the same root is presented in a multitude of examples, both Minoan and Tyrrhenian, but if in most cases they differ in lexical meaning (cf., for example, κεικύνη : *ki-ki-na*, κικένδα, and κικίρδης as the words for different plants, Aegean and Etruscan derivatives from **p:al-* "top, head"; φύλαξ "guard"; φύλοπις "battle"; etc.), some Etruscan derivatives with different suffixes are always translated equally (cf., a free alternation in *flexumines* and *flexuntes*, etc.).[211] In the chain of affix layers, one cannot always differentiate word-formational and morphological elements. Moreover, some of them could play both roles. However, the meaning of certain lexemes is actually explicable when the combinatory analysis is used.

There is no generally adopted classification of word-formational suffixes. It is also quite difficult to be guided by the frequency of their occurrence (it does not coincide in Minoan and Etruscan texts and relic lexica), so the order of their description usually is unconditioned. Sometimes attempts are made to systematize them most generally.[212]

However, even here, the classification of the suffix is not very trustworthy. For example, we know that the suffixes -*na* and -*um* in Etruscan can join both nominal and verbal roots/stems. But they are the two most widespread uses, and with regard to rare ones, it is not possible to affirm if they join only one part of stems. Newer findings may show the contrary.

---

211. Typologically, see also the uncertainty of Latin parallels of the types -*men* and -*mentum* (third and second declensions correspondingly), -*ia* and -*ies* (abstract nouns, formed in the first and fifth declensions), etc.

212. Particularly, in Chapter 7: Word Formation in Pfiffig's grammar (1969, 163–73), the following order of description is accepted: *deverbale Verba, denominale Verba, denominale Nomina, deverbale Nomina*. At the same time, proper, ethnic, and place names are analyzed separately.

Some suffixes (the same *-na* and *-um*, Minoan *-oπ*) form proper names and common nouns in the broadest sense. The others are more specific, as, for example, the suffix -νθ-/-*te*, showing the origin or belonging, or an Etruscan diminutive formant *-zV*. It should be especially emphasized that we are dealing almost exclusively with the noun formants. Attempts to describe derivative verbs (cf., Pfiffig 1969, 164) are unconvincing in large part, and the formants which had been marked out belong mostly to morphological, not to word-formational, elements (cf., again the suffix -*in*- with supposedly inchoative meaning).

We shall be analyzing the word-formational elements in the following order: (a) prefixes (on Minoan material); (b) nominal suffixes *-na*, *-ur-*, *-um-*, *-uk-*, *-u(m)b-*, *-uf-* (with their variants), and also their combinations among themselves and with the other elements; (c) special suffixes, particularly, Minoan *-op-*, adjectival ones, the often mentioned indicator of belonging -νθ-/-*te*, and diminutive ones; and (d) that part of forms with pronominal enclitics where the latter act as substantivizing.

PREFIXATION

Prefixation as a morphological phenomenon in the languages being analyzed is peculiar only to Minoan (but even here it is unclear if it was produced during the period when the known inscriptions were being created, or if we are dealing with fossilized forms). It is also not clear if there are fused forms with the prefixes that had been forgotten long before in Tyrrhenian inscriptions and borrowings (theoretically they can be discerned only in rare roots of the type VCVC and rarest CVCVC).

The main Minoan prefixes were marked out by Molchanov (cf., for example, [Molchanov et al., 1988, 172.]). To them belong *a-* (with a variant containing parasitic semivowel: *ja-*), *u-/i-*, *no-*, *ra-*, and, apparently, some others.

The prefix *a-* is found in the name of one of the main (pre-)Greek goddesses, Ἀθανᾶ and Ἀθηνᾶ, along with the name of the Cretan town Τάνος, with the pure root, and the name of another Cretan town Ἴτανος (Mycenaean *u-ta-no*), with another prefix. The supposed deity name *a-sa-sa-ra*, *ja-sa-sa-ra* (if the version from the previous chapter is not confirmed), can be brought into correlation with the root of the word σάσαμον, σήσαμον "sesame," formed with the suffixes -αρ- and -αμ- correspondingly (both with dialectal vowel, see below). The lexeme *a-su-pu-wa* (ARKH 2) is likely to be compared with σιπύη, *su-pu2-* [HT 8] "bin," in the latter inscription (cf., also *si-da-te* and *a-si-da-to-no*, etc.).

An indubitable merit of Molchanov's analysis is the suggestion that the name *no-da-ma-te* (AR Zf 1) be read as a parallel with Ῥαδάμανθυς (Minos's brother, one of the three judges of the underworld). Moreover, a pure stem is also known to us: *da-ma-te* (KY Za 2), Δαμυρίας, Sicilian river, Δαμύλος (Lucian.), a proper name with typical Minoan suffixes -νθ- and -υρ-, which will be discussed below, too. Dybo pointed out to the author that such prefixing can reflect the relics of nominal classes, but this supposition has not been concretized yet.

We should also distinguish from the prefixing principle the appearance of prothetic *e-* known both in Minoan and Etruscan: cf., ἕλμινς, ἕλμινθος, along with Hesychius's gloss λίμινς "parasitic worm," Etruscan *esl-* along with *zal-* "two," the title *eprt-* : *purt-* : πρύτανις, and the name *Etrusci* itself along with Τυρσηνοί and Umbrian *Turskum*. In Etruscan, this phenomenon can be observed also in the syntactic morphemes: *epl* along with *pul*. The word λεβίνθιος (in Stephan also a place name Λέβινθος) along with ἐρέβινθος is unclear (if here we admit the alternation ρ : λ), because in the other cases when prothetic *e-* appears, the root vowel is dropped.

Tyrrhenian languages of the first millennium BCE are characterized by the whole absence of prefixing (but as was shown above, there are single cases of word combination). A very interesting example of how to compensate for the absence of prefixes, which are unknown in Etruscan, is the word *tuśurθi* (TLE 586), *tuśurθii* (TLE 627) "spouse," *tusurθir* (TLE 587) "spouses." From our point of view, it is a calque of Latin *consors*, Gen. *consortis*. In consideration of the fact that the Latin root is *sort-* (*sors* "fate"), and *con-* is a prefix which expresses the unity, the Etruscan element *-surθ-* is almost identical to Latin *sort-*. Further, we can analyze the meaning of *tu*. It seems that when the Latin word had been borrowed, its structure was understood quite clearly, and, in the absence of an analogous prefix for showing the unity, they used the numeral "one" (*tu*[*n*], *θu*[*n*]), which is quite close semantically.

MAIN NAME FORMANTS AND THEIR COMBINATIONS[213]

There are eight main word-formation elements in the forms analyzed below. If we omit for a time their phonetic variants, they can be presented as follows. For Greek transfers: -οπ-, -να, -νθ-, -υρ-, -υμ-, -υκ-, -υ(μ)β-, -υφ-; for Etruscan and Latin: -*na*(-), -*te*/-*nt*-/-*t*-, -*ur*(-), -*um*(-) (it is doubtful whether there were the analogues for -υκ-, -υ(μ)β-, -υφ- in Etruscan, or not,[214] *-*op*- is absent). As was said above, -οπ- and -νθ-/-*te* will be examined separately.

In Greek writings, for the forms containing the latter five suffixes, there are three main types of variation: two of them reflect the specific features of Minoan phonetics, and the third one seems to be evidence of dialectal differences within the Minoan language. The alternation ι/υ and the mixing of λ and ρ belong to the first two types. On the other hand, in every suffix, with the exception of the seldom found -υφ-, the vowel ι/υ may alternate with α, which, from our point of view, reflects the features of a normal local dialect. With due regard for these alternations, the most widespread Minoan suffix, written below as -υρ- for simplicity, is presented in six variants. It is also possible to observe three variants for three suffixes, each:

---

213. There are plenty of possible suffix combinations and alternations of suffixes, and an attempt to characterize them all would bring this chapter to an unexpectedly huge size. Below we shall give the most typical variants, whereas the brief description of the suffixes added to the very root are shown in the Index.

214. In particular, it is not clear if the Etruscan suffix *-uc*, *-uχ* may correspond to -uk- or had been borrowed from Hurrian. There is also something similar in Eteo-Cypriote; see below in detail.

-υρ-	-ιρ-	-αρ-
-υλ-	-ιλ-	-αλ-
-υμ-	-ιμ-	-αμ-
-υκ-	-ικ-	-ακ-
-υ(μ)β-	-ι(μ)β-	-α(μ)β-
-υφ-	*-ιφ-	*-αφ-

There are two reasons to consider the totality of these suffixal derivatives as a single system. On the one hand, the alternations of different suffixes with the same roots, and, on the other, the varied combinations of the suffixes among themselves (by all appearances, there are no more than two or three suffixes with the root and no case of redoubling has been observed).

It is possible that the word formation suffix -να/-νη/-na, -nV[215] is one of the most widespread in Minoan and doubtless most often seen in Tyrrhenian. In pre-Greek it is discovered, in particular, in Hesychius' lexemes ἄττανα "frying pan,"[216] βουκανῆ "anemone flower" (Cypriote gloss of Hesychius), βασύνιας (Semus, Fr., 3) "sacrificial donation to Hecate in Delos" (cf., Etruscan *pesna*, CIE 252, etc.), γάρσανον "brushwood" (Cretan Hesychius's gloss), δρεπάνη "sickle," ἐλεδώνη "mollusk species" (*Eledone moschata?*), ζιζάνιον "darnel, *Lolium temulentum*," καπάνα (Thessalian) "vehicle," καπάνη (in Hesychius) "hair cap," κεκῆνας (acc. pl.) "hare" (Cretan Hesychius's gloss), κορύνη "staff; club," κόσκινον "sieve, bolter," κόττανα, a kind of small fig, μυρσίνη "myrtle," ῥυκάνη "plane," σαγήνη "seine, net," σιβύνη "hunting spear, bear spear," συβήνη, συβίνη "leather case," τήβεννα "cloak," τορύνη "stirring rod," possibly βαθανία "nest" (in Hesychius), βαλίνος, fish species, δάφνη "lauret, *Laurus nobilis*," δελκανός, fish species, σαργάνη "cord," Σελήνη, σελάννα "moon,"[217] σκαπάνη "mattock," τίτανος "gypsum"; among the names: Ἅρπινα (with a variant Ἅρπιννα), town in Elys, Γαλήνη (Etruscan *calaina*), Nereid, Ἑλένη, Καμάρινα, nymph Oceanis and a town in Sicily (cf., *Camars, Camertes*), Κερκίνη (mountain range in Paeonia), Κισθήνη (town in Aeolis), possibly, Κρῶμνος, towns in southern Arcady and Aeolis, Κρῶμνα in Paphlagonia, Μοστινή (Lydian town), Μύρινα in Lemnos (*morina-* in the Stele inscription), Περσεφόνη, Πιτάνη, Mysian town, facing Lemnos, and one of the five districts (κῶμαι) of Sparta, Ῥάμνους, Attic town and deme, Σιληνός, Σειληνός, also Σικύνη, Συκίνη (Macedonian locality), and Ὑττηνία, Ὑτέννα, mentioned above (cf., also possible feminine variants with -ni/-ni in the previous chapter).

In Linear A inscriptions, forms ending in -na occur quite often, but, without some evident parallels, and because of the morphological uncertainty of the words obscured

---

215. The relatively rare Etruscan variants -nu, -ne should be understood rather as dialecticisms. Judging by the forms like *capevane/i* (see below), it could join the feminine suffix -i when the derivatives concerned human beings (the example given is an ethnonym).

216. "τήγανα καὶ πλακοῦς ὁ ἐπ' αὐτῶν σκευαζόμενος" (Hes.).

217. The word σελήνη should be investigated independently as a derivative of σέλας "light, shining," which does not have any reliable etymology.

by the peculiarities of Linear writing, it would hardly make sense to list them here. Obvious parallels with the borrowings in Greek are: MA 1 *qe-de-mi-nu* : Βελεμίνα, HT 54, HT Wc 3014 *ku-mi-na-qe* : κύμινον, HT 88 *ki-ki-na* : κεικύνη, etc., given above.

In the first millennium BCE, the suffix *-na* appears not only in the inscriptions of Etruscan, in Rhaetic proper, in the inscription of the Lemnian stele (and, supposedly, in Eteo-Cypriote inscriptions) but also in Etruscan loanwords in Latin, transfers of the names and place names. In Etruscan, the suffix can join both verbal and nominal stems. As examples, we can adduce some forms from the inscriptions: *spurana* "urban" from *śpur-* "town" (TLE 165, 183); *suθina* "funeral" from *śuθi* "grave" (TLE 264, 750); *paχana-* "belonging to the worship of Bacchus" (TLE 131, 137); *ziχina* from *ziχ-* "to write" (TLE 331); it is possible that the form *ceχan-* (TLE 1, 90, 126) from an unclear verbal root should also go here. The same type is the basis of the original name of the Etruscans: *rasna-* (TLE $1^{11\ \gamma V}$, 87, 137), *Rasenna* (Dionysius of Halicarnassus shows just such a meaning of Ῥασέναι [I, 30]) (cf., also *Rasinius*).

In some cases, we can try to ascertain the meaning of the verbal root if we detach the suffix. So, the word *malena* "mirror" (TLE 695) is formed from the root *mal-* with the possible meaning "to look" (cf., Latin *speculum* from *specio*). When we compare the Etruscan word *cabanna* (*capanna*) "hut, shack," borrowed in Latin, with the pre-Greek καπάνη "knitted hat" (in Hesychius), we can reconstruct the root *Kap-* with the meaning "to weave"[218] (cf., also pre-Greek κάπη "crib" without suffixation. A consonant, but not the same Tyrrhenian root, is presented in Thessalian: καπάνη "vehicle," along with the Tyrrhenian gloss of Hesychius TLE 832 γάπος with the same meaning.

Judging by the borrowings in Latin and forms like Ὑττηνία, the main meaning of this suffix is nominal, but adjectival use is also known (cf., *spurana*, usually "urban" in translations, etc.; one of the most typical examples is the inscription TLE 762, containing the combination *aska mi eleivana* "I (am an) askos (Greek ἀσκός) for olive oil." It seems that the same type, as in Ὑττηνία, we find in the names of boards *śarvena-* (TLE 170) and *zelarvena-* (TLE 172, 195). These names, as it follows from the numeral meanings, should be understood as "duodecim viri" and "duo viri" accordingly.

A considerable number of words formed with the given suffix were preserved in Latin and Greek. Separate forms, structurally similar to the latter, are known in Oscan and Umbrian. Having penetrated into classical languages, these words could join masculine endings, form plurals according to Greek and Latin rules, gain a parasitic vowel (cf., again Ὑττηνία, etc.), but in most cases they preserved their original ending *-na*.

In Etruscan borrowings in Latin, the suffix *-na* seems to occur most often. Compare the following forms: *afannae* "(lame) excuse"; *agina*[219]; *arena* (Faliscan *fasena*) "sand"; not

---

218. This Etruscan-Latin example typologically can be compared with Egnlish "wattle," Russian плетень, or German *Wand* "wall" from *winden* "to weave" (i.e., *Wand* is suitable for the primitive German dwelling *Mauer* [from Latin *murus*] to the Roman-type building).

219. "*agina est, quo inseritur scapus trutinae, id est, in quo foramine trutina se vertit*" (Paul. Fest., 10).

very clear *arvina* "fat"[220]; already given *cabanna* "hut," possibly here also *Capena*, Etruscan town on the Tiber, also *porta Capena* in Rome; *catena* "chain"; *cortina* "tripode"; possibly, *lamina* "plate"; *marrucina,* kind of fig or sloe (*Rhamnus paliurus*); *persona* "mask" : Etruscan φersu (TLE 80); *popina* "inn"; compare above the title *Porsen(n)a* (< *purśvana*), wrongly understood as a king's name; *sagina* "fattening (up)"; *sculna* "arbitrator" (in Aulus Gellius, Macrobius, and Varro; here also *Scultenna* with a more complicated suffixation and *schola* without any); *surena* "prime minister"; *trasenna* "fowler"s net," *urna* (along with *urceus* "jug"), *vagina.* The word *damnum* "damage" is neuter gender. It is also possible that the word "soft" (from Sabinian) dates from Etruscan, too.

Similar Etruscisms also penetrated other Italic dialects (especially Umbrian). A very characteristic example is the Umbrian word *esono* "sacrifice" (= Etruscan *aisuna, eisna* from *ais* "god"). About the suffix *-na* in Eteo-Cypriote inscriptions, see below (cf., also the gloss βουκανῆ [in Hesychius] "anemone flower").[221]

It was also possible to form loanwords with this suffix in Etruscan. Sometimes such forms are found in Latin, like *carina* (from Greek καρύα) "nut shell" > "vessel."

It seems that the given Minoan and Tyrrhenian words had not undergone serious changes. This can be seen from the comparison of these lexemes with forms like Etruscan *malena* "mirror," where the ending does not differ at all, at least graphically.

As was shown by Tronskij, the Etruscan suffix *-na* had been borrowed into Latin as an independent word formational element (cf., the forms *levenna, sociennus,* probably, *dossennus* [stage humpback in *atellana*][222] "unceremonious lexica, already used the assimilated Etruscan suffix" [Tronskij 1953, 124]). On the other hand, the form *barginna* seems to be Etruscan rather than Latin, dating from the name *parc-na* (Walde-Hofmann 1938-56, s. v. *bargena*).

The suffix *-na* is found in many names, primarily family ones, attested in Etruscan inscriptions (see the examples, occurring in the inscriptions in the previous chapters). Sometimes we also know the meaning of the root itself (cf., *pulena* [TLE 131, etc.] from *pul-* "top, heaven," *uselnas* [TLE 934] from the borrowed *us(i)l-* "sun"]). In some cases, we find them in Latin with another suffixation. Compare, for example, Etruscan *śatnal* along with Latin *satelles, Satellius.* It is quite interesting that the derivatives of the same root, ending with *-na,* can have different meanings. See the most typical of them: *pupliana* (TLE 763 *velθur pupliana*) along with *pupluna* "Populonia" and *spuriana*[223] (TLE 78 *araθ spuriana*) along with *spurana* "urban." An assumption, suggested by Pallottino, that such word formation is typologically similar to Latin *rex* : *regius,* Greek πολεμοί : πολεμιοί (1978: 435), does not seem convincing, at least for the fact that we do not know of a morphological element *-i-* with the meaning, different from dative, instrumental, and locative cases. Such an interpretation was influenced by Greek and Latin morphology. On the other hand, if we analyze the forms with *-na* and *-a-na*, the difference in their

---

220. A coincidence with Sicilian is mysterious: "ἀρβίννη· κρέας Σικελοί" (Hes.). However, this Etruscan-Sicilian parallel is not unique; they can be explained principally by maritime contacts.

221. "βουκανῆ· ἀνεμώνη τὸ ἄνθος. Κύπριοι."

222. Probably, it should be compared with *dorsum* "back."

223. It seems that the name *Spurin(n)a* originates from the same model.

grammatical meaning would seem to be bound with the element -a-. The most interesting example is provided by the Roman inscription REE 47/29 in the context *araz silqetenas spurianas*, where we see two names formed with -na at the same time.

From our point of view, the element -a- can give the family name the same meaning, as Latin composite -a-no-, used for forming family names after adoption.[224] In principal, this inscription can be presented as *Arruns Seligius Popilianus*. When the whole model of Latin names developed under Etruscan influence (Tronskij 1953, 123), it seems to be likely that the element -an- had been borrowed from Etruscan, having later combined with the Latin suffix -no-. Theoretically, the element -a- can be compared with the archaic Etruscan genitive suffix.

Sometimes the suffix -nV is used to form ethnonyms: *veiane* from *Veii* (TLE 707, etc.), *capevane/i* from *Capua* (CIE 4096, etc.), *hep(a)ni* from *Heba* (TLE 920, etc.). In this case, it can join -i, supporting gender differentiation.

So, Latin in Greek preserved numerous names and toponyms containing the suffix under study. We shall adduce the following examples: the name *Adenna* (possibly, here also *ati* "mother"); *Andena*, a river in Etruria; *Caecina* (Etruscan *ceicna*), cognomen of a noble family from Volaterrae (Volterra); *Camenae* "*Quellgöttinnen*" (cf., above *Capena*); *Cotena*, Faliscan name; *Fidena(e)*, Sabinian town in Latium; *Freganae*, town in southern Etruria; *Larinum*, town of Frentani; *Lucina* "Lady, mistress" (epithet of Juno, from *lauk:-* "to rule"); *Mevania* (town in Southern Umbria; a derivative for their inhabitants, Etruscan *mefanate*, Latin *Mevanates*): Μηονίη (Ionic Maionja, with the loss of *digamma*), name for eastern Lydia[225]; *Misena*, cape and town in Campania; *Numana*, town in Picenum (here also the Etruscan name *num[e]na*); *Mutina*, modern *Modena*, from the same root a place name Μυτιλήνη (later Μιτυλήνη), town in Lesbos; *Ortona*, town of Aequi in Latium; (*Anna*) *Peranna* "Goddess of the beginning and end of the year" (Etruscan *perna*, Oscan *Pernai*); *Populonia*, one of the greatest Etruscan cities; *Ramnes*, name for the Roman tribe, here also *Ramnii* and *Ramennii* (in Capua and Ostia accordingly); *Ravenna* (the name has not changed up to our day); *Sisenna*, cognomen of Cornelii; *Tolenus*, Sabinian river, etc. The suffix -nV can combine with different elements, particularly with the suffixes -um- and -(u)r- (the main cases of such usage will be shown below, after a characteristic of -um and -ur properly).

The word formational suffix -υμ- rarely appears beyond the combinations in pre-Greek. Compare, for example, the forms ἔλυμος "millet, *Panicum*"; ὄστριμον "shed"; place name Αἰσύμη along with Αἴσυμνος. Somewhat more often we find this suffix in a dialectal variant -αμ-; besides the plant names βάλσαμον, κάγκαμον, κάρδαμον, σάσαμον, given above, to this type belong: ἄρταμος "cook"; then "butcher" (cf., ἄρτος "bread")[226]; θάλαμη "burrow, gorge, grave"; and θάλαμος "room, house"; κάδαμος "blind" (in Hesychius; cf., Latin *calamitas* < *cadamitas* "misfortune, distress"); καλάμη "stalk," κάλαμος "reed" and καλαμίνθη kind of mint, with double suffixation;

---

224. That is, the name *Octavi-an-us* was formed after he had been adopted by *Julii*.

225. The name is formed from the root *mav-*, preserved in the name of the Anatolian goddess, using the Tyrrhenian model.

226. Interesting to compare with Basque *arto* "Mais(brot)" (Frisk 1960, s. v. ἄρτος).

κέραμος "clay"; κύγχραμος, κύχραμος "quail, *Coturnix*"; possibly χηραμός "burrow, cave"; among the toponyms the name Σαλαμίς is formed similarly.[227]

It seems possible that this suffix can be found in a pre-Indo-European theonym Ἄρτεμις, Doric Ἄρταμις. It is interesting that in Lydian inscriptions this name appears as *artímu-ś* (with variants). Theoretically, it is permissible that the voicing -υμ- is reflected in Lydian, -αμ- in Doric. The root itself can be compared with Minoan ἄρτος "bread." Some connections of this goddess with the agricultural cult are attested in Sparta. It can also be observed in the myth of the Calydonian hunt.

In Etruscan, the suffix -*um*(-) > -(*V*)*m*(-) is seldom used independently (more often it is combined with -*na*). Compare the following examples: **met:(u)l*- "city, town" : Eteo-Cypriote *a-na ma-to-ri* = Greek ἡ πόλις (KS 5), Etruscan *metl* (TLE 792), *meχl* (TLE 87)[228] has a suffixal derivative **met:l-um: metlum*- (TLE 719), *meθlum*- (TLE 1 [several times], 99, 131, 237, 901), *meχlum* (TLE 233). Compare the examples *zilaθ amce meχl rasnal* (TLE 87) "was (a) zilath of Etruscan cities" (i.e., of the main 12 cities (= "praetor Etruriae"), *śpureri meθlumeric* (TLE 1$^{II\,8}$) ≈ "for city and state," etc. The latter conditional context, suggested above, is quite typical. It is possible that the derivative *met:l-um* should be properly translated as "state" typologically (cf., Greek πολιτεία from πόλις). The word **p:ul-um* "star" is formed in the same way (cf., above *pulum-χva, fulum-χva*), from the root **p:al(a)* "top, heaven, head."

The numeral *zaθr-um* "twenty," as was shown above, appears once without a suffix. This suffix also forms some names of different vessels, borrowed from Greek: *pruχum* "mug" (from Greek πρόχους, TLE 5, 62), along with *prucuna* (TLE 1$^{IX\,\gamma\,1}$) with another suffixation and *pruχś* (TLE 1$^{IV\,22}$) without a suffix, *qutum* "flask, canteen" (from κώθων, TLE 63, 865). In the second case, this suffix is likely to appear during a reconsideration of the Greek ending.[229] Below, compare also the forms *leχtumuza, qutumuza*. It is also possible that the same suffix is presented in the plural form *mesnamer* (TLE 366), "deity" or "idol" (from Anatolian).[230]

The suffix -*Vm*- has not been reliably attested in Etruscan toponymy. We can speak about it with surety only in regard to the Thracian place name Αἰσύμη from the widespread root *ais* "god."

We should also consider the main combinations between the suffixes -*Vm*- and -*na*. Words of this type are widely presented in pre-Greek, Etruscan, and Latin. The quantitative correlation of borrowings in these languages, as well as the relationships between the common nouns on the one hand, and proper and place names on the other, show them to be virtually the same as in the group with simple -*nV*. Among the others, the Aegean word *aisunna "sanctuary" (*ais* "god"), preserved in the town name Αἴσυμνος (Il. XI, 303), was used to form the verb αἰσυμνῶ "to rule over" in Greek (it

---

227. Here is also the name Σαλύνθιος with another suffix.
228. Here also Latin *Metellus* = Etruscan *metli* (TLE 888), *meteliś* (TLE 651), etc.
229. It is preserved, in particular, in the forms *qutun* (TLE 28), *qutunas* (TLE 767).
230. Cf., Anatolian *massanalli-.

is fused and may possibly join personal endings to final -*a*, borrowed from Minoan or Tyrrhenian: *αἰσυμνάω).

We shall adduce the main forms with -(υ)μ-να preserved in pre-Greek: ἀτάλυμνος (in Nicander) "plum, *Prunus L.*"; θέλυμνα "foundation"; συκάμινος "mulberry tree"; names and place names: Ἄμυμνοι, unknown tribe; possibly, here also Ἀμυμώνη, Danaide; Ἐλύμνιος, according to Hesychius, Neptune in Lesbos; here also Ἐλύμνιον, locality in Euboea; Ἐρυμναί, Ἐρυμνά, towns in Lycia and Lydia correspondingly; Κάλυμνα, one of the Isles of Sporades; Καρτεμνίδες, name of inhabitants of Gortyn, in Hesychius; Λάρυμνα, Boeotian town; Λάτυμνον (in scholias to Theocrites), mountain near Croton; Λύκαμνος, unclear place name; Λεπέτυμνος, mythological hero; Μάθυμνα, Μήθυμνα, town in Lesbos; Πόλυμνον (in Pausanius), unclear place name; Πρόσυμνα, ancient town in Argolis; Ῥίθυμνα (in Stephan), Cretan town (= Etruscan *ritumena*). In Mycenaean Greek, the same type includes, for example, the name *o-pi-ri-mi-ni-jo* (**Opilimnios*)[231] from the Knossos tablet Sc 230. It should be noted that more archaic pre-Greek words persistently retain the vowel *u*, often changed in Etruscan (cf., Etruscan-Latin *antemna* and many others).

In Etruscan, among the forms with -*Vmna*, the word *lauχumneti* "in royal (palace)," also from the root *lauk:-* "to rule," is of special grammatical interest. It, equally with *aisunal* (TLE 1[VI 9]), clarifies the ways of declension in the -*nV-* type as a whole. The same word is known also in the Aegean area. It is preserved by Strabo (VIII, 6, 11) as Λίκυμνα; it had been the older name for the acropolis of Tiryns. The name *velimna* (i.e., Ἐλύμνιος, where *digamma* was lost) is widely presented in Etruscan inscriptions, and there are also some more interesting forms.

In Eteo-Cypriote, we know the words *pu-e-ne-mi-na* (KS 2) and *e-ne-mi-na* (KS 3, twice). It seems that, in their formation, they are identical to the given Etruscan and Aegean-Tyrrhenian terms. The meaning of the lexeme(s) has not been clarified yet, but, by all appearances, we are dealing with the same form. (With the absence of prefixing in the Tyrrhenian languages, we would rather suppose an unclear word division. As was shown above, *pu-* can be compared with the semi-independent Etruscan grammar element *pi*).

See the following examples of lexemes, passed through Latin, such as *aerumna* "hard labor"[232]; *antemna* "(ship) yard" (from *ant-* "wind"); *autumnus* "autumn" (cf., the name *autu*, *Autius* without a suffix); *columna* "column"; *flexumines* "royal horsemen," etc. Names and place names: *Celemna*, town in Campania; *Clitumnus*, river in Umbria and a deity of the same name; *fescemnoe* (Fest.) : *Fescennia*, town in southern Etruria; not fully clear Νώνυμνα, town in Sicily (in Stephan); possibly, *Pilumnus* and *Picumnus*, deities who patronized the newborn; *Ratumenna*, gate between Quirinalis and Capitolium (in Pliny); Ῥίθυμνα, a town not only in Crete but also in Italy[233] (= Etruscan *ritumenas* in the epitaph CIE 4950); *Vitumnus*, one of the gods patronizing children;

---

231. Cf., Etruscan-Latin *opilio*!
232. From **ais-um-na* "sacrifice," with rhotacism, which happened in earlier borrowings.
233. Stephan calls the inhabitants of the town Βοβωνία Ῥιθυμνιάτης along with Βοβωνιάτης.

Voltumna, goddess in the temple of the 12 allied Etruscan cities; *Volumnius*, Roman *nomen*; *Vortumnus* (*Vertumnus*), one of the main Etruscan gods, etc.[234]

One more suffix common to Minoan and Tyrrhenian languages played the key role for studying Cretan lexica. This suffix happened to be -υρ-/-υλ-. When Neumann had discovered the word νικύλεον and had bound some plant names with it (see also in Russian [Neumann 1976]), there appeared real prospects of clarifying the most diverse cross-models of word formation. Unfortunately, Neumann did not notice the relationship between -υλ- and -υρ- (although the alternation r : l had been known long before) and, accordingly, their ties with -ιλ- and -ιρ-. It delayed further research for a long time. We have managed not only to expand the number of lexemes formed in the same way but also to find variants with the alternation mentioned for at least five of them: properly νικύλεον : Νικυρίς, ἀγγύλη, a kind of missile weapon, and ἄγγυρα "bunch of grapes"; ἄγγυρος, a kind of flat cake (both in Hesychius); ἄμυλος "pie (of fine-ground flour)"; Ἄμυρος, Thessalian river; Δαμυρίας : Δαμύλος (see above), and also μορμύλος : μορμύρος (fish species, *Pagellus mormo*).

See more examples: ἀκανθυλλίς, bird species (also see -νθ- below); ἄκυλος, ἀκύλος, ἄχυλος "edible acorn"; ἀμαρυλλίς "*Amaryllis*"; ἄρμυλα "sandal, (high) boot" (Cypriote Hesychius's gloss); ἄσκυρον "St. John's wort, *Hypericum*"; ἄχνυλα "hazel, hazel grove" (Cretan Hesychius's gloss)[235]; βαίτυλος (again in Hesychius) "stone, swallowed by Cronus (instead of Zeus)"; βαλλιρός, species of fresh-water fish; βατύλη (Sch. Arph.) "woman"; βράβυλον "sloe"; γαθύλλις, γηθύλλις "onion"; possibly, γογγύλη "turnip"; γόργυρα "cave, dungeon"; δάκτυλος "date"; δάσκιλλος, fish species (*Sciaena?*); ἔρπυλλος "thyme, *Thymus erpyllum*"; ζέφυρος "wind from the west"; ζιζουλά (Alex. Med.) "millet"; κάδυρος (in Hesychius) "κάπρος ἄνορχις" (cf., above κάδαμος, *calamitas*); καμπύλη "staff"; κίττυλα (in Hesychius) "peel"; κολλύρα "barley bread"; κορδύλος "newt"; κοτύλη "cup"; κρώβυλος "crest, plume"; see below λάβιρος, λαβύρινθος; μαίκυλον, with the reduplication μιμαίκυλον "fruit of the strawberry tree"; possibly μάρτυρος "eyewitness"; μέσπιλον "medlar, *Mespilus germanica*"; μιστύλη, μυστίλη "piece of bread used as a spoon"; οἴκυλος[236]; πάπυρος "*papyrus, paper*"; πίτυρον "bran"; ῥόβιλλος "kinglet, *Regulus*"; σίβυλλα "prophetess"; σταφυλή "bunch of grapes"; τίτυρος "sheep *or* goat" (Theocr.) and bird species (Hesychius); τόρδυλον, τόρδιλον "*Seseli* or *Tordylium officinale*"; φιλύρα "linden." Names and placenames: Ἔλυρος, Cretan town; Κέρκυρα, island in Ionian Sea; Σάτυρος "Satyr." It is not fully clear if the toponyms Ἄστυρα (settlement in Mysia),[237] Λάμυρα and Λίμυρα (Lycian town), and Κίβυρα (Phrygian town) are of Minoan or Tyrrhenian origin (see also the comparison of Stoltenberg (1961, 82). It is evident that the word *littera* (< διφθέρα) should not be included here (although it might be borrowed in Tyrrhenian languages).

---

234. "*Deus Etruriae princeps*" (Varro, lL, V, 46).
235. Possibly related to ἄχυλος (*αχ-ν-?).
236. "οἴκυλος, τό ὄσπριον" (Theogn.).
237. Along with pre-Greek ἄστυ "town" (cf., also Boeotian Ϝάστιος).

The dialectal variant -αρ- beyond the combinations can possibly be observed in the words βασσάρα "fox," γαλλαρίας (Athen.), καλλαρίας (Hesychius),[238] fish species, χίμαρος "she-goat," and with the alternation λ in ἀμύγδαλον "almond," κίδαλον (Hesych.) "onion," κοδύμαλον (Hes., Athen.) "quince, *Cydonia*," κορυδαλ(λ)ός "crested skylark, *Alauda cristata*"; ὀμφαλός "cone, navel."

This suffix, with alternate vowels or even without a vowel, seems to correspond to Etruscan final *-r(a)*, which also passed through Latin (*-ra*). The suffix *-r(a)* in its independent usage is presented in such Etruscan forms as *neθśra* "fortune-telling using entrails" (see above), names *lucer* (TLE 119; Latin *Luceres*, pre-Greek Λοκροί), *θucer* (TLE 709), *śertur* (TLE 597, Latin *Sertorius*), etc., and also in some borrowings in Latin (Tronskij 1953, 124). Included in such borrowings may be the following: *acerra* "censer" (here also cognomen *Acerra* and 'Αχέρραι (Stephan et al.), name of trans-Padan town), *saburra* "sandy ballast," *vacerra* "stake" (in plural "fence"), possibly some others (for example, *tessera* "die (pl. dice), tile, mosaic," *viverra* "polecat"), and without final vowel, *vultur* "(black) kite" (see above *Volturnus*).

We can also observe the combinations between the suffixes *-(u)r-* and *-na* in the languages under study. In pre-Greek they are: κίσιρνις, bird species (in Hesychius); λεχέρνα, "rite in honor of Hera in Argos" (again in Hesychius); σίσυρνα "sheep *or* goat skin" (more often appears as σίσυρα with a single suffix; compare also the cognomen *Sisenna*); 'Αλίκυρνα, settlement in Acarnania (Steph.); possibly Μηκύβερνα, town in Chalcidice, and Μυτιλήνη, Μιτυλήνη, the main town in Lesbos (with dialectal reflection *r > l*?).

Words of the same type had also passed through Latin (cf., *laburnum* "broom, *Cytisis laburnum*"; *pincerna* "cupbearer"; *santerna* "borax"; possibly *taberna* "tavern" [originally "plank/boarded house"]). It is probable that the stems, borrowed into Tyrrhenian, could be formed in such a way. Compare κιστέρνα (Hes.), *cisterna* along with Greek κίστη. The word *lanterna* "lamp" does not belong to this type, because here, it seems, the Greek ending of λαμπτήρ is reflected.

These combinations are also widely presented in toponymy and names: *Aesarnia*, town of Samnites on river *Vulturnum* (the name of the same type); 'Αγάθυρνα, Sicilian town (Steph.); *Angerona* "Totengottheit" (along with Etruscan *anχari, ancar*); *Avernus*, lake in Campania (beside Sibylla's cave and the entrance to the realm of shadows); *Claterna*, town not far from Modena; *Cliternum*, town of Aequi; *Falernus* (*ager*), locality in Campania; *Laverna*, goddess of gain and locality in Latium; *Liternus*, river in Campania; *Minturnae*, town of Aurunci in southern Latium, etc.

Other suffixes, such as -υκ-, -υ(μ)β-, and -υφ-, are now known only from pre-Greek, and we do not find any reliable Etruscan correspondences. Let us cite the main examples. For -υκ-: ἄλλιξ (in Hesychius) "chlamys"; βόμβυξ "silkworm, *Bombyx*"; δοίδυξ "pestle"; ἐρπυξή (in Disocorides), kind of plant; κεκύκη (in Hesychius) "staff"; κώρυκος "leather sack"; μιρύκεον (in Hesychius) "reed"; πέρδιξ, πῆριξ "partridge"; φιλύκη, kind of shrubs, *Rhamnus alaternus* (?); dialectal (-ακ-): δέλφαξ "swine"; θρῖδαξ,

---

238. Here also γάρος, "fish soup, caviar"; γαλεός "spotted shark," Γαλήνη, Nereid.

θρῖναξ "lettuce"; κάμαξ "pole, spear, handle"; κλῖμαξ "ladder"; κόνδαξ (?) "peg"; λάβραξ "grouper"; λάρναξ "box, coffin"; ὄμφαξ "unripe grapes" (cf., ὀμφαλός); ὄστρακον "crock, shell"; πάπραξ, fish species; πιθάκνη "keg" (without a suffix πίθος "barrel"); πίναξ "board, tablet, picture"; πόρταξ "heifer"; πύνδαξ "lid *or* bottom of a vessel"; σάμαξ "reed"; σκύλαξ "puppy, cub"; τίταξ (in Hesychius) "lord" (cf., Etruscan *tit-* everywhere); ὕραξ (in Nicander) "swine" (onomatopoetic?); φάρμακον "medicine"; φύλαξ "guard."

For -υ(μ)β-: κισσύβιον "cup"; κόλλυβος "~ penny"; κόρυμβος "stern"; κοσύβατας "donator"; μόλυβδος (also -ιβδ-) "lead"; σίλλυβον "fringe, chain, thorn"; σισύμβριον "*Iris sisyrinchion*"; dialectal (-α(μ)β-): κάραβος "*crab*"; κόλλαβος (cf., κόλλοψ) "pin, handle"; κορίαμβλον "coriander"; κότταβος, κόσσαβος, well-known game; μάτταβος (in Hesycius) "unwise, foolish." It is tempting to mention here also θρίαμβος, but the root structure becomes unclear then (to be precise, the final consonant cannot be seen). However, a similar root is presented in some plant names, including the ones with typical Minoan suffixation.[239]

From the word ἐρυσίβη, ἐρισύβη (in Rhodes ἐρυθίβη) "mealy dew, rust in plants," formed with the same suffix, the verb ἐρυσιβάω was derived "to be affected with mealy dew."

For -υφ-: Ἀκύφας, Doric town; ἀσύφη (in Dioscorides) "*Cassia*"; ζίζυφον "*Rhamnus jujuba*" (along with ζιζουλά and ζιζάνιον "darnel"); κέλυφος "pellicle, shell"; κορυφή "top, summit"; κόττυφος, κόσσυφος "blackbird, *Turdus merula*"; σέσυφος (in Hesycius) "cheat, swindler"; Σίσυφος "Sisyph"; dialectal variants (*-αφ-) have not yet been observed.

SPECIAL FORMANTS

MINOAN SUFFIX -*op*- (-οπ-)

The suffix -οπ- in Minoan seems to be one of the most characteristic and the most solitary at the same time. It appeared to be an element for which only a combination (with -ακ-) is visible to us (cf., σκολόπαξ "woodcock" or "snipe," the name itself has evidently arisen because of the typical form of the beak [σκόλοψ means "hook"]). However, such rarity cannot be an argument against its "participation" in our system. First, this element is attested directly in the Linear A inscriptions. Second, it can be joined to the roots for which the cases of combination with other suffixes are noted (cf., for example, φύλοπις "battle" and φύλαξ "guard (< "warrior")"; κόλλαβος and κόλλοψ with the same meaning of "pin, handle." It is possible that here the derivatives of the root καρδ- are the most characteristic examples: κάρδ-οπ-ος (HT 31 *ka-ro-pa₃*), κάρδ-αμ-ον (*ka-da-mi-ja* in Linear B), καρδ-αμ-ίς, καρδ-αμ-άλ-η, καρδ-αμ-ί-νη (see in the Index in

---

239. Cf., θρῖδαξ, θρῖναξ "lettuce"; θρινία "grapes" (In Hesychius: "ἄμπελος ἐν Κρήτῃ"); θρῖον "fig leaf"; θρύον "reed."

detail). The almost complete absence of combinations allows us to consider the suffix to be not productive even for the Minoan epoch. It fully agrees with the fact of its loss in the Tyrrhenian inscriptions of the first millennium BCE.

We shall adduce the main Minoan lexemes, where the suffix -οπ- is found: Ἀέροπες, ethnos in Argolis and bird species (in Hesychius); Ἀερόπη, Minos's granddaughter, ἀερόπος (in Hesychius "κοχλίας"), mollusk with a spiral shell); Δόλοπες, Thessalina tribe; δρύοψ, woodpecker species and Δρυόπες, tribe beside the mountain of Oeta; ἔλλοψ (ἔλλοπος), sea fish species and "snake" (in Nicander); possibly, ἦνοψ "glaring" (in Hesychius "λαμπρόν") (cf., in Homerus ἤνοπι χαλκῷ "glittering [with] copper"); Εὐρώπη, Phoenician princess, mother of Minos, Radamanthus, and Sarpedon; Καλλιόπη, poetic muse; κάρδοπος "(kneading) trough": in Linear A *ka-ro-pa₃* (HT 31)[240]; Κασσιόπη, Cepheus's wife, Andromeda's mother; κέδροπα (in Hesychius), χέδροπα "beans"; Κέκροψ, mythical founder of Athens; κόλλοψ "pin, handle"; κόρνοψ : πάρνοψ (Aeolian, Boeotian (in Strabo) πόρνοψ) "locust"; Μέροπες, ethnonym, earlier inhabitants of Cos,[241] and Μέροψ, name of three mythological kings; Μοψοπία, ancient name of Attica[242]; ὀνόπη, kind of black grapes (in Hesychius); Παρθενόπη, isle in Tyrrhenian sea; Πέλοψ, Tantalos's son, king of Elys and Argos; Πενελόπα (Πηνελόπα), Odysseus's wife, πηνέλοψ, Doric πανέλοψ "teal, *Anas Penelope*"; σκάλοψ "mole," σκόλοψ "tree, stake, hook"; Τρίοψ (Τριόπας), founder of Cnidus, Merops's father; φύλοπις "battle."[243]

The main (appellative) meaning of the suffix -οπ- was attested quite a long time ago (Dejanov 1976: 84). The root **wel-* "snake," which was to be reconstructed while using Greek archaisms (Nicander, Aristotle), is reflected in the acrophonic sign 075 ϟ *we* (from ἔλλοπος, ἔλλοψ [*ϝελ-] "snake-like" appears as the name for the sea species).

ADJECTIVE SUFFIXES

The suffix -*Vk:* in Tyrrhenian, being presented in a few examples, belongs to the group of grammar elements with an exact, precisely known meaning—a situation quite typical for Etruscologists. It could appear in different phonetic variants: -*ac*, -*αχ*, -*ίχ*, -*υχ*, -*χ*, and possibly some others. The suffix finds a parallel in Eteo-Cypriote inscriptions (-*o-ko-*), but it has not been attested in the other Tyrrhenian languages.

If we do not accept that the suffix had been borrowed from the Hurrian-Urartian group of languages (cf., Hurrian -*oh̬=h̬e*, -*h̬=h̬e*, -*h̬e* "manly" *h̬=uroh̬=h̬e* "Hurrian," *ninuari* [ninuaγe] "Ninevian"), Urartian -*uh̬=i/e*, -*h̬=i/e* (*Minua-h̬=i/e-ni/e* "(son) of Minua," *Diau-h̬=i/e-ni/e* "of (a tribe) D.," etc.) (D'jakonov 1961, 383), it cannot be excluded that it correlates with Minoan -υκ-.

Coming from Etruscan, the most interesting examples of the ways in which the suffix -*Vk:* could be used are bound with ethnonyms. Compare the inscription TLE 300:

---

240. Cf., also *da-ro-pa* (HT 38).
241. From which the older name for the isle derives Μεροπίς.
242. From Μόψος.
243. In classical language gen. -ιδος, epic voice preserves acc. φύλοπιν.

cneve tarχunies rumaχ "Gnaeus Tarquinius Romanus"[244] (cf., below *rumaθeś*, etc.), that is, here we find direct ties with the man who belonged to the family of Roman kings: *Tarquinii*. We can also observe an adjective formed in the same way: *velznaχ* "inhabitant of Volsinii" in the inscription CIE 5269 (along with *velznal* in CIE 2421, 2650).

A well-known title also has a derivative: *marunuχ*. It occurs in the inscriptions TLE 137, 165, 234: cf., TLE 137 *marunuχ paχanati* "*maro in Bacchi collegio*"; TLE 165 *amce marunuχ spurana* "was (a member) of urban *maros*"; in TLE 234 in unclear context. Evidently, the title *parniχ* (TLE 131) was formed in the same way. It is even possible that the word *frontac* from an oft-cited inscription TLE 697 can be ascribed to the same group. An ordinal numeral, given above, is also formed with this suffix: *θunχ-* "first."

The same suffix, as has been shown, is known also from Eteo-Cypriote. In the bilingual from Amathus, there is a correspondence *a-ra-to-va-na-ka-so-ko-o-se* to the name Ἀριστώνακτος (father of Ariston, mentioned in the inscription), which is used in the genitive case. It can be seen that the suffix *-o-ko-* forms the meaning of possession. In its turn, the composite is added with the genitive suffix *-se*. Thus, even a suffix not having the same meaning in Etruscan was used in Eteo-Cypriote patronyms, and Tyrrhenian-wide "redetermination" worked under the same rules.

Other widespread Tyrrhenian suffixes coincide with genitive ones (-[a]*l* and –[a]*s*). Accordingly, we understand them as borrowings: compare Hittite adjective forms and *nomina auctoris* with *-ala-*[245] and adjectives with *-ili-*[246] (Friedrich 2001: 56). Numerous adjective and nominal derivatives with the suffix *-(a)l* are known to us. Compare Etruscan *raśnal* "Etruscan" (it may seem that the original meaning of the word actually was "*populus*," as in many other original names), *śpural*, probably, an adjective "urban," *truial* "Trojan" (CIE 5263), *puinel* "Carthagenian" (TLE 724). Compare the form *velznal* "inhabitant of Volsinii," mentioned above, Eteo-Cypriote *ke-ra-ke-re-tu-lo-se* "noble" (gen.), etc. In the inscription of the Lemnian Stele, there are some more words formed in the same way: φokiaśial-e "Phocian" (dat.), *morinail* "inhabitant of Myrina" : Greek Μύρινα, Μυρίνη. Here also "Μύρινα· ἡρωΐς παρὰ Ἰλιεῦσι" (in Hesychius). The ordinal numeral *hutila* "fourth," cited above, was also formed with the same suffix (it is possibly used in the [feminine] genitive form).

In some cases, the suffix being analyzed is joint with the root to such a degree that its original adjectival meaning cannot be perceived (cf., Etruscan *hinθial* "soul" (TLE 88, 295, 330). This suffix seems to be one of the most productive. It is possible that its importance increased during the later period of the language. In any case, such forms noticeably leave the derivatives with *-Vk:* behind, if we look at the frequency of usage.

Another well-known suffix, *-(a)s*, was also used while forming family names, and there it cannot be treated only as a genitive. It is often present in masculine family names, put in the direct case: *karcuna tulumneś* (TLE 36), *vel matunas* (TLE 51), *mamarce velχanas* (TLE 57). On the other hand, in feminine names the suffix *-(a)i*, analyzed above,

---

244. We should remember that, in the archaic period, the name *Gnaeus* looked like *Gnaivos*.

245. Cf., *genzuwala-* "friendly" from *genzu* "inclination," *tuwala-* "distant" from *tuwa* "far (away)," *išpantuzziiala-* "cupbearer" from *išpantuzzi-* "vessel for wine."

246. Cf., *karuili-* "old" from *karu* "earlier."

corresponds to it: compare family names *huzcnai* (TLE 122), *zertnai* (TLE 123), *apatrui* (TLE 138), etc. It can be seen that such a suffix -(a)s, which finds a corresponding feminine -(a)i, may be rather understood as word formational. This conclusion is also confirmed by the fact that the suffixes -(a)l and -(a)s are never mixed while being used as word formational, which cannot be said about declension.

By all appearances, this suffix is presented in some Etruscan borrowings into Latin: cf., *cerussa* "whitewash," *mantissa(e)* "makeweight," *favissa(e)* "underground room of a temple," and also in some Aegean-Tyrrhenian lexica (cf., for example, Λάρισ[σ]α, formed from the well-known Tyrrhenian root [here also a typical Λάρυμνα]).

SUFFIX OF BELONGING -NΘ-/-*TE*

In the languages of the group under study, one of the most typical forms appeared to be an element which looks like -*te*(-) in the inscriptions of Linear A, -νθ- in Greek transfers, and -*te* in Etruscan and Rhaetic. In the inscriptions of Linear A -*te*(-) (‡, 004) usually occurs in word-final position. The sign itself, evidently, dates from the image of a certain plant and could also be used as a logogram. We should cite the main examples where this sign is used (with the exception of badly damaged inscriptions) and seems to reflect the Minoan suffix.

Compare the inscription from Hagia Triada: -*du-ri-te* (HT 4, line 2), *qa-ti-da-te* (HT 12, line 1), *312-te-te* (HT 26, line 1), *da-ju-te* (HT 34, line 1), *mi-nu-te* (HT 86, line 5; HT 95, lines 2, 2–3r, HT 106, line 1), *ma-ka-ri-te* (HT 78, lines 1-2, HT 117, line 1), *ra-[.]-de-me-te* (HT 94, line 5r), *a-123-te* (HT 96, lines 1–2), *di-re-di-na-te-pe* (HT 98, lines 2–3), *da-ru-ne-te* (ibid., line 2r), *pi-034-te* (HT 116, line 4), and *su-ki-ri-te-no-ja* (HT Zb 158 r).

In the inscriptions on different artifacts, this element occurs in the following cases: -*ku-pa3-na-tu-na-te* (AP Za 2, line 1), *pi-mi-na-te* (ibid., line 2), *no-da-ma-te* (AR Zf 1), *si-da-te* (ARKH 2, line 1), *de-su[.]-47-te* (ARKH 4, line 3-4), *si-ru-te ta-na-ra-te-u-ti-nu* (IO Za 2, line 2), *si-ru-te* (IO Za 14, IO Za 15, KO Za 1), *au-re-te* (KH 6, line 7), *a-ki-pi-e-te* (KH 10, lines 3-4), *a-da-ri ku-ni-te* (KH 92), *a-re-ne-si-di-pe-pi-ke-pa-ja-ta-ri-se-te-ri-mu-a-ja-ku* (KN Zf 13), *ti-di-te-qa-ti* (KN Zf 31), *da-ma-te* (KY Za 2), *qe-si-te* (MA Ze 11), *ta2-ti-te* (PK1, line 1), *ma-ti-za-no-te* (ibid., line 7), *ja-na-ki-te-te-du-pu2-re* (PK Za 8), *a-di-ki-te-te . . .* (PK Za 11), *a-di-ki-te-* (PK Za 12), *ja-di-ki-te-te-du-pu2-re* (PK Za 15), *me-ta-ni-te* (PK Zb 21), *no-ja-te* (PH Zb 4), *ta-na-su-te* (PR Za 1), 1 *ku-pa3-na-tu-na-te*[2]*pi-mi-na-te* (AP Za 2).

As all the variants of old Cretan writing are, by all appearances, bound with one another, one cannot exclude that the same sign could also appear in the inscription of the Phaistos disk. In the inscription of the disk, we find a sign ⚘,[247] representing a branch with leaves (i.e., structurally close to ‡). We can try to give it the reading *te. Then we will get eleven substitutions: A9 31-26-*te*, A10 02-12-41-19-*te*, A17, A29

---

247. It has been given the number 35 by scholars (here and below the numeration according to [Ipsen 1976, 39]).

02-12-27-27-*te*- 37-21, A27 23-19-*te*, B2 27-45-07-*te*, B10 07-24-40-*te*, B13 29-24-24-20- *te*, B16 06-*te*-32-39-33, B23 07-18-*te*, B28 02-06-*te*-23-07 (i.e., ten words as a whole [one is repeated]). It can be seen that, in seven cases among the ten available, the word is ended by the sign, and such similarity with the Linear A examples cannot be ignored.

Further, we can compare some of the given Linear A word forms given with pre-Greek lexemes. The roots *kar-* and *tan-*, which are presented in the forms *ma-ka-ri-te* and *ta-na-su-te*, should be understood as Minoan, but they do not occur in Greek with the suffix being analyzed. But a certain part of the forms given (three lexemes by now) has detailed correspondences. In all cases we find -νθ- (because the final consonant of a syllable is omitted in Linear writing). We should adduce them in alphabetical order.

The root of the names (?) *da-ma-te* and *no-da-ma-te* (with a prefix, that was mentioned above), corresponds to the same in the name Ῥαδάμανθυς. Thus, we can add *no-* and *ra-* to the prefixes known to us. It is quite probable that the same root, not with suffix, but with a prefix *no-*, is presented in the form *no-da-mi* from the inscription SY Za 1.

The word *da-ru-ne-te* seems to be formed from the same stem as the name Λαρυνθίῳ (dat. sg.), mentioned by Lycophron (Alex., 1092), which in "Scholias" has been explained as an epithet of Zeus or Apollo (in principle, we can make a supposition about the place name *Λάρυνθος), but in this case we must reconstruct some more suffixes (e.g., *da-ru-ne(n)-te*). Such a word is not known in Greek, but we know well the names of the towns Boeotian (Hesychius, Strabo) and Thessalian ("Scholias" to Lycophron) Λάρυμνα. The peculiarities of Linear writing allow us to read the exact inscription as *da-ru(m)-ne(n)-te* (i.e., to see the full correspondence to the cited toponym here). In the form *si-ru-te*, we find the name of the Cretan town Σύρινθος, preserved by Stephan and Herodianus.

It is quite probable that the suffix -νθ- had originally been of an adjectival meaning, but some forms (they will be cited below) are appropriate to be understood as substantivized. Further, some of the words cited find correspondences in relic lexica, but without -νθ-. The form *mi-nu-te*, occurring twice, is quite interesting, as it has been thought for a long time that Μίνως seems to be rather a title than a name, so we could presuppose a translation for *mi-nu(n)-te*: "royal" (in Etruscan *mi-na-te*).

Thus, we can postulate a real correspondence between Minoan -*te* (in Linear A graphics) and the well-known pre-Greek -νθ-, and, having accepted it, have the possibility of ascribing to the Minoan period numerous lexemes formed in a similar way. This suffix occurs both in pure categorematic words, mainly plant names: ἄκανθ-[248] "thorn, sloe," ἀλένθη "night" (in Hesychius, ἀσάμινθος (ibid.) "trough, vat, tub," ἀψίνθιον "wormwood, *Artemisia absinthium*," βόλινθος "wild bull," ἕλμινς, ἕλμινθος "*helminthos*" (in Hesychius also λίμινς), ἐρέβινθος "*Cicer arietinum*" (in Hesychius also γάλινθος, λεβίνθιος, and ὀδόλυνθος with the same meaning), καλαμίνθη "*Nepeta*

---

248. Cf., ἄκανθα "thorn, sloe", ἀκανθίας "shark," ἀκανθίς "goldfinch," *Carduelis carduelis L.*, ἀκανθίων "hedgehog," ἀκανθυλλίς, species of bird.

cataria or *Melissa altissima*," κήρινθος "bee-bread, pollen," κολοκύνθη "pumpkin, *Lagenaria vulgaris*," κυλίνθιον (in Hesychius) "wooden mask," μυάκανθα (in Dioscorides) "asparagus," ὄλυνθος "winter (= unripe) fig," πείρινς, πείρινθος "chariot," σμήρινθος, μήρινθος "thread,"[249] τερέβινθος, τέρμινθος "*Pistacia terebinthus*," also in a famous etymological riddle λαβύρινθος),[250] as well as in numerous toponyms: Ἀμάρυνθος, settlement in Euboea, Ἀράκυνθος, mountains in Attica, Boeotia, and Aetolia, Ἀρίνθη, town of Oenotri, Ἄψυνθος, Thracian town, Βερέκυνθος, Cretan mountain, Βισάνθη, Macedonian town, Ἐρύμανθος, river and mountain in Arcadia, Ζάκυνθος, island facing Elys, Ζήρυνθος, Thracian town, Κήρινθος, Euboean town, Κόρινθος, main city on the Isthmus, Κόσκυνθος, Euboean river, Οἰάνθη, town of *Locri*, Πέρινθος, Thracian town, Πρεπέσινθος (evidently, with a Greek prefix), small island in the Aegean sea, Προβάλινθος (with indubitable Greek prefix) *demos* in the Attic *phyle* Πανδιονίς, Πύρανθος, town and its surroundings in Crete close to Gortyn, Σάμινθος, locality in Argolis, Σικύνθος, unclear toponym, mentioned by Plutarch, Τρικόρυνθος, one of Attic "four-towns" (seems to be the same as Κόρινθος, only joining Greek τρι-), Φάλανθος, mountain and town in Arcadia; here also the names Ἀργάνθος (Orph.), Ἀργανθώνη, Σαλύνθιος, and Ὑάκινθος.

A comparison of the word-formational elements allows us to suggest an etymology for two words, having become international and, in fact, cultural for the whole of Europe: λαβύρινθος and the name Ὑάκινθος. The name of mythological heroes, later preserved even in the plant name and the name of the gem, must be bound with the word ὕαξ, preserved by Hesychius, "πηδάλιον," (i.e., "scull" [so, ὑάκινθος "helmsman"]). It has been said above that the initial phoneme had been reflected exactly in the Linear A syllabogram number 010 𐘀 *u*, depicting the helm. This comparison seems to be one of the most reliable, which can be developed from a brilliant suggestion by Neumann.

One more of Hesychius's glosses can throw light on the origin of another word: λαβύρινθος (Mycenaean *da-pu2-ri-to*). Of course, here we reject an older comparison with the Lydian gloss preserved by Plutarch: *λάβρυς ("Λυδοὶ γάρ λάβρυν τὸν πέλεκυν ὀνομάζουσι"). It is the typical image of the double-edged axe already known from Cretan hieroglyphs (Linear sign number 008 𐘁 that also has a reading *a*). Hesychius saved for us another, simpler form λάβιρος "pit, hole," the evident etymology for an underground cult building. It can easily be seen that, in the word λαβύρινθος, we are dealing with two suffixes, whereas in λάβιρος with only one (as was shown above, the suffix -υρ- quite often appears as -ιρ-).

A widely presented suffix can be found in Etruscan and Rhaetic corresponding to that given above: *-te* (in feminine *-ti*), the main meaning of which was to show belonging to a certain community, such as a family, district, town, or locality (see above). In plural, as has been shown, it appeared as *-θur*, so during an analysis of such forms a more precise formulation is needed if one means a complicated suffix, always mentioning multiple persons.

---

249. Cf., also μηρύομαι "to wind."
250. Some of the words cited were also used as toponyms, for example, Ὄλυνθος, Thracian town.

We shall cite the following examples: *vipiθur cucrinaθur* "(brothers) Vibii from (the kin) Cucrina"[251] (TLE 635), *cusuθur-as* "members of (the family) Cusu" (TC, gen.), *paχaθur-as* "Bacchanti" (TLE 190, gen.). It is quite probable that one word, preserved by Hesychius, had been formed in the same way (TLE 802): ἀγαλήτορα (acc.) "child." If we suggest a reservation that the plural had been distorted (i.e., to presuppose the meaning "children"), the word itself can be understood as "the members of *agela*."[252] The following ethnonyms are of the simplest structure: *rumaθeś* (CIE 4883), *rumates* (CIE 4885) "Roman," *rumati* (CIE 1559) "Roman (for women),"[253] *nulaθe* (SE 26/90) "inhabitant of Nola."

In Latin transfers, we find *Caerites* (along with Etruscan χeritne, CIE 1506, etc.), *Camertes* (inhabitants of Clusium), and in the geographical Etrurian part by Pliny, given above: *Attidiates, Camertes, Dolates, Matilicates*, but more often this suffix is joined to geographical points formed with the help of *-na*, and *-m-na*. Compare the following examples: CIE 4810 *carpnatesa* (gen.), REE 53/4 *carpnati*,[254] TLE 609 *frentinate* (*Frento*), TLE 630 *mefanate* = *MEVANATES* in Pliny (*Mevania*), TLE 218 *petinate*, TLE 469 *sentinate*, TLE 582 *sentinati* (*Sentinum*), *urinate/i* (CIE 5632, etc.); in Pliny *Asisinates, Arnates, Aesinates*; quite unusual *Interamnates* (*Inter-Ramnates* [?] along with the tribe name *Ramnes*); here also Etruscan-Latin *Maecenas*, gen. *Maecenatis* along with Faliscan *MACENA* (CIE 8384) and *Carrinas*, gen. *Carrinatis*. In the inscription of Octavianus Augustus mentioned before, we find Rhaetic inscriptions of the same type: *FOCVNATES, RVCINATES, CATENATES*.

In Greek transfers, some forms of the same type are known: Ἀντεμνάτης, Ῥαβεννάτης (in Stephan, mentioning Italian towns), which find full Aegean correspondences. Only once, in Pausanius (VI, 21, 8), a river name is given: Ἁρπινάτης, with an indication that it flows not far from the town Ἅρπινα (mentioned above, when the *-na* forms had been cited). The name Πιτανάτης from Πιτάνα (also given above) belongs to the same circle, Ῥιθυμνιάτης from Ῥίτυμνα. There are possibly more examples. It is not always evident to us if the suffix had been joined to a stem of a place name, unknown to us, or had just explained belonging to a kin name (cf., for example, *harpite* [CIE 2280], *TARQUTTI* [CIE 5910]). However, we cannot find any principal differentiation here.

In certain cases, a derivative with *-te* has the added suffix *-na*: *taiχvetenas* (CIE 4922), *silqetenas* (REE 47/29), *vipiθenes* (TLE 286), *vipitenes* (CIE 5662). The meaning of such forms is not clear to us. Here also *Libitina* (archaic *Lubitina*), the name of the

---

251. That is, the first form is a *praenomen*, the second a *nomen*.

252. That is, something like youth detachment (ἀγέλη). Compare in Plutarch: "πάντας ἑπταετεῖς γενομένους ... εἰς ἀγέλας κατελόχιζε" "all (the boys who) have reached the age of 7, (Lycurgus) divided into detachments" (Lyc., 16, 4). So, borrowing of the Greek word is supposed here (according to Frisk, an isolated derivative from ἄγω, comparable with Latin *agolum* "Hirtenstab" ("shepherd's staff"), (Frisk 1960, s. v. ἀγέλη]).

253. We also know the genitive form *rumatesa* (CIE 1944).

254. This appears quite often in the inscriptions of Clusium. We can suppose the corresponding settlement had existed not far from there.

goddess, who was a patroness ("matroness" in fact!) of the death and burial rites (from *lup-* "to die").

It can be seen that, in the suffix under analysis, we should reconstruct a sonant which had been omitted in writing. It would be presented as *-nTe* (cf., above the statement about weak **n*). Such an element can be quite easily found in different reliable or presupposed Etruscan lexemes from Latin sources: *falando, flexuntes, frons, -ntis* and *frons, -ndis, hirundo* (cf., also the gloss TLE 825 κικένδα "*Gentiana*"). It is possible that the name of the underworld river *Accheruns, -ntis*[255] should be included here. At the same time, the suffix **-nt-* is seldom observed in proper Etruscan texts. In those cases when we face *-nt* or *-nθ*, it belongs to the root (which is quite probable for the goddess *vanθ*) or can be distributed into independent elements (cf., *nunθ-en-θ* [TLE 1$^{II\ 10}$, etc.]), where *-θ* is an imperative formant (cf., *nunθ-en-a* [TLE 878], *nunθ-eri*).

In Latinisms, the suffix *-nt-* can alternate with *-(m-)na*. At the same time, in trustworthy examples, one cannot find clear lexical differences as, for example, in an alternation *flexuntes* and *flexumines*. An externally similar alternation can be seen in the above given plant names κικένδα and κεικύνη "συκάμινος" (in Hesychius).

DIMINUTIVE SUFFIXES

There are several suffixes in Etruscan, which, with a higher or lower degree of confidence, can be understood as diminutive. In the other Tyrrhenian languages, such indicators have not been found. Pfiffig adduces the following elements as diminutive: *-ce, -za, -icu, -iu, -la, -le* (Pfiffig 1969, 164-67). We shall analyze them in a different order.

The suffix *-za* (rather, evidently, *-zV*), can be considered the most reliable. Its meaning is not disputed now (cf., the glossary [Pallottino 1976, 375-80], etc.). The meaning of the suffix was clarified owing to the fact that we know some cases when it is added to Greek words for different vessels: *leχtumuza* (TLE 761) "little lekythos" (Greek λήκυθος), *qutumuza* (REE 49/30) "little flask" (κώθων), *putiza* (TLE 11) "little cup" (Greek ποτήρ; cf., *putere* in TLE 344, 914). A "disclosure" of this suffix in the word *murzua* (TLE 619) "urn" by Pfiffig is evidently erroneous (here we observe only a phonetic alternation with *murs-*), as in the names *arnza, larza* as well (the result of phonetic development of *arnθia, larθia*). On the other hand, it is present in the names *veliza* (CIE 531, etc., along with *velia*), *ravntza* (CIE 109, along with *ravnθu*), *veneza* (CIE 412, along with *venel*), etc. The signature *mi lartlizi* on a bone stylus (TLE 361) also probably shows that the utensil belonged to a child.

Evidently, the suffix *-ce* spread to a very limited extent. Pfiffig finds it only in names, such as *larice* along with *laris, petke* along with *peθe*, and *sapice* along with *sapu*. The name *rustice* (CIE 622) is obviously borrowed from Latin *rusticus* and cannot be a

---

255. The widespread name *Arruns, -ntis* < Etruscan *arunt:* (Tronskij 1953, 124) is sometimes ascribed to the same type, but such a comparison is not persuasive from the phonetic point of view.

derivative from *ruste*, etc. (CIE 164). We suppose that exactly the same type is reflected in Latin *urceus* "jug," whereas the word *urna* designated a larger vessel.[256]

The "suffixes" *-icu* and *-iu*, in Pfiffig's opinion, form feminine and masculine pet names, respectively (ibid., 165). Such distribution is extremely doubtful, although we share his thesis about the meaning of the element *-iu* (for example, in the epitaph CIE 5870 with the name *velθuriu*, the age is given as eight years). In some cases, it is difficult to define the gender of the name to which the suffix was added (cf., *velicu* along with *vel* and *velia*, *larθiu* along with *larθ* and *larθia*, and *arnziu* along with *arnθ* and *arnθia*).

Along with those, there occur the reliable forms *θanicu* (TLE 897, etc., along with *θana*), *auliu* (CIE 2245, etc., along with *aule*), *velθuriu*, etc. From our perspective, we are faced with the diminutive suffix *-u*, which could be used both independently or in combination with *-c(e)* given above. The vowel *i* is of a different origin in different cases. It is connecting in the forms like *θanicu*, but is a result of a dissimilation on the basis of openness or closedness of the vowel in *auliu* from *aule* (cf., Etruscan *sa* "six" : Etruscan *sealχ-*, Lemnian *śialχv-* "sixty"). In the form *atiu* (TLE 549), the suffix under analysis is added to the word *ati* "mother," with an unproductive gender formant.

The combination *aisiu himiu* is found in an inscription on the bronze helmet TLE 360 (with the evident root *ais-* "god"). Unfortunately, the meaning of the second word is unclear.

Attempts to differentiate the suffixes *-la* and *-le* (Pfiffig 1969, 167) are absolutely insecure. Such derivatives are understood as feminine and masculine forms, respectively, although it contradicts the phonetic data. It is more appropriate to presuppose the evolution of the same sound here, maybe, of a dialectal character. The separation of the suffix itself is fully justified (cf., the forms *ranθula* "the little Ravnthu," *larile* "the little Laris*," etc.). The given suffix could possibly have been borrowed from Latin. The interpretation of some other less widespread suffixes is quite indeterminate.

So, Pfiffig suggested understanding the element *-k:vil* as a formant of a feminine theophoric (Pfiffig 1969, 167), which could have explained *tinścvil* as a feminine name or a feminine hypostasis of a supreme god (from *tin*), but, in the case of the widespread *θanakvil* : *θana*, we are primarily faced with a simple feminine name to which the same component had been added. This makes the whole correlation unclear.

Some word-formational suffixes occur in singular words but in a large number of inscriptions. For example, *-θur* in the name *velθur* (in TLE it occurs thirty-two times), and the incomparably rarer *larθurniś* from *larθ* (TLE 730), perhaps the very well-known combination *-ur-na-* had been added only once to the name, which is found everywhere. Of course, it can accidentally coincide with the plural forms ending with *-θur*. In the other forms, this suffix is practically impossible to be found (only *Numitor* is related, if

---

256. It is likely that we should reconstruct the root *ur-* "clay"; its derivative also will be Etruscan *urθanike* "shaped, sculpted" (cf., Greek κεραμεύω "to shape" from κέραμος "clay"), the name *urnasis* (TLE 591, etc.), an ethnonym *urinate* from a supposed place name *urina* (cf., Greek Κεραμεικός).

one considers it a borrowing from Etruscan, formed from *Numa*,[257] and also *Sertorius* : *serθur*).

FORMS WITH ENCLITICS

As has been shown above, the forms complicated with enclitics presented in Etruscan can be interpreted with some difficulty. It is not always clear if the enclitic is used to express case relationships or if it works as a substantivizing (i.e., independent word-formational) element. However, some such words passed through Latin (and some other Italic dialects) and Greek languages. All of them are nouns.

It also has been shown above that the pronoun *tV* that could act as an enclitic is sometimes complicated with the elements -*r*- and -*l*-, not seeming to be quite clear. The first alternation we can also observe in the corresponding borrowings. Thus, as the presupposed Tyrrhenian loanwords in Latin and Greek, we shall adduce some forms with -*ta* and –*tra* (accordingly, -τ-, -τρ- in Greek), with possible phonetic changes of final vowels and different grammar/gender formations. This type includes a number of words in Etruscan inscriptions of which the clearer meanings are *malstria* (TLE 752), "mirror" (cf., TLE 695 *malena*), *hiχvetra* "ten" (see above), and some others.

One of the words of this type has a direct indication of Etruscan origin: it is the gloss *lanista* "one who manages a troop of gladiators" (TLE 841). Some other derivatives of the same root also had been borrowed into Latin: *lanio* "butcher" (*nomen agentis*) and *laniena* "butcher shop" (formed with -*na*).[258] By analogy, the words *arista* "ear" (cf., CIE 4824 *arista*, etc.) and the plant name *genesta, genista* "greenweed, *Spartium junceum* or *Genista tinctoria*" also had been formed. The root of the latter is also reflected in the Etruscan gloss TLE 825 γεντιανή "gentian." The word *locusta, lucusta* "spiny lobster, locust" may also belong to the same group.[259]

Among the words given, the plant name *genesta* has a variant *genestra*. The alternation with the sonant and its absence coincide in detail with the data from Etruscan texts. The word *ballista*, not having any reliable etymology, also appears as *ballistra*. The town name *Numistro* (in northern Lucania) occurs with the element -*r*-, but the root is also present in the town name *Numana* (in Picenum), formed, in its turn, with the typical Etruscan suffix -*na*. All of these facts make us consider the cited words as Etruscisms. Their semantic attribution (of course, with the exception of place names) fully confines itself into lexical strata, defined by Tronskij (see above in Chapter 4: The Interpretation of the Vocabulary).

We may notice that all the forms given join pronominal enclitics after the element -*s*, which (under the root structure CVC) is reasonable to be considered as a genitive suffix.

---

257. An analogy, suggested long ago (cf., Pfiffig 1969, 172). Here, it is also possible to cite a suffixal form *Numana* of an evident Etruscan appearance.

258. That is, *lanista* "carnifex."

259. An old etymology which bound this word with different Indo-European verbs, including Greek ληκᾶν "jump" (Walde-Hofmann, s. v. *locusta*), is absolutely unconvincing. It may be that the root reflects some common identifier of Arthropoda.

It again fully coincides with Etruscan forms (cf., *vipina-l-tra* [TLE 398], with another genitive formant.)[260]

One must also analyze the Latin word *fenestra*, "window." It can have at least two possible explanations: (a) Graecism, along with *fēstra*, or (b) a form complicated with a pronominal enclitic (i.e., **fenes-tra*).

One opinion about the Greek origin of the lexeme was suggested by Peruzzi, who, having shown quite convincingly a number of borrowings into Latin (seemingly, some with Oscan mediation) from the Arcadian dialect of the Mycenaean period (cf., above the records about Evander), deduced a general phonetic regularity for some other similar lexemes—namely, the loss of initial anteconsonant σ-[261] (Peruzzi 1975). In the number of supposed borrowings were also (erroneously) included some forms where an initial sibilant had never existed, such as *fenestra*, *forma*, *fucus*, *funda*, and *fur*.

Thus, an archaic variant *fēstra*, preserved by Festus (Fest. Paul., 91) and Macrobius (with the reference on Salii brethren an Enius [Sat., III, 12]), was derived from **phaustēr* (from φάος "light"), along with the known Hesychius's gloss "φωστήρ· θυρίς." However, it was necessary to find the earlier form for *fenestra* where the variant given did not work. Willing to correlate *fēstra* and *fenestra*, Peruzzi introduced a derivative **phawestēr*, but the change **w > n*[262] was given an extremely untrustworthy explanation and no more similar examples were given.

In addition, in classical Latin etymology, *fenestra* is treated as an Etruscan word (Walde-Hofmann, 1938–56, s.v. *fenestra*). Acting in the capacity of one of the important correspondences, there is the Etruscan-Latin name *Fenestius* (accordingly, with an enclitic without a sonant). From Etruscan inscriptions, we also know the forms *fniścial* (TLE 746), *fnesci* (CIE 5041), *fnescial* (CIE 3064), but they seem to be formed from a different root of the type CSVC, where S is a sonant, when the root under analysis must have looked like *fen-* (CVC).

In accordance with the facts given, we come to the conclusion that *festra* and *fenestra* are borrowings from different languages (i.e., Greek and Etruscan, respectively), and only later, with the loss of *festra* in spoken language, has the understanding of the difference between them been lost. Moreover, certain external similarities drew these words together in vulgar etymology. The independent origin of *fenestra* and *festra* is also confirmed by considerable lexical differences. Along with a few meanings for *fenestra*, another lexeme, *festra*, is of highly specialized meaning, as Macrobius says in a fragment

---

260. In principle, even Tronskij in the late 50s noticed that words ending with *-stra* (in particular, *fenestra*) are Etruscan in origin, so he separated the Indo-European Latin forms with *-tro-*, *-trū*, and coglutinative *-s-tro-* (Tronskij 2001, 359), but at that time Etruscan grammar had not been investigated enough to single out a pure Etruscan enclitic (i.e., to separate a genitive suffix *-s*).

261. That is, *capis* < σκάφις, *capula* < **skáphula* (in Pylos tablet Un 1321 *ka-pu-ra*), etc. On the other hand, Greek words in their classical form cannot act as *terminus post quem* while judging earlier Arcadian sources.

262. In particular, he presupposes vulgar etymological ties with *fenum* "thatch" in an associative line with the roof, *fenum* "material for roof" and *fenestra* "small window in the roof."

mentioned earlier[263]; although Peruzzi speaks about specialization as a general feature of borrowing, he did not explain the wide meaning of *fenestra* and its derivatives.

Some Latin words with *-ta/-tra* (i.e., supposed Etruscisms) find parallels in Greek. These include, in particular, *aplustre* (more often plural *aplustria* or *aplustra*), "stern-post of a ship." By tradition, it has been understood as a borrowing from Greek (ἄφλαστον with the same meaning) through Etruscan mediation (Walde-Hofmann 1938–56, s.v. *aplustra*). But, from our point of view, that cannot explain the appearance of *-r-* in the Latin word. Really, it is hard to assume that the stem with a consonant *-t-*, not perceived as an enclitic component, could be formed in such a way in Etruscan (in fact, we do not know any other examples where *-r-* or *-l-* appears beyond the pronominal paradigm). The change *a* > *u* is also not fully clear. In principle, it is possible to assume that these lexemes are independent borrowings into Greek and Latin from Tyrrhenian dialects quite close to each other. (If this assumption is right, it [as also δέπαστρον] will show that, in Aegean-Tyrrhenian, there were also pronominal enclitics similar to Etruscan.)

To the same circle of lexemes belongs Latin *lepesta, lepista* "cup" (cf., the same alternation in *genesta, genista*). It is also often thought to be a borrowing of Greek λεπαστή "cup (shell-shaped)." The latter is related to λεπάς (gen. άδος) lit. "saucer" (sea mollusk species). It is easily seen that λεπαστή cannot be a direct derivative from λεπάς. The reconstructed root **dep-* (see below about the consonant), extended into λεπαδ- only in Greek, dates, according to phonetics, from the Minoan age, and is changed into λεπαστή with a pronominal enclitic in the standard way (with genitive suffix *-s-*). It is typical that, in both Greek examples under analysis, we can see a (ἄφλαστον, λεπαστή), when in Etruscan-Latin words an alternation of vowels is observed (*aplustra, lepesta, lepista*). The consonant **d* can be reconstructed owing to a parallel with pre-Greek δέπας, δέπαστρον "cup" (the appearance of *-r-* again attracts our attention). An alternation *d : l* is, as has been shown, Minoan. A variant with *l* was also preserved in Greek with the enclitic *-tr-*. In Hesychius, we find λέπαστρον "kind of fishing tackle"[264] (evidently, here ceramic vessels are meant, which, since the earliest times, have been used by Mediterranean fishermen to catch octopi).

Similar substantivized forms can be found not only in Latin but also in some other Italic dialects. To them belongs, in particular, the word *esaristrom* (in Tabula Veliterna) borrowed into the Volscan. This word in the context *façia esaristrom* is to be translated as "*faciat sacrificium.*" The derivative *esaristrom* can be interpreted as a nominal form from the root *ais* "god," complicated with the same genitive suffix *-s-*. So far as rhotacism was peculiar to the dialect of Volsci and Umbrian, the stem can be more easily reconstructed by Oscan *aisusis* "*sacrificiis.*" We probably find the same enclitic in Umbrian *persontro* with the conjectural meaning "image, figmentum" from the cited stem.

It seems that variants with another pronominal enclitic—namely *-K(r/l)-*, could have passed through Latin, too (cf., *molucrum* "log for sacrifice" [from *mul-*]); *marisca*, kind

---

263. "*Cicero . . . frequentabat, Salios Herculi datos probat in eo volumine quo disputat quid sit festra, quod est ostium minusculum in sacrario, quo verbo etiam Ennius usus est.*"

264. "σκεῦός τι ἁλιευτικόν."

of figs (from the Tyrrhenian root *mar-* "plant; wood"). They could be preserved in Etruscan-Latin place names (cf., the name of the Etruscan town *Graviscae* [again genitive type with *-s*]. Its root finds some parallels in the inscriptions [TLE 176 *cravzaθuras*, CIE 659 *craupznal*, CIE 1902 *craufa*], although it had a vulgar etymology among the Romans).[265] Also compare (*Trebula*) *Mutuesca* from the root, often seen in the inscriptions.

---

265. Erroneously from *gravis* "heavy (air)."

APPENDICES

Appendix 1

Phaistos Disk Inscription with Its Full Text and Stable Enumeration

Side A

Side B

Side A	Side B
1. 02-12-13-01-18	1. 02-12-22-40-07
2. 24-40-12	2. 27-45-07-35
3. 29-45-07	3. 02-37-23-05
4. 29-29-34	4. 22-25-27
5. 02-12-04-40-33	5. 33-24-20-12
6. 27-45-07-12	6. 16-23-18-43
7. 27-44-08	7. 13-01-39-33
8. 02-12-06-18-?	8. 15-07-13-01-18
9. 31-26-35	9. 22-37-42-25
10. 02-12-41-19-35	10. 07-24-40-35
11. 01-41-40-07	11. 02-26-36-40
12. 02-12-32-23-38	12. 27-25-38-01
13. 39-11	13. 29-24-24-20-35
14. 02-27-25-10-23-18	14. 16-14-18
15. 28-01	15. 29-33-01
16. 02-12-31-26	16. 06-35-32-39-33
17. 02-12-27-27-35-37-21	17. 02-09-27-01
18. 33-23	18. 29-36-07-08
19. 02-12-31-26	19. 29-08-13
20. 02-27-25-10-23-18	20. 29-45-07
21. 28-01	21. 22-29-36-07-08
22. 02-12-31-26	22. 27-34-23-25
23. 02-12-27-14-32-18-27	23. 07-18-35
24. 06-18-17-19	24. 07-45-07
25. 31-26-12	25. 07-23-18-24
26. 02-12-13-01	26. 22-29-36-07-08
27. 23-19-35	27. 09-30-39-18-07
28. 10-03-38	28. 02-06-35-23-07
29. 02-12-27-27-35-37-21	29. 29-34-23-25
30. 13-01	30. 45-07
31. 10-03-38	

Appendix 2

Eteocretan Inscriptions

1. 1 ... ΝΚΑΛΜΙΤΚΕ 2 ΟΣ | ΒΑΡΖΕ | Α ... | Ο 3 ΑΡΚ ... ΑΓΣΕΤ|ΜΕΔΓ 4 ΑΡΚΡΚΟΚΛΕΣ | ΔΕΓ 5 ΑΣΕΓΔΝΑΝΙΤ.

2. 1 ... ΟΝΑΔΕΣΙΕΜΕΤΕΠΙΜΙΤΣϜΑ 2 ... ΔΟ ... ΙΑΡΑΛΑϜΡΑΙΣΟΙΙΝΑΙ 3 ... ΡΕΣΤΝ ΜΤΟΡΣΑΡΔΟϜΣΑΝΟ 4 ... ΣΑΤΟΙΣΣΤΕϜ.ΣΑΤΙΥΝ 5 ... ΑΝΙΜΕΣΤΕΠΑΛΥΝΕΥΤΑΤ 6 ... ΣΑΝΟΜΟΣΕΛΟΣϜΡΑΙΣΟΝΑ 7 ... ΤΣΑΑΔΟϜΤΕΝΑ ... 8 ... ΜΑΠΡΑΝΑΙΡΕΡΙ ... 9 ... ΙΡΕΙΡΕΡΕΙΕ ... 10 ... ΝΤΙΡΑΝΟ ... 11 ... ΑΣΚΕΣ ... 12 ... ΙΤ ...

3. 1 ... ΝΝΥΜΙΤ 2 ... ΑΤΑΡΚΟΜΝ 3 ... ΗΔΗΣΔΕΑ 4 ... ΣΩΠΕΙΡΑΡΙ 5 ... ΕΝ ΤΑΣΕΤϜΣΕΥ 6 ... ΝΝΑΣΙΡΟΥΚΛΕΣ 7 ... ΙΡΕΡΝΗΙΑΜΑΡϜ 8 ... ΕΙΡΕΡϜΙΝΣΔΑΝ 9 ... ΜΑΜΔΕΔΙΚΑΡΚ 10 ... ΡΙΣΡΑΙΡΑΡΙϜ 11 ... ΝΝΕΙΚΑΡΧ 12 ... ΤΑΡΙΔΟΗΙ 13 ... ΕΝΒΑ 14 ... ΔΝΑΣ.

4. (Eteocretan part) 1 ... (Ι)ΡΜΑϜ ΕΤ ΙΣΑΛΑΒΡΕ (Τ?) ΚΟΜΝ 2 ... Δ ΜΕΝ Ι(Ζ ?)ΝΑΙ ΙΣΑΛΥΡΙΑ ΛΜΟ (Greek part) 3 ... ΣΤΟΝΤΥΡΟΝΜΗΑ (Τ?) ΟΑΟΙΕϜΑΔ 4 ... ΕΤΥΡΟ ... ΜΥΝΑ . ΟΑ . ΕΝΗ 5 ... ΜΑΤΡΙΤΑΙΑ.

5. (Eteocretan part) 1 ... ΟΣΤΥΠΡΜΗΡΙΗΙΑΟΜΟ (Greek part) 2 ΣΑΙΔΑΠΕΡΕΝΟΡΚΙΟΙΣΙΑ 3 ... ΚΑΘΑΡΟΝΓΕΝΟΙΤΟ.

Appendix 3

Tabula Cortonensis

Side A

01: et . pɜtruiś . scɜvɜś . ɜliuntś .
02: vinac . restmc . cenu . tɜnθur . śar .
03: cusuθuraś . larisalisvla . pesc . spante . tɜnθur .
04: sa . śran . śarc . clθii . tɜrsna . θui . span θi . ml
05: ɜśieθic . raśnas IIIIC inni . pes . pɜtruś . pav
06: ac . trau lac . tiur . tɜn[θ]urs . tɜnθa[ś] . za cina tpr
07: iniserac . zal[six] \\ cś . ɜsiś vere cusuθurśum .
08: pes . pɜtruśta . scɜv[aś] \\ nu θanatur . lart pɜtr
09: uni . arnt . pini . lart . [v]ipi . lusce . laris . salini
10: vɜtnal . lart . vɜlara . larθal'isa . lart vɜlara.
11: aulesa . vɜl . pumpu . pruciu . aule cɜl atina . sɜ
12: tmnal . arnza . fɜlśni . vɜlθinal . vɜl . luisna
13: lusce . vɜl uslna . nufresa . laru . slanzu . larz
14: a lartle vɜlaveś arnt . pɜtru . ra ufe \\ ɜpru
15: ś . ame . vɜlχe . cusu larisal . clenia rc . laris
16: cusu . larisalisa larizac clan . larisal . pɜtr
17: uni . scɜ[va]ś arntlei . pɜtruś . puia
18: cen . zic . ziχuχe . spa-rzɜ-śtiś śazleiś in
19: θuχti . cusuθuraś . suθiu . ame . tal suθive
20: naś . rat-m . θuχt . ceśu . tlt eltɜi . sianś .
21: spa-rzɜ-te . θui . saltzic . fratuce . cusuθuraś .
22: larisalisvla . pɜtruśc . scɜvaś . peśś . tarχ ian
23: eś \\ cnl . nuθe . mal ec . lart . cucrina . lausisa .
24: zilaθ meχ l.raśnal .[la]ris . cɜl atina lau
25: sa clanc . arnt luscni [a]rnθal . clanc . larz
26: a . lart . turmna . salin[ial . larθ cɜl atina . a
27: pnal . clenia rc . vɜlχe[ś][. . .][papal]
28: śerc . vɜlχe . cusu . aule[sa][. . .]
29: aninalc . laris . fuln[folnius][clenia]
30: rc . lart . pɜtce . uslnal[. . .][cucrina]
31: inaθur . tɜcsinal . vɜl[. . .]
32: uś . larisc . cusu . uslna[l][. . .]

Side B

1: aule . salini . cusual
2: zilci . larθal . cusuś . titinal
3: larisalc . saliniś . aulesla . celti nɜitis
4: ś . tar sminaśś . spa rz a in θuχt ceśu .
5: rat-m . suθiu . suθiusa . vɜlχeś . cusuśa
6: ulesla . vɜlθuruś . t[.]lniś . vɜlθurusla .
7: larθalc . cɜl atina ś . vetnal . larisalc .
8: cɜl atina ś . pitlnal

Appendix 4

Bilingual from Pyrgi (TLE 874) and Its "Synopsis" (TLE 875)
(Example of the Analysis)

Phoenician (Punic) Text

lrbt lʻštrt ʼšr qdš ʼz ʼš pʻl wʼš ytn tbryʼ wlnš mlk ʻl kyšryʼ byrḥ zbḥ šmš bmtnʼ bbt wbm tw kʻštrt ʼrš bdy lmlky šnt šlš III byrḥ krr bym qbr ʻlm wšnt lʼmš ʼlm bbty šnt km hkkbm ʻl

Note 1: in the last word the writing ✗ *aleph* should be understood as erroneous (instead of ⵔ *ayin*), which was caused by the confusion of gutturals in the later (Punic) language, so we are to read ʻ*l* 'above, overhead' instead of ʼ*l* 'these,' which sometimes appears in published research.

Phoenician part translated: "To lady Astarte this holy place, which Tiberius Veliana, a king over Caere, built and donated during the month of the sacrifice to the Sun, as a gift to the temple and its (holy) plot, as Astarte chose her servant as a king. Three years have passed in the month of Churvar, in the day of the burial of the divinity. (And may) the years of the statue of the divinity in her house (be) as years of the stars above."

Note 2: *kyšryʼ* reflects the Etruscan place name *keizra*, from which Latin *Cisra/Caere* (Pyrgi was a seaport of Caere).

Note 3: month name *krr* is a distorted Etruscan *χosfer* 'October' from *cezp* 'eight.'

Etruscan Text

ita tmia icac heramasva vatieχe unialastres θemiasa meχ θuta θefariei velianas sal cluvenias turuke munistas θuvas tameresca ilacve tulerase nac ki avil teśiameitale ilacve alśase nac atranes zilacal seleitala acnaśvers itanim heramve avil eniaca pulumχva

Clear Forms from Etruscan Text

ita: demonstrative pronoun, along with *ta*

tmia: 'sacred plot,' by analogy with the Phoenician part; probably, from Greek τέμενος

ica-c: demonstrative pronoun, along with *ca*; *c* = Latin *-que*

heramasva: (genitive), also *heramve*, 'sanctuary' below (by analogy with the Phoenician part), with an enclitic that can probably be translated as "here"

vatieχe: 'to/for Lady' (only by analogy with the Phoenician part); phonetic appearance of the dative-locative suffix *-e/-i* depends on its environment

unialastres: double name, 'Astarte' is added to Etruscan *uni* 'Juno'; both parts in genitive

θemiasa: part. pres. I from well known root 'to donate'

meχ θuta: title, borrowed from Oscan *meddix tuticus*

θefariei velianas: name of the king of Caere; family name appears in genitive according to the general rule

sal cluvenias: see below

turuke: perf. 'donated,' possibly from Greek δῶρον

tulerase: aor. 'determined,' formed with the suffix *-s*, along with

tular: 'boundary' (from Umbrian *tuder*)

nac: adverb, probably, 'thus, so, well'

ki avil: 'three years,' see also in the Phoenician part

teśiameitale: substantived form (with the suffix *-al*) from the root 'to sacrifice/donate' with a typical suffixation *-am-*; *-e*, probably, it should be understood as ablative indicator

alśase, also aor.: formed with the suffix *-s-*, from the root *al-* 'to donate'

atranes: 'servant,' by analogy with the Phoenician part and Mylian *atran*, 'friend, bodyguard' used in genitive

zilacal: magistrate's name (also with *-al*); *zil(a)c*, ruler of the town, whereas *zilaθ*, 'praetor Etruriae'

ita-ni-m: derivative from *ita*, with a particle -*m* 'and, while,' suffix -*ni* is unclear

eniaca: possibly related to demonstrative pronoun *an*, with unclear suffixation

pulumχva: 'stars,' with the suffix of collective plural -*χva*

Text of the Brief Inscription

nac tefarie veliiunas θamuce cleva etanal masan tiurunias šelace vacal tmial avilχval amuce pulumχva *snutuφ

Note 4: We should pay attention to the extremely rare variant ? for (s) in *šelace*.

Note 5: writing *snutuφ* is reconstructed by the analogy with *snuiaφ* with the Zagreb text, where this form appears three times.

Clear Forms from the Etruscan Text (Except Repeated):

θamuce: perf. with an unknown meaning

cleva etanal: most likely 'annual nail,' which was driven into the temple wall; this rite is described, for example, in Livy [VII, 3]; the same rite seems to be possibly reflected in *sal cluvenias* in the main inscriptions (cf., Latin *clavus* and *eta-* 'Idus,' new year started in the first full moon [i.e., Idus], after vernal equinox)

masan: borrowed from Anatolian word for cult object (probably statue of a divinity)

tiurunias: unclear combination of *tiv* with the meaning 'month' and 'moon' with a theonym 'Juno'

selace: perf. with an unknown meaning

avil-χva-l: 'years,' collective plural in genitive

amuce: perf. of a well-known verb *am-* 'to be'; but the usage of the past is also unclear.

Appendix 5

Lemnos Stele Inscription

Front:

(left): *1. aker tavarśio 2. vanalasial śeronai morinail*

(right): *3. holaieś naφoθ śiaśi*

(middle): *4. maraś mav 5. sialχveiś aviś 6. evisθo śeronaiθ 7. śivai.*

Side:

1. holaieśi φokiaśiale śeronaiθ evisθo toveronai 2. rom haralio śivai epiteśio arai tiś φoke[ś?] 3. śivai aviś sialχviś maraś-m aviś aomai.

Middle lines are to be read as 6-7-5-4; such an order is confirmed by the sequence *śivai aviś sialχviś maraś-m* ... on the side; on the front a similar combination is preceded by *evisθo śeronaiθ* 'buried (part.) here.'

Appendix 6

Main Eteo-Cypriote Inscriptions[*]

KS 1 *vi-ti-le ra-nu ta-na mu-no-ti/a-i-lo e-ki ja-no-ti ma-na ko-/to-u-pa-ra* (or *ki*; or *la*)-*mi ra-nu ta-na mu-/no-ti*

KS 2 *a-na ta-si tu-sa e-ki vi-ja-ki ma-na/a-po-i e-ki ma-ri ma-na tu-mi-ra/i-mi-ka-ni pu-e-ne-mi-na pa-na-mo/vo* (or *ka*)-*ni-o ta-ra-vi ka-va-li-ja ma-na mi-?*

KS 3 *tu a-li-ra-ni o-i-te tu-tu* (or *su*) *ta-le-ja pa-ku-ke a-no-ti ta-so-ti/a-pu-e-ma o-i-te a-?-ra* (or *le*)-*ma ma-na a-so-na tu-ka i-mi-no-na/a-ja-i-a ko-?-? a-na ta-? a-so-na tu-ka e-ne-mi-na o-/i-te ta-ra-vo e-ne-mi-na ? -ti* (or *ka*)-*la-va-ka* (or *ti*)-*ke mu* (or *va*)-*so-ti*

KS 5 *ta ve-ta-re-se*

KS 11 (bilingual from Amathus)

(Greek part) ἡ πόλις ἡ Ἀμαθουσίων Ἀρίστωνα Ἀριστώνακτος εὐπατρίδην

(Eteo-Cypriote part) *a-na ma-to-ri u-mi-e-sa-i-mu-ku-la-i-la-sa-na a- ri-si-to-no-se a-ra-to-va-na-ka-so-ko-o-se ke-ra-ke-re-tu-lo-se(-)ta-ka-na- ku? no?-so-ti a-lo ka-i-li-po-ti*

---

[*] According to: J. Friedrich, *Kleinasiatische Sprachdenkmäler* (Berlin: W. de Gruyter & Co., 1932), 50–52; Tom B. Jones, "Notes on the Eteo-Cypriote inscriptions," *American Journal of Philology* 71, no. 4 (1950): 401–7.

PRELIMINARY INDEX OF MINOAN AND TYRRHENIAN WORDS, PRESERVED IN GREEK

The present index is intended primarily for systemizing borrowings, put in clusters by the roots; since these clusters are built mainly according to word formational models, it helps us to avoid numerous repetitions in different chapters. In each alphabetical section we enumerate separate words or groups formed from the same root, which for different reasons (and with unequal degrees of probability) can be bound with pre-Greek (i.e., Minoan or Tyrrhenian strata). Any criterion by which we find it possible to consider some lexeme as Minoan or Tyrrhenian is given in square brackets; it may be typical suffixation, direct indications of the authors, Etruscan and other foreign parallels, etc. Also, we found it useful to adduce some words considered "Mediterranean" or "not having etymology" in the authoritative dictionary by H. Frisk, if their phonetic type or morpheme structure does not contradict the criteria described above. Below we list not only the words which appear in the main text, but also some not included in it.

A

ἄβαξ: avaks "calculating board" (-ακ- -ak-).

ἀγγ-: aggos ἄγγος, different kinds of vessels; "basket"; "trunk" ("*Mittelmeerwort*" ["Mediterranean"], Frisk); ἀγγύλη aggíli (Eudem.), kind of missile weapon.

ἄγγυρα: aggira (Hes.) "vine"; ἄγγυρος aggiros (Hes.), kind of cookie (-υ/ιρ/λ-).[266]

ἄγλις: aglis, see γαλ- gal-.

ἀγόρ: agor "eagle" (Hes. "ἀετός. Κύπριοι"; Etruscan-Latin *aquila, Aquilo*).

---

266. Below -υρ- for simplicity.

ἀερ-: aer- Ἀέροπες Aeropes (Hes.), ethnos in Argolis; bird species; Ἀερόπη Aeropi, Minos's granddaughter; ἀερόπος aeropos (Hes.), kind of mollusc (-οπ- -op-).

Ἀθηνᾶ: Athina see ταν- tan-.

αἰγυπιός: aigipios (?) "kite" (-υπ-? -ip-?).

αἰσ-: ais- αἴσακος aisakos "stalk of laurel" (plant, devoted to gods) (-ακ- -ak-); αἰσιμία aisimia "happiness"; αἴσιμος aisimos "fatal"; "just"; αἰσυμνάω aisimnao "to rule," "to reign"; Αἴσυμνος Aisimnos, Αἰσύμη Aisimi, different toponyms (Etruscan *ais* "god"; "god," *aisuna* "sacrifice" (> Umbrian *esono*); -υμ -im (-να -na).

ἀκαλήρ-: akalir- ἀκακαλλίς akakallis, flower of narcissus (Hes. "ἄνθος ναρκίσσου. Κρῆτες": red.; ἀγαλλίς agallis "iris"; Ἀκάλλη Akalli (Apollod.), Minos's daughter; ἄκαρα akara "leg"; "thigh" (Hes. "τὰ σκέλη. Κρῆτες"); ἀκαλανθίς akalanthis (Arph.) "young goldfinch" (-νθ- [-nth-]) (cf., καρ- kar- [?]).

ἀκανθ-: akanth- "sloe": ἄκανθα akantha "thorn"; ἀκανθίας akanthias "shark"; ἀκανθίς (akanthis) "goldfinch, *Carduelis carduelis L.*"; ἀκανθίων akanthion "hedgehog" (-νθ-); ἀκανθυλλίς akanthilis, bird species (-νθ-υρ- -nth-ir-).

ἀκαρν-, ἀκάρναξ: akarn- akarnaks (Hes.) "grouper, *Labrax lupus* or *Sebastes marinus*" (-ακ- -ak-); ἀχάρνας "*Anarrhichas lupus* or *rufus* (?)"; ἀχαρνώς "perch (?)" (-αρ-να -ar-na?) (cf., Ἀκαρνανία "*Acarnania*").

ἄκορον: akoron, see κορ-έ kor-e.

ἀκτέα: aktea "elder, elderberry, *Sambucus nigra*" (-ε/ι+GI.)[267]

ἄκυλος, ἀκύλος, ἄχυλος: akilos "edible acorn" (-υρ- -ir-) (cf., Ἀκύφας [?] Akifas [?] [-υφ- -if-]).

Ἀκύφας: Akifas (Steph.), Doric town (-υφ- -if-) (cf., ἄκυλος [?] [akilos]).

ἄλαρα: (EtM, Hes.) alara, ἐλάραι elarai (Herod.) "spike," "point" (KN Zf 31 *a-da-ra* [woman's silver hairpin]).

ἀλένθη: alenthi (Hes.) "night" (-νθ- -nth-).

Ἀλίκυρνα: Alikirna (Steph.), Acarnanian area (-υρ-να -ir-na) (cf., Ἁλικαρνασ(σ)ός [?] Alikarnas[s]os [?]).

---

267. Greek inflection.

ἄλλιξ: (?) alliks (Hes.) "chlamys [short cloak]" (-υκ- -ik-).

αμ-1: am-e ἀμάδεα amadea (acc. pl.), kind of fig (Athen. "Ἑρμῶναξ δ' ἐν Γλώτταις") Κρητικαῖς σύκων γένη ἀναγράφει ἁμάδεα καὶ νικύλεα" -ε/ι+GI); ἄμυλος amilos "pie (of fine-ground flour)"; Ἄμυρος Amiros, Thessalian river (-υρ- -ir-);Ἄμυμνοι Amimnoi, unknown tribe; Ἀμυμώνη Amimoni, Danaid (-υμ-να -im-na); poss. ἀμύγδαλον: amigdalon "almond, Amygdalus" ("*Fremdwort unbekannten Ursprungs*" ["Foreign word of unknown origin"], Frisk; -αρ- -ar- ?).

αμ-2: am-e ἀμία amia, tuna species (-ε/ι+GI; < Egypt. *mehī*?); ἀμύς amis (gen. -ύδος -idos) (Gal.) "fresh-water turtle."

αμαρ-: amar (ἀμέ-αρ-? ame-ar-?): ἀμαρυλλίς amarillis "*Amaryllis*" (-υρ- -ir-); ἀμάρακον amarakon "marjoram" (-ακ- -ak-); Ἀμάρυνθος Amarinthos, town in Euboea (-νθ- -nth-).

Ἀμνισός: Amnisos (?), Cretan river and city (Mycenaean *A-mi-ni-so*).

ἄμπελος: ampelos "grapes"; "vine (plant)" (Etruscan gloss TLE 805 *Ampiles* "May" (usual time for the engrafting of grape vines) (Geopon., V, 1).

ἄναξ: anaks (F-, Mycenaean *wa-na-ka*) "lord" (-ακ- -ak-).

ἀνθ-: anth- ἀνθέριξ antheriks "awn; ear"; ἀνθερίκη (antheriki) "asphodel" (-υκ- -ik-).

ἄνθραξ: anthraks "coal" (-ακ- -ak-).

Ἄπταρα: Aptara (Hes.), Ἄπτερα Aptera, Cretan city (Mycenaean *A-pa-ta-wa*).

ἄρακις: arakis "cup" (KO Zf 2 [inscribed bronze cup]): *a-ra-ko-* (cf., Athen. "Αἰολεῖς δὲ τὴν φιάλην ἄρακιν καλοῦσι"; Hes. "ἄρακιν φιάλην, καὶ ἀράκτην").

Ἀράκυνθος: Arakinthos mountain in Boeotia (Etruscan gloss TLE 810 ἄρακος arakos "falcon; hawk"; -νθ- -nth-).

Ἀργάνθον: Arganthon mountain in Mysia (Latin *Moesia*); Ἀργανθώνη Arganthoni, personal name[268] (Etruscan; -νθ- -nth-; -να-na [?]).

Ἀρίνθη: Arinthi (Hecat., Steph.), town of *Oenotri* (-νθ- -nth-).

ἄρμυλα: armila "sandal; (high) boot" (Hes. "ὑποδήματα. Κύπριοι"; -υρ- -ir-).

---

268. PN below.

ἀρτ-: art- ἄρτος artos "bread"; ἄρταμος artamos "cook"; "butcher" (-αμ- am-) (cf., Ἄρτεμις Artemis, Doric Ἄρταμις Artamis [?]).

ἀσάμινθος: asaminthos "tub, bath" (-νθ- -nth-).

ἄσκυρον: askiron "St. John's wort, *Hypericum*" (-υρ- -ir-).

ἀσπ-: asp- ἀσπάλαξ aspalaks "mole" (-ακ- -ak-) (cf., ἀσπάλατος aspalatos (?), suppos. *Genista acanthoclada*).

ἀστ-: ast- (?) (Ϝἀστ- wast-; Boeot. Ϝάστιος wastios, etc.): ἄστυ asti "city (mainly capital)."

Ἄστυρα: Astira, settlement in Mysia (-υρ- -ir-).

ἀστακός: astakos "lobster, *Homarus* or *Astacus marinus*" (-ακ- -ak).

ἀσύφη: asifi (Diosc.) "*Cassia*" (-υφ- -if-).

ἀτάλυμνος: atalimnos (Nicander) "plum; plum tree, *Prunus L.*" (-υμ-να -im-na).

Ἄταρνα: Atarna, see ταρ- tar-.

ἀχαρν-: axarn- see ἀκαρν- akarn-.

ἄχνυλα: axnila "hazel, hazel grove" (Hes. "καρύα karia. Κρῆτες"; -υρ- -ir).

ἄχυρα: axira "chaff" (-υρ- -ir-).

ἀψίνθιον: apsinthion "wormwood, *Artemisia absinthium*"; Ἄψυνθος Apsinthos, city in Thrace (-νθ- -nth) (cf., Ἄψυρτος Apsirtos [?], Medea's brother.)

B

Βαθανία: vathania "nest" (Hes. "νεοσσείαν neosseian. Κρῆτες"; -να? -na).

βαίτυλος: vaitilos (Hes.) "stone, swallowed by Cronus (instead of Zeus)" (-υρ- -ir-).

βαλ-: val- βάλαγρος valagros; βάλερος valeros; βαλίνος valinos (-να -na); βαλλιρός valliros (-υρ- -ir-), species of freshwater fish (carp, *Cyprinus*?) (cf., *Βάλινθος? *valinthos?).

*Βάλινθος: *valinthos (Προβάλινθος Provalinthos, with Greek προ- pro-), Attic town (-νθ- -nth) (cf., βαλ-? val- ?).

βάλσαμον: valsamon (> Hebrew bāśām) "*Balsamum gileadense*" (-αμ- -am-).

βασιλεύς: (?)vasileis "king" (Mycenaean *qa-si-re-u*).

βασσάρα: vassara "fox" (-αρ- -ar-; "*ohne Etimologie*" ["Without etymology"], Frisk).

βασύνιας: vasinias (Semus, Fr., 3) "sacrificial donation to Hecate in Delos." (Etruscan *pesna*, CIE 252 etc.; -να -na).

βάτος: vatos "blackberry; sloe" ("*Mittelmeerwort*" ["Mediterranean word"], Frisk).

Βατύλη: vatili (Sch. Arph.) "woman (?); female dwarf" (-υρ- -ir-).

Βελεμίνα: Velemina (Paus.), Laconic toponym (MA 1 *qe-de-mi-nu*, *q > b, *D > l, -να -na, -μι-να? -mi-na?).

βήραξ: viraks (Hes.) (βαρ- var-, παρ- par-), kind of bread (-ακ- -ak-).

βήρυλλος: virillos "beryl" (-υρ- -ir-).

Βισάνθη: Visanthi, Macedonian city (-νθ- -nth-).

βόλινθος: volinthos "wild bull" (-νθ- -nth) (cf., Βόλισσος Volissos), town in Chios.

βόμβυξ: vomviks "silkworm, *Bombyx*" (-υκ- -ik-).

βότρυς: votris "bunch of grapes" (*Unbefriedigendeidg. Etymologien* ["Unsatisfactory etymology"], Frisk).

βουκανῆ: voukani "narcissus" (Hes. "ἀνεμώνη τὸ ἄνθος. Κύπριοι"; -να -na).

βράβυλον: vravilon "sloe" (-υρ- -ir-).

βρέτας: vretas "wooden statue, idol" ("*Mittelmeerwort ohne Etymologie*" ["Mediterranean word without etymology"], Frisk).

Γ

γαθύλλις, γηθύλλις: gathillis, githillis "onion" (-υρ- -ir-) (cf., γηθύον githion, γήτειον giteion).

γαλ-, ἄγλις, γέλγις: gal-, aglis, gelgis "clove" (-θ- -th-; Red.); γάλινθος galinthos (see ἐρέβινθος erevinthos). γαλλ- gall- see γαρ- gar-.

γαρ-: gar- γάρος garos "fish soup; caviar"; γαλεός galeos "spotted shark"; γαλλαρίας gallarias. (Athen.), καλλαρίας kallarias (Hes.), fish species (-αρ- -ar-); Γαλήνη Galini, Nereid (-να -na).

γάρσανον: garsanon "brushwood" (Hes. "φρύγανα frigana. Κρῆτες"; -να? -na?).

Γέλχανος: Gelxanos, see ἐλ- el-.

γογγ-: (gogg-) "round" (?): γόγγρος (goggros) "eel"; γογγύλη (goggili) "turnip" (-υρ- -ir-). Cf., γογγών: (goggon) (Hes.) "foolish" (-να -na) (?).

γόργυρα: (gorgira) "cave, dungeon" (-υρ- -ir).

γορδήτ-: (gordit-) (< Hittite *gurta-*) "city" (Mycenaean *ko-tu*): Γορδιας (Gordias) (Thessaly, legend on coin); Γόρτυν (Gortin) (Crete), Γόρτυς (Gortis) (Arcadia), Gortunja, Gordunja (Macedonia), Γυρτών (Girton) (Thessaly); Hes. "Κορτύνιοι· οἱ Ἀρκάδες· ἡ γὰρ Κόρτυς τῆς Ἀρκαδίας"; Κυρτώνη (Kirtoni) (Steph., Boeotia); Etruscan *curtun* > Latin, Italian *Cortona*; Hes. Καρτεμνίδες (Kartemnides) ("οἱ Γορτύνιοι. Κρῆτες") (-μ- να -m-na).

γραψαῖος: (grapsaïos) (Athen.) "crab" ("*Mittelmeerwort*" ["Mediterranean word"], Frisk).

Δ

δαγύς: dagis (?) "waxen puppet" (intended for witchcraft) ("*Technisches Fremdwort ohne Etymologie*" ["Technical foreign word with etymology"], Frisk).

δάκτυλος: daktilos "date (fruit)" (-υρ- -ir-).

δαμ-: dam- Δαμυρίας Damirias, river in Sicily; Δαμύλος Damilos (Lucian.) PN (-υρ- -ir-); Ῥαδάμανθυς Radamanthis, Minos' brother (KY Za 2 *da-ma-te*; AR Zf 1 *no-da-ma- te*; -νθ- -nth-).

δάσκιλλος: daskillos "kingfish; meadow-wort" (*Sciaena*?) (-υρ- -ir-).

δάφνη: dafni λάφνη lafni "laurel, *Laurus nobilis*" (-να -na, "*unerklärtes Mittelmeerwort*" ["Unexplained Mediterranean word"], Frisk).

δελκανός: delkanos (Athen.), fish species (-να -na).

δέλφαξ: delfaks "sow" (-ακ- -ak-).

δεπ-: dep- δέπας depas "cup, bowl, goblet" (Mycenaean *di-pa*); λεπάς lepas, mollusc species; δέπαστρον depastron "cup"; λεπαστή lepasti "cup (looking like shell)" > Latin *lepesta, lepista*); λέπαστρον lepastron (Hes.) "kind of fishing tackle" ("*Mittelmeerwort ohne Etymologie*" ["Mediterranean word without etymology"], Frisk; enclitics).

δοίδυξ: doidiks "pestle" (-υκ- -ik-).

Δόλοπες: Dolopes, Thessalian tribe (-οπ- -op-).

δρεπάνη: drepani "sickle" (-να -na).

δρύοψ: driops, kind of woodpecker. Δρυόπες: Driopes, tribe near the mountain *Oeta* (-οπ- -op-).

E

ἐλ- (ϝελ-): el (wel); Γέλχανος Gelxanos (< *ϝέλχανος) (Hes. "ὁ Ζεύς, παρὰ Κρησίν"; Etruscan *velχana* > Latin *Vulcanus*); Ἐλύμνιος Elimnios (Hes. "Ποσειδῶν ἐν Λέσβῳ"; Etruscan *vel-im-na*); Ἐλύμνιον Elimnion, locality in Euboea; Ἑλένη (?) Eleni, daughter of Zeus and Leda ("*alte minoische Vegetationsgöttin*" ["Old Minoan vegetation goddess"], Frisk; -να -na (cf., Ἔλυρος? Eliros).

ἐλεδώνη: eledoni, mollusk species (*Eledone moschata*?) (-να -na; "*Mittelmeerwort*" ["Mediterranean word"], Frisk).

Ἑλένη: Eleni see ἐλ- el-.

ἐλλ- (ϝελλ-): ell (well) "snake": ἔλλοψ ellops, ἔλλοπος ellopos "snake" (Nicander); "eel" (< "serpentine") (-οπ- -op-); Ἐλλώτια Ellotia, ritual in honor of Athena ("*Schlangengöttin der minoischen Zeit*" ["Time of the Minoan snake goddess"], Frisk); Ἑλλωτίς Ellotis, former name of Gortyn (Steph. "Γόρτυν, πόλις Κρήτης . . . ἐκαλεῖτο δὲ καὶ Λάρισσα. πρότερον γὰρ ἐκαλεῖτο Ἑλλωτίς. . .") (LA, LB 75 ? we).

ἕλμινς: Elmins see λίμινς limins.

ἔλυμος: elimos "millet; panic grass, *Panicum*" (-υμ- -im-; Hes. "ἔλεμος· σπέρμα ὅπερ ἑψῶντες Λάκωνες ἐσθίουσιν").

Ἔλυρος: Eliros (Steph.) Cretan town (-υρ- -ir-) (cf., 6l-?).

ἐρέβινθος: erevinthos (Hes. γάλινθος galinthos, λεβίνθιος levinthios (= ἐρέβινθος erevinthos, without prothetic ε-?), ὀδόλυνθος odolinthos, with the same meaning), "kind of peas, *Cicer arietinum*" (-νθ- -nth-). ἐρπ- erp-: ἔρπυλλος erpillos "thyme, *Thymus serpyllum*" (-υρ- -ir-); ἐρπυξή erpiksi (Diosc.), kind of plant ("ἐλαφικόν elafikon, νέβρειον nefrion") (-υκ- -ik-) (cf., Egypt. ἔρπις erpis (Eust.) "wine" (?).

Ἐρυμ- Erim-, Ἐρύμανθος Erimanthos: mountain and river in Arcadia; Ἐρυμναί Erimnai.

Ἐρυμνά Erimna: Lycian and Lydian towns (-νθ- -nth-, -μ-να -m-na).

ἐρυσίβη erisivi, ἐρισύβη erisivi, in Rhodes ἐρυθίβη erithivi: "powdery mildew"; ἐρυσιβάω erisivao "to be affected with powdery mildew" (-υ(μ)β- -i(m)v-).

Εὐρώπη: Evropi "Europe" (-οπ- -op-) (cf., Εὖρος Evros "wind from the east").

Z

ζέφυρος: zefiros "wind from the west" (-υρ- -ir).

ζιζ-: ziz- ζιζουλά zizoula (Alex. Med.) "millet" (-υρ- -ir-); ζίζυφον zizifon (Geopon., Galen.) "*Rhamnus jujuba*" (-υφ- -if-) (cf., Syr. *zūzfā*; ζιζάνιον zizanion "darnel, cockle" *Lolium temulentum*" (-να -na-).

Ζάκυνθος: Zakinthos, island in the Ionian Sea (modern *Zante*) (-νθ- -nth-).

Ζήρυνθος: Zirinthos, city and cave-temple in Thrace (-νθ- -nth-).

H

ἦνοψ: inops (?) "flaring" (-οπ- -op-).

Θ

θάλαμη: thalami "burrow; gorge; grave"; θάλαμος thalamus "room; house" (-αμ- -am-).

θρίαμβος: thriamvos "hymn in honor of Dionysus" (Latin (< Etruscan) *triumphus*).

θριήν-: thrini- θρῖδαξ thridaks, θρῖναξ thrinax "lettuce" (-ακ- -ak-); θρινία thrinia "vine" (Hes. "ἄμπελος ἐν Κρήτῃ"; -να -na); θρῖον thrion "fig leaf"; θρύον thrion "reed" (cf., also θρίαμβος thriamvos [?]).

θύννος: thinnos (?) "tuna, *Thunnus*" ("*Mittelmeerwort*" ["Mediterranean word"], Frisk).

I

ἰέττας: (I.-E.?) iettas "father" (Hes. "πατέρας Κρῆτες").

Ἴκαρος: Ikaros, see καρ- kar-.

Ἰλαττία: Ilattia, Cretan town (N.-Pic. *vilatos*?).

ἰόβλης: iovlis "reed" (Hes. "κάλαμος παρὰ Κρησίν").

Ἴτανος: Itanos, see ταν- tan-.

Ἴσμαρος: Ismaros, see μαρ- mar-.

ἰτέα: itea "willow, *Salix*," Ἰτέα Itea, Attic toponym (-ε/ι+GI).

K

κάγκαμον: kagkamon (> Akkadian *kurkānu*, Hebrew *karkōm*) "saffron" (-αμ- -am-).

καδ-: kad- "mutilation": κάδαμος kadamos "blind" (-am-; Hes. "τυφλός· Σαλαμίνιοι"); κάδυρος kadiros (Hes.) "κάπρος ἄνορχις" (-υρ- -ir-); Latin *calamitas* (< *cadamitas*) "disaster, misery."

καδμ-: kadm- κάδμος kadmos (Hes. "δόρυ. λόφος. ἀσπίς. Κρῆτες"); myth. Κάδμος Kadmos; Καδμῖλος Kadmilos (-υρ- -ir-; Sch. Lyc. "Καδμῖλος λέγεται ὁ Ἑρμῆς παρὰ τοῖς Τυρσηνοῖς"; "Καδμίλος ὁ Ἑρμῆς Βοιωτικῶς"; Etruscan gloss TLE 819 b "casmillae ... *apud Tuscos* Camillum *appellari Mercurium*").

κάδος: kados "jug" (> Hebrew *kad* "tub; scoop"; Latin *cadus*). ("*Mittelmeerwort*" ["Mediterranean word"], Frisk) (cf., κάθιδοι? kathidoi?).

κάθιδοι: kathidoi (< Hittite *gazzi*), kind of vessel (Hes. "ὑδρίαι· Ἀρκάδες"; HT 63, Mycanaean *ka-ti*) (cf., κηθάριον kitharion, "vessel for voting").

καλαμ-: kalam- καλάμη kalami "stem, stalk"; κάλαμος kalamos "reed" (-αμ- -am-); καλαμίνθη kalaminthi "kind of mint" *Nepeta cataria* or *Melissa altissima*; Καλαμίνθη Kalaminthi (Steph.), African town (in Cyrene?) (-αμ-ινθ- -am-inth-).

καλλαρίας: kallarias, see γαρ- gar-.

Καλλιόπη: Kalliopi, muse who presides over epic poetry (-οπ- -op-).

Κάλυμνα: Kalimna, Aegean island (-υμ-να -im-na) (cf., Κάλυνδα Kalinda (?), Carian city (-νθ- -nth-).

κάμαξ: kamaks "pole, spear, handle" (-ακ- -ak-).

καμ(αρ)-: kam(ar)- καμάρα kamara "covered wagon"; Καμάρα Kamara (Steph.), Cretan town.

Καμάρινα: Kamarina, Oceanus's daughter (-να -na); here also *Camars, Camers*, early Etruscan name for Clusium.

καμπύλη: kampili "staff" (-υρ- -ir-).

Κάνηθος: Kanithos, mountain in Euboea (-θ- -th-).

κάνθαρος: kantharos "scarab"; fish species (-αρ- -ar-).

κανθύλη: kanthili "swelling abscess" (-υρ- -ir-).

κάνναβις: kannavis (< Sumerian *kunibu* [?]) "hemp, *Cannabis*."

καπάνα: kapana (Thess.) "cart, vehicle" (Etruscan gloss TLE 832 γάπος· ὄχημα. Τυρρηνοί"; -να -na).

καπάνη: kapani (Hes.) "hair-cap" (-να –na).

κάππαρις: kapparis "capers, *Capparis*" (-αρ- -ar-).

καρ-1: kar-e (Hes.): "κάρα· αἴξ ἥμερος Πολυρρήνιοι. ὑπὸ Γορτυνίων ... ἄλλοι δὲ ἡ συκῆ Ἴωνες τὰ πρόβατα. καὶ τὴν κεφαλήν; καρανῶ· τὴν αἶγα. Κρῆτες."

καρ-2: kar-e, Karja "Caria"; Ἴκαρος Ikaros, Aegean island; "Icarus" (P271) (cf., ἀκαλήρ- akalir- [?]).

κάραβος: karavos "crab" ("*Mittelmeerwort*" ["Mediterranean word"], Frisk; -α[μ]β- -a[m]v-).

καρδ-: kard- "dough, pastry; bread": κάρδαμον kardamon, Mycanaean *ka-da-mi-ja* "cardamom" (as a kind of spice) (-αμ- -am-) (cf., καρδαμίς kardamis; καρδαμύλη kardamili, καρδαμάλη kardamali (Hes.) "unleavened cookie" (-υμ-αρ- -im-ar-); καρδαμίνη kardamini (Hes.) "*Sium latifolium*" (-αμ-[ι]-να -am-[i]-na); κάρδοπος kardopos "kneading trough" (-οπ- -op-; HT 31 *ka-ro- pa₃*).

καρορύς: karoris, kind of vessel (Hes. "ὑδρία. Κρῆτες"; Mycanaean *ka-ra-re-we*).

καρτ-: kart-, see gord/t-.

καρύκη: kariki (< Lydian?), kind of dish (-υκ -ik).

Κασσιόπη: Kassiopi, Andromeda's mother (-οπ- -op-).

καυ-: see κυδ- kid-.

κεδρ-: κέδρος kedros "cedar"; χέδροπα xedropa, Hes. κέδροπα kedropa (nom. pl.) "beans" (-οπ- -op-).

κεκῆνας: (acc. pl.) kekinas "hare" (Hes. "λαγωούς. Κρῆτες"; -να -na).

κεκρ-: kekr- Κέκροψ Kekrops, founder of Athens (-οπ- -op-); κεκρύφαλος kekrifalos "headband" (-υφ-? -if-?).

κεκύκη: kekini (?) (Hes.) "staff" (-υκ- -ik-).

κελ-: kel- κέλυφος kelifos "peel; shell" (-υφ- -if-); κελέβη kelevi "cup" ("*Mittelmeerwort*" ["Mediterranean word"], Frisk).

κέραμος: keramos "clay" (-αμ- -am-) (cf., Didym. κεραμύλλιον "ἀλλὰ καὶ Πέτρου" (-υρ- -ir-).

κερκ-: kerk- Κερκίνη Kerkini, Paeonian mountain range; Κέρκινα Kerkina, town in North Africa (-να -na); Κέρκυρα Kerkira, Ionic island (*Corfu*) (-υρ- -ir-).

κηθάριον: kitharion, see κάθιδοι kathidoi.

κήρινθος: kirinthos "bee-bread; pollen"; Κήρινθος Kirinthos, Euboean town (-νθ- -nth-).

κιβ-: kiv- κίβισις kivisis, κυβισίς kivisis "bag" (Hes. "πήρα· Κύπριοι"; LA, LB 67 𒆠 *ki*); κιβώριον kivorion "seed cavity of water lily" (-ε/ι+GI); Κίβυρα Kivira, Phrygian town (-υρ- -ir-).

κιδ-: kid- κίδαλον kidalon (Hes.) "onion"; κίδαρις kidaris, κίταρις kitaris, kind of high headdress (-αρ- -ar-).

κιθάρα: kithara "*cithara*" (-αρ- -ar-).

κικ-: kik- κεικύνη keikini (Hes.) "mulberry, *Morus nigra*": *ki-ki-na* after the logogram *FICus* (HT 88; -να -na); Κικύνηθος Kikinithos, island in Pagasean cove (Thessaly) (-νθ-); κικένδα kikenda "*Gentiana*" (Etruscan gloss TLE 825; -νθ- -nth-); κικίρδης kikirdis (Hes.) "fig" (-ρδ- -rd-). Here also Etruscan γιγάρουμ gigaroum (Diosc.) βῆτα λεπορίνα vita leporine (cf., also κίκιννος kikinnos "curl, ringlet" [?]).

κισ(θ)-: kis(th)- κίσθος kisthos, κισσός kissos "ivy, *Hedera helix*," derivative κίσθαρος kistharos, κίσσαρος kissaros (-αρ- -ar-) (cf., Diosc.: "κίσθος, ὅν ἔνιοι κίσθαρον ἢ κίσσαρον καλοῦσι"; Κισθήνη Kisthini, town in Aeolis [-να –na]).

κίσιρνις: kisirnis (?) (Hes.), bird species (-υρ-να -ir-na).

κισσύβιον: kissivion "cup" (-υ(μ)β- -i(m)v-; -ε/ι+GI).

κιστ-: kist- κίστη kisti "box, chest; basket"; κιστέρνα kisterna "cistern" (-ερ-να -er-na).

κίταρις: kitaris, see κιδ- kid-.

κίττυλα: kittila (Hes.) "peel" (-υρ- -ir-).

κλῖμαξ: klimaks "stairs, ladder" (-ακ- -ak-).

κοδύμαλον: kodimalon (Athen., Hes.) "quince, quince tree, *Cydonia*" (-υμ-αλ- -im-al-).

Κόκυνθος: kokinthos (Polyb.), colonial toponym in Italy (-νθ- -nth-).

κολλ-: koll- κόλλιξ kolliks "barley bread" (-υκ- -ik-); κόλλαβος kollavos, κόλλοψ kollops "pin; handle" (-α[μ]β- -a[m]v-; -οπ- -op-); κόλλυβος kollivos (> Hebrew ḥālap "paper, bill") "penny" (-υ[μ]β- -i[m]v-); κολλύρα kollira = κόλλιξ kolliks (?) (-υρ- -ir-).

κολοκύνθη: kolokinthi "pumpkin, *Lagenaria vulgaris*" (-νθ- -nth-).

κόμαρος: komaros "strawberry tree, *Arbutus unedo*" (-αρ- -ar-; Hes. "κόμαρος· φυτόν τι, ὅπερ φέρει καρπὸν μιμαίκυλον" (cf., μαίκυλον maïkilon; LA, LB 70?).

κόνδαξ: kondaks (?) "peg" (-ακ- -ak-).

κοράλ(λ)ιον: koral(l)ion, see κορ-έ kor-e.

κόραξ: koraks "raven, *Corvus corax*" (-ακ- -ak-).

κορδύλος: kordilos "newt" (cf., κορδύλη kordili "bump, tumor" [-υρ- -ir-]).

κορ-έ: kor-e κόρι kori (Hes.) "*Coriandrum sativum*," derivative κορίαμβλον koriamvlon (-α[μ]β- -a[m]v-), κορίαννον koriannon, Mycanaean *ko-ri-ja-do-no*, *ko-ri-a-g-da-na* ("*Mittelmeerwort*" ["Mediterranean word"], Frisk); κορίανδρον koriandron, vulgar etymology; ἄκορον akoron "blueflag, *Iris pseudacorus*" (P); possibly, κοράλ(λ)ιον koral(l)ion "coral"; κορίαξος koriaksos (Alex. Med.), fish species (?).

κορ-ὲ kor-e "top, head": κορυδαλ(λ)ός koridal(l)os "crested skylark, *Alauda cristata*"; κόρυμβος korimvos "aft" (-υ[μ]β- -i[m]v); κόρυς koris "helmet"; κορυφή korifi "crown (of the head); top, peak" (-υφ- -if-) (cf., Κόρινθος korinthos?)

κορθίλος: korthilos (?) (Hes.), bird species (-υρ- -ir-).

Κόρινθος: Korinthos "Corinth"; Τρι-κόρυνθος Tri-Korinthos, Attic town (-νθ- -nth-).

κορν-: korn- (*qʷ-): κόρνοψ kornops, πάρνοψ parnops, πόρνοψ pornops "locust" (-οπ- -op-).

κόρσεον: korseon "lotus tuber" (-ε/ι+GI).

κορύνη: korini (?) "crook, cudgel" (-να -na).

κοσ-: kos- κοσύμβη kosimvi "woman's headband"; κόσυμβος kosimvos (Hes.) "cup"; κοσύβατας kosivatas. (Suppl. Epigr.) "donor" (-υ[μ]β- -i[m]v-).

κοσκ-: kosk- κόσκινον koskinon "sieve, bolter" (-να -na); Κόσκυνθος (Lycophr.), river in Euboea (-νθ- -nth-).

κόσσ-: koss- see κοττ- kott-.

κοττ-: kott- "small" (< Semitic or > Semitic (?) (cf., Hebrew *qātān* "small"): κόττος kottos "bullhead, goby, *Cottus gobio*"; κότταβος kottavos, κόσσαβος kossavos, popular game in Athens; κοτταβία kottavia (Hes.) "curly(-head)" (-α[μ]β-? -a[m]v-?); κοττάνη kottani (Aelian.), fish species; κόττανα kottana, kind of small figs; "girl" (Hes. "κόττανα· εἶδος σύκων μικρῶν. καὶ παρθένος παρὰ Κρησὶ κόττανον"; -να -na); κοττάρια kottaria (Hes.) "millet" (-αρ- -ar-); κόττυφος kottifos, κόσσυφος kossifos "blackbird, *Turdus merula*" (-υφ- -if-).

κοτύλη: kotili "cup"; liquid / dry measure (0.274 l) (-υρ- -ir-).

κύγχραμος, κύχραμος: kigxramos, kixramos "quail, *Coturnix*" (-αμ- -am-).

κύδνος, κύκνος: kidnos, kiknos "swan, *Cygnus*" (LA, LB 81 ✝ *ku*).

κυδ- (*καυδ-): kid (*kavd-) Κύδωνες Kidones, Cretan tribe; Κυδωνία Kidonia, famous Cretan city (HT 13, 85 *ku-do-ni*; HT 26 *ka-u-do-ni*; HT 13 *ka-u-de-ta*; -να -na, -νθ-? -nth-?); Καυλικοί Kavlikoi (Steph.), Ioniac tribe (cf., Ital. *Caudium, Caulonia*?)

κύδαρος (-ον): kidaros (-ον -on), kind of ship (-αρ- -ar-).

κυλίνθιον: kilinthion (Hes.) "wooden mask" (-νθ- -nth-).

κύμινον: kiminon "caraway, cumin" (HT 54, HT Wc 3014 *ku-mi-na-qe*; -να -na).

κυπάρισσος: kiparissos "cypress" ("*Mittelmeerwort unbekannten Ursprungs*" ["Mediterranean word of unknown origin"], Frisk).

κύταρον: kitaron (Hes.), scoop (-αρ- -ar-) (cf., κύδαρος kidaros).

κώρυκος: korikos "leather sack" (-υκ- -ik-).

Λ

λαβ-: lav- λάβιρος laviros (Hes.) "pit, hole" (-υρ- -ir-); λαβύρινθος lavirinthos "labyrinth" (-υρ-ινθ- -ir-inth-). Comparison with *λάβρυς *lavris (Plut. "Λυδοὶ γάρ λάβρυν τὸν πέλεκυν ὀνομάζουσι") seems to be mistaken.

λάβραξ: lavraks "grouper, *Labrax lupus* or *Sebastes marinus*" (-ακ- -ak-).

Λάμυρα, Λίμυρα: Lamira, Limira. Lycian river and town (-υρ- -ir-).

λαρ-: lar- Λάρισ(σ)α Laris(s)a, Aeolian and Thessalian towns; Λάρυμνα Larimna, Boeotian town (-υμ-να -im-na); Λαρύνθιος (Sch. Lyc.), epithet of Zeus (Etruscan *lar-* everywhere; HT 98 *da-ru-ne-te*; -νθ- -nth-).

λάρναξ: larnaks "box, coffin" (-ακ- -ak-).

Λάτυμνον: Latimnon (Sch. Theocr.), mountain near Croton (-υμ-να -im-na).

λαυκ-: lavk- "to rule": Λίκυμνα Likimna (Strabo), acropolis ("palace") of Tiryns (Etruscan perf. *luc-a-ir-c-e*, NA *-um-u* > Latin *lucumo*, *laχumni* (loc. *lauχumne-ti*) "palace," Λυκομίδαι Likomidai (Hes.) "γένος ἰθαγενῶν"; Latin *Lucina* "Our Lady" (epithet of Juno) (-να -na); Etruscan-Latin *Lucretius* (cf., Λυκάμβης Likamvis, PN; Λύκαμνος Likamnos (Arcad.), unclear toponym (-αμ-να -am-na) (cf., δαῦκος davkos (Hes.) ("θρασύς. καὶ βοτάνη τις Κρητική").

Λαύρ(ε)ιον: Lavr(e)ion, mountain in Attica (Etruscan-Latin *laurus*).

λέβνθος: levnthos, see ἐρέβινθος erevinthos.

Λεπέτυμνος: Lepetimnos (myth.), Methymna's husband (a town in Lesbos was named in her honor) (-υμ-να -im-na).

λεχέρνα: lexerna (Hes.), rite in honor of Hera in Argos (-ρ-να -r-na).

Λῆμνος, Λᾶμνος: Limnos, Lamnos "Lemnos" (Etruscan *lemni-*).

λίμινς, ἕλμινς, ἕλμινθος: limins, elmins, elminthos "helminth" (-νθ- -nth-; cf., Etruscan. *zal-* : *esl-*; *purt-* : *eprt-* (> πρύτανις pritanis); *Etrusci* : Umbrian *Turskum*).

Λίκυμνα: Likimna, see λαυκ- lavk-.

Λυκάμ-: Likam, see λαυκ- lavk-.

M

Μάθυμνα, Μήθυμνα: Mathimna, Mithimna, town in Lesbos (Etruscan *mat-* "to devote"; -υμ-να -im-na).

μαίκυλον, μιμαίκυλον: maikilon, mimaikilon, "fruit of the strawberry tree" (-υρ- -ir-; Red.). See κόμαρος komaros.

μαλ-: mal- μαλέα malea, μηλέα milea "apple-tree" (-ε/ι+GI); μᾶλον malon, μῆλον milon "apple"; μάλβαξ malvaks (Luc.), μαλάχη malaxi "Malva" (-ακ-? -ak-?).

μαρ-: mar- Doric μαρύομαι marvomai "to bind"; μέρμις mermis (-q-; Red.); μήρινθος mirinthos "thread, cord" (-νθ- -nth-).

μάριν: marin (acc. sg.) (Hes.) "swine" ("τὴν σῦν. Κρῆτες").

μάρτυρος: martiros "eyewitness" (-υρ- -ir-) (not connected with Egypt. *metre).

μάτταβος: mattavos (Hes.) "unwise, foolish" (-α[μ]β- -a[m]v-).

μέθλην: methlin (acc. sg.) (Hes.) "sheep, ram" (LA, LB 13 ℞ me).

μέμβραξ: memvraks (Aelian.), cicada species (-ακ- -ak-).

Μέροπες: Meropes, ancient inhabitants of Cos; Μέροψ Merops, Μερόπη Meropi, mythical personages (-οπ- -op-).

μέσπιλον: mespilon "medlar, *Mespilus germanica*" (-υρ- -ir-).

Μήθυμνα: Mithimna, see Μάθυμνα Mathimna.

Μηκύβερνα: Mikiverna (?), town in Chalcidice (-ρ-να -r-na).

μηλ-: mil-, see μαλ- mal-.

μήρινθος: mirinthos, see μαρ- mar-.

μιμαίκυλον: mimaikilon, see μαίκυλον maikilon.

μιν-: min- Μίνως Minos, probably, the title of some Cretan kings, taken as a name (> Etruscan *mine, mina-te*); Μινώα Minoa, Cretan town.

Μιρύκεον: Mirikeon (Hes.) "reed" (-υκ- -ik-; -ε/ι+GI).

μιστύλη, μυστίλη: mistili "piece of bread, used as a spoon" (-υρ- -ir-).

μολ-: mol- μόλυβδος molivdos (also -ιβδ-) "the element lead" (-υ[μ]β-); μολύβδαινα molivdaina "leadweight, ball" (-υ[μ]β- -i[m]v-; -να -na?); Μολύκρειον Molikreion, Aetolian town (-uk-).

μορμύρος, μορμύλος: mormiros, mormilos, fish species, *Pagellus mormo* (-ur-).

Μοστινή: Mostini, Lydian town (-να -na).

μοψ-: mops Μόψος Mopsos, mythical personages; Μοψοπία Mopsopia, ancient inhabitants of Attica (-op-).

μυ-: μύαξ miaks "mussel" (-ακ- -ak-); μυάκανθα miakantha (Geopon., Diosc.) "asparagus" (-ακ-α-νθ- -ak-a-nth).

μυρ-: mir- "fish" (Hes. "μύλλον· ... καὶ εἶδος ἰχθύος μύλλος"; "μύρος· ἰχθῦς ποιός. καὶ ἡ ἄρρεν μύραινα"; Μυrina (Lemn. *morina*[-*il*]), city in Lemnos (Etruscan *murin-; -na*, LA, LB 73 |ᛌ *mi*).

μυρσίνη: mirsini "myrtle" (-να -na); name Μυρσίλος Mirsilos is more likely Anatolian.

Μυτιλήνη, Μιτυλήνη: Mitilini, main city in Lesbos (-υρ-να -ir-na).

μῶλυ: moli (?), unknown officinal plant ("*Fremdwort unbekannter Herkunft*" ["Foreign word of unknown origin"], Frisk).

N

ναϝός: nawos (?), Lesbian ναῦος navos "temple" (PH 6 *no-na-wa* [?] (cf., *da-ma-te*: Ῥαδάμανθυς Radamanthis: *no-da-ma-te*).

ναπ-: nap "plant, tangle": νάπα napa, νάπη napi, νάπος napos "woody valley" (Etruscan *nap-ti* (loc.) "in (sacred) grove"; Latin *nepeta* "*Nepeta cataria*," Tusc. *nepa* "greenweed, *Genista*"; Latin (Fest.) *napurae* "cord").

νηδύς: nidis "stomach; entrails" (Etruscan *neθśra* "haruspicy, a kind of fortune-telling (using entrails)"; *netśvis* "foreteller").

νηρ-: nir- "water": Modern Greek νέρο nero, id.; Νηρεύς nirevs, Νηρεῖς nireis (Νηρηΐς nirnis), sea deities; νηρίτης niritis (νηρείτης nireitis), mollusk species; Milyan *nere* "nymph" (dat. pl.) (Etruscan *neri* "water"; NP *nerina*[*l*]). Here I also find it possible to adduce Νεῖλος Neilos "Nile" (cf., alternation r : l); this root is unknown in Egyptian and may happen to be Minoan.

νικύλεον: nikileon (Athen.), kind of fig; Νικυρίς nikiris (Suda), unknown toponym ("Ἑρμῶναξ δ᾽ ἐν Γλώτταις Κρητικαῖς σύκων γένη ἀναγράφει ἁμάδεα καὶ νικύλεα"; LA, LB 30 Ύ *ni*; -υρ- -ir -; -ε/ι+GI).

O

ὀΔόλυνθος: odolinthos, see ἐρέβινθος erevinthos. Οἰάνθη Oianthi, town of Locri (-νθ- -nth-).

οἴκυλος: (Theogn.) ("οἴκυλος, τό ὄσπριον" [see ὄσπριον osprion]; -υρ- -ir -).

ὄλυνθος: olinthos "winter fig"; Ὄλυνθος, Chalcidian town (-νθ- -nth-).

ομφ-: omf-, ὄμφαξ omfaks "green grapes" (-ακ- -ak-); ὀμφαλός omfalos "cone; navel" (-αρ- -ar-).

ὀνόπη: onopi (Hes.), kind of black grapes (-οπ- -op-).

ὀπυίω: opnio "to marry" (Etruscan *puia* "wife").

ὄρνις: ornis "bird" (-θ- -th-).

ὄσπρεον, ὄσπριον: "leguminous plant," mainly "bean" (-ε/ι+GI).

οστρ-: ostr- 1. "crock; shell": ὄστρακον ostrakon id. (-ak-); ὄστρειον ostreion "mollusk, covered with shell" (-ε/ι+GI?); 2. "wall, fence: ὄστριμον ostrimon "shed, cattle shed" (-υμ- -im-) (cf., also ὀστρύα ostria [Theophr.] "hop hornbeam, *Ostrya caprinifolia Scop*."

Π

παν-: pan- πανέλοψ panelops, πηνέλοψ pinelops "teal, *Anas Penelope*"; Πενελόπα, Πηνελόπα Penelopa, Pinelopa "Penelope" (-οπ- -op-).

πάπραξ: papraks (Her.), fish species (-ακ- -ak-).

πάπυρος: papiros "paper" (-υρ- -ir-).

παρθ(εν)-: parth(en)- παρθένος parthenos "virgin"; Παρθενόπη Parthenopi, Tyrrhenian island; Παρθενόπεια Parthenopeia, ancient name of Naples; Παρθενοπαῖος, Parthenopaios, mythological hero (-οπ- -op-).

Πάρνηθος: Parnithos, mountain wood in Attica (-θ- -th-).

πάήόρνοψ: Paiornops, see κόρνοψ kornops.

πείρινς, πείρινθος: peirins, peirinthos "chariot" (-νθ- -nth-; HT 116 *pi-ri₂[n]-te GRAnum ₃*).

Πέλοψ: "Pelops" (-οπ- -op-).

πεν-: pen- see παν- pan-.

Πεπάρηθος: Peparithos, Cycladian island (-θ- -th-).

πέρδιξ, πῆριξ: perdiks, piriks (Hes.) "partridge" ("Κρῆτες"; - υκ- -ik-).

Πέρινθος: Perinthos, Thracian town (-νθ- -nth-).

περσ-: pers- περσέα, persea, kind of Egyptian plant (-ε/ι+GI); Περσεύς, Persefs, Perseis.

Περσεφόνη (Περσέφασσα, Φερσέφασσα): Persefoni, Persefassa, Fersefassa, mythological personages (-να, -σσ- -na, -ss-).

πην-: pin- see παν- pan.

πιθ-: pith- πίθος pithos "barrel"; πιθάκνη, φιδάκνη pithakni, fidakni "keg" (-ακ-να -ak-na).

πίναξ: pinaks "table, plate, picture" (-ακ- -ak-).

Πίνη: pini (?) "pearl" ("*Mittelmeerwort unbek. Ursprung*" ["Mediterranean word of unknown origin"] Frisk).

Πιτάνη: Pitani, Mysian town and district in Sparta (-να -na).

πίτυρον: pitiron "bran" (-υρ- -ir-).

Πόλυμνον: Polimnon (Paus.), unknown toponym (-υμ-να -im-na-).

πόρταξ: portaks "heifer" (-ακ- -ak-).

Πρεπέσινθος: Prepesinthos (Strabo), Cycladian island (-νθ- -nth-).

Προβάλινθος: Provalinthos, see *Βάλινθος valinthos.

Πρόσυμνα: Prosimna, ancient town in Argolis (-υμ-να -im-na).

πρύτανις: pritanis "lord, ruler" (Etruscan *purt-/eprt-* id.; Latin *Frutis*, epithet of Venus, *Frutinal* "*templum Veneris Frutis*"; Etruscan *purtśvana* > Latin *Porsenna*); seems to be a borrowing from Asia Minor (cf., Lycian *epriti* "deputy," Hattic *puri* "lord."

πτελέα: ptelea, Mycenaean *pte-re-wa* "elm, *Ulmus campestris*" (-ε/ι+GI) (cf., μήλεα milea, ἰτέα itea).

πύνδαξ: pindaks "lid *or* bottom of a vessel" (-ακ- -ak-).

Πύρανθος: Piranthos (Steph.), Cretan town (-νθ- -nth-).

πώλυπος: polipos "Cephalopoda" (> vulgar etymology πολύπους polipous) ("*Mittelmeerwort unbekannter Herkunft*" ["Foreign word of unknown origin"], Frisk).

P

Ῥαδάμανθυς: Radamanthis, see δαμ-.

ῥάξ, ῥώξ: raks, roks "berries, grapes" ("*Sonst isoliert; wohl Mittelmeerwort*" ["Otherwise an isolate; probably a Mediterranean word"], Frisk).

*Ῥήσκυνθος: *Riskinthos (Ρησκύνθιον ὄρος, Riskinthion oros, Nic.), mountain in Thrace (-νθ- -nth-).

Ῥίθυμνα: Rithimna (Steph.) Cretan town (Etruscan PN *ritumena*; -υμ-να -im-na).

ῥόβιλλος: rovillos (Hes.) "kinglet, *Regulus*" (-υρ- -ir-).

ῥυκάνη: rikani "hand plane" (-να -na).

ῥυστόν: riston (Hes.) "spear" ("δόρυ· Κρῆτες").

Σ

σαγήνη: sagini "seine, net" (-να -na).

σάκκος: sakkos (?) "bag, sack" (< Hebrew *śaq* id.).

σαλ-: sal- Σαλαμίς "Salamis" (-αμ- -am-) (cf., σαλαμάνδρα salamandra [similar to κορί- ανδρον? kori- andron?]).

Σαλύνθιος: Salinthios (Thuc.), Acarnanian princelet.

σάλπη: salpi (?) fish species, "*Box salpa*" ("*Unerklärtes Mittelmeerwort*" ["Unexplained Mediterranean word"], Frisk).

σαμ-: sam-, locality in Argolis (-νθ- -nth-); Σάμος Samos, Aegean island (cf., σάμαξ samaks "reed" (-ακ- -ak-).

σαμβύκη: samviki, kind of harp (-υκ- -ik-) (cf., Hebrew *šebākā* "net").

σάνδυξ: sandiks "*Bezüglich eines hellroten Farbstoffes, einer hellroten Mineralfarbe*" (-υκ- -ik-).

σαπ-: sap- σηπία sipia "cuttlefish"; σαπέρδης saperdis (Hes.) "ὄνομα ἰχθύος. οἱ δὲ ταρίχου εἶδος. ἄλλοι ὑπὸ Ποντικῶν τὸν κορακίνον ἰχθύν" (-ρδ- -rd-) (cf., Coptic *šaburí*?).

σαργ-: sarg- σαργός sargos (?) φιση σπεχιες, "*Sparus sargus* or *Sargus Rondeletti*" ("*Mittelmeerwort unbek. Herkunft*" ["Mediterranean word of unknown origin"], Frisk); unclear σαργάνη sargani "cord" (-να -na).

σάσαμον, σήσαμον: sasamon, sisamon "sesame" (HT 32 *sa-sa-me*; -αμ- -am-; LA, LB 31 Υ *sa*).

Σάτυρος: Satiros "Satyr" (-υρ- -ir-); Etruscan (-ur-); Etruscan *satna* (-να -na); Etruscan-Latin *Saturnus* (-υρ-να -ir-na); Etruscan-Latin *Saturejum* (-υρ- -ir-).

σηπία: sipia, see σαπ- sap-.

Σειληνός: Seilinos, see σιλ- sil-.

σελ- (?): sel-, σελας selas "light; shining; lightning"; Σελήνη, σελάννα selini, selanna "moon" (-να -na).

Σέρῑφος: Serifos, Cycladian island (-υφ- -if-). Σερμύλη Sermili, town in Chalcidice (-υρ- -ir-).

σέσυφος: sesifos (Hes.) "cheat, swindler" (-υφ- -if-).

σίβυλλα, Σίβυλλα: sivilla, Sivilla "prophetess, *Sibyl*" (-υρ- -ir-).

σιβύνη: sivini "hunting spear; bear spear" (-να -na).

Σίβυρτος: (?) Sivirtos (Steph.), Cretan town (-υρ-? -ir-?).

σικ-: sik-, see συκ- sik-.

Σιληνός, Σειληνός: Silinos, Seilinos, rural deities (-να -na).

σίλλυβον: sillivon "fringe; chain; pin" (-υ[μ]β- -i[m]v-).

σιπύη: sipii "chest for bread" (HT 8 *su-pu₂-188*).

σισ-: sis- σισύμβριον sisimvrion (Theophr.) "*Iris sisyrinchion*" (-υ[μ]β- -i[m]v-); σίσυρα sisira "sheep's *or* goat's fell" (-υρ- -ir-); σίσυρνα sisirna id. (-υρ-να –ir-na); Σίσυφος Sisifos "Sisyphus" (-υφ- -if-).

σῖτος: sitos "cereals; bread; food" (LA 041 m *si*; "*ohne überzeugende Etymologie*" ["Without a convincing etymology"], Frisk).

σκάλοψ: skalops, see σκολ- skol-.

σκαπάνη: skapani "hoe, mattock" (-να -na).

σκολ-: skol- σκόλοψ, skolops "staje; hook" (-οπ- -op-); σκολόπαξ skolopaks "woodcock" (-op-ak-); unclear σκάλοψ skalops "mole" (-οπ- -op -).

σκύλαξ: skilaks "puppy" (-ακ- -ak-).

σμαρίς: smaris, small sea fish ("*Herkunft unbekannt; gewiß Mittelmeerwort*" ["Origin unknown; certainly Mediterranean"], Frisk).

σμήρινθος: smirinthos, see μερ- mer-.

σταφ-: staf- "grapes": σταφυλή stafili "bunch of grapes" (-υρ- -ir-), σταφίς stafis "raisins."

συβήνη, συβίνη: sivini, sivini, "leather case" (-να -na).

συκ- (*συλκ-?): sik- (*silk-?) σικύα sikia "pumpkin *or* melon"; σίκυος sikios "cucumber"; συκέα sikea "fig"; συκάμινος sikaminos "mulberry tree, *Morus nigra*" (-αμ-να -am-na) (> Semitic *šiqmīn*); Σικύνη Sikini Συκίνη Sikini, different toponyms (-na); Σικύνθος Sikinthos (Plut.), unclear toponym (-νθ- -nth-); HT 8, *si-ki-ra*; HT Zb 185, *su-ki-ri-te- no-ja* (-υρ- -ir-). Unclear Etruscan PN *silqetena* (-νθ-ε-να? -nth-e-na?), Latin *siliqua* "bean" (cf., Hebrew σικέρα sikera "grain *or* fruit wine" (?).

Σύρινθος: Sirinthos (Steph.), Cretan town (-νθ- -nth-).

T

ταν-: tan-, Τάνος Tanos, Cretan town; Ἀθηνᾶ Athina "Ατηενε"; Ἴτανος Itanos (Mycenaean *u-ta-no*), Cretan town (P).

τερέβινθος, τέρμινθος: Terevinthos, Terminthos "*Pistacia terebinthus*" (-νθ- -nth-).

τήβεννα: tivenna "cloak" (-να -na).

τιβήν: tivin (?) "tripod" (LA, LB 37 𓉔 *ti*; "*Unerklärtes Fremdwort*" ["Unexplained foreign word"], Frisk).

Τίρυνς, Τίρυνθον: Tirins, Tirinthon, city in Argolis (-νθ- -nth-).

τιτ-: tit τίταξ titaks (Hes.) "lord"; Τιτακός, Titakos PN (Etruscan *tit-*; -ακ- -ak-); unclear τίτανος titanos "gypsum" ("*Technisches Wort unbekannten Ursprungs*" ["Technical word of unknown origin"], Frisk; -να -na). τίτυρος: titiros "sheep *or* goat" (Theocr.); bird species (Hes.) (-υρ- -ir-).

τολύπη: tolipi "hank of wool" (-υπ- -ip-).

τόρδυλον, τόρδιλον: tordilon (Diosc.) "*Seseli* or *Tordylium officinale*" (-υρ- -ir-).

τορύνη: torini "stirring rod" (-να -na).

Τρικόρυνθος: Trikorinthos, see Κόρινθος Korinthos.

Τρίοψ, Τριόπας: Triops, Triopas, mythological personage (-οπ- -op-).

τροχίλος, τροχῖλος, τροχεῖλος: Troxilos, Troxeilos (?) "plover; wren, *Pluvianus* or *Carsorius Aegyptius*; *Troglodytes parvulus*" (-υρ- -ir-). τύβαριν: tivarin (acc. sg.) (Pollux.), kind of spice (-αρ- -ar-).

τυΐ: tii (Hes.) "here" ("ὧδε. Κρῆτες"; Etruscan *θui* id.).

τύραννος: tirannos "lord" ("*Unerklärtes Fremdwort aus der kleinasiat-ägäischen Kultursphäre*" ["Unexplained foreign word from the Asia Minor/Aegean cultural sphere"], Frisk; Etruscan *turan* "Venus").

Τυρσηνοί, Τυρρηνοί: Tirsinoi, Tirrinoi, probably the original name (Egyptian *trš*; E-*trus*-*ci*, Umbrian *turskum*, etc.).

ὑακ-: iak *ax (Hes.) "rudder oar" (LA, LB 10 ʄ *u*); Ὑάκινθος, Ὑάκυνθος gakinthos "hyacinth" ("helmsman") (-νθ- -nth-).

ὕραξ: iraks (Nic.) "swine" (-ακ- -ak-).

ὑτ- "4": it- Ὑττηνία Ittinia (Steph.) (= Τετράπολις Tetrapolis; Etruscan *huθ* "4").

Ὑτέννα: Itenna (Steph.), Lycian town.

Φ

Φαιστός: Faistos, ancient Cretan city (Mycenaean *Pa-i-to*).

φαλ-: fal- "top; head": φάλα fala (Hes.) "head"; Φάλανθος Falanthos, Arcadian mountain and town (-νθ- -nth-); φαλακρός, φάλανθος falakros, falanthos "bald" ~ φαληρίς, φάλαρις faliris, falaris, "common coot, *Fulica atra*" (Etruscan (Fest.) *falado* (*falando*) "sky"; *palatum* "palate"; *Palatium*; -αρ- -ar-); probably, also Φαλάσαραν Falasaran, Cretan town.

φάρμακον: farmakon "potion; medicine"; φάρμακος "wizard"; "victim" (-ακ- -ak-).

φιδάκνη: fidakni, see piq-.

φιλ-: fil- φιλύκη filiki, kind of shrubs, *Rhamnus alaternus* (?) (-υκ- -ik-); φιλύρα filira "limetree" (-υρ- -ir-).

φυλ-: fil- φύλαξ filaks "guard" (-ακ-); φύλοπις filopis "battle" (-οπ- -op-).

Χ

Χάρυβδις: Xarivdis (?) "Charybdis" (-υ[μ]β-? -i[m]v-?).

χεδρ-: xedr-, see κεδρ- kedr-.

χηραμός: xiramos (?) "hole; cave" (-αμ- -am-).

χίμαρος: ximaros (?) "goat" (-αρ- -ar-).

GLOSSARY

This glossary contains both reconstructed Tyrrhenian roots and stems and some full forms (mainly ἅπαξ λεγόμενα), given in Latin alphabetical order. Also, a number of inevitable repeats occur in the "Index . . .," if the root (stem) is reconstructed in Etruscan or Italic and has clear parallels in Aegean (however, in the "Index . . ." itself Etruscan and Italic correspondences are given, if they can clarify the origin of the pre-Greek forms).

I have not included in the glossary any separable grammatical elements (i.e., suffixes, sometimes described as postpositions), as well as theonyms, proper and place names, if their roots (stems) do not have reliable interpretations (in the Index similar ones are given in abundance for Minoan and Aegean even without an etymology). Glosses are supplied with indications of the sources, but without numbering, because all the enumeration is provided in Chapter 4, and vague glosses are not repeated. Pre-Greek lexemes, understood by us as borrowings from Minoan or the local Tyrrhenian dialect, are marked as Aegean equally with the forms in the Lemnian inscription; for all that, they also should be collated with the Index.

The main grammatical forms are given in brackets directly after the stem for all words, known from Tyrrhenian inscriptions, with the exception of the demonstrative pronouns.

The roots/stems being reconstructed, given in boldface, and grammatical elements (in brackets) do not differentiate special signs for *k* and *s* (i.e., *c, q, ś, š, ṣ* are not used), *vh, hv* (for *f*), aspirated *χ, φ, θ* – in the examples, where it is possible to reconstruct a strong consonant, we use *k:, p:, t:,* and where the phoneme is unclear – *K, P, T*. The differentiation of signs like *k:, k, K* does not influence the alphabetical order; the roots containing the vowel, unclear from the etymological point of view (*CV-*), are put after the roots like *Ca-, Ce-, Ci-, Cu-*. The signs *c, q, ś, š, ṣ, χ, φ, θ*, digraphs *vh, hv* are reproduced when the concrete forms from the inscriptions are cited.

A

a/eis(-) (dat.-instr. IIb -(*ı*)-*al-e*, pl. -*a/er*; gen. pl. -*er-as*, fem. -*er-a* (??); demin. *aisiu* "god"; glosses.: Suet. *aesar* id. (erroneously sg.), Hes. αἰσοί "gods"; Oscan *aisusis* (dat. pl.) "religious rite." Derivatives *a/eis(u)na* (gen. -*l*) "sacrifice" > Umbrian *esono* id., Volscan *esaristrom* "religious rite"; *aisumna > pre-Greek Αἴσυμνος ("ὄνομα κύριον," Suda), also as a place name; here αἰσυμνάω "to rule"; Αἰσύμη, town in Thrace, *Aesar*, river in Bruttium, *Aesarnia*, Samnian town on the river Volturnus.

aK- a possible root for **aKas-* and **aKil-*.

aKal-1 (gen. fem. *-ia*) menonime; *acale*, glossed *Aclus* "June."

aKal-2 "youth command" (< Greek ἀγέλη); cf., the derivative gloss (Hes.) ἀγαλ/τορα acc. "child."

aKas- (Perf. *-k:-e*, Ger. *-ri*) "to make; to put together, to donate (?)"; *ziχ neθśrac acasce* "completed haruspicinal book"; subst. *acaz-r* (pl.) "funeral offerings."

aKil(-) (NA *-u*) "to do *or* work" (?); derivative *-une*.

akVr(-) (1) "eagle": Eteo-Cypriote ἀγὸρ (Hes.), Latin *aquila* id.; Aegean NP *aker*; here also Umbrian *Akeřuniam* (acc.), Oscan *Akudunniad* (abl.) etc.; (2) "northerly wind": Latin *Aquilo* id.

aKn- (part. pres. I trans. *-[an]-asa*, aor. *-[e]-s-e*) "to make, to create," "to give birth" or "to leave" (?); derivative *-i-na*.

al- (pres. *-e*, perf. *-k:-e*, perf. M.-P. *-k:-u*) "to give, to donate"; derivative *alpan, alpnu* "gift"; also a connection with Latin *aleae* "dice" is not excluded.

alaP- "gesture": Latin *alapa* (including the meaning "a gesture when somebody sets free his servent," later "slap in the face"); Etruscan-Latin NP *Alaponius*.

am- (pres. *-e*, perf. *-k:-e*, unclear *-a*) "to be"; Aegean perf. *aom-ai* "was."

amPVl- (1) "sun, spring": gloss (TLE 805) *Ampiles* "May"; (2) Aegean ἄμπελος "grapes."

an (1) pron. demonstr. "this" (only independently); here also Eteo-Cypriote *a-na*; (2) pron. rel. "who, which," also known with reduplication *an-an(-c)*.

anT- gloss (Hes.) (1) "eagle": ἄνταρ id.; (2) "(north) wind": ἄνδας id.; here also ἄντας "whiff"; derivatives: Latin *antemna* "yard"; toponyms: town *Antemna* (*Antemnates*, its inhabitants), river *Andena, Andes*, village near Mantua (Virgil's birthplace), etc.

ap:- (Gen. *-s*, Rhaetic *-(n)-in*) "father"; *aper (Gen. Pl. *af-r-s*) "ancestors"; apparently, here also Aegean *epi-te-śi-o*.

aPK-ar, Latin *abacus* id. (< Greek ἄβαξ; cf., in the "Index . . .").

aPlusT- "stern detail"; here also Aegean ἄφλαστον "upper part of the stern"; borrowed in Latin *aplustra* (gen. *-orum*) and *aplustria* (gen. *-ium*).

ar- (perf. *-k:-e*) "to be; to become" (?); Aegean perf. *ar-ai* "was."

araK- gloss (Hes.) "hawk"; apparently, here also Ἀράκυνθος, mountain in Boeotia (Steph.).

arim- gloss (Hes., Serv., Strab.) "ape."

asK- kind of a vessel (< Greek ἀσκός).

at:r- part of the room, possibly, also "house": Latin *atrium* (an origin from Punic *hats.ar* id. is not excluded).

aT- (gen. *-[i]-al*, allat. *-eri* [?]) "mother"; *ati nacn(v)a*, probably, "grandmother."

aTran- "man-at-arms" (< Milyan id.)

avil (gen. *-s*, coll. pl. (Gen.) *-k:va-l*, sg. with numerals) "year"; Aegean *aviś* id. (sg., also with numerals).

E

e/il- (perf. *-k:-e*, Perf. M.-P. *-k:-u*, Ger. *-ri*, unclear *ilacve*) verb, designating a religious rite (prayer?).

eleiva "olive" < pre-Greek ἐλαίϜα; *eliun(i)-* "olive oil" < Greek ἔλαιον; adj. *eleiva-na*.

e/iT- "Idus, middle of the month" (goes back to Near East: cf., Sumerian *itu* "full moon." Both Etruscan and earlier Roman month began from a new moon and years from the last full moon before a vernal equinox). Derivatives: *etia-sa-s* (gen.) like *favissa*, borrowed in Latin *Idus* (dialectal *ir-*), Oscan *eidulis* "Idibus"; adj. *eta-na-* (*cleva etanal* "New Year's nail").

eiTv- < Oscan *eítiuva* "money" (?).

eTer- < Umbrian *etr-* "alter" (gen. *-[Ⅵ.s*) "foreigner," social group (~ Roman *peregini*), *zilaθ eterau* "*tribunus peregrinorum*.

et: conjunction (probably, final. Latin *ut*?), or with several meanings (Latin *cum*?); also known *et:nam* (as an enclitic *-tnam*).

F

fan- (aor. *-[u]-s-e*, NA *-u*, Ger. *-[l]-ri*) "to devote" (< Latin *fanum*?).

fas- (gen. -[*l*]*s*) kind of sacrificial gifts ("milk," "honey," etc.?); derivative -(*e*)*na*, a vessel for it.

fav- (gen. -*in*, loc. -*ti*) "subterranean part of a temple" > Latin *favis*(*s*)*a*.

fer- (pres. -*in-e*) "to make, to manufacture."

fir- (gen. -*in*) "fire" (< IE; cf., Greek πῦρ, Deutsch *Feuer*, etc.); not very clear *fir-a*, apparently borrowed into Latin (Fest.) *ex-fir* "*purgamentum, unde adhuc manet suffitio.*"

fler- (gen. -*es*, allat. -*eri*, coll. pl. -*k:va*) kind of sacrificial gifts.

fronT-ac (adj.) "fulgurator" (probably, from Greek βροντή "lightning"; also not excluded is some ethnonyms [< *Ferentum*?]).

ful- (NA -*u*) "to felt wool" (?); NA *fulu* > Latin *fullo* "fuller, launderer"; not very clear *fuluna* > Etruscan-Latin *Fullonius*, Umbrian *Fulunie* (cf., also *p:al-*).

H

halχ (-) "ten": adv. *halχ-ze* "ten times"; -*alχ* in tens (*ki-alχ-* "thirty," etc., Aegean *śi-alχv-* "sixty"); here also NP *hulχena*, * *Decimius*.

hamp:- (gen. -*es*) adj. "right."

heK- (perf. -*k:-e*, imper. -*s-t:*, ger. -*z-ri*, unclear -*i*, -*ia*, -*z*) "to put" or "to make stand."

herm- (1) gloss (TLE 836) "(month) August"; (2) kind of ritual statues (< Greek ἑρμῆς?).

hint:- (gen. -*in*) "place; underworld"; not fully clear what the difference is among the variants with -*a*, -*u*, -*ia*; derivative *hinθial* "soul; ghost."

hiuls "owl" (onomatopoetic).

huc- "fire" (??) (> Latin [non-IE] *fŏcus*).

huPn- (gen. -*is*) "grave"; derivative *hupnina* (loc. -*t:i*).

hus(-) (pl. -*ur*) "child; boy"; -*na*, -(*l*)*na* adj. "young" (?) (cf., *vinum husina*; derivative *huzrna-tre-* > Milyan *xuzrñta-*) (dat. pl.) (?).

hut:(-) (gen. -*s*, allat. -*eri*) "four"; *huθ-zar-* "sixteen" (4 + 12); the form "forty" is unknown; in Aegean, the derivative {Υττηνία "Τετράπολις" (Steph.) < * *hut:ena* "four"; here also Lycian Ὕτεννα (Steph.).

I

ik: "as; and"; Eteo-Cypriote *e-ki* (?); *ἴχ-nac* "so, as."

iKV- see *KV*.

iTV- see *TV*.

K

-K postpositive copulative conjunction (< IE [?]; cf., Vedic, Avestan *ca*). Borrowed rather in Asia Minor (Hittite *-ki*, Lydian *-k*) than in Italy (Latin *-que*, Faliscan *-cue*); in Etruscan could be reduplicated (*apa-c ati-c* "both father and mother").

KV, iKV (probably, *k:*) pron. dem.; could be used independently or as an enclitic (in the latter case more often as *-k-l-*, *-k-n-*); also reduplicated *cn- ti-cn-θ* (loc.). Compound forms: *ce-hen, ca-ti-ca*, etc.

Kail- "heaven": Latin *caelum* id.; here also NP *cailinal, caili vipinas* = Latin *Caele Vibenna*; Latin *Caelius*; Faliscan NP *cailio, celio*. Probably here also Eteo-Cypriote *ka-i-li-po-ti*.

kal- "lump; hillock" (?): Latin *galea* "(leather) helmet; crest"; Aegean Κάλυμνα (one of Sporades); possibly here also Etruscan *calu*, etc.

Kant:- (pres. *-e*, perf. *-k:-e*) "fulfill some duties"; possibly also a derivative title (?) *kamθi*.

kaP- "kind of a vehicle, carriage": gloss (Hes.) γάπος, Thessalian καπάνη (Eust.) id.

Kap- "to weave": Etruscan-Latin *cabanna* (*capanna*) "hut"; καπάνη "knitted hat" (Hes.); here also *Capena*, Etruscan town on Tiber, and also *porta Capena* in Rome (cf., also pre-Greek κάπη "crib").

Kapr- gloss (Hes.) "she-goat" (< Latin *capra*); possibly here also gloss (TLE 818) *Cabreas* "April" (if the word is connected with the type of cattle-breeding work [cf., *Ampiles*]).

Kar- "nut(wood)" (< pre-Greek κάρυον); derivative Latin (from Etruscan) *carina* "nut shell," later "ship; keel"; NP *Carrinas* (gen. *-atis*).

Kaup- verb, not fully clear; here also Latin *caupo* (?), dialectal *cōpo* "innkeeper" (< NA **Kaup-u*); derivative NP *caupna-l* (gen.), *caup-is* (gen.), Etruscan-Latin NP *Coponius*.

Kaut:- (gen. *-in*, *-[a]-s*) "sun"; gloss (Diosc.) kaut= "marjoram" > Tuscan *cota* "*occhio di sole*"; possibly here also derivative *cauzna* < **kaut:na*.

Kek:- (unclear *-am*) "rite" or "law, order"; *ca ceχa ziχuχe*, possibly "wrote this law"; derivative *-se* (*ceχasieθur* [pl.], members of some collegium); *-ne* (allat. *-ri*).

Kel- menonym root: Etruscan *celi*, gloss Latin *Celius* "September"; possibly here also *Celemna* (Campanian town).

ken- plant name: Latin *genista, genesta* "greenweed, *Spartium junceum* or *Genista tinctoria*"; gloss (Diosc.) γεντιάνη "gentian."

KeP- root for some cultural terms; *kep-en, kip-en* "priest": Sabinian *cupencus* id. (Serv.); not fully clear derivatives *cep-ar, cep-ta*.

Ker- (opt. *-en*, caus. *-iχ-*; perf. trans. *-un-k:-e*, NA *-u*) "to set up"; with the suffix *-in-* "to get up, to rise" (*usil cerine* "*Sol oritur*").

Kes- (pres. M.-P. *-u*) "to lie; to rest"; *ces-eθ-* (perf. *-k:-e*) "to put."

ki(-) (gen. *-s*) "three"; *ki-aχ-* "thirty," *ciś śariś* "fifteen" (gen.; 3 + 12), adv. *ki-z(i)* "three times." By all appearances borrowed in Asia Minor (cf., Hurrian *ki̯g*] id.; cf., also Basque **hiru-* [dialectal *hiru, iru-r*]).

Kilen(-) (gen. *-s, -sl*) "night" (??) and nocturnal deity.

kik- plant name; gloss (Diosc.) κικένδα "gentian," here also Aegean (Hes.) κεικύνη "mulberry"; here also γιγάρουμ (Diosc.) "βῆτα λεπορίνα."

klan(-) (gen. *-in, -(a)s*, dat.-instr. IIa *-s-i*; pl. *-ar*, gen. *-ar-as*, dat.-instr. IIa *-ar-as-i*) "son"; NP *clante, clanti* (Etruscan and Rhaetic); Rhaetic gen. pl. *klan-t-ur-us*.

Klaruk:- (gen. *-es*) "settlement, community" (< Doric κλαρουχία instead of Ionic κληρουχία).

KleTr- (gen. *-al*) "(ritual) stretcher *or* sedan chair" (< Umbrian *kletranr*; here also Latin *clitellae* "pack saddle"; Gothic *hleiþra*, Welsh *cledren* "Sparren, Latte, Zaun," Russian *клеть*); derivative *cletr-am* id.

Klev- "nail" (< Latin *clavus*).

krum- "setsquare" (< Greek γνώμων): Latin *groma* (*gromaticus* "land surveyor").

k:ulik:na "cup" (< Greek κυλίχνη).

KuPe "cup" (< Greek κύπη or Latin *cupa*).

KuT- (*-un, -um*) kind of vessel (< Greek κώθων).

k:Vzp:(-) (gen. -s) "eight," cezp-aχ "eighty," adv. cezp-z "eight times"; gloss *Xosfer* (**Ch-*; here also dialectal, rhotacistic χurvar) = *October*; here also the "eighth" Roman hill *Cespius, Cispius* (Varro).

L

laiv- (gen. -s) adj. "left" (< Latin *laevus*).

lan- "meat, flesh": Latin *lanio* "butcher," *laniena* "butcher's" (Etruscan word formation); here also the gloss (Isid.) *lanista* "keeper of gladiators' school" (= "carnifex"); possibly here also Etruscan *lanti*.

lauk:- (dialectal *au > a, u*, perf. *luc-a-ir-c-e*, NA *-um-u*) "to rule"; NA *lucumnu* > Latin *lucumo* (title; here also the form Λοκόμων [Dion. Hal.], erroneously understood as NP); derivative *laχumni* (loc. *lauχumne-ti*) "royal (palace)," the same in Aegean Λίκυμνα (acropolis of Tiryns); Λυκομίδαι ("γένος ἰθαγενῶν," Hes.); NP *laucanias, laucis, lauχusieś, lavcisla, luχrias*; NP *lucer* > Latin *Luceres* (Roman tribe); here also Latin *Lucina* "Lady" (Juno's epithet); here also Λοκροί (town in Bruttium) and Latin *Lucretius*.

lauTn- (dialectal *au > a, u*) "family" (< IE **leudh-*); θ*aure lautn-eś-cle* "family tomb"; *lautni* (fem. -θ*a*) "house serve" (cf., Latin *famul, famulus*, Oscan, Pelignian *famel* id.) or "freedman"; *lautneteri* "Klient der Familie."

lein- (pres. -e) "to die" (??).

lek:T- kind of vessel (< Greek λήκυθος); demin. *leχt-um-u-za*.

lup- (pres. M.-P. -*u*, perf. -*k:-e*) "to die"; extended *lup(V)n-* in *lupven-as* (part. pres. I) and Rhaetic *lup(i)n-u* (pres. M.-P.). Here also Latin *Libitina* (archaic *Lubitina*), goddess of death and burial.

lut:- (loc. -*ti*, coll. pl. -*k:va*) "stone" (?) or "stone construction" (?).

M

mal- (NA -*u*?) "to look" (?): derivative *malena, malstria* "mirror."

makstr-ev title (< Latin *magister*); Etruscan *macstrna*, secondarily borrowed in Etruscan-Latin *Mastarna*.

man- (unclear -*i, -inr*, allat. -*im-eri*) "the deceased" (= Latin *Manes*); derivative *man-in-c-e* (perf.) verb, designating a sacrifice to the deceased.

manT- (< *man-t-*??) epithet for an underworld deity: *Mantus* (Serv.), here also toponym *Mantua*, *mantrn-śl*; Latin *Manturna* (Aug.). Unclear gloss (Fest.) *mantis(s)a* "makeweight."

mar-1 (Part. Praes. I *marv-as*, NA *-u*) verb for some official duties (from IE? [cf., Lycian *mar-* "to order"]); subst. NA (pl. coll. *-k:va*) *maru* > Latin *Maro*, Umbrian *maron-*; derivative *mar(u)n-* (pl. coll. *-k:va*); Aegean part. pres. I *mar-aś*.

mar-2 "plant; tree": borrowed into Latin *Marica*, woodland nymph (wife of Faunus, mother of Latinus; a grove near the Etruscan town of Minturnae was devoted to her), *marisca*, kind of fig, *marrubium* "hoarhound, *Marrubium vulgare*," *marrucina*, kind of fig or sloe (*Rhamnus paliurus*), *marruria* "lettuce."

mas(a)n "statue of deity" (?) < Anatolia **massan-* "deity" (Luwian *massanalli-* "divine," etc.).

mat:- (pres. M.-P. *-u*) "to devote" or something similar; subst. *maθ-cva* (pl. coll.), kind of gifts; probably here also Aegean Μήθυμνα ("sanctuary?").

maTam/n adv. "before" or "above."

mazb(a) "altar" < Punic *mzbḥ* id. (from *zbḥ* "to make sacrifice").

men- (pres. *-e*, pres. M.-P. *-u*, perf. *-k:-e*, part. pres. I *-as*) verb for sacrifice; subst. *menitla*, unclear derivatives *mena*, *menaθa*, *menaχzi*, *menica*.

met:(u)l- (dialectal *meχl*, gen. *-(e)s*, loc. *-t:*, allat. *-eri*) "town"; Eteo-Cypriote *ma-to-ri* id.; derivative *meθl-um*, rather, "state" or "region." Here also NP *metli*, *meteliś*, Latin *Metellus*.

mi (acc. *mi-ni*, dat.-allat. [?] *mi-[ni]-pi*) pron. pers. 1 sg. "I"; variant *ni*, *ni-pe*.

mul-1 (pres. M.-P. *-u*, perf. trans. *-n-i-k:-e*, inf. *-nr*, not fully clear with *-na*, *-ne*) "to bring, to devote, to sacrifice"; probably here also Latin *molucrum* (Fest.) "block for sacrifice."

mul-2 "good" (?) (if *mlak:* < **mul-ak:*, with adjective suffix); the combination *mlaχ mlakas* seems to correspond to "duenom duenos" or "καλός καλῷ"); unclear *mlak:(u)ta*.

mun- "place, subterranean room" (= Latin *locus*); derivative with *-T-* > Latin *mundus*; not fully clear are the forms with *-klet:*, *-sulet:*.

murs- (pl. *-l*, *-a*) "urn"; might be compared with Aegean μυρσίνη, μυρρίνη "myrtle" (plant, used in the funeral rites?).

muT- "to project, to go beyond" (?): Latin *Mutunus* "*priapische Gottheit*"; here also toponyms *Mutina* : modern *Modena*, Aegean Μυτιλήνη with the earlier variant Μύτων; Etruscan-Latin NP *Mutellius* (cf., also μύτιλον ["ἔσχατον," Hes.]).

mVT- (NA *mat-u*) "to die, to go to (ancestors)"; possibly here also *mut-na* (loc. *-ia-θi*) "sarcophagus."

mVχ- (gen. *-s*) "five"; *muv-alχ-* "fifty."

N

naK adv. "so; then" (cf., also *ik:-naK*).

naP- "plant; bush": *nap-ti* (loc.) "in (sacred) grove" (?); Aegean νάπα, νάπη, νάπος (gen. -εος) "wooded valley," Latin *nepeta*, kind of mint, modern Tuscan *nepa* "greenweed"; derivative *nap-er* (dat.-instr. *-i*) lice *luc-er*; Latin *napurae* (Fest.) "rope (of fiber)."

neft- "grandson" (< IE; cf., Latin *nepos*, Vedic *nápāt*, Avestan *napāt-*, etc.); Aegean *ναφοθ* id.

ner-i (gen. *-es*) "water"; here also NP *nerina(i)*; Modern Greek νέρο id. Pre-Greek Νηρεύς, Νηρεῖς (Νηρηΐς), sea deities; νηρίτης (νηρείτης) kind of sea mollusk; Milyan *nere* "nymph" (dat. pl.).

nes- (part. perf. I *-(i)θv-as*) "to die"; adj. *-i*; also a derivative with *-na*.

net- "stomach; entrails": pre-Greek νηδύς id.; derivative *netśvis* "foreteller," (*ziχ*) *neθśra* "*liber haruspicinus*."

nunt:- (< Milyan *nuni-* "to bring" (?); opt. *-en*, imper. (?) *-en-t:*) "to make a sacrifice"; unclear derivatives with *-ena*, *-ene*.

nurφ(-) "nine": adv. *nurφ-zi* "nine times"; possibly, *nuzlχne* "ninetieth."

P

p:al- "top," "dome of heaven," "head": φάλα "small head" (Hes.). Derivatives: **p:alanT-*: gloss (Fest.) *falado* (*falando*) "heaven," *Palatum, Palatium*; possibly **p:ul-um-*: "star" (pl. *-k:va*); word formations like in **met:l-* and **zat:r-*. The forms *falaś*, *falzati* are also not excluded (possible month name) (cf., also Faliscan-Latin *Falerii* < **Falesii*, *Falisci*. In pre-Greek φαλακρός, φάλανθος "bald," φαληρίς, φάλαρις "coot" (*Fulica atra*), φάλος "top of a helmet," φάλαρα, also a detail of the helmet.

Pak:a theonym "Bacchus"; derivative *paχa-te* (pl. *-θ-ur*) "Bacchans," *paχa-na* (loc. *-ti*) "sanctuary of Bacchus."

PaP- "grandfather" (< Greek πάππος?); derivative *papaK/ls* (pl. *-er*) "grandson."

Pent:- "stone" (?): derivative with *-(u)na* "column; tombstone."

p:ers- (NA *-u*) verb for a ritual game; adj. *-na* borrowed into Latin as *persona* (an attribute of NA); with the enclitic in Umbrian *persontro*.

PisiKe "doctor, physician" (?) (< Greek φυσικός).

p:lek:- (NA *-u*) "to ride" (?); Latin *flexuntes, flexumines* (*x* instead of Greek χ) = "trossuli."

Pruk:- (gen. *-s*) kind of vessel (< Greek πρόχους); derivatives *-um, -una*.

Prum(a)t:- "great grandson" (< Latin *pronepos*); here also PN *prumaθnal, prumaθni*.

pui(a)- (gen. *-an*?) "wife"; here also pre-Greek ὀπυίω "to marry."

p:up:(V)l- "people" > Latin *populus*; here also the name *p:up:luna* (Latin *Populonia*).

purt:- (variant *eprt-*) title; *purtśvavc-ti* (loc.) "while being prytanis"; here also Latin *Frutis*, epithet of Venus, *Frutinal* "*templum Veneris Frutis*," Aegean πρύτανις; derivative *purtśvana* > Latin *Porsenna*. Possibly borrowed in Asia Minor (cf., Lycian *epriti* "deputy," Hattic *puri* "lord."

Put(er)- kind of vessel (< Greek ποτήρ); demin. *puti-za*.

p:Vk:- (perf. M.-P. *-k:-u*) "to accomplish a ritual"; probably here also Eteo-Cypriote *pa-ku-ke* (perf.?).

R

rasna- (gen. *-s*) "people; Etruscans"; adj. *-I*; here also {Ras1nna (Dion. Hal.) and Etruscan-Latin NP *Rasinius*.

rat- plant name: gloss (Diosc.) ῥαδία "thorny yew" or "dog rose"; *ratsna*, Latin *radia*; Etruscan-Latin NP *Ratius, Ratinius*.

ril (indecl.) "age, at the age"; possible *ta-rils* "lifelong."

S

sa (gen. -s) "six" (possible borrowing); *se-alχ-*, Aegean *śi-alχv-* "sixty"; pl. *sa-r* "twelve" (derivative *śarvena*); *ciś śariś* (gen.) "fifteen" (3 + 12), *huθ-zar-* "sixteen" (4 + 12); "22" (??).

saK- (Ger. -*ri*, inf. -*ni*) verb for some rite (< Latin *sacer*?).

se/il(V)k- word for domestic plants: Latin *siligo*, *siliqua*; here also Etruscan-Latin NP *Seligius*.

sek: (gen. -*is*) "daughter."

semp:(-) (gen. -*s*) "seven," *semφ-alχ-* "seventy."

ser- (trans. -*on-*) "to bury" (Aegean-Lusitanian isogloss): Aegean perf. -*ai*, Aegean part. perf. -*ai-θ* : Lusitanian -*ah*; unclear *sarunθoa*.

sian(s)- "copper; bronze" (adj. -*l*?).

sis- "small cattle"; derivative Aegean σίσυρα, σίσυρνα "sheep, goat fell"; cogn. *Sisenna*.

snen- (part. pres. II -*at:*) "to serve, to work" (??).

spur- (gen. -*es*, -*al*, loc. -*t:i*, acc. -*ni*) "town"; adj. -*al*, -*ana*; NP *spurina* > Etruscan-Latin *Spurinna*, *spuriana*, probably like *Octavi-an-us*; unclear Latin *spurium* "*vasculum muliebre*," *spurius* (law) "son of an unknown father."

sren- (pl. -*k:ve*) "painting" (??).

suPl-u (probably NA) "flautist" > gloss (Varr., Fest.) *subulo* id.

sut:-i (gen. -*s*, loc. -*t:*(*i*)) "sepulchre"; derivative -*na*, probably "funeral offerings."

sval- (perf. -*k:-e*, part. pres. I -*as* (instr. -*as-i*), part. perf. I -*t:-as*) "to live" (in perf. "who has lived," i.e., "dead").

T

TV, iTV (*t:*?) pron. dem., both independent and enclitic (in the latter case more often -*tl-*, -*tr-*, -*tn-*); *θui* "here," possibly fossilized locative; Aegean *tiś* (gen.), Eteo-Cypriote *ta*.

t:a/em- (perf. -*k:-e*, perf. M.-P. -*k:-u*, part. pres. I *θemiasa*) "to place; to found"; derivative *tamia-*, kind of collegium, *tamiaθuras* (gen. pl.) its members.

t:an- (part. pres. I -*asa*, pl. -*ri*) verb for ritual rite.

t:aur- "grave"; adj. -k: (*cepen θaurχ* "priest for funeral rites").

t:ei(v)- "god" (< Italic *deiv-): gloss (Hes.) δέα "θεὰ"; *θeiviti faviti-c* (loc.) "in the temple and in the subterranean room (of the temple)."

Ten- (pres. -*in-e*, Praes. M.-P. -*u*, part. perf. I -*t:-as*) "to hold a post."

Tes- (part. pres. I -*am-sa*, part. pres. II -*in-t:*) "to place, to put" (?). Derivatives: *teśiameit-al-e* (dat.-instr. IIb), probably "interment," also -*ne*, -*im*.

t:es(a)n(-) (gen. -*in*, -*s*) "dawn, morning"; also as a name of the dawn goddess (= Latin *Aurora*, Greek Ἕως).

TeT-a "grandmother"; *tetalś* "grandson (in the female line)" (cf., *papaK/ls*).

t:eur- "bull" (related to Latin *taurus* and pre-Greek ταῦρος); *θevru-mine-s* "Minotaurus."

t:ez- (pres. -*in-e*, perf. -*in-k:-e*, Ger. -*eri*, unclear -*i*, -*in*) verb for some ritual.

Tin(-) (gen. -*s*, -*s-in*, dat.-instr. IIa -*si*) (1) "day" (2) theonym "Tin" (i.e., Jupiter; variant -*ia*).

Tiv(-) (gen. -*s*, gen. pl. -*r-s*) "Moon; month" (< Anatolian; cf., Luwian *Tiw-*, Lydian *tiv-*).

Tmia "devoted place" (< Greek τέμενος?).

Trin- (perf. -*k:-e* (also Rhaetic), part. pres. II -*t:*, part. perf. I -*t:-asa*) "to pray" or "to claim."

Tular(-) (gen. -*is*) "border, confines" or "boundary stone" (< Umbrian *tuder* "finem" with dialectal *d* > *l* (nom. pl. *tuderor*, acc. pl *tudero*, *tuderato est* "*finitum ibit*"); here also Latin *tundo* (*tutudi*, *tu(n)sum*) "to hew of stone." Also used as a verb (aor. -*a-s-e*): "defined."

t:u(n)(-) (gen. -*s*, loc. -*t:*) "one," ord. *t:un-k:* "first" (gen. pl. -*er-s*), here also possibly *t:un-s-na*, adv. *θun-z* "once"; pl. *t:un-ur* "singuli"; *t:u-surt:ir* "conjoints" (partial calque of Latin *con-sortes*); unclear *t:unk:ul-*.

Tup- (-*i* fem,?) "punishment" < Milyan *tupi-* "to punish."

t(u)r- "power" (< Minoan **tur-* (from here also Greek τύραννος): gloss δροῦνα (Hes.) id.; *turan*, divine epithet; here also gloss (TLE 854) *Traneus* "July."

Tur- (pres. M.-P. -*u*, perf. -(*n*)-*k:-e*) "to give, to donate" (< Greek δῶρον?); not fully clear derivative *turu-ne*.

t:ut:- (gen. -*in*) "people; community" (< Umbrian *tuta* or Oscan *touto*); *meχ θuta* < Oscan *meddix tuticus*; adj. *tuθi-neś* (gen.) "state, public."

TVvVr- (part. pres. II -(a)t:) "to establish"; *tevar-aθ* "judge" (?); Aegean perf. trans. *tover-on-ai* "(he) established."

U

ur- "clay" > "vessel": Latin *urna*, demin. *urceus*; derivative Etruscan *urθanike* (perf. trans.) = Greek ἐκεραμεύσαν; PN *urnasis*; unclear *urin(a)te* (from a toponym **urina*).

usil(-) (gen. -s) "sun" (< Sabinian *ausel* from IE **ausos-* and **sol-*); derivative *usla-ne* "midday" or "day (adj.)" (?).

V

ve/iTVl- (1) "bull; neat (horned oxen) cattle": gloss (Apollod.) ἰταλὸν id.; the same root in Latin *vitulus*, *vitellus*, Umbrian *vithuf* (acc. pl.); Etruscan-Latin *Vetulonia*, NP *Vitellius*, possibly here also Eteo-Cypriote *vi-ti-le*; (2) "money": on the coins from Populonia χ*a fufluna vetalu* (cf., Latin *pecunia* from *pecu*).

vers- "fire" (gen. -in): gloss (Fest.) *verse* id.; *kauθaś ... versie*, probably "sunlight"; derivative NP *versni*, unclear *verśena-s*.

vin-um "wine" (< Umbrian *vinu* or Latin *vinum*).

Z

zal- (in indirect and derivative forms mostly *es(a)l-*; gen. -s) "two"; pl. *zel-ur* "bini," adv. **eslsi* (in writing *elsśi*) "twice"; derivative *zelarve-na-* (gen. -s) "duumviri" (?).

zat:r- (gen. -(i)s) "twenty"; more widespread derivative *zaθr-um* (type *meθl-um*, *pul-unr*, gen. -s); *zaθrumsne*, probably ordinal numeral.

zik:- (perf. -k:-e, trans. -n-k:-e-, NA -u) "to write"; subst. *ziχ* "book."

zil- title-making verb root; derivatives with -(V)k: (gen. [?] -al, instr. -i, loc. -t:i) and -(V)t: call the officials of different levels; *zilaθ meχl rasnal* "*praetor Etruriae*"; adj. (?) -(ak)-al; derivative *zil(V)k:-n-* of the same meaning (perf. -k:-e, NA -u, part. perf. I -t:-as).

ziv- (part. pres. I -as) "to live."

zusl- (gen. -[v]es) kind of sacrifice, possibly "oblatory animal."

ABBREVIATIONS

Place names

Al: Alalia (Corsica)
Arr: Arretium
Camp: Campania
Cl: Clusium
Cort: Cortona
Faes: Faesulae
Hort: ager Hortanus
Per: Perusia
Pop: Populonia
R: Roma
Rus: Rusellae
Sp: Spina
Tarq: Tarquinia
V.C.A.: agri inter Volaterras, Clusium et Arretium
Vet: Vetulonia
Volat: Volaterrae (Volterra)
Volc: Volcii

JOURNALS

AG: Furtwaengler A. *Die antiken Gemmen.*
AIΩN: *Annali del Seminario di Studi del Mondo Classico, Sezione linguistica.* Istituto Orientale, Napoli.
ARE: Breasted, J. *Ancient Records of Egypt.*
CHIC: Godart, L., and J.-P. Olivier. *Corpus hieroglyficarum inscriptionum Cretae.*
CIL: *Corpus inscriptionum Latinarum.*
CIE: *Corpus inscriptionum Etruscarum.*
CT: Raison, J., and M. Pope. *Corpus transnuméré du linéaire A.* Rix H. *Etruskische Texte.*
GO: Godart L., and J. P. Olivier. *Recueil des inscriptions en Linéaire A.*
LDIA: *Lingue e dialetti dell'Italia antica.* Roma, 1978.
LF: Giacomelli, G. *La lingua falisca.*
NRIE: Buffa, M. *Nuova raccolta di iscrizioni etruschi.*
PID: Conway, R. S., et al. *The Prae-Italic Dialects of Italy.*
PdP: "La Parola del Passato," Napoli.
REE: *Rivista di epigrafia etrusca* (SE).
ScAnt: *Scienze dell'Antichità*, Roma.
SE: *Studi Etruschi*, Firenze.
TDP: *Tajny drevnikh pismen.* M. 1976 (Mysteries of Ancient Scripts).
TLE: Pallottino, M. *Testimonia linguae Etruscae.*
VDI: *Vestnik drevnej istorii.* M. (The Journal of Ancient History).
VJa: *Voprosy jazykoznanija.* M. (The Aspects of Linguistics).

OTHER

orig. inc.: originis incertae vel ignotae.
rec.: aetatis recentioris.

ALPHABETICAL BIBLIOGRAPHY

Agostiniani, L. 1981. "Duenom duenas: Kalos kalô: Mlaχ mlakas." *Studi Etruschi*, 49: 95-111.

Agostiniani, L., and F. Nicosia. 2000. *Tabula Cortonensis "L'Erma" di Bretschneider*. Rome: La Libreria dello Stato.

Benelli, E. 1994. *Le iscrizioni bilingui etrusco-latine* [Bilingual Etruscan-Latin inscriptions]. Florence: Olschki.

Boisacq, E. 1916. *Dictionnaire étymologique de la langue grecque* [Etymological dictionary of the Greek language]. Heidelberg.

Boisson, C. 1989-90. "Note typologique sur le systéme des occlusives en étrusque" [Typological note on the system of occlusives in Etruscan]. *Studi Etruschi* 56: 175-87.

Bonfante, G. 1968. *La pronunzia della z in etrusco* [The pronunciation of the *z* in Etruscan]. *Studi Etruschi* 36: 57-64.

Bonfante, G. 1974. "L'opposizione *k* : *ch* (*k* : χ) in etrusco" [The opposition of *k* : *ch* (*k* : χ) in Etruscan]. *Studi Etruschi* XLII.

Bonfante, G. 1983. "Il suono 'f' in Europa di origine etrusca" [The sound "f" in Europe of Etruscan origin]. *Studi Etruschi* 51: 161-62.

Bonfante, L. 1990. *Reading the Past: Etruscan*. London: British Museum Press.

Borodina, M. A. 1969. *Sovremennyj literaturnyj retoromanskij jazyk Shveitsarii* [*Modern literary Romansh language of Switzerland*]. Leningrad: Nauka Publishing.

Breasted, J. 1906. *Ancient Records of Egypt*, 3. Chicago: University of Chicago Press.

Buffa, M. 1935. *Nuova raccolta di iscrizioni etrusche* [New collection of Etruscan inscriptions]. Florence: Rinascimento del Libro.

Buonamici, G. 1928. "L'ipogeo e l'iscrizione etrusca di S. Manno presso Perugia" [The hypogeum and Latin inscription of S. Manno near Perugia]. *Studi Etruschi* 2: 334-402.

Cataldi, M. 1988. *I sarcofagi etruschi delle famiglie Partunu, Camna e Pulena* [The Etruscan sarcophagi of the Partunu, Camna, and Pulena families]. Rome: Procom.

Chadwick, J. 1958. *The Decipherment of Linear B.* Cambridge: Cambridge University Press.

Chelysheva, I. I. 2001. "Dialekty Italii" [Dialects of Italy] *Yazyki mira. Romanskie yazyki* [Languages of the world. Romance languages]. Academia Publishing. 90-146.

Colonna, G. 1989-90. "'Tempio' e 'santuario' nel lessico delle lamine di Pyrgi" [Temple and sanctuary in the lexicon of the Pyrgi sheets]. *Scienze dell'Antichità* 3-4: 197-98.

Colonna, G. 1994. "A proposito degli dei del Fegato di Piacenza" [Concerning the gods of the Piacenza liver]. *Studi Etruschi* 59: 123-36.

Conway, R. S. 1897. *The Italic Dialects Edited with a Grammar and Glossary*, 1-2. Cambridge: Cambridge University Press.

Conway, R. S., J. Whatmough, and S. E. Johnson. 1933. *The Prae-Italic Dialects of Italy*, 1-3. Oxford: Oxford University Press.

Cortsen, S. P. 1935. *Glossar Runes M. Der etruskische Text der Agramer Mumienbinde* [The Etruscan text of the Agramer (*Liber Linteus*) mummy bindings]. Göttingen: Vandenhoeck & Ruprecht.

Cristofani, M. 1973. "Ancora sui morfemi etruschi *-ke* : *-khe*" [Again on the Etruscan morphemes *-ke* : *-khe*]. *Studi Etruschi* 41: 181-92.

Cristofani, M. 1974. *Tabula Capuana. Un calendario festivo di età arcaica* [The Capuan table. A festival calendar of the ancient age].

Cristofani, M. 1978. *L'alfabeto etrusco* [The Etruscan alphabet]. In *Lingue e dialetti dell'Italia antica*. Rome: Biblioteca di Storia Patria, 403-28.

D'yakonov, I. M. 1961. "Sravnitel'no-grammatičeskij obzor khurritskogo i urartskogo jazykov" [Comparative grammar review of the Hurrian and Urartian languages] *Palestinskij sbornik* [Palestinian Collection]. Moscow, 369-423.

de Simone, C. 1970. "I morfemi etruschi *-ce* (*-ke*) e *-che*" [The Etruscan morphemes *-ce* (*-ke*) e *-che*]. *Studi Etruschi* 38: 115-39.

de Simone, C. 1975. "Il nome de Tevere" [The name of Tevere]. *Studi Etruschi* 43: 119-57.

de Simone, C. 1976. "Ancora sul nome di Caere" [Again on the name of Caere]. *Studi Etruschi* 44: 163-84.

de Simone, C. 1978. "Sull'esito del dittongo etrusco *ai*" [On the outcome of the Etruscan diphthong *ai*]. *Studi Etruschi*, 46: 177.

de Simone, C. 1992. "Il nome etrusco del poleonimo Mantua" [The Etruscan name of Mantua]. *Studi Etruschi* 63: 197-200.

de Simone, C. 1994. "I tirreni a Lemnos: L'alfabeto" [The Tyrrhenians at Lemnos: The alphabet]. *Studi Etruschi* 60: 145-63.

de Simone, C. 1996. "Etrusco **usel-* 'sole.'" *Studi Etruschi* 33: 537-38.

de Simone, C. 1996. "Il morfo etrusco -*si*: 'dativo' o 'agentivo'? Questioni di principio" [The Etruscan morpheme -*si*: "Dative" or "agentive"? Principle problems]. *ParPass* 51: 401-21.

Dejanov, A. F. 1976. "Linejnoe pis'mo A" [Linear script A], In *Tajny drevnih pis'men: problemy deshifrovki* [Secrets of ancient writings: Decryption problems]. Moscow: Progress Publishing, 83-84, 99-100.

Devine, A. M. 1973. "Etruscan Language Studies and Modern Phonology: The Problem of the Aspirates." *Studi Etruschi* 42: 123-51.

Devoto, G. 1970. "Protolatini e tirreni" [Proto-Latins and Tyrrhenians] (II). *Studi Etruschi* 37: 141-51.

Durante M. 1978. "Nord piceno: La lingua delle iscrizioni di Novilara" [Northern Piceno: The language of the Novilara inscriptions]. In *Lingue e dialetti dell'Italia antica*. Rome: Biblioteca di Storia Patria, 393-400.

Dvoretskij, I. Kh. 1958. *Drevnegrechesko-russkij slovar'* [Ancient Greek-Russian dictionary]. Moscow.

Dvoretskij, I. Kh. 1995. *Latinsko-russkij slovar'* [Latin-Russian dictionary]. Moscow.

Ernout, A., and Meillet, A. 1951. *Dictionnaire étymologique de la langue latine: Histoire de mots* [Etymological dictionary of the Latin language: History of words]. Paris: C. Klincksieck.

Ernshtedt, P. V. 1953. *Egipetskie zaimstvovanija v grecheskom* [Egyptian loan-words in Greek]. Academia Publishing.

Fedorova, E. V. 1982. *Vvedenie v latinskuju epigrafiku* [Introduction to Latin Epigraphy]. Moscow: Moscow State University Publishing.

Fedorova, E. V. 1991. *Rann'aja latinskaja pis'mennost' (VII-II vv. do n. e.)* [Early Latin writing. 8th-2nd centuries BC]. Moscow: Moscow State University Publishing.

Fiesel, E. 1922. *Das grammatikalische Geschlecht im Etruskischen*. Göttingen.

Friedrich, J. 1932. *Kleinasiatische Sprachdenkmäler* [Language inscriptions of Asia Minor]. Berlin: Mouton de Gruyter.

Friedrich, J. 1979. *Istoriya pis'ma* [A history of Writing]. Moscow: Editorial URSS Publishing.

Friedrich, J. 2001. *Kratkaja grammatika khettskogo jazyka* [A brief grammar of the Hittite language]. Moscow: Editorial URSS Publishing.

Frisk, H. 1960. *Griechisches etymologisches Wörterbuch* [Etymological Greek dictionary]. Heidelberg.

Furtwaengler, A. 1900. *Die antiken Gemmen*. Bd. 1-3, Leipzig. Berlin.

Furumark, A. 1956. *Linear A und die altkretische Sprache: Entzifferung und Deutung* [Linear A and the ancient Cretan language: Decipherment and meaning]. Berlin.

Gelb, I. E. 1982. *Opyt izuchenija pis'ma* [A study of writing]. Moscow: Editorial URSS Publishing.

Georgiev, V. 1958. *Issledovanija po sravnitel'no-istoricheskomu yazykoznaniju* [Studies in comparative historical linguistics]. Moscow: Inoizdat Publishing.

Gernot, W. 2004. Hurrian. *The Cambridge Encyclopedia of the World's Ancient languages*. Cambridge: Cambridge University Press, 95-118.

Giacomelli, G. 1963. *La lingua falisca* [The Faliscan language]. Florence.

Giacomelli, G. 1978. "Il falisco" [Faliscan]. In *Lingue e dialetti dell'Italia antica*. Rome: Biblioteca di Storia Patria, 505-42.

Gianecchini, G. 1996. "'Destra' e 'sinistra,' e lo strumentale in etrusco" ["Right" and "left," and the instrumental in Etruscan]. *Studi Etruschi* 62: 281-310.

Godart, L., and J. P. Olivier. 1976-85. *Recueil des inscriptions en Linéaire A* [Collection of Linear A inscriptions], 1-5. Paris: Dépositaire, P. Geuthner.

Godart, L., and J. P. Olivier. 1996. *Corpus hieroglyficarum inscriptionum Cretae* [Corpus of hieroglyphic inscriptions of Crete]. Études crétoises. Paris: Dépositaire, de Boccard.

Halbherr, F., and M. Guarducci. 1942. *Inscriptiones Creticae* [Cretan inscriptions], III. Rome: La Libreria dello Stato.

Heurgon, J. 1961. *La vie quotidienne chez les Étrusques* [Everyday life of the Etruscans]. Oxford: Oxford-Hachette.

Hualde, J. I., and J. O. de Urbina. 2003. *A Grammar of Basque*. Berlin: Mouton de Gruyter.

Ipsen, G. 1976. "Festskij disk (Opyt dešifrovki)" [Phaistos Disc (Decryption experience)]. In *Tajny drevnih pis'men: problemy deshifrovki* [Secrets of ancient writings: Decryption problems]. Moscow: Progress Publishing, 32–65.

Ivanov, V. V. 1980. "Novye dannye o sootnoshenii maloaziatskoj, likijskoj, etrusskoj i rimskoj pis'mennykh traditsij. Oboznachenija chisel" [New data on the correlation of Asia Minor Lycian, Etruscan and Roman written traditions. Number designation] *Antičnaja balkanistika* [Antique balkanistics]. Moscow.

Ivanov, V. V. 1988. "Drevnevostochnye sv'azi etrusskogo jazyka" [Ancient Eastern relations of the Etruscan language]. In *Drevnij Vostok: Etnokul'turnye sv'azi* [Ancient East: Ethnocultural Relations]. Moscow.

Ivanov, V. V. 2008. *Trudy po etimologii indoevropejskikh i drevneperedneaziatskikh jazykov* [Proceedings on the etymology of Indo-European and ancient Asian languages], 5.

Jatsemirskij, S. A. 2001. "Nadpis' lemnosskoj stely" [Inscription on the Lemnos stele]. *XII čtenija pam'ati prof. S. I. Arkhangel'skogo*, part 1: 112–21.

Jatsemirskij, S. A. 2005. Jazyk nadpisi lemnosskoj stely v sravnitel'nom osveshenii [Language of the Lemnos stele in a comparative light]. *Orientalia et classica* 11, part 1: 317–38.

Jatsemirskij, S. A. 2006. *Problemy morfologii tirrenskikh jazykov* [Morphological problems of the Tyrrhenian languages]. Doctoral dissertation. Moscow.

Jatsemirskij. S. A. 2007. "Etrusskie cislitel'nye: Problemy i itogi issledovanija" [Etruscan numerals: Problems and results of the study]. *Orientalia et clássica* 11, part 2: 187–96.

Jatsemirskij, S. A. 2008. *Etruscan Numerals (Problems and Results of Research): Bygone Voices Reconstructed*. Copenhagen.

Jatsemirskij, S. A. 2009. "Labyrinthos: Suffiks -*nth*- v minojskom i tirrenskikh jazykakh" [Labyrinthos: The suffix -*nth*- in the Minoan and Tyrrhenian languages]. *Orientalia et classica* 2, part 4: 98–111.

Jones, T. B. 1950. "Notes on the Eteo-Cypriote Inscriptions." *American Journal of Philology* 71: 401–7.

Jones, T. B. 1975. "Zametki ob eteokiprskom jazyke" [Notes on the Eteocypriot inscriptions]. In *Tajny drevnih pis'men: problemy deshifrovki* [Secrets of ancient writings: Decryption problems]. Moscow: Progress Publishing, 257-60.

Krall, J. 1892. *Die Etruskischen Mumienbinde des Agramer Österreichischen Nationalmuseums: Denkschriften der österreichischen Akademie der Wissenschaft* [The Etruscan Agramer (*Liber Linteus*) mummy bindings of the Austrian National Museum: memoranda of the Austrian Academy of Science]. Vienna: Austrian Academy of Science.

Krasnovskaja, N. A. 1964. *K voprosu ob etnogeneze retoromantsev* [On the question of Rhaeto-Romance ethnogenesis]. *Sovetskaja etnografija*: 89-101.

Kretschmer, P. 1942. "Die tyrrhenischen Inschriften der Stele von Lemnos" [The Tyrrhenian Inscriptions of the Lemnos stele]. *Glotta*, 29: 96-8.

Kretschmer, P. 1976. "Tirrenskie nadpisi Lemnosskoj stely" [Tyrrhenian inscriptions of the Lemnos stele]. *Tajny drevnih pis'men: problemy deshifrovki* [Secrets of ancient writings: Decryption problems]. Moscow: Progress Publishing, 336-37.

Liddell, H. G., and R. Scott. 1996. *A Greek-English Lexicon*. Oxford: Oxford University Press.

Maggiani, A. 1982. "Qualche osservazione sul fegato di Piacenza" [Some observations on the Liver of Piacenza]. *Studi Etruschi* 50: 53-54.

Maggiani, A. 1987-88. "Casi di scanbio $\varphi : \theta$ nell'Etruria settentrionale" [Cases of switching between $\varphi : \theta$ in western Etruria]. *Studi Etruschi* 55: 195-202.

Malzahn, M. 1999. "Das lemnische Alphabet: eine eigenstaendige Entwicklung" [The Lemnos alphabet: An independent development]. *Studi Etruschi* 63: 259-79.

Mancini, A. 1973. "Retico" [Rhaetic]. *Studi Etruschi* XLI: 363-409.

Mancini, A. 1975. "Iscrizioni retiche" [Rhaetic inscriptions]. *Studi Etruschi* 43: 223-306.

Masson, E. 1974. *Cyprominoica. Répertoires. Documents de Ras Shamra. Essais d'interprétation* [Cyprominoaca. Inventories. Documents of Ras Shamra. Interpretive essays]. Göteborg: Paul Aströms Förlag.

Masson, O. 1961. *Les inscriptions chypriotes syllabiques* [Syllabic Cypriote inscriptions]. Paris: Dépositaire, de Boccard.

Mastrelli, A. 1976. "Etrusco-piceno *frontac* e greco *keraunos*" [Etruscan-Piceno *frontac* and Greek *keraunos*]. *Studi Etruschi* 44: 149-62.

Mayak, I. L. 1983. "Novyj trud o drevnejšem Latsii" [New book on ancient Latium]. *Vestnik drevnej istorii* [Journal of ancient history] 1: 187-99.

Melikishvili, G. A. 1964. *Urartskij yazyk* [Urartian language]. Moscow.

Modestov, B. I. 1868. *Rimskaya pis'mennost' v period tsarej* [Roman writing during the period of kings]. Kazan.

Molchanov, A. A. 1988. Neroznak V. P., Sharypkin S. *Pam'atniki drevneishei grecheskoi pis'mennosti (Vvedenie v mikenologiyu)* [Inscriptions of ancient Greek writing (Introduction to mycenology)]. Moscow.

Molchanov, A. A. 1992. *Poslantsy pogibshikh tsivilizatsij (Pis'mena drevnej Egeidy)* [Envoys of Fallen Civilizations (Letters of ancient Aegeid)]. Moscow.

Nemirovskij, A. I. 1983. *Etruski. Ot mifa k istorii* [Etruscans. From myth to history]. Moscow.

Nemirovskij, A. I. 1986. "Bronzovaya model' pecheni iz P'yachentsy kak kalendarnaya Sistema" [Piacenza bronze liver model as a calendar system]. *Vestnik drevnej istorii* [Journal of ancient history] 4: 109–18.

Nemirovskij A. I., and A. I. Xarsekin 1969. *Etruski* [Etruscans]. Voronež. 26–67.

Neumann, G. 1957. "Zur Sprache der kretischen Linearschrift A" [On the language of Cretan Linear A]. *Glotta* 36 (1-2): 156–58.

Neumann, G. 1976. *O jazyke kritskogo linejogo pis'ma A* [About the Cretan language of Linear A], 97–100.

Olzscha, K. 1939. *Interpretation der Agramer Mumienbinde* [Interpretation of the Agramer (*Liber Linteus*) mummy bindings]. Leipzig: Dieterich'sche Verlagsbuchhandlung.

Olzscha, K. 1962. "Studie über die VII Kolumne der Agramer Mumienbinde" [Study on the seventh column of the Agramer (*Liber Linteus*) mummy bindings]. *Studi Etruschi* 30: 157–92.

Olzscha, K. 1966. "Die punisch-etruskischen Inschriften von Pyrgi" [The Punic-Etruscan inscriptions from Pyrgi]. *Glotta* 44: 60–108.

Pallottino, M. 1936. *Elementi di lingua etrusca* [Elements of Etruscan language]. Florence: Rinascimento del Libro.

Pallottino, M. 1948. "Sulla lettura e sul contenuto della grande iscrizione di Capua." [On the reading and the contents of the great inscription of Capua]. *Studi Etruschi* 20: 159–60.

Pallottino, M. 1958. "Der Akkusativ im Etruskischen" [The accusative in Etruscan]. *Glotta* 37: 305–11.

Pallottino, M. 1963. *Studien zu der Agramer Mumienbinden* [Studies of the Agramer (*Liber Linteus*) mummy bindings]. Denkschriften der philosophisch-historischen Klasse. T. 81. Vienna: Böhlaus.

Pallottino, M. 1967. "Eine Nennung Hannibals in einer Inschrift des 2. Jahrhunderts v. Ch. aus Tarquinia" [Hannibal's mention of an inscription of the second century BC from Tarquinia]. *Studi Etruschi* 35: 659–63.

Pallottino, M. 1968. *Testimonia linguae Etruscae* [Testimonials of the Etruscan language], 2nd ed. Florence: Olschki.

Pallottino, M. 1969. *Die etruskische Sprache. Versuch einer Gesamt-Darstellung* [The Etruscan language. The search for a total account]. Graz: Akademische Druck, u. Verlagsanstalt.

Pallottino, M. 1972. Etruskische Bauinschriften [Etruscan building inscriptions]. Vienna: Böhlaus.

Pallottino, M. 1976. "Problema etrusskogo jazyka" [Problems of the Etruscan language]. *Tajny drevnih pis'men*, 349–80.

Pallottino, M. 1978. *Lingue e dialetti dell'Italia antica*. Rome: Biblioteca di Storia Patria, 429–68.

Pauli, K. 1893–1902. *Corpus Inscriptionum Etruscarum* (CIE). Continued by A. Danielsson, G. Herbig, and E. Sittig until 1936; M. Cristofani, 1970, II (tit. 5607–6324); M. Cristofani, M. Pandolfini Angeletti, and G. Coppola, 1996, (tit. 8601–880, *inscriptiones et in Latio et in Campania repertae*); M. Pandolfini Angeletti (tit. 10001–520, *Tarquinii cum Agro*), 1982; G. Magini Carella Prada and M. Pandolfini Angeletti, 1987 (tit. 10521–943, *Volsinii cum agro*); M. Pandolfini Angeletti, 1994 (tit. 10951–1538).

Peruzzi, E. 1975. "Mikenskie yazykovye elementy v latyni" [Mycenaean language elements in Latin]. *Voprosy yazykoznaniya* [Issues in linguistics] 5: 104–9.

Pisani, V. 1953. *Le lingue dell'Italia antica oltre il latino* [Languages of ancient Italy other than Latin]. Turin: Rosenberg and Sellier.

Pokorny, J. 1959. *Indogermanisches etymologisches Wörterbuch* [Dictionary of Indo-European etymologies]. Bern-München.

Poup, M. 1976. "Linejnoe pis'mo i problema egejskoj pis'mennosti" [Linear writing and the problem of Aegean literature]. In *Tajny drevnih pis'men*, 85–96.

Pugliese Carrattelli, G. 1945. "Le iscrizioni preelleniche di Haghia Triada in Creta e della Grecia Peninsulare" [The pre-Hellenic inscriptions of Hagia Triada in Crete and of peninsular Greece]. *Monumenti Antichi* 40: 421–610.

Pugliese Carrattelli, G. 1963. *Le epigrafi di Haghia Triada in lineare A* [The writings of Hagia Triada in Linear A]. Salamanca: Seminario de Filología Clásica, Universidad de Salamanca.

Raison J., and M. Pope. 1994. *Corpus transnuméré du linéaire A* [Cross-numbered corpus of Linear A]. BCILL 74. Louvain-la-Neuve.

Rix H. 1991. *Etruskische Texte* [Etruscan Texts]. Editio Minor. I. Einleitung, Konkordanz, Indices, II. Texte. Tübingen: G. Narr.

Rix, H. 1963. *Das etruskische Cognomen* [Etruscan cognomens]. Wiesbaden: O. Harrassowitz.

Rix, H. 1983. "Norme i variazioni nell'ortografia etrusca" [Norms and variations in Etruscan orthography]. *Annali dell'Istituto Universitario Orientale di Napoli* 5: 132-33.

Rix, H. 1984. Etrusco *mex rasnal* = Latino *res publica*. In *Studi di antichità in onore di Guglielmo Maetztke*. Rome.

Rix, H. 1984. "Scrittura e Lingua" [Writing and language]. In *Gli Etruschi: una nuova immagine*, edited by M. Cristofani. Florence: Giunti.

Rix, H. 1987. "Zur Morphostruktur des etruskischen *s*-Genetivs" [On the morphemic structure of Etruscan *s* genitives]. *Studi Etruschi* 60: 169-93.

Rix, H. 1991. "Etrusco *un, une, unu* 'te, tibi, vos.'" *Archeologia Classica*: 43 (1): 665-89.

Rix, H. 1998. *Rätisch und Etruskisch* [Rhaetic and Etruscan]. Innsbruck: Institut für Sprachwissenschaft der Universität Innsbruck.

Rix, H. 2000. "Osservazioni Preliminari ad una Interpretazione dell'Aes Cortonese" [Preliminary observations toward an interpretation of Aes Cortonese]. *Incontri linguistici*: 11-31.

Robertson, E. 2006. "Etruscan's Genealogical Linguistic Relationship with Nakh-Daghestanian: A Preliminary Evaluation." Unpublished manuscript.

Rodriguez, Ramos J. 2000. "La lectura de las inscriptiones sudlusitano-tartesias" [The reading of the inscriptions of South Lusitania and Tartessos]. *Faventia* 22 (1): 21-48.

Schumacher, S. 1992. *Die rätischen Inschriften: Geschichte und heutiger Stand der Forschung* [The Rhaetic inscriptions: History and current knowledge of the research]. Innsbruck: Instituts für Sprachwissenschaft.

Shifman, I. 2003. *Finikijskij yazyk* [Phoenician language]. Moscow: Editorial URSS Publishing.

Stoltenberg, H. L. 1943. Die Bedeutung der etruskischen Zahlnamen [The meaning of the Etruscan numerals]. *Glotta* 30: 234–44.

Stoltenberg, H. L. 1953. Übersetzung der Tontafel von Capua [Translation of the Capua clay tablet]. *Studi Etruschi* 22: 158–65.

Stoltenberg, H. L. 1957. *Etruskische Gottnamen* [Names of Etruscan gods]. Leverkusen: Gottschalksche Verlagsbuchhandlung.

Šul'ten, A. 1941. "Tirseny v Ispanii (Novye dannye ob iberijskom jazyke)" [Tyrrhenians in Hispania (New data from the Iberian language)]. *Vestnik drevnej istorii* [Journal of ancient history], 1: 8–30.

Syrom'atnikov, N. A. 2002. *Drevnejaponskij jazyk* [Old Japanese]. Moscow.

Tagliavini, C. 1959. *Le origini delle lingue neolatine* [The origins of the Neo-Latin languages]. Bologna: Patron.

Talocchini, A., Giacomelli, G. 1966. "Il nuovo alfabeto di Vetulonia" [The new alphabet of Vetulonia]. *Studi Etruschi* 34: 239–57.

Tronskij, I. M. 1953. *Ocherki iz istorii latinskogo yazyka* [Essays from the history of the Latin language]. Moscow.

Tronskij, I. M. 2001. *Istoricheskaja morfologija latinskogo yazyka. Obšheindoevropejskoe jazykovoe sostojanie (Voprosy rekonstruktsii)* [The historical morphology of the Latin language. Common Indo-European language state (Reconstruction issues)]. Moscow.

Tronskij, I. M. 2004. *Voprosy yazykovogo razvitija v anticnom obschestve* [Issues of language development in ancient society]. Moscow.

Turcan, R. 1976. "Encore la prophétie de Vegoia" [Again the Vegoia prophecy]. In *L'Italie préromaine et la Rome républicaine*. Rome: Collection de L'École Française de Rome.

Untermann, J. 2000. *Wörterbuch des Oskisch-Umbrischen* [Osco-Umbrian dictionary.] Heidelberg.

Urbanová, D., and V. Blažek. 2008. *Národy staroveké Itálie, jejich jazyky a písma* [The peoples of ancient Italy, their languages and writing]. Brno: Host.

Walde, A., and J. B Hofmann. 1938–56. *Lateinisches etymologisches Wörterbuch* [Latin etymological dictionary]. Heidelberg.

Woodhouse, S. C. 1910. *English-Greek Dictionary*. London: George Routledge and Sons, Ltd.

Xarsekin, A. 1963. *Voprosy interpretatsii pam'atnikov etrusskoj pis'mennosti* [Questions on the interpretation of Etruscan literary inscriptions]. Stavropol.

Xarsekin, A. 1964. "K interpretatsii etrusskikh čislitel'nykh" [Contribution to the interpretation of Etruscan numerals]. *Vestnik Drevnej Istorii* [*Journal of Ancient History*] 2 (88): 48–61.

Xarsekin, A. 1969. Etrusskaja epigrafika i etrusskij jazyk [Etruscan epigraphy and Etruscan language]. Voronež.

Xarsekin, A. 1976. "Eteokiprskie nadpisi" [Eteo-Cypriote enscriptions]. *Tajny drevnih pis'men: problemy deshifrovki* [Secrets of ancient writings: Decryption problems]. Moscow: Progress Publishing.

Xarsekin, A. 1976. "Lemnosskie nadpisi" [Lemnos inscriptions]. *Tajny drevnih pis'men: problemy deshifrovki* [Secrets of ancient writings: Decryption problems]. Moscow: Progress Publishing, 335, 337–38.

Xarsekin, A. I., and M. L. Helzer. 1965. "Novye nadpisi iz Pirgi na finikijskom i etrusskom jazykakh" [New inscriptions in Phoenician and Etruscan from Pyrgi]. *Vestnik Drevnej Istorii* [Journal of ancient history] 3 (93): 108–31.

Zhirmunskij, V. M. 1964. *Vvedenie v sravnitel'no-istoricheskoe izuchenie germanskikh yazykov* [Introduction to the comparative historical study of Germanic languages]. Moscow: Nauka Publishing.

CATEGORICAL BIBLIOGRAPHY

TEXTS

Agostiniani, L., and F. Nicosia. 2000. *Tabula Cortonensis "L'Erma" di Bretschneider.* Rome: La Libreria dello Stato.

Breasted, J. 1906. *Ancient Records of Egypt*, 3. Chicago: University of Chicago Press.

Buffa, M. 1935. *Nuova raccolta di iscrizioni etrusche* [New collection of Etruscan inscriptions]. Florence: Rinascimento del Libro.

Conway, R. S. 1897. *The Italic Dialects Edited with a Grammar and Glossary*, 1-2. Cambridge: Cambridge University Press.

Conway, R. S., Whatmough, J., Johnson, S. E. 1933. *The Prae-Italic Dialects of Italy*, 1-3. Oxford: Oxford University Press.

Friedrich, J. 1932. *Kleinasiatische Sprachdenkmäler* [Language inscriptions of Asia Minor]. Berlin: Mouton de Gruyter.

Godart, L., and J. P. Olivier. 1976-85. *Recueil des inscriptions en Linéaire A* [Collection of Linear A inscriptions], 1-5. Paris: Dépositaire, P. Geuthner.

Godart, L., and J. P. Olivier. 1996. *Corpus hieroglyficarum inscriptionum Cretae* [Corpus of hieroglyphic inscriptions of Crete]. Études crétoises. Paris: Dépositaire, de Boccard.

Halbherr, F., and M. Guarducci. 1942. *Inscriptiones Creticae* [Cretan inscriptions], III. Rome: La Libreria dello Stato.

Mancini, A. 1975. *Iscrizioni retiche* [Rhaetic inscriptions]. *Studi Etruschi* 43: 223-306.

Pallottino, M. 1968. *Testimonia linguae Etruscae* [Testimonials of the Etruscan language], 2nd ed. Florence: Olschki.

Pauli, K. 1893-1902. *Corpus Inscriptionum Etruscarum* (CIE). Continued by A. Danielson, G. Herbig, and E. Sittig until 1936; M. Cristofani, 1970, II (tit. 5607-6324); M. Cristofani, M. Pandolfini Angeletti, G. Coppola, 1996, (tit. 8601-880, *inscriptiones et in Latio et in Campania repertae*); M. Pandolfini

Angeletti (tit. 10001-520, *Tarquinii cum Agro*), 1982; G. Magini Carella Prada and M. Pandolfini Angeletti, 1987 (tit. 10521-943, *Volsinii cum agro*); M. Pandolfini Angeletti, 1994 (tit. 10951-1538).

Pugliese Carrattelli, G. 1945. "Le iscrizioni preelleniche di Haghia Triada in Creta e della Grecia Peninsulare" [The Pre-Hellenic inscriptions of Hagia Triada in Crete and of peninsular Greece]. *Monumenti Antichi* 40: 421-610.

Pugliese Carrattelli, G. 1963. *Le epigrafi di Haghia Triada in lineare A* [The writings of Hagia Triada in Linear A]. Salamanca: Seminario de Filología Clásica, Universidad de Salamanca.

Raison J., and M. Pope. 1994. *Corpus transnuméré du linéaire A* [Cross-numbered corpus of Linear A]. BCILL 74. Louvain-la-Neuve.

Rix H. 1991. *Etruskische Texte* [Etruscan Texts]. Editio Minor. I. Einleitung, Konkordanz, Indices, II. Texte. Tübingen: G. Narr.

Schumacher S. 1992. *Die rätischen Inschriften: Geschichte und heutiger Stand der Forschung* [The Rhaetic inscriptions: History and current knowledge of the research]. Innsbruck: Instituts für Sprachwissenschaft.

DICTIONARIES

Boisacq, E. 1916. *Dictionnaire étymologique de la langue grecque* [Etymological dictionary of the Greek language]. Heidelberg.

Dvoretskij, I. Kh. 1958. *Drevnegrechesko-russkij slovar'* [Ancient Greek-Russian dictionary]. Moscow.

Dvoretskij, I. Kh. 1995. *Latinsko-russkij slovar'* [Latin-Russian dictionary]. Moscow.

Ernout, A., and A. Meillet. 1951. *Dictionnaire étymologique de la langue latine: Histoire de mots* [Etymological dictionary of the Latin language: History of words]. Paris: C. Klincksieck.

Frisk, H. 1960. *Griechisches etymologisches Wörterbuch* [Etymological Greek dictionary]. Heidelberg.

Liddell, H. G., and R. Scott. 1996. *A Greek-English Lexicon*. Oxford: Oxford University Press.

Pokorny, J. 1959. *Indogermanisches etymologisches Wörterbuch* [Dictionary of Indo-European etymologies]. Bern-München.

Untermann, J. 2000. *Wörterbuch des Oskisch-Umbrischen* [Osco-Umbrian dictionary.] Heidelberg.

Walde, A., and J. B. Hofmann. 1938–56. *Lateinisches etymologisches Wörterbuch* [Latin etymological dictionary]. Heidelberg.

Woodhouse, S. C. 1910. *English-Greek Dictionary.* London: George Routledge and Sons, Ltd.

RESEARCH

Agostiniani, L. 1981. "Duenom duenas: Kalos kalô : Mlaχ mlakas." *Studi Etruschi* 49: 95–111.

Benelli, E. 1994. *Le iscrizioni bilingui etrusco-latine* [Bilingual Etruscan-Latin inscriptions]. Florence: Olschki.

Boisson, C. 1989–90. "Note typologique sur le systéme des occlusives en étrusque" [Typological note on the system of occlusives in Etruscan]. *Studi Etruschi* 56: 175–87.

Bonfante, G. 1968. "La pronunzia della *z* in etrusco" [The pronunciation of the *z* in Etruscan]. *Studi Etruschi* 36: 57–64.

Bonfante, G. 1974. "L'opposizione *k* : *ch* (*k* : χ) in etrusco" [The opposition of *k* : *ch* (*k* : χ) in Etruscan]. *Studi Etruschi* 62.

Bonfante, G. 1983. "Il suono "f" in Europa di origine etrusca" [The sound "f" in Europe of Etruscan origin]. *Studi Etruschi* 51: 161–62.

Bonfante, L. 1990. *Reading the Past: Etruscan.* London: British Museum Press.

Borodina, M. A. 1969. *Sovremennyj literaturnyj retoromanskij jazyk Shveitsarii* [Modern literary Romansh language of Switzerland]. Leningrad: Nauka Publishing.

Buonamici, G. 1928. "L'ipogeo e l'iscrizione etrusca di S. Manno presso Perugia" [The hypogeum and Latin inscription of S. Manno near Perugia]. *Studi Etruschi* 2: 334–402.

Cataldi, M. 1988. *I sarcofagi etruschi delle famiglie Partunu, Camna e Pulena* [The Etruscan sarcophagi of the Partunu, Camna, and Pulena families]. Rome: Procom.

Chadwick, J. 1958. *The Decipherment of Linear B.* Cambridge: Cambridge University Press.

Chelysheva, I. I. 2001. "Dialekty Italii" [Dialects of Italy]. In *Yazyki mira. Romanskie yazyki* [Languages of the world. Romance languages]. Academia Publishing, 90-146.

Colonna, G. 1989-90. "'Tempio' e 'santuario' nel lessico delle lamine di Pyrgi" [Temple and sanctuary in the lexicon of the Pyrgi sheets]. *Scienze dell'Antichità* 3-4: 197-98.

Colonna, G. 1994. "A proposito degli dei del Fegato di Piacenza" [Concerning the gods of the Piacenza liver]. *Studi Etruschi* 59: 123-36.

Cortsen, S. P. 1935. *Glossar Runes M. Der etruskische Text der Agramer Mumienbinde* [The Etruscan text of the Agramer (*Liber Linteus*) mummy bindings]. Göttingen: Vandenhoeck & Ruprecht.

Cristofani, M. 1973. "Ancora sui morfemi etruschi *-ke* : *-khe*" [Again on the Etruscan morphemes *-ke* : *-khe*]. *Studi Etruschi* 41: 181-92.

Cristofani, M. 1974. *Tabula Capuana. Un calendario festivo di età arcaica* [The Capuan table. A festival calendar of the ancient age].

Cristofani, M. 1978. "L'alfabeto etrusco" [The Etruscan Alphabet]. In *Lingue e dialetti dell'Italia antica*. Rome: Biblioteca di Storia Patria, 403-28.

D'yakonov, I. M. 1961. "Sravnitel'no-grammatičeskij obzor khurritskogo i urartskogo jazykov" [Comparative grammar review of the Hurrian and Urartian languages]. In *Palestinskij sbornik* [*Palestinian collection*]. Moscow, 369-423.

de Simone, C. 1970. "I morfemi etruschi *-ce* (*-ke*) e *-che*" [The Etruscan morphemes *-ce* (*-ke*) e *-che*]. *Studi Etruschi* 38: 115-39.

de Simone, C. 1975. Il nome de Tevere [The name of Tevere]. *Studi Etruschi* 43: 119-57.

de Simone, C. 1976. "Ancora sul nome di Caere" [Again on the name of Caere]. *Studi Etruschi* 44: 163-84.

de Simone, C. 1978. "Sull'esito del dittongo etrusco *ai*" [On the outcome of the Etruscan diphthong *ai*]. *Studi Etruschi* 46: 177.

de Simone, C. 1992. "Il nome etrusco del poleonimo Mantua" [The Etruscan name of Mantua]. *Studi Etruschi* 63: 197-200.

de Simone, C. 1994. "I tirreni a Lemnos: L'alfabeto" [The Tyrrhenians at Lemnos: the alphabet]. *Studi Etruschi* 60: 145-63.

de Simone, C. 1996. "Etrusco **usel-* 'sole.'" *Studi Etruschi* 33: 537-38.

de Simone, C. 1996. "Il morfo etrusco *-si*: 'dativo' o 'agentivo'? Questioni di principio" [The Etruscan morpheme *-si*: "dative" or "agentive"? Principle problems]. *ParPass* 51: 401-21.

Dejanov, A. F. 1976. "Linejnoe pis'mo A" [Linear A script]. In *Tajny drevnih pis'men: problemy deshifrovki* [Secrets of ancient writings: Decryption problems]. Moscow: Progress Publishing, 83-4, 99-100.

Devine, A. M. 1973. "Etruscan Language Studies and Modern Phonology: The Problem of the Aspirates." *Studi Etruschi* 42: 123-51.

Devoto, G. 1970. Protolatini e tirreni [Proto-Latins and Tyrrhenians] (II). *Studi Etruschi* 37: 141-51.

Durante M. 1978. "Nord piceno: La lingua delle iscrizioni di Novilara" [Northern Piceno: The language of the Novilara inscriptions]. In *Lingue e dialetti dell'Italia antica*. Rome: Biblioteca di Storia Patria, 393-400.

Ernshtedt, P. V. 1953. *Egipetskie zaimstvovanija v grecheskom* [Egyptian loan-words in Greek]. Academia Publishing.

Fedorova, E. V. 1982. *Vvedenie v latinskuju epigrafiku* [Introduction to Latin Epigraphy]. Moscow: Moscow State University Publishing.

Fedorova, E. V. 1991. *Rann'aja latinskaja pis'mennost' (VII-II vv. do n. e.)* [Early Latin writing. 8th-2nd centuries BC]. Moscow: Moscow State University Publishing.

Fiesel, E. 1922. Das grammatikalische Geschlecht im Etruskischen. Göttingen.

Friedrich, J. 1979. *Istoriya pis'ma* [A history of writing]. Moscow: Editorial URSS Publishing.

Friedrich, J. 2001. *Kratkaja grammatika khettskogo jazyka* [A brief grammar of the Hittite language]. Moscow: Editorial URSS Publishing.

Furtwaengler, A. 1900. *Die antiken Gemmen*. Bd. 1-3, Leipzig. Berlin.

Furumark, A. 1956. *Linear A und die altkretische Sprache: Entzifferung und Deutung* [Linear A and the ancient Cretan language: Decipherment and meaning]. Berlin.

Gelb, I. E. 1982. *Opyt izuchenija pis'ma* [A Study of Writing]. Moscow: Editorial URSS Publishing.

Georgiev, V. 1958. *Issledovanija po sravnitel'no-istoricheskomu yazykoznaniju* [Studies in comparative historical linguistics]. Moscow: Inoizdat Publishing.

Gernot, W. 2004. "Hurrian." In *The Cambridge Encyclopedia of the World's Ancient Languages*. Cambridge: Cambridge University Press, 95-118.

Giacomelli, G. 1963. *La lingua falisca* [The Faliscan language]. Florence.

Giacomelli, G. 1978. "Il falisco" [Faliscan]. In *Lingue e dialetti dell'Italia antica*. Rome: Biblioteca di Storia Patria, 505–42.

Gianecchini, G. 1996. "'Destra' e 'sinistra,' e lo strumentale in etrusco" ["Right" and "left," and the instrumental in Etruscan]. *Studi Etruschi* 62: 281–310.

Heurgon, J. 1961. *La vie quotidienne chez les Étrusques* [Everyday life of the Etruscans]. Oxford: Oxford-Hachette.

Hualde, J. I., and J. O. de Urbina. 2003. *A Grammar of Basque*. Berlin: Mouton de Gruyter.

Ipsen, G. 1976. "Festskij disk (Opyt dešifrovki)" [Phaistos Disc (Decryption experience)]. In *Tajny drevnih pis'men: problemy deshifrovki* [Secrets of ancient writings: Decryption problems]. Moscow: Progress Publishing, 32–65.

Ivanov, V. V. 1980. "Novye dannye o sootnoshenii maloaziatskoj, likijskoj, etrusskoj i rimskoj pis'mennykh traditsij. Oboznachenija chisel" [New data on the correlation of Asia Minor Lycian, Etruscan and Roman written traditions. Number designation]. In *Antičnaja balkanistika* [Antique balkanistics]. Moscow.

Ivanov, V. V. 1988. "Drevnevostochnye sv'azi etrusskogo jazyka" [Ancient Eastern relations of the Etruscan language]. In *Drevnij Vostok: Etnokul'turnye sv'azi* [Ancient East: Ethnocultural Relations]. Moscow.

Ivanov, V. V. 2008. *Trudy po etimologii indoevropejskikh i drevneperedneaziatskikh jazykov* [Proceedings on the etymology of Indo-European and Ancient Asian languages], 5.

Jatsemirskij, S. A. 2001. "Nadpis' lemnosskoj stely" [Inscription on the Lemnos stele]. XII čtenija pam'ati prof. S. I. *Arkhangel'skogo*, part 1: 112–21.

Jatsemirskij, S. A. 2005. Jazyk nadpisi lemnosskoj stely v sravnitel'nom osvešhenii [Language of the Lemnos stele in a comparative light]. *Orientalia et classica* 11, part 1: 317–38.

Jatsemirskij, S. A. 2006. *Problemy morfologii tirrenskikh jazykov.* [Morphological problems of the Tyrrhenian languages]. Doctoral dissertation. Moscow.

Jatsemirskij. S. A. 2007. "Etrusskie cislitel'nye: problemy i itogi issledovanija" [Etruscan numerals: Problems and results of the study]. *Orientalia et classica* 11, part 2: 187–96.

Jatsemirski, S. A. 2008. *Etruscan Numerals (Problems and Results of Research): Bygone Voices Reconstructed*. Copenhagen.

Jatsemirskij, S. A. 2009. Labyrinthos: suffiks -*nth*- v minojskom i tirrenskikh jazykakh [Labyrinthos: The suffix -*nth*- in the Minoan and Tyrrhenian languages]. *Orientalia et classica* 28, part 4: 98-111.

Jones, T. B. 1975. "Zametki ob eteokiprskom jazyke" [Notes on the Eteocypriot inscriptions]. In *Tajny drevnih pis'men: problemy deshifrovki* [Secrets of ancient writings: Decryption problems]. Moscow: Progress Publishing, 257-60.

Jones, T. B. 1950. "Notes on the Eteo-Cypriote Inscriptions." *American Journal of Philology*, 71: 401-7.

Krall, J. 1892. *Die Etruskischen Mumienbinde des Agramer Österreichischen Nationalmuseums: Denkschriften der österreichischen Akademie der Wissenschaft* [The Etruscan Agramer (*Liber Linteus*) mummy bindings of the Austrian National Museum: Memoranda of the Austrian Academy of Science]. Vienna: Austrian Academy of Science.

Krasnovskaja, N. A. 1964. "K voprosu ob etnogeneze retoromantsev" [On the question of Rhaeto-Romance ethnogenesis]. *Sovetskaja etnografija*: 89-101.

Kretschmer, P. 1942. "Die tyrrhenischen Inschriften der Stele von Lemnos" [The Tyrrhenian inscriptions of the Lemnos stele]. *Glotta*, 29: 96-98.

Kretschmer, P. 1976. Tirrenskie nadpisi Lemnosskoj stely [Tyrrhenian inscriptions of the Lemnos stele]. *Tajny drevnih pis'men: problemy deshifrovki* [Secrets of ancient writings: Decryption problems]. Moscow: Progress Publishing. 336-37.

Maggiani, A. 1982. "Qualche osservazione sul fegato di Piacenza" [Some observations on the Liver of Piacenza]. *Studi Etruschi* 50: 53-54.

Maggiani, A. 1987-88. Casi di scanbio $\varphi : \theta$ nell'Etruria settentrionale [Cases of switching between $\varphi : \theta$ in western Etruria]. *Studi Etruschi* 55: 195-202.

Malzahn, M. 1999. Das lemnische Alphabet: eine eigenstaendige Entwicklung [The Lemnos alphabet: An independent development]. *Studi Etruschi* 63: 259-79.

Mancini, A. 1973. Retico [Rhaetic]. *Studi Etruschi*, XLI, 363-409.

Masson, O. 1961. Les inscriptions chypriotes syllabiques [Syllabic Cypriote inscriptions]. Paris: Dépositaire, de Boccard.

Masson, E. 1974. *Cyprominoica. Répertoires. Documents de Ras Shamra. Essais d'interprétation* [Cyprominoaca. Inventories. Documents of Ras Shamra. Interpretive essays]. Göteborg: Paul Aströms Förlag.

Mastrelli, A. 1976. "Etrusco-piceno *frontac* e greco *keraunos*" [Etruscan-Piceno *frontac* and Greek *keraunos*]. *Studi Etruschi* 44: 149-62.

Mayak, I. L. 1983. "Novyj trud o drevnejšem Latsii" [New book on ancient Latium]. In *Vestnik drevnej istorii* [Journal of ancient history] 1: 187–99.

Melikishvili, G. A. 1964. *Urartskij yazyk* [*Urartian language*]. Moscow.

Modestov, B. I. 1868. *Rimskaya pis'mennost' v period tsarej* [Roman writing during the period of kings]. Kazan.

Molchanov, A. A., V. P. Neroznak, and S. Sharypkin. 1988. *Pam'atniki drevneishei grecheskoi pis'mennosti (Vvedenie v mikenologiyu)* [Inscriptions of ancient Greek writing (Introduction to mycenology)]. Moscow.

Molchanov, A. A. 1992. *Poslantsy pogibshikh tsivilizatsij (Pis'mena drevnej)* [Ambassadors of fallen civilizations (Ancient's writings)]. Moscow.

Nemirovskij, A. I. 1983. *Etruski. Ot mifa k istorii* [Etruscans. From myth to history]. Moscow.

Nemirovskij, A. I. 1986. "Bronzovaya model' pecheni iz P'yachentsy kak kalendarnaya sistema" [The Piacenza bronze liver model as a calendar system]. *Vestnik drevnej istorii* [Journal of ancient history], 4: 109–18.

Nemirovskij A. I., and A. I. Xarsekin. 1969. *Etruski* [Etruscans]. Voronež, 26–67.

Neumann, G. 1957. "Zur Sprache der kretischen Linearschrift A" [On the language of Cretan Linear A]. *Glotta* 36 (1–2): 156–58.

Neumann, G. 1976. *O jazyke kritskogo linejogo pis'ma A* [About the Cretan language of Linear A], 97–100.

Olzscha, K. 1939. *Interpretation der Agramer Mumienbinde* [Interpretation of the Agramer (*Liber Linteus*) mummy bindings]. Leipzig: Dieterich'sche Verlagsbuchhandlung.

Olzscha, K. 1962. "Studie über die VII Kolumne der Agramer Mumienbinde" [Study on the seventh column of the Agramer (*Liber Linteus*) mummy bindings]. *Studi Etruschi* 30: 157–92.

Olzscha, K. 1966. "Die punisch-etruskischen Inschriften von Pyrgi" [The Punic-Etruscan Inscriptions from Pyrgi]. *Glotta* 44: 60–108.

Pallottino, M. 1936. *Elementi di lingua etrusca* [Elements of Etruscan language]. Florence: Rinascimento del Libro.

Pallottino, M. 1948. "Sulla lettura e sul contenuto della grande iscrizione di Capua" [On the reading and the contents of the great inscription of Capua]. *Studi Etruschi* 20: 159–60.

Pallottino, M. 1958. "Der Akkusativ im Etruskischen" [The accusative in Etruscan]. *Glotta* 37: 305-11.

Pallottino, M. 1963. *Studien zu der Agramer Mumienbinden* [Studies of the Agramer (*Liber Linteus*) mummy bindings]. Denkschriften der philosophisch-historischen Klasse. T. 81. Vienna: Böhlaus.

Pallottino, M. 1967. "Eine Nennung Hannibals in einer Inschrift des 2. Jahrhunderts v. Ch. aus Tarquinia" [Hannibal's mention of an inscription of the second century BC from Tarquinia]. *Studi Etruschi* 35: 659-63.

Pallottino, M. 1969. *Die etruskische Sprache. Versuch einer Gesamt-Darstellung* [The Etruscan language. The search for a total account]. Graz: Akademische Druck, u. Verlagsanstalt.

Pallottino, M. 1972. *Etruskische Bauinschriften* [Etruscan building inscriptions]. Vienna: Böhlaus.

Pallottino, M. 1976. "Problema etrusskogo jazyka" [Problems of the Etruscan language]. *Tajny drevnih pis'men*, 349-80.

Pallottino, M. 1982. *Lingue e dialetti dell'Italia antica*. Rome: Biblioteca di Storia Patria, 429-68.

Peruzzi, E. 1975. "Mikenskie yazykovye elementy v latyni" [Mycenaean language elements in Latin]. *Voprosy yazykoznaniya* [Issues in Linguistics] 5: 104-9.

Pisani, V. 1953. *Le lingue dell'Italia antica oltre il latino* [Languages of ancient Italy other than Latin]. Turin: Rosenberg and Sellier.

Poup, M. 1976. "Linejnoe pis'mo i problema egejskoj pis'mennosti" [Linear writing and the problem of Aegean literature]. In *Tajny drevnih pis'men*, 85-96.

Rix, H. 1963. *Das etruskische Cognomen* [Etruscan cognomens]. Wiesbaden: O. Harrassowitz.

Rix, H. 1983. "Norme i variazioni nell'ortografia Etrusca" [Norms and variations in Etruscan orthography]. *Annali dell'Istituto Universitario Orientale di Napoli* 5: 132-33.

Rix, H. 1984. "Etrusco *mex rasnal* = Latino *res publica*." In *Studi di antichità in onore di Guglielmo Maetztke*. Rome.

Rix, H. 1984. "Scrittura e Lingua" [Writing and language]. In *Gli Etruschi: una nuova immagine*, edited by M. Cristofani. Florence: Giunti.

Rix, H. 1987. "Zur Morphostruktur des etruskischen *s*-Genetivs" [On the morphemic structure of Etruscan *s* genitives]. *Studi Etruschi* 60: 169-93.

Rix, H. 1991. "Etrusco *un, une, unu* 'te, tibi, vos.'" *Archeologia Classica* 43 (1): 665–89.

Rix, H. 1998. *Rätisch und Etruskisch* [Rhaetic and Etruscan]. Innsbruck: Institut für Sprachwissenschaft der Universität Innsbruck.

Rix, H. 2000. "Osservazioni Preliminari ad una Interpretazione dell'Aes Cortonese" [Preliminary observations toward an interpretation of Aes Cortonese]. *Incontri linguistici*, 11–31.

Robertson, E. 2006. "Etruscan's Genealogical Linguistic Relationship with Nakh-Daghestanian: A Preliminary Evaluation." Unpublished manuscript.

Rodriguez, Ramos J. 2000. "La lectura de las inscriptiones sudlusitano-tartesias" [The reading of the inscriptions of South Lusitania and Tartessos]. *Faventia* 22 (1): 21–48.

Shifman I. 2003. *Finikijskij yazyk* [Phoenician language]. Moscow: Editorial URSS Publishing.

Stoltenberg, H. L. 1943. "Die Bedeutung der etruskischen Zahlnamen" [The meaning of the Etruscan numerals]. *Glotta* 30: 234–44.

Stoltenberg, H. L. 1953. "Übersetzung der Tontafel von Capua" [Translation of the Capua clay tablet]. *Studi Etruschi* 22: 158–65.

Stoltenberg, H. L. 1957. *Etruskische Gottnamen* [Names of Etruscan gods]. Leverkusen: Gottschalksche Verlagsbuchhandlung.

Šul'ten A. 1941. "Tirseny v Ispanii (Novye dannye ob iberijskom jazyke)" [Tyrrhenians in Hispania (New data from the Iberian language)]. *Vestnik drevnej istorii* [Journal of ancient history] 1: 8–30.

Syrom'atnikov, N. A. 2002. *Drevnejaponskij jazyk* [Old Japanese]. Moscow.

Tagliavini, C. 1959. *Le origini delle lingue neolatine* [The origins of the Neo-Latin languages]. Bologna: Patron.

Talocchini, A., and G. Giacomelli. 1966. "Il nuovo alfabeto di Vetulonia" [The new alphabet of Vetulonia]. *Studi Etruschi* 34: 239–57.

Tronskij, I. M. 1953. *Ocherki iz istorii latinskogo yazyka* [Essays from the history of the Latin language]. Moscow.

Tronskij, I. M. 2001. *Istoricheskaja morfologija latinskogo yazyka. Obšheindoevropejskoe jazykovoe sostojanie (Voprosy rekonstruktsii)* [The historical morphology of the Latin language. Common Indo-European language state (Reconstruction issues)]. Moscow.

Tronskij, I. M. 2004. *Voprosy yazykovogo razvitija v anticnom obschestve* [Issues of language development in ancient society]. Moscow.

Turcan, R. 1976. "Encore la prophétie de Vegoia" [Again the Vegoia prophecy]. In *L'Italie préromaine et la Rome républicaine.* Rome: Collection de l'Ecole française de Rome.

Urbanová, D., and V. Blažek. 2008. *Národy staroveké Itálie, jejich jazyky a písma* [The peoples of ancient Italy, their languages and writing]. Brno: Host.

Xarsekin, A. 1963. *Voprosy interpretatsii pam'atnikov etrusskoj pis'mennosti* [Questions on the interpretation of Etruscan literary inscriptions]. Stavropol.

Xarsekin, A. I. and Helzer, M. L. 1965. "Novye nadpisi iz Pirgi na finikijskom i etrusskom jazykakh" [New inscriptions in Phoenician and Etruscan from Pyrgi]. *Vestnik Drevnej Istorii* [*Journal of Ancient History*] 3 (93): 108-31.

Xarsekin, A. 1964. "K interpretatsii etrusskikh čislitel'nykh" [Contribution to the interpretation of Etruscan numerals]. *Vestnik Drevnej Istorii* [*Journal of Ancient History*] 2 (88): 48-61.

Xarsekin, A. 1969. *Etrusskaja epigrafika i etrusskij jazyk* [Etruscan epigraphy and Etruscan language]. Varonezh.

Xarsekin, A. 1976. Eteokiprskie nadpisi [Eteo-Cypriote inscriptions]. *Tajny drevnih pis'men: problemy deshifrovki* [Secrets of ancient writings: Decryption problems]. Moscow: Progress Publishing.

Xarsekin, A. 1976. "Lemnosskie nadpisi" [Lemnos inscriptions]. In *Tajny drevnih pis'men: problemy deshifrovki* [Secrets of ancient writings: Decryption problems]. Moscow: Progress Publishing, 335, 337-38.

Zhirmunskij, V. M. 1964. *Vvedenie v sravnitel'no-istoricheskoe izuchenie germanskikh yazykov* [Introduction to the comparative historical study of Germanic languages]. Moscow: Nauka Publishing.

INDEX

Abkhazian, 131
ablaut, 133
accusative, 134-36, 143-45, 160, 164, 166-67, 261, 275
acrophonic, viii, 51
adjectives, 125, 139, 189
adverbs, 127, 152
Aegean-Tyrrhenian, 16, 19, 45, 90, 95, 110, 126, 158, 164-65, 170, 198
affixes, 18, 68, 123, 134, 146, 176
agglutinative, 123-25, 133-35, 146, 159, 165
Akkadian, 69, 223
Alaric, 11
allative, 123, 134, 137, 140-41, 145, 150
allophones, 90, 97, 109
alternations, 67, 85-89, 94, 96, 100-2, 107-9, 111-12, 114-17, 124, 133, 169, 175, 178-79
Anatolian, 3, 7, 67, 80, 182-83, 230, 250
animals, 73
animate, 124, 128-30, 135, 137, 141, 143, 144
Arabian, 69
Aramaic, 69, 73, 82
articles, 42, 69, 86, 139, 145
Ashmolean Museum, 25
Asia Minor, 3, 7, 19, 67, 83, 131, 139, 149, 232, 243, 244, 248, 258-59, 267, 272
aspect, 13, 55, 126, 139, 157, 166, 168-70
aspirates, 31, 87-88, 96-98, 100, 108-9, 149
aspiration, 98-99, 104, 108-9, 112-13, 135, 146, 152

Bacchus, 131, 140, 162, 180, 248
Basque, 121, 149, 156-57, 182, 244, 259, 272
boustrophedon, 25, 29-30, 35, 44
Bruttium, 15, 95, 240, 245
Caere, 20, 37, 40, 58, 61, 81, 93-94, 96, 100, 103-4, 106, 112-14, 116, 122, 257, 270
calendar, 31-32, 37-38, 80, 149-50, 256, 261, 270, 274
Campania, 9-10, 40, 72, 99, 182, 184, 186, 253, 262, 267
Capua, 9, 35, 182, 261, 264, 274, 276
cardinal numbers, 147
Carians, 4
Carthage, 9
case, ii, 4, 8, 17, 18, 19, 30, 38, 39, 47, 53, 57-58, 63, 67, 70, 76, 79-81, 91, 94-95, 97-101, 103-4, 107, 109, 115-17, 123-25, 127, 129-138, 140-46, 148, 150-52, 155, 157-58, 161-62, 164-67, 169-71, 174, 176, 179, 182-83, 189, 191, 195-96, 235, 243, 249
causative, 158, 161, 168
Celtic, 10, 11, 82, 136
Cicero, 45, 46, 198
Cimbri, 9, 10
classical Cypriote, 54-58
Clusium, 9, 31, 41, 94, 95, 101-2, 104, 105, 112, 193, 223, 253
collective plural, 111, 129-30, 137, 162
consonant, vi, viii, 12, 52, 57, 63, 77, 79, 87-89, 97, 99-105, 108, 110-11, 117, 122-23, 155, 160, 180, 187, 191, 198, 239

copulative, 127
Corsica, 8, 19, 22, 253
Cortona, 5, 15, 31, 35, 82, 95, 112, 220, 253
Cretan, vi, 2-6, 23-25, 28-29, 44, 47-50, 52, 54, 57, 67, 68-69, 82, 88-89, 94, 129, 177, 179, 184-85, 190-92, 217, 221-23, 227, 229, 232-36, 258, 261, 267, 271, 274
Cretan hieroglyphics, 23, 25, 48, 52, 57
Crete, i- ii, 2-5, 13, 23-24, 26-27, 29-30, 47-49, 52, 59-60, 68, 87-89, 105, 184, 192, 220, 258, 262, 267-68
Cydonia, 5, 186, 226
Cydonians, 4, 6
Cypriote syllabary, 1, 17, 47, 50, 54-55, 58
Cyprus, 2, 5, 8, 16, 44, 47, 49, 55, 76, 90, 105
dative, 130, 134, 140-41, 143, 146, 150, 159, 161, 166-67, 181, 271
demonstrative, 28, 99, 121, 135, 143-44, 239
dialectal features, 86, 101, 104
dialecticisms, 34, 68, 109, 119, 179
diminutive, 78, 81, 177, 194, 195
Diodorus, 8, 13, 15, 18, 21-22
Dion Cassius, 74
Dionysius I, 10
Dioscorides Pedanius, 72
diphthongs, 86-87, 89-90, 92-95, 117-18, 122
Doric, 5-6, 53, 68, 81, 122, 134, 183, 187, 188, 216, 218, 229, 244
Dorics, 4, 15
Dreros, 6, 29, 30
enclitics, vii
Engadine, 12
Enkomi, 17, 44, 55
epigraphy, 28, 97, 265, 277
epitaphs, 32, 34, 37, 76, 78, 125, 140, 144, 147, 149, 155, 158, 162
Eteo-Cypriote, v, i, 7, 8, 16-18, 44, 55, 57, 76, 81-82, 90, 106, 126-27, 133, 139-40, 144-45, 147, 165-66, 178, 180-81, 183-84, 188-89, 240, 243, 246, 248-49, 251, 259, 265, 273, 277
ethnonyms, 12, 27, 182, 188, 193, 242
Etruria, 8-10, 14-15, 20, 22, 30, 33, 75, 153, 182, 184, 260, 273
Etruscan, i, ii, v, vii-viii, 1, 2, 5, 6, 8-13, 15-20, 23, 28, 30-64, 68-83, 85-87, 89-105, 107-19, 121-136, 138-41, 143-173, 175-84, 186, 188-199, 215-17, 219-25, 228-36, 239-49, 251, 255-65, 267-77
Etruscan-Latin, 34, 38, 61, 69, 90, 94, 100, 112, 146, 163, 180, 184, 193, 197-99, 215, 228, 234, 240, 242, 243, 245, 247-48, 249, 251, 255, 269
Etruscology, 40, 86, 135
Euboea, 13, 61, 184, 192, 217, 221, 224, 227
Eustathius, 69
Faliscan, 1, 83, 93, 96, 99, 111-12, 115, 117, 119, 128, 139, 180, 182, 193, 243, 247, 258, 272
Festus, 10, 38, 39, 80, 99, 130, 163, 169, 197
finitary, 126, 165
First Punic War, 11
flapped, 98
folk etymology, 14, 81-82
Gallo-Romance, 11
Gascon, 112
Gauls, 10
gender, vi, 79, 106, 124-29, 144, 181-82, 195, 196
gerundive, 126, 133, 141, 158, 160, 169, 171-73
Hagia Triada, vii, 26, 54, 262-63, 268
Hannibal, 10, 77, 262, 275
harmonization, 83, 91, 100, 129, 162
haruspices, 11
Heba, 36, 182
Hebrew, 69, 73, 218, 223, 226-27, 233, 235
Herodotus, 4, 9, 13-15, 18

Hesychius, 4-6, 13-14, 16, 18, 38-39, 44, 52, 54, 63, 68-69, 74, 76, 82-83, 88-89, 91-92, 105, 122, 129-30, 140, 175, 178-82, 184-89, 191-94, 197-98
Hittite-Luwian, 3
Homer, 4, 5, 14
hortative, vi, 158, 160, 171-72, 174
Hurrian, 44, 80, 121, 139, 149, 155-57, 178, 188, 244, 256, 258, 270-71
Hurro-Urartian, 67, 80
Iberia, vii, 18, 57
Iberian, 8, 18, 19, 45, 47, 57, 58-59, 264, 276
Ibero-Romance, 45
Ibero-Tyrrhenian, 18, 45
Iliad, 14
Imbros, 13, 43
imperatives, 125, 171
inanimate, 124, 129, 130, 141, 143
inchoative, 158, 167, 171, 177
indicative, 126, 146, 157, 158
Indo-European, v, 1, 2, 4-5, 12, 19, 39, 42, 67, 70, 75-76, 79-81, 85-86, 92-94, 96-97, 105, 115, 121, 128, 133-34, 136-37, 148-49, 153, 165, 183, 196-97, 259, 262, 264, 268, 272, 276
Indo-Iranian, 94
infinitive, 72, 164
inscription of Novilara, 92
instrumental, 130, 134, 140, 161, 166, 181, 258, 272
interdental, 106-8
John the Lydian, 58, 74
Jupiter, 31, 137, 250
Knossos, 5, 6, 24-25, 27, 29, 184
labiodental, 102
labiovelar, 98, 110-11, 119, 123, 149
Laris Pulena, 36, 38, 135-36, 144
Latium, 8, 9, 40, 58, 61, 64, 95, 182, 186, 260, 274
Lemnian, i, 6, 13, 19, 43, 45, 59, 61, 80, 95-97, 105, 110, 113, 118, 131, 139, 140, 144-45, 149, 160, 164-65, 170, 180, 189, 195, 239
Lemnos stele, vii, 8, 13, 15, 42-43, 45, 59, 71, 76, 90-91, 121, 160, 260, 273
lexemes, 3, 8, 31, 37-39, 44-45, 63, 67-72, 75-83, 85, 91, 93, 101, 109, 116, 125, 128-29, 133-34, 137, 146, 164, 175-76, 179, 181, 184-85, 188, 191, 194, 197-98, 239
Liber Linteus, 31-33, 78, 94, 100, 145, 153, 256, 260-62, 270, 273-75
Libyans, 7, 8
Linear A, viii, i, iii, 2-5, 23-24, 26, 28-29, 47-48, 49-50, 52-56, 67-69, 87, 89, 128, 175, 179, 187-8, 190-92, 258, 261, 263, 267-68, 271, 274
Linear B, 2- 5, 26, 28, 47, 49, 50, 52, 53-56, 87, 89, 187, 256, 269
liquid, 98, 227
Livy, 10, 38-39, 58, 83
loanwords, 19, 50, 67, 75, 79, 81, 85, 88, 90, 94, 96-97, 102, 105, 110, 134, 180-81, 196
locative, 83, 94, 98, 105, 123, 130, 134-35, 140-41, 144-45, 161, 170, 181, 249
logogram, 26-27, 48, 50, 52-55, 136, 190, 225
Lombard, 42
Lucretius, 33, 228, 245
Lusitanian, v, i, 7-8, 16, 18, 45, 57, 59, 90, 126, 139, 164-65, 170, 172, 249
Lycian, 80, 83, 136, 147-48, 185, 221, 228, 232, 236, 242, 246, 248, 259, 272
Lydia, 19, 182, 184
Lydians, 14, 19
Macedonian, 5, 76, 179, 192, 219
Macrobius, 72, 150, 181, 197
Magliano, 36
Mallia, 26, 27
Mars, 31, 137
Mavro Spelio, vii, 27, 28
mediopassive, 158-61, 168, 170, 173
Mediterranean, vii, i, 1-3, 7, 8, 11, 17,

19, 76, 85, 94, 198, 215
Merneptah, 7
metathesis, 122
Middle East, 69, 131
Minoan, i–ii, v–vii, 2–5, 8, 16–18, 23–24, 26, 29, 44, 47–50, 52–58, 63, 67–69, 74, 77–78, 81–83, 85–90, 92–93, 102, 116, 121–24, 135, 146, 160–61, 163, 168, 170, 175–79, 181, 183–85, 187–88, 190–91, 198, 215, 230, 239, 250, 259, 273
Modern Greek, 82, 230, 247
monophthongized, 94–95
Monte Pitti, 33, 36, 138, 152
mood, 126, 157–60, 165
morphemes, vi, 121, 123, 157, 178, 256, 270, 257
morphology, vi, 13, 19, 32, 37, 39, 93, 105, 118
Museum of Perugia, 35
Mycenaean Greece, 49
Mysia, 19, 185, 217, 218
nasal, 57, 81, 88, 97, 98, 116–17, 123
National Archaeological Museum in Athens, 25
National Museum in Zagreb, 31
Neptune, 31–32, 157, 171, 184
nominal, 94, 95, 99, 102, 105, 107, 110, 114–16, 124–26, 131, 133, 135, 141, 144–46, 148, 157, 161, 167, 176, 177, 180, 189, 198
noun, vi, 18, 78, 98, 100, 103, 123, 133, 148, 152, 163, 169, 177
number, i–ii, 2, 4–5, 7–10, 12, 23, 25, 27, 35, 36, 38–40, 42, 44, 48, 50, 52–55, 57–58, 67–70, 73, 78, 81, 83, 85–88, 90, 94, 100–1, 103, 105–6, 108–10, 124–26, 128, 130, 133, 136, 143, 145–47, 150–51, 153, 159, 161–63, 165–66, 169, 173, 175, 180, 185, 190, 195–97, 239
numerals, vi, viii, 25, 27, 34, 37, 55, 59, 121, 124–25, 129–30, 147–57, 241, 259, 264–65, 272, 276–77

Odyssey, 14
optative, 126, 158, 171
palatalization, 103
Paphlagonia, 19, 179
participial, 126, 132, 158, 164–65, 170–71, 173
particles, 70, 127
passive, 33, 157, 159, 166–68
Pelasgian, 15
Pelasgians, 4, 13–15
Periphrastic, vi
Perugia, 37, 255, 269
Perusia, 20, 31, 35, 38, 95, 102, 112–13, 115–16, 253
Phaistos, vii–viii, 2–3, 5, 23–24, 27–28, 48–49, 190, 259, 272
Phaistos disk, 3, 24, 28, 48, 190
Phoenician, 37, 57, 77, 97, 131, 147, 188, 263, 265, 276–77
phonetic, 5, 9, 16, 34, 36, 39, 40, 47, 52, 55–57, 61, 63–64, 67–68, 70, 76, 78–79, 81, 83, 85–86, 89–92, 94–102, 104–6, 108–12, 114–15, 117, 119, 124, 129, 132, 137, 140–41, 143–44, 148–49, 151–53, 163, 166–67, 178, 188, 194–98, 215
Piacenza, 37, 81, 256, 260–61, 270, 273–74
Pillars of Hercules, 18
Pisaurum, 20, 38, 41
Placentia, 21, 37
Pliny the Elder, 8, 12
plural suffix, 123, 125, 130, 132, 151–52
Populonia, 19, 22, 82, 98, 102, 181, 182, 248, 251, 253
possessive, 90–91, 94, 137, 143–44, 174
postpositions, 123, 127, 134, 140, 143, 239
prefixation, vii, 122–24, 176–77
pre-Greek, 5, 8, 28, 39, 44, 83, 92, 104, 176, 179–80, 182–86, 191, 198, 215, 239–41, 243, 247–48, 250

present tense, 160-61, 164-65, 168, 171
pronominal enclitics, 124, 133-34, 145-46, 177, 196, 198
pronouns, vi, 116, 121, 127, 130, 136, 143-44, 146, 149, 239
pronunciation, 85, 88-90, 96-97, 101, 106, 114, 117, 255, 269
Proto-North-Caucasian, 149
Punic, 11, 37, 39, 41, 77, 82, 96-97, 131, 147, 159, 173, 241, 246, 261, 274
Pyrgos, 27
Ramesses III, 7
reduplication, 110, 117, 122-23, 138, 143, 185, 240
reflexive, 33, 161, 167, 168
reflexivity, 157
Rhaetic, v, i, 1, 6-8, 11-13, 16, 42, 59, 89-90, 92-93, 96-97, 100, 111, 126, 132, 136, 138-41, 145, 159-61, 164-66, 168, 170, 180, 190, 192-93, 240, 244-45, 250, 260, 263, 267, 268, 273, 276
Rhaeto-Romance, 11-12, 260, 273
Roman, v, 8, 10-13, 31, 33, 42, 63-64, 71, 74, 75, 81, 83, 90, 93, 95, 99, 106, 114, 149, 153, 169, 180, 182, 185, 189, 193, 241, 245, 259, 261, 272, 274
Rome, 9, -11, 34-35, 39, 95, 106, 150, 181, 243, 255-58, 262-64, 267, 269-72, 275, 277
root syllable, 86, 92, 93
Sabinian, 75, 110, 112, 159, 181-82, 244, 251
Samnites, 10, 186
San Manno, 37, 173
Santa Marinella, 36
Sardinia, 7-8, 19
Sea Peoples, 7
Semitic, 3-4, 67, 69, 73, 80, 227, 235
semivowel, 83, 87-90, 98, 112, 117-18, 177

sibilants, 98, 110, 114, 122
Sicels, 8
Sicily, 7-8, 15, 18-19, 179, 184, 220
Social War, 32
sonants, 52, 88-89, 98, 110, 116, 122, 144
Spanish, 112
sprachbund, 139
stems, 26, 28, 34, 70, 78, 82, 101, 104, 106-7, 109-10, 115, 125, 135, 141, 145-46, 148, 157, 160-61, 164, 166, 171, 176, 180, 186, 239
Strabo, 5, 14, 115, 184, 188, 191, 228, 232
stress, 86, 91, 93, 116, 133
substrate, 68, 74, 87
suffixation, 69, 122, 125, 136, 180-82, 183, 187, 215
suffixes, vii, 4, 5, 12, 17, 69, 80-81, 87-88, 101, 116-17, 121, 123-26, 129-131, 133-35, 137-41, 150, 157, 160, 162, 164-65, 170, 176-79, 182-83, 186-87, 189-92, 194-95, 239
Sulla, 11, 31, 261, 274
Sumerian, 67, 69, 72, 224, 241
syllabary, 17, 47, 48
syllabic writing, 44, 50, 55, 57, 89
syllabograms, 48, 52-53, 55-57, 87
syntax, 33, 161, 167, 169
Tablet HT 54, 116
Tabula Cortonensis, 132, 159, 255, 267
Tages, 30, 33, 45, 80
Tarquinia Tomb, vii, 9
Tarquinii, 36-37, 40, 94, 97, 102, 106, 110, 114, 131, 135, 140, 164, 169, 189, 262, 268
Tarquitius Priscus, 33
Tartessos, vii, 17-18, 263, 276
Tenses, vi
Thracian, 4, 14, 136, 183, 192, 232
Thucydides, 13
Tiberius, 11, 37
tin, 31, 81, 134, 137, 142, 250
Titus Livy, 12

tone, 91
toponyms, 3, 13, 19, 27, 41, 44, 70, 75-76, 82, 85, 87, 129, 148, 182-83, 185, 192, 216, 235, 240, 247
Trojan War, 61
Tuscany, 6, 8, 58, 75, 94-95, 98, 104, 114
Tyrolean, 42
Tyrrhenian, i, v-viii, 2, 5-20, 23, 33, 39, 41-45, 47-48, 57-59, 61, 63-64, 67-71, 74-83, 85-93, 95-97, 105, 109-10, 113, 116-18, 121-30, 133-41, 143-44, 146, 148-49, 157-58, 160-66, 170-73, 175-82, 184-86, 188-90, 194, 196, 198-99, 215, 231, 239, 259-60, 272-73
Tyrsenians, 8, 13
Ugarit, 44
Umbri, 9, 20, 72
Umbrian, 1, 6, 9-10, 31-32, 38, 61, 70-71, 76, 81-82, 90, 93, 95, 110-12, 115-16, 119, 122, 127-28, 130, 136-37, 146, 163, 165, 168, 178, 180-81, 198, 216, 228, 236, 239, 240-42, 244, 246, 248, 250-51, 264, 269
Val di Cembra, 42
Vegoia, 33, 36, 167, 264, 277
Veii, 10, 59, 103, 162, 182

Venetic, 60, 82, 104
Ventris, 28, 50, 52, 87
verb, vi, 124
verbal, 13, 17, 28, 36, 100-1, 118, 124-26, 133, 135-37, 141, 143, 145-46, 157-58, 161, 164-67, 169-71, 173, 176, 180
Villanova, 9
Villanovan, 9
Virgil, 96, 148, 240
Viterbo, 61, 62
vocabulary, i, 8, 13, 16-19, 23, 28, 30, 32-33, 38, 40, 44, 50, 52, 58, 67-71, 73, 75-76, 78, 80, 82-83, 85-86, 90, 92, 116
voice, 126, 157, 166, 188
voiced, 52, 57, 59, 63, 87-88, 93, 96-98, 100-1, 103-4, 107-10, 115
voiceless, 31, 52, 77, 87, 96-98, 101-2, 104-5, 107, 109, 111, 114-15
Volsinii, 32, 38, 40, 90, 94, 106, 112, 114-16, 131, 135, 140, 170, 189, 262, 268
Volterra, 19, 36
vowels, vi, 5, 7, 31, 52, 57, 86, 89-92, 94, 96, 100, 103, 116, 118, 152, 186, 196, 198
Vulgar Latin, 11
Zagreb mummy text, 31, 141

Printed in Great Britain
by Amazon